American Prisoners of the Revolution

Danske Dandridge

Table of Contents

Table of Contents

Table of Contents

American Prisoners of the Revolution

American Prisoners of the Revolution

Danske Dandridge

Kessinger Publishing reprints thousands of hard-to-find books!

Visit us at http://www.kessinger.net

Dedication

TO THE MEMORY OF MY GRANDFATHER

Lieutenant Daniel Bedinger, of Bedford, Virginia

"A BOY IN PRISON"

AS REPRESENTATIVE OF ALL THAT WAS BRAVEST AND MOST HONORABLE IN THE LIFE AND CHARACTER OF THE PATRIOTS OF 1776

PREFACE

The writer of this book has been interested for many years in the subject of the sufferings of the American prisoners of the Revolution. Finding the information she sought widely scattered, she has, for her own use, and for that of all students of the subject, gathered all the facts she could obtain within the covers of this volume. There is little that is original in the compilation. The reader will find that extensive use has been made of such narratives as that Captain Dring has left us. The accounts could have been given in the compiler's own words, but they would only, thereby, have lost in strength. The original narratives are all out of print, very scarce and hard to obtain, and the writer feels justified in reprinting them in this collection, for the sake of the general reader interested in the subject, and not able to search for himself through the mass of original material, some of which she has only discovered after months of research. Her work has mainly consisted in abridging these records, collected from so many different sources.

The writer desires to express her thanks to the courteous librarians of the Library of Congress and of the War and Navy Departments; to Dr. Langworthy for permission to publish his able and interesting paper on the subject of the prisons in New York, and to many others who have helped her in her task.

DANSKE DANDRIDGE.

December 6th, 1910.

CHAPTER I. INTRODUCTORY

It is with no desire to excite animosity against a people whose blood is in our veins that we publish this volume of facts about some of the Americans, seamen and soldiers, who were so unfortunate as to fall into the hands of the enemy during the period of the Revolution. We have concealed nothing of the truth, but we have set nothing down in malice, or with undue recrimination.

It is for the sake of the martyrs of the prisons themselves that this work has been executed. It is because we, as a people, ought to know what was endured; what wretchedness, what relentless torture, even unto death, was nobly borne by the men who perished by thousands in British prisons and prison ships of the Revolution; it is because we are in danger of forgetting the sacrifice they made of their fresh young lives in the service of their country; because the story has never been adequately told, that we, however unfit we may feel ourselves for the task, have made an effort to give the people of America some account of the manner in which these young heroes, the flower of the land, in the prime of their vigorous manhood, met their terrible fate.

Too long have they lain in the ditches where they were thrown, a cart-full at a time, like dead dogs, by their heartless murderers, unknown, unwept, unhonored, and unremembered. Who can tell us their names? What monument has been raised to their memories?

It is true that a beautiful shaft has lately been erected to the martyrs of the Jersey prison ship, about whom we will have very much to say. But it is improbable that even the place of interment of the hundreds of prisoners who perished in the churches, sugar houses, and other places used as prisons in New York in the early years of the Revolution, can now be discovered. We know that they were, for the most part, dumped into ditches dug on the outskirts of the little city, the New York of 1776. These ditches were dug by American soldiers, as part of the entrenchments, during Washington's occupation of Manhattan in the spring of 1776. Little did these young men think that they were, in some cases, literally digging a grave for themselves.

More than a hundred and thirty years have passed since the victims of Cunningham's cruelty and rapacity were starved to death in churches consecrated to the praise and worship of a God of love. It is a tardy recognition that we are giving them, and one that is most imperfect, yet it is all that we can now do. The ditches where they were interred have long ago been filled up, built over, and intersected by streets. Who of the multitude that daily pass to and fro over the ground that should be sacred ever give a thought to the remains of the brave men beneath their feet, who perished that they might enjoy the blessings of liberty?

Republics are ungrateful; they have short memories; but it is due to the martyrs of the Revolution that some attempt should be made to tell to the generations that succeed them who they were, what they did, and why they suffered so terribly and died so grimly, without weakening, and without betraying the cause of that country which was dearer to them than their lives.

We have, for the most part, limited ourselves to the prisons and prison ships in the city and on the waters of New York. This is because such information as we have been able to obtain concerning the treatment of American prisoners by the British relates, almost entirely, to that locality.

It is a terrible story that we are about to narrate, and we warn the lover of pleasant books to lay down our volume at the first page. We shall see Cunningham, that burly, red–faced ruffian, the Provost Marshal, wreaking his vengeance upon the defenceless prisoners in his keeping, for the assault made upon him at the outbreak of the war, when he and a companion who had made themselves obnoxious to the republicans were mobbed and beaten in the streets of New York. He was rescued by some friends of law and order, and locked up in one of the jails which was soon to be the theatre of his revenge. We shall narrate the sufferings of the American prisoners taken at the time of the battle of Long Island, and after the surrender of Fort Washington, which events occurred, the first in August, the second in November of the year 1776.

What we have been able to glean from many sources, none of which contradict each other in any important point, about the prisons and prison ships in New York, with a few narratives written by those who were imprisoned in other places, shall fill this volume. Perhaps others, far better fitted for the task, will make the necessary researches, in order to lay before the American people a statement of what took place in the British prisons at Halifax, Charleston, Philadelphia, the waters off the coast of Florida, and other places, during the eight years of the war. It is a solemn and affecting duty that we owe to the dead, and it is in no light spirit that we, for our part, begin our portion of the task.

CHAPTER II. THE RIFLEMEN OF THE REVOLUTION

We will first endeavor to give the reader some idea of the men who were imprisoned in New York in the fall and winter of 1776, It was in the summer of that year that Congress ordered a regiment of riflemen to be raised in Maryland and Virginia. These, with the so–called "Flying Camp" of Pennsylvania, made the bulk of the soldiers taken prisoners at Fort Washington on the fatal 16th of November. Washington had already proved to his own satisfaction the value of such soldiers; not only by his experience with them in the French and Indian wars, but also during the siege of Boston in 1775–6.

These hardy young riflemen were at first called by the British "regulars," "a rabble in calico petticoats," as a term of contempt. Their uniform consisted of tow linen or homespun hunting shirts, buckskin breeches, leggings and moccasins. They wore round felt hats, looped on one side and ornamented with a buck tail. They carried long rifles, shot pouches, tomahawks, and scalping knives.

They soon proved themselves of great value for their superior marksmanship, and the British, who began by scoffing at them, ended by fearing and hating them as they feared and hated no other troops. The many accounts of the skill of these riflemen are interesting, and some of them shall be given here.

One of the first companies that marched to the aid of Washington when he was at Cambridge in 1775 was that of Captain Michael Cresap, which was raised partly in Maryland and partly in the western part of Virginia. This gallant young officer died in New York in the fall of 1775, a year before the surrender of Fort Washington, yet his company may be taken as a fair sample of what the riflemen of the frontiers of our country were, and of what they could do. We will therefore give the words of an eyewitness of their performances. This account is taken from the *Pennsylvania Journal* of August 23rd, 1775.

"On Friday evening last arrived at Lancaster, Pa., on their way to the American camp, Captain Cresap's Company of Riflemen, consisting of one hundred and thirty active, brave young fellows, many of whom have been in the late expedition under Lord Dunmore against the Indians. They bear in their bodies visible marks of their prowess, and show scars and wounds which would do honour to Homer's Iliad. They show you, to use the poet's words:

  "'Where the gor'd battle bled at ev'ry vein!'

"One of these warriors in particular shows the cicatrices of four bullet holes through his body.

"These men have been bred in the woods to hardships and dangers since their infancy. They appear as if they were entirely unacquainted with, and had never felt the passion of fear. With their rifles in their hands, they assume a kind of omnipotence over their enemies. One cannot much wonder at this when we mention a fact which can be fully attested by several of the reputable persons who were eye−witnesses of it. Two brothers in the company took a piece of board five inches broad, and seven inches long, with a bit of white paper, the size of a dollar, nailed in the centre, and while one of them supported this board perpendicularly between his knees, the other at the distance of upwards of sixty yards, and without any kind of rest, shot eight bullets through it successively, and spared a brother's thigh!

"Another of the company held a barrel stave perpendicularly in his hands, with one edge close to his side, while one of his comrades, at the same distance, and in the manner before mentioned, shot several bullets through it, without any apprehension of danger on either side.

"The spectators appearing to be amazed at these feats, were told that there were upwards of fifty persons in the same company who could do the same thing; that there was not one who could not 'plug nineteen bullets out of twenty,' as they termed it, within an inch of the head of a ten−penny nail.

"In short, to evince the confidence they possessed in these kind of arms, some of them proposed to stand with apples on their heads, while others at the same distance undertook to shoot them off, but the people who saw the other experiments declined to be witnesses of this.

"At night a great fire was kindled around a pole planted in the Court House Square, where the company with the Captain at their head, all naked to the waist and painted like savages (except the Captain, who was in an Indian shirt), indulged a vast concourse of people with a perfect exhibition of a war–dance and all the manoeuvres of Indians; holding council, going to war; circumventing their enemies by defiles; ambuscades; attacking; scalping, etc. It is said by those who are judges that no representation could possibly come nearer the original. The Captain's expertness and agility, in particular, in these experiments, astonished every beholder. This morning they will set out on their march for Cambridge."

From the *Virginia Gazette* of July 22nd, 1775, we make the following extract: "A correspondent informs us that one of the gentlemen appointed to command a company of riflemen to be raised in one of the frontier counties of Pennsylvania had so many applications from the people in his neighborhood, to be enrolled in the service, that a greater number presented themselves than his instructions permitted him to engage, and being unwilling to give offence to any he thought of the following expedient: He, with a piece of chalk, drew on a board the figure of a nose of the common size, which he placed at the distance of 150 yards, declaring that those who came nearest the mark should be enlisted. Sixty odd hit the object.—General Gage, take care of your nose!"

From the *Pennsylvania Journal*, July 25th, 1775: "Captain Dowdle with his company of riflemen from Yorktown, Pa., arrived at Cambridge about one o'clock today, and since has made proposals to General Washington to attack the transport stationed at Charles River. He will engage to take her with thirty men. The General thinks it best to decline at present, but at the same time commends the spirit of Captain Dowdle and his brave men, who, though they just came a very long march, offered to execute the plan immediately."

In the third volume of American Archives, is an extract from a letter to a gentleman in Philadelphia, dated Frederick Town, Maryland, August 1st, 1775, which speaks of the same company of riflemen whose wonderful marksmanship we have already noted. The writer says:

"Notwithstanding the urgency of my business I have been detained here three days by a circumstance truly agreeable. I have had the happiness of seeing Captain Michael Cresap marching at the head of a formidable company of upwards of one hundred and thirty men from the mountains and backwoods; painted like Indians; armed with tomahawks and rifles; dressed in hunting shirts and moccasins; and, tho' some of them had travelled hundreds of miles from the banks of the Ohio, they seemed to walk light and easy, and not with less spirit than at the first hour of their march.

"I was favored by being constantly in Captain Cresap's company, and watched the behavior of his men and the manner in which he treated them, for is seems that all who go out to war under him do not only pay the most willing obedience to him as their commander, but in every instance of distress look up to him as their friend and father. A great part of his time was spent in listening to and relieving their wants, without any apparent sense of fatigue and trouble. When complaints were before him he determined with kindness and spirit, and on every occasion condescended to please without losing dignity.

"Yesterday, July 31st, the company were supplied with a small quantity of powder, from the magazine, which wanted airing, and was not in good order for rifles: in the evening, however, they were drawn out to show the gentlemen of the town their dexterity in shooting. A clap board with a mark the size of a dollar was put up; they began to fire offhand, and the bystanders were surprised. Few shots were made that were not close to, or into, the paper. When they had shot some time in this way, some lay on their backs, some on their breasts or sides, others ran twenty or thirty steps, and, firing as they ran, appeared to be equally certain of the mark. With this performance the company were more than satisfied, when a young man took up the board in his hand, and not by the end, but by the side, and, holding it up, his brother walked to the distance, and coolly shot into the white. Laying down his rifle he took the board, and holding it as it was held before, the second brother shot as the former had done.

"By this exhibition I was more astonished than pleased, but will you believe me when I tell you that one of the men took the board, and placing it between his legs, stood with his back to a tree, while another drove the centre?

"What would a regular army of considerable strength in the forests of America do with one thousand of these men, who want nothing to preserve their health but water from the spring; with a little parched corn (with what they can easily procure by hunting); and who, wrapped in their blankets in the dead of night, would choose the shade of a tree for their covering, and the earth for their bed?"

The descriptions we have quoted apply to the rifle companies of 1775, but they are a good general description of the abilities of the riflemen raised in the succeeding years of the war, many indeed being the same men who first volunteered in 1775. In the possession of one of his descendants is a letter from one of these men written many years after the Revolution to the son of an old comrade in arms, giving an account of that comrade's experiences during a part of the war. The letter was written by Major Henry Bedinger of Berkeley County, Virginia, to a son of General Samuel Finley.

Henry Bedinger was descended from an old German family. His grandfather had emigrated to America from Alsace in 1737 to escape persecution for his religious beliefs. The highest rank that Bedinger attained in the War of the Revolution was that of captain. He was a Knight of the Order of the Cincinnati, and he was, after the war, a major of the militia of Berkeley County. The document in possession of one of his descendants is undated, and appears to have been a rough copy or draught of the original, which may now be in the keeping of some one of the descendants of General Finley. We will give it almost entire. Such family letters are, we need scarcely say, of great value to all who are interested in historical research, supplying, as they do, the necessary details which fill out and amplify the bare facts of history, giving us a living picture of the times and events that they describe.

PART OF A LETTER FROM MAJOR HENRY BEDINGER TO A SON OF GENERAL SAMUEL FINLEY

"Some time in 1774 the late Gen'l Sam'l Finley Came to Martinsburg, Berkeley County, Virginia, and engaged with the late Col'o John Morrow to assist his brother, Charles Morrow, in the business of a retail store.

"Mr. Finley continued in that employment until the spring of 1775, when Congress called on the State of Virginia for two Complete Independent Volunteer Companies of Riflemen of 100 Men each, to assist Gen'l Washington in the Siege of Boston &to serve one year. Captains Hugh Stephenson of Berkeley, &Daniel Morgan of Frederick were selected to raise and command those companies, they being the first Regular troops required to be raised in the State of Virginia for Continental service.

"Captain Hugh Stephenson's rendezvous was Shepherd's Town (not Martinsburg) and Captain Morgan's was Winchester. Great exertions were made by each Captain to complete his company first, that merit might be claimed on that account. Volunteers presented themselves in every direction in the Vicinity of these Towns, none were received but young men of Character, and of sufficient property to Clothe themselves completely, find their own arms, and accoutrements, that is, an approved Rifle, handsome shot pouch, and powder horn, blanket, knapsack, with such decent clothing as should be prescribed, but which was at first ordered to be only a Hunting shirt and pantaloons, fringed on every edge and in Various ways.

"Our Company was raised in less than a week. Morgan had equal success.—It was never decided which Company was first filled—

"These Companies being thus unexpectedly called for it was a difficult task to obtain rifles of the quality required &we were detained at Shepherds Town nearly six weeks before we could obtain such. Your Father and some of his Bosom Companions were among the first enrolled. My Brother, G. M. B., and myself, with many of our Companions, soon joined to the amount of 100—no more could be received. The Committee of Safety had appointed Wm Henshaw as 1st Lieut., George Scott 2nd, and Thomas Hite as 3rd Lieut to this Company, this latter however, declined accepting, and Abraham Shepherd succeeded as 3d Lieut—all the rest Stood on an equal footing as *Volunteers* —We remained at Shepherds Town untill the 16th July before we could be Completely armed, notwithstanding the utmost exertions. In the mean time your Father obtained from the gunsmith a remarkable neat light rifle, the stock inlaid and ornamented with silver, which he held, untill Compelled, as were all of us—to ground our arms and surrender to the enemy on the evening of the 16th day of November 1776.

"In our Company were many young men of Considerable fortune, &who generally entered from patriotic motives ... Our time of service being about to expire Captain Hugh Stephenson was commissioned a Colonel; Moses Rawlings a Lieutenant Colonel, and Otho Williams Major, to raise a Rifle Regiment for three years: four companies to be raised in Virginia and four in Maryland.

"Henshaw and Scott chose to return home. Abraham Shepherd was commissioned Captain, Sam'l Finley First Lieutenant, William Kelly Second Lieutenant, and myself 3rd Lieutenant. The Commissions of the Field Officers were dated the 8th July, 1776, &those of our Company the 9th of the same month. Shepherd, Finley and myself were dispatched to Berkeley to recruit and refill the old Company, which we performed in about five weeks. Col'o Stephenson also returned to Virginia to facilitate the raising the additional Companies. While actively employed in August, 1776, he was taken sick, and in four days died. The command of the Regiment devolved on Lieutenant Colonel Moses Rawlings, a Very worthy and brave officer.

"Our Company being filled we Marched early in September to our Rendezvous at Bergen. So soon as the Regiment was formed it was ordered up the North River to the English Neighborhood, &in a short time ordered to cross the River and assist in the defence of Fort Washington, where were about three thousand men under the command of Col'o Magaw, on New York Island. The enemy in the mean time possessed New York, and had followed General Washington to the White Plains, from whence, after several partial actions, he returned, and approached us by the way of King's bridge, with a force of from 8 to 12000 Men. Several frigates ran up the Hudson from New York to cut off our intercourse with Fort Lee, a fort on the opposite bank of the North River: and by regular approaches invested us on all sides.

"On the 15th November, 1776, the British General Pattison appeared with a flag near our Guards, demanding a surrender of Fort Washington and the Garrison. Col'o Magaw replied he should defend it to the last extremity. Pattison declared all was ready to storm the lines and fort, we of course prepared for the Pending contest.

"At break of day the next morning, the enemy commenced a tremendous Cannonade on every side, while their troops advanced. Our Regt. tho weak, was most advantageously posted by Rawlings and Williams, on a Small Ridge, about half a mile above Fort Washington. The Ridge ran from the North River, in which lay three frigates, towards the East River. A deep Valley divided us from the enemy, their frigates enfiladed, &their Cannon on the heights behind the advancing troops played incessantly on our party (consisting of Rawling's Regiment, say 250 men, and one other company from Maryland, and four companies of Pennsylvania Flying Camp, also for the present commanded by Rawlings and Williams).

"The Artillery were endeavoring to clear the hill while their troops crossing the Valley were ascending it, but without much effect. A few of our men were killed with Cannon and Grape Shott. Not a Shott was fired on our side untill the Enemy had nearly gained the Sumit. Though at least five times our numbers our rifles brought down so many that they gave way several times, but by their overwhelming numbers they at last succeeded in possessing the summit. Here, however, was great carnage, each making every effort to possess and hold so advantageous a position. This obstinacy continued for more than an hour, when the enemy brought up some field pieces, as well as reinforcements. Finding all resistance useless, our Regiment gradually gave way, tho' not before Col'o Rawlings, Major Williams, Peter Hanson, Nin Tannehill, and myself were wounded. Lt. Harrison

[Footnote: Lieutenant Battaille Harrison of Berkeley County, Va.] was the only officer of our Regiment Killed. Hanson and Tannehill were mortally wounded. The latter died the same night in the Fort, &Hanson died in New York a short time after. Capt. A. Shepherd, Lieut. Daniel Cresap and myself, with fifty men, were detailed the day before the action and placed in the van to receive the enemy as they came up the hill.

"The Regiment was paraded in line about fifty yards in our rear, ready to support us. Your Father of course on that day, and in the whole of the action commanded Shepherd's Company, which performed its duty admirably. About two o'clock P. M. the Enemy obtained complete possession of the hill, and former battle-ground. Our troops retreated gradually from redoubt to redoubt, contesting every inch of ground, still making dreadful Havoc in the ranks of the enemy. We laboured too under disadvantages, the wind blew the smoke full in our faces. About two o'clock A. Shepherd, being the senior Captain, took command of the Regiment, [Footnote: After Rawlings and Williams were disabled.] and by the advice of Col'o Rawlings &Major Williams, gradually retreated from redoubt to redoubt, to &into the fort with the surviving part of the Regiment. Col'o Rawlings, Major Williams, and Lt Hanson and myself quitted the field together, and retreated to the fort. I was slightly wounded, tho my right hand was rendered entirely useless. Your Father continued with the regiment until all had arrived in the fort. It was admitted by all the surviving officers that he had conducted himself with great gallantry and the utmost propriety.

"While we were thus engaged the enemy succeeded much better in every other quarter, &with little comparative loss. All were driven into the fort and the enemy began by sundown to break ground within 100 yards of the fort.

"Finding our situation desperate Col'o Magaw dispatched a flag to Gen. Howe who Commanded in person, proposing to surrender on certain conditions, which not being agreed to, other terms were proposed and accepted. The garrison, consisting of 2673 privates, &210 officers, marched out, grounded arms, and were guarded to the White House that same night, but instead of being treated as agreed on, and allowed to retain baggage, clothes, and Side Arms, every valuable article was torn away from both officers and soldiers: every sword, pistol, every good hat was seized, even in presence of Brittish officers, &the prisoners were considered and treated as *Rebels*, to the king and country. On the third day after our surrender we were guarded to New York, fourteen miles from Fort Washington, where in the evening we received some barrels of raw pork and musty spoiled biscuit, being the first Morsel of provision we had seen for more than three days. The officers were then separated from the soldiers, had articles of parole presented to us which we signed, placed into deserted houses without Clothing, provisions, or fire. No officer was permitted to have a servant, but we acted in rotation, carried our Cole and Provisions about half a mile on our backs, Cooked as well as we could, and tried to keep from Starving.

"Our poor Soldiers fared most wretchedly different. They were crowded into sugar houses and Jails without blankets or covering; had Very little given to them to eat, and that little of the Very worst quality. So that in two months and four days about 1900 of the Fort Washington troops had died. The survivors were sent out and receipted for by General Washington, and we the officers were sent to Long Island on parole, and billetted, two in a house, on the families residing in the little townships of Flatbush, New Utrecht, Newlots, and Gravesend, who were compelled to board and lodge us at the rate of two dollars per week, a small compensation indeed in the exhausted state of that section of country. The people were kind, being mostly conquered Whigs, but sometimes hard run to provide sustenance for their own families, with the addition, generally, of two men who must have a share of what could be obtained. These people could not have furnished us but for the advantage of the fisheries, and access at all times to the water. Fish, oysters, clams, Eels, and wild fowl could always be obtained in their season.

"We were thus fixed on the inhabitants, but without money, or clothing. Sometimes a companion would receive a few hard dollars from a friend through a flag of truce, which was often shared by others to purchase a pair of shoes or a shirt.

"While in New York Major Williams received from a friend about forty silver dollars. He was still down with his wound, but requested Captain Shepherd, your Father and myself to come to his room, and there lent each of us ten Dollars, which enabled each of us to purchase a pair shoes, a shirt, and some other small matters: this liberality however, gave some offence. Major Williams was a Marylander, and to assist a Virginian, in preference to a Marylander, was a Crime almost unpardonable. It however passed off, as it so happened there were some refugees in New York from Maryland who had generosity enough to relieve the pressing wants of a few of their former acquaintances.

"We thus lived in want and perfect idleness for years: tho sometimes if Books could be obtained we made out to read: if paper, pen, and ink could be had we wrote. Also to prevent becoming too feeble we exercised our bodies by playing fives, throwing long bullets, wrestling, running, jumping, and other athletick exercises, in all of which your Father fully participated. Being all nearly on the same footing as to Clothing and pocket money (that is we seldom had any of the latter) we lived on an equality.

"In the fall of 1777 the Brittish Commander was informed a plan was forming by a party of Americans to pass over to Long Island and sweep us off, release us from captivity. There were then on the Island about three hundred American officers prisoners. We were of course ordered off immediately, and placed on board of two large transports in the North River, as prison ships, where we remained but about 18 days, but it being Very Cold, and we Confined between decks, the Steam and breath of 150 men soon gave us Coughs, then fevers, and had we not been removed back to our billets I believe One half would have died in six weeks. This is all the imprisonment your———"

The rest of this valuable letter has been, most unfortunately lost, or possibly it was never completed.

We have given a great deal of it because of its graphic description of the men who were captured at Fort Washington, and of the battle itself. Major Bedinger was a dignified, well–to–do, country gentleman; honored and respected by all who knew him, and of unimpeachable veracity.

CHAPTER III. NAMES OF SOME OF THE PRISONERS OF 1776

As we have seen, the officers fared well in comparison with the wretched privates. Paroled and allowed the freedom of the city, they had far better opportunities to obtain the necessities of life. "Our poor soldiers fared most wretchedly different," says Major Bedinger.

Before we begin, however, to speak of the treatment they received, we must make some attempt to tell the reader who they were. We wish it were possible to give the name of every private who died, or rather who was murdered, in the prisons of New York at this time. But that, we fear, is now an impossibility. As this account is designed as a memorial to those martyred privates, we have made many efforts to obtain their names. But if the muster rolls of the different companies who formed the Rifle Regiment, the Pennsylvania Flying Camp, and the other troops captured by the British in the summer and fall of 1776 are in existence, we have not been able to find them.

The records of the Revolution kept in the War Department in England have been searched in vain by American historians. It is said that the Provost Marshal, William Cunningham, destroyed his books, in order to leave no written record of his crimes. The names of 8,000 prisoners, mostly seamen, who were confined on the prison ship Jersey, alone, have been obtained by the Society of Old Brooklynites, from the British Archives, and, by the kind permission of this Society, we re-publish them in the Appendix to this volume.

Here and there, also, we have obtained a name of one of the brave young riflemen who died in torment a hundred times worse, because so much less swift, than that endured on a memorable occasion in India, when British soldiers were placed, during a single night, into one of their own "Black Holes." But the names of almost all of these our tortured countrymen are forgotten as completely as their places of interment are neglected.

In the hands of the writer, however, at this time [Footnote: This muster roll was lent to the writer by Henry Bedinger Davenport, Esq, a descendant of Major Bedinger] is the pay-roll of one of these companies of riflemen,—that of Captain Abraham Shepherd of Shepherdstown, Virginia. It is in the handwriting of Henry Bedinger, one of the lieutenants of the company.

We propose to take this list, or pay roll, as a sample, and to follow, as well as we can, at this late day, the misfortunes of the men named therein. For this purpose we will first give the list of names, and afterwards attempt to indicate how many of the men died in confinement, and how many lived to be exchanged.

MUSTER ROLL

The paper in question, falling to pieces with age, and almost illegible in places, is headed, "An ABSTRACT of the Pay due the Officers and Privates of the Company of Riflemen belonging to Captain Abraham Shepherd, being part of a Battalion raised by Colonel Hugh Stevenson, deceased, and afterwards commanded by Lieut Colonel Moses Rawlings, in the Continental Service from July 1st, 1776, to October 1st, 1778." The paper gives the dates of enlistment; those who were killed; those who died; those who deserted; those who were discharged; drafted; made prisoners; "dates until when pay is charged;" "pay per month;" "amount in Dollars," and "amount in lawful Money, Pounds, Shillings and pence." From this account much information can be gleaned concerning the members of the company, but we will, for the present, content ourselves with giving the muster roll of the company.

MUSTER ROLL OF CAPTAIN ABRAHAM SHEPHERD'S COMPANY OF RIFLEMEN RAISED IN JULY, 1776

Captain Abraham Shepherd. First Lieutenant, Samuel Finley. Second Lieutenant, William Kelly. Third Lieutenant, Henry Bedinger. First Sergeant, John Crawford. Second Sergeant, John Kerney. Third Sergeant, Robert Howard. Fourth Sergeant, Dennis Bush. First Corporal, John Seaburn. Second Corporal, Evert Hoglant. Third Corporal, Thomas Knox. Fourth Corporal, Jonathan Gibbons. Drummer, Stephen Vardine. Fifer, Thomas Cook. Armourer, James Roberts.

Privates, William Anderson, Jacob Wine, Richard Neal, Peter Hill, William Waller, Adam Sheetz, James Hamilton, George Taylor, Adam Rider, Patrick Vaughan, Peter Hanes, John Malcher, Peter Snyder, Daniel Bedinger, John Barger, William Hickman, Thomas Pollock, Bryan Timmons, Thomas Mitchell, Conrad Rush, David Harman, James Aitken, William Wilson, John Wilson, Moses McComesky, Thomas Beatty, John Gray, Valentine Fritz, Zechariah Bull, William Moredock, Charles Collins, Samuel Davis, Conrad Cabbage, John Cummins, Gabriel Stevens, Michael Wolf, John Lewis, William Donnelly, David Gilmore, John Cassody, Samuel Blount, Peter Good, George Helm, William Bogle (or Boyle), John Nixon, Anthony Blackhead, Christian Peninger, Charles Jones, William Case, Casper Myre, George Brown, Benjamin McKnight, Anthony Larkin, William Seaman, Charles Snowden, John Boulden, John Blake, Nicholas Russell, Benjamin Hughes, James Brown, James Fox, William Hicks, Patrick Connell, John Holmes, John McSwaine, James Griffith, Patrick Murphy, James Aitken.

Besides the names of this company we can give a few privates of the Pennsylvania Flying Camp who are mentioned by Saffel. He adds that, as far as is known, all of these perished in prison, after inscribing their names high up upon the walls.

SOME PRIVATES OF THE PENNSYLVANIA FLYING CAMP WHO PERISHED IN PRISON IN 1776–7

"Charles Fleming, John Wright, James McKinney, Ebenezer Stille, Jacob Leinhart, Abraham Van Gordon, Peter D'Aubert, William Carbury, John McDowell, Wm. McKague, Henry Parker, James Burns, Henry Yepler, Baltus Weigh, Charles Beason, Leonard Huber, John McCarroll, Jacob Guiger, John May, Daniel Adams, George McCormick, Jacob Kettle, Jacob Miller, George Mason, James Kearney, David Sutor, Adam Bridel, Christian Mull, Daniel McKnight, Cornelius Westbrook, Luke Murphy, Joseph Conklin, Adam Dennis, Edward Ogden, Wm. Scoonover, James Rosencrants."

The names of the officers who were prisoners in New York after the battle of Long Island and the surrender of Fort Washington, can easily be obtained. But it is not with these, at present, that we have to do. We have already seen how much better was their treatment than that accorded to the hapless privates. It is chiefly to commemmorate the sufferings of the private soldier and seaman in the British prisons that this account has been written.

CHAPTER IV. THE PRISONS OF NEW YORK—JONATHAN GILLETT

We will now endeavor to describe the principal places of confinement used by the British in New York during the early years of the war. Lossing, in his Field Book of the Revolution, thus speaks of these dens of misery: "At the fight around Fort Washington," he says, "only one hundred Americans were killed, while the British loss was one thousand, chiefly Hessians, But the British took a most cruel revenge. Out of over 2600 prisoners taken on that day, in two months & four days 1900 were killed in the infamous sugar houses and other prisons in the city.

"Association of intense horror are linked with the records of the prisons and prison ships of New York. Thousands of captives perished miserably of hunger, cold, infection, and in some cases, actual poison.

"All the prisoners taken in the battle near Brooklyn in August, 1776 and at Fort Washington in November of the same year, were confined in New York, nearly 4000 in all. The New Jail and the New Bridewell were the only prisons. The former is the present

Hall of Records. Three sugar houses, some dissenting churches, Columbia College, and the Hospital were all used as prisons. The great fire in September; the scarcity of provisions; and the cruel conduct of the Provost Marshal all combined to produce intense sufferings among the men, most of whom entered into captivity, strong, healthy, young, able–bodied, the flower of the American youth of the day.

"Van Cortlandt's Sugar House was a famous (or infamous) prison. It stood on the northwest corner of Trinity church–yard.

"Rhinelander's Sugar House was on the corner of William and Duane Streets. Perhaps the worst of all the New York prisons was the third Sugar House, which occupied the space on Liberty Street where two buildings, numbers 34 and 36, now stand.

"The North Dutch Church on William Street contained 800 prisoners, and there were perhaps as many in the Middle Dutch Church. The Friends' Meeting House on Liberty and several other buildings erected for the worship of a God of love were used as prisons.

"The New Jail was made a Provost Prison, and here officers and men of note were confined. At one time they were so crowded into this building, that when they lay down upon the floor to sleep all in the row were obliged to turn over at the same time at the call, 'Turn over! Left! Right!'

"The sufferings of these brave men were largely due to the criminal indifference of Loring, Sproat, Lennox, and other Commissaries of the prisoners.

"Many of the captives were hanged in the gloom of night without trial and without a semblance of justice.

"Liberty Street Sugar House was a tall, narrow building five stories in height, and with dismal underground dungeons. In this gloomy abode jail fever was ever present. In the hot weather of July, 1777, companies of twenty at a time would be sent out for half an hour's outing, in the court yard. Inside groups of six stood for ten minutes at a time at the windows for a breath of air.

"There were no seats; the filthy straw bedding was never changed. Every day at least a dozen corpses were dragged out and pitched like dead dogs into the ditches and morasses beyond the city. Escapes, deaths, and exchange at last thinned the ranks. Hundreds left names and records on the walls."

"In 1778 the hulks of decaying ships were moored in the Wallabout. These prison ships were intended for sailors and seaman taken on the ocean, mostly the crews of privateersmen, but some soldiers were also sent to languish in their holds.

"The first vessels used were transports in which cattle and other stores had been brought over by the British in 1776. These lay in Gravesend Bay and there many of the prisoners taken in battle near Brooklyn in August, 1776, were confined, until the British took possession of New York, when they were moved to that city. In 1778 the hulks of ships were moored in the Wallabout, a sheltered bay on the Long Island shore, where the Navy Yard now is."

The sufferings of the prisoners can be better understood by giving individual instances, and wherever this is possible it shall be done. We will commence by an abstract of

THE CASE OF JONATHAN GILLETT OF WEST HARFORD

This man with seven others was captured on Long Island on the 27th of August, 1776, before they could take to their boats. He was at first confined in a prison ship, but a Masonic brother named John Archer procured him the liberty of the city on parole. His rank, we believe, was that of a lieutenant. He was a prisoner two years, then was allowed to go home to die. He exhibited every symptom of poison as well as starvation.

When he was dying he said to his son, Jonathan Gillett, Junior, "Should you enlist and be taken prisoner as I was, inquire for Mr. John Archer, a man with whom I boarded. He will assist you."

In course of time his son enlisted, was taken prisoner, and confined in the Old Sugar House on Liberty Street. Here he was nearly starved to death. The prisoners ate mice, rats, and insects. He one day found in the prison yard the dry parings of a turnip which seemed to him a delicious banquet. It is recorded that Jonathan Gillett, Jr., was finally freed from captivity through the efforts of the same gentleman, Mr. John Archer, who had aided his father.

American Prisoners of the Revolution

In 1852 Jacob Barker offered to present survivors who had been confined in the Old Sugar House with canes made from the lumber used in its construction. Four of these survivors were found. Their names were William Clark, Samuel Moulton, Levi Hanford, and Jonathan Gillett, Jr. The latter's father during his confinement wrote a letter to his friends which has been preserved, and is as follows:

My Friends,

No doubt my misfortunes have reached your ears. Sad as it is, it is true as sad. I was made prisoner the 27th day of August past by a people called heshens, and by a party called Yagers the most Inhuman of all Mortals. I can't give Room to picture them here but thus much—I at first Resolved not to be taken, but by the Impertunity of the Seven taken with me, and being surrounded on all sides I unhapily surendered; would to God I never had—then I should never (have) known there unmerciful cruelties; they first disarmed me, then plundered me of all I had, watch, Buckles, money, and sum Clothing, after which they abused me by bruising my flesh with the butts of there (guns). They knocked me down; I got up and they (kept on) beating me almost all the way to there (camp) where I got shot of them—the next thing was I was allmost starved to death by them. I was keept here 8 days and then sent on board a ship, where I continued 39 days and by (them was treated) much worse than when on shore—after I was set on (shore) at New York (I was) confined (under) a strong guard till the 20th day of November, after which I have had my liberty to walk part over the City between sun and sun, notwithstanding there generous allowance of food I must inevitably have perished with hunger had not sum friends in this (city) Relieved my extreme necessity, but I cant expect they can always do it—what I shall do next I know not, being naked for clothes and void of money, and winter present, and provisions very skerce; fresh meat one shilling per pound, Butter three shillings per pound, Cheese two shillings, Turnips and potatoes at a shilling a half peck, milk 15 Coppers per quart, bread equally as dear; and the General says he cant find us fuel thro' the winter, tho' at present we receive sum cole. [Footnote: I have made no changes in this letter except to fill up some blanks and to add a few marks of punctuation.]

"I was after put on board siezed violently with the disentarry—it followed me hard upwards of six weeks—after that a slow fever, but now am vastly better * * * my sincere love to you and my children. May God keep and preserve you at all times from sin, sickness, and death * * * I will Endeavor to faintly lead you into the poor cituation the soldiers are in, espechally those taken at Long Island where I was; in fact these cases are deplorable and they are Real objects of pitty—they are still confined and in houses where there is no fire—poor mortals, with little or no clothes—perishing with hunger, offering eight dollars in paper for one in silver to Relieve there distressing hunger; occasioned for want of food—there natures are broke and gone, some almost loose there voices and some there hearing—they are crouded into churches &there guarded night and day. I cant paint the horable appearance they make—it is shocking to human nature to behold them. Could I draw the curtain from before you; there expose to your view a lean Jawd mortal, hunger laid his skinny hand (upon him) and whet to keenest Edge his stomach cravings, sorounded with tattred garments, Rotten Rags, close beset with unwelcome vermin. Could I do this, I say, possable I might in some (small) manner fix your idea with what appearance sum hundreds of these poor creatures make in houses where once people attempted to Implore God's Blessings, &c, but I must say no more of there calamities. God be merciful to them—I cant afford them no Relief. If I had money I soon would do it, but I have none for myself.—I wrote to you by Mr. Wells to see if some one would help me to hard money under my present necessity I write no more, if I had the General would not allow it to go out, &if ever you write to me write very short or else I will never see it—what the heshens robbed me of that day amounted to the value of seventy two dollars at least. * * * I will give you as near an exact account of how many prisoners the enemy have taken as I can. They took on Long Island of the Huntingon Regiment 64, and of officers 40, of other Regiments about 60. On Moulogin Island 14, Stratton Island (Staten) 7, at Fort Washington 2200 officers and men. On the Jersey side about 28 officers and men. In all 3135 and how many killed I do not know. Many died of there wounds. Of those that went out with me of sickness occasioned by hunger eight and more lie at the point of death.

"Roger Filer hath lost one of his legs and part of a Thigh, it was his left. John Moody died here a prisoner.

"So now to conclude my little Ragged History * * * I as you know did ever impress on your mind to look to God, for so still I continue to do the same—think less of me but more of your Creator, * * * So in this I wish you well and bid you farewell and subscribe myself your nearest friend and well wisher for Ever

John'a Gillett

New York, Dec. 2nd, 1776. To Eliza Gillett at West Harford

The figures given in this pathetic letter may be inaccurate, but the description of the sufferings of the prisoners is unexaggerated. Of all the places of torment provided for these poor men the churches seem to have been the worst, and they were probably the scenes of the most brutal cruelty that was inflicted upon these unfortunate beings by the wicked and heartless men, in whose power they found themselves. Whether it was because the knowledge that they were thus desecrating buildings dedicated to the worship of God and instruction in the Christian duties of mercy and charity, had a peculiarly hardening effect upon the jailers and guards employed by the British, or whether it was merely because of their unfitness for human habitation, the men confined in these buildings perished fast and miserably. We cannot assert that no prisoners shut up in the churches in New York lived to tell the awful tale of their sufferings, but we do assert that in all our researches we have never yet happened upon any record of a single instance of a survivor living to reach his home. All the information we have gained on this subject we shall lay before the reader, and then he may form his own opinion of the justice of these remarks.

CHAPTER V. WILLIAM CUNNINGHAM, THE PROVOST MARSHAL

We will condense all that we have to say of this man, whose cruelty and wickedness are almost inconceivable, into one chapter, and have done with the dreadful subject. As far as we have been able to learn, the facts about his life are the following.

William Cunningham was an Irishman, born in Dublin Barracks in 1738. His father was a trumpeter in the Blue Dragoons. When he was sixteen he became an assistant to the riding–master of the troop. In 1761 he was made a sergeant of dragoons, but peace having been proclaimed the following year, the company to which he belonged was disbanded. He afterwards commenced the business of a scaw–banker, which means that he went about the country enticing mechanics and rustics to ship to America, on promise of having their fortunes made in that country; and then by artful practices, produced their indentures as servants, in consequence of which on their arrival in America they were sold, or at least obliged to serve a term of years to pay for their passage. This business, no doubt, proved a fit apprenticeship for the career of villainy before him.

About the year 1774 he appears to have embarked from Newry in the ship Needham for New York, with some indentured servants he had kidnapped in Ireland. He is said to have treated these poor creatures so cruelly on the passage that they were set free by the authorities in New York upon their arrival.

When Cunningham first appeared in New York he offered himself as a horse–breaker, and insinuated himself into the favor of the British officers by blatant toryism. He soon became obnoxious to the Whigs of that city, was mobbed, and fled to the Asia man–of–war for protection. From thence he went to Boston, where General Gage appointed him Provost Marshal. When the British took possession of New York he followed them to that city, burning with desire to be revenged upon the Whigs.

He is said to have compassed the death of thousands of prisoners by selling their provisions, exchanging good for spoiled food, and even by poisoning them. Many also fell victims to his murderous violence. About two hundred and fifty of these poor creatures were taken out of their places of confinement at midnight and hung, without trial, simply to gratify his bloodthirsty instincts. Private execution was conducted in the following manner. A guard was first dispatched from the Provost, about midnight, to the upper barracks, to order the people on the line of march to shut their window shutters and put out their lights, forbidding them at the same time to presume to look out of their windows on pain of death. After this the prisoners were gagged, and conducted to the gallows just behind the upper barracks and hung without ceremony there. Afterwards they were buried by his assistant, who was a mulatto.

This practice is said to have been stopped by the women along the line of march from the Provost to the barracks. They appealed to General Howe to prevent further executions, as the noise made by the sufferers praying for mercy, and appealing to Heaven for justice was dreadful to their ears.

It would seem from this account that, although the wretched men were gagged as they were conveyed along the streets, their ferocious murderer could not deny himself the pleasure of hearing their shrieks of agony at the gallows.

Watson, in his "Annals of New York," says that Cunningham glutted his vengence by hanging five or six of his prisoners every night, until the women who lived in the neighborhood petitioned Howe to have the practice discontinued.

American Prisoners of the Revolution

A pamphlet called "The Old Martyrs' Prison," says of Cunningham: "His hatred of the Americans found vent in torture by searing irons and secret scourges to those who fell under the ban of his displeasure. The prisoners were crowded together so closely that many fell ill from partial asphyxiation, and starved to death for want of the food which he sold to enrich himself."

They were given muddy and impure water to drink, and that not in sufficient quantities to sustain life. Their allowance was, nominally, two pounds of hard tack and two of pork *per week*, and this was often uncooked, while either the pork, or the biscuit, or both, were usually spoiled and most unwholesome.

Cunningham's quarters were in the Provost Prison, and on the right hand of the main door of entry. On the left of the hall was the guard room. Within the first barricade was the apartment of his assistant, Sergeant O'Keefe. Two sentinels guarded the entrance day and night; two more were stationed at the first and second barricades, which were grated, barred, and chained.

"When a prisoner was led into the hall the whole guard was paraded, and he was delivered over to Captain Cunningham or his deputy, and questioned as to his name, age, size, rank, etc., all of which was entered in a record book. These records appear to have been discreetly destroyed by the British authorities.

"At the bristling of arms, unbolting of locks and bars, clanking of enormous iron chains in a vestibule dark as Erebus, the unfortunate captive might well sink under this infernal sight and parade of tyrannical power, as he crossed the threshold of that door which probably closed on him for life.

"The north east chamber, turning to the left on the second floor, was appropriated to officers of superior rank, and was called Congress Hall. * * * In the day time the packs and blankets used by the prisoners to cover them were suspended around the walls, and every precaution was taken to keep the rooms clean and well ventilated.

"In this gloomy abode were incarcerated at different periods many American officers and citizens of distinction, awaiting with sickening hope the protracted period of their liberation. Could these dumb walls speak what scenes of anguish might they not disclose!

"Cunningham and his deputy were enabled to fare sumptuously by dint of curtailing the prisoners' rations, selling good for bad provisions, etc., in order to provide for the drunken orgies that usually terminated his dinners. Cunningham would order the rebel prisoners to turn out and parade for the amusement of his guests, pointing them out with such characterizations as 'This is the d——d rebel, Ethan Allen. This is a rebel judge, etc.'"

Cunningham destroyed Nathan Hale's last letters containing messages to his loved ones, in order, as he said, that "the rebels should not know that they had a man in their army who could die with such firmness."

From Elias Boudinot's "Journal of Events" during the Revolution we extract the following account of his interview with Cunningham in New York. "In the spring of 1777 General Washington wrote me a letter requesting me to accept of a Commission as Commissary General of Prisoners in the Army of America. I waited on him and politely declined the task, urging the wants of the Prisoners and having nothing to supply them."

Washington, however, urged him not to refuse, saying that if no one in whom he could trust would accept the office, the lot of the prisoners would be doubly hard. At last Boudinot consented to fill the position as best he could, and Washington declared that he should be supplied with funds by the Secret Committee of Congress. "I own," he says, "that after I had entered on my department, the applications of the Prisoners were so numerous, and their distress so urgent, that I exerted every nerve to obtain supplies, but in vain—Excepting L600 I had received from the Secret Committee in Bills of exchange, at my first entrance into the Office—I could not by any means get a farthing more, except in Continental Money, which was of no avail in New York. I applied to the General describing my delicate Situation and the continual application of the Officers, painting their extreme distress and urging the assurance they had received that on my appointment I was to be furnished with adequate means for their full relief. The General appeared greatly distressed and assured me that it was out of his power to afford me any supplies. I proposed draining Clothing from the public stores, but to this he objected as not having anything like a sufficient supply for the Army. He urged my considering and adopting the best means in my power to satisfy the necessities of the Prisoners, and he would confirm them. I told him I knew of no means in my Power but to take what Monies I had of my own, and to borrow from my friends in New York, to accomplish the desirable purpose. He greatly encouraged me to the attempt, promising me that if I finally met with any loss, he would divide it with me. On this I began to afford them some supplies of Provisions over and above what the Enemy afforded them, which was very small and very indifferent.

"The complaints of the very cruel treatment our Prisoners met with in the Enemy's lines rose to such a Heighth that in the Fall of this Year, 1777 the General wrote to General Howe or Clinton reciting their complaints and proposing to send an Officer into New York to examine into the truth of them. This was agreed to, and a regular pass–port returned accordingly. The General ordered me on this service. I accordingly went over on the 3rd of Feb. 1778, in my own Sloop."

The Commandant at this time was General Robertson, by whom Boudinot was very well treated, and allowed, in company with a British officer, to visit the prisons. He continues: "Accordingly I went to the Provost with the Officer, where we found near thirty Officers from Colonels downwards, in close confinement in the Gaol in New York. After some conversation with the late Ethan Allen, I told him my errand, on which he was very free in his abuse of the British. *** We then proceeded upstairs to the Room of their Confinement. I had the Officers drawn up in a Ring and informed them of my mission, that I was determined to hear nothing in secret. That I therefore hoped they would each of them in their turn report to me faithfully and candidly the Treatment they severally had received,—that my design was to obtain them the proper redress, but if they kept back anything from an improper fear of their keepers, they would have themselves only to blame for their want of immediate redress. That for the purpose of their deliverance the British officer attended. That the British General should be also well informed of the Facts. On this, after some little hesitation from a dread of their keeper, the Provost Martial, one of them began and informed us that * * * some had been confined in the Dungeon for a night to await the leisure of the General to examine them and forgot for months; for being Committee men, &c, &c. That they had received the most cruel Treatment from the Provost Martial, being locked up in the Dungeon on the most trifling pretences, such as asking for more water to drink on a hot day than usual—for sitting up a little longer in the Evening than orders allowed—for writing a letter to the General making their Complaints of ill–usage and throwing (it) out of the Windows. That some of them were kept ten, twelve, and fourteen weeks in the Dungeon on these trifling Pretenses. A Captain Vandyke had been confined eighteen months for being concerned in setting fire to the City, When, on my calling for the Provost Books, it appeared that he had been made Prisoner and closely confined in the Provost four days before the fire happened. A Major Paine had been confined eleven months for killing a Captain Campbell in the Engagement when he was taken Prisoner, when on examination it appeared that the Captain had been killed in another part of the Action. The charge was that Major Paine when taken had no commission, though acknowledged by us as a Major.

"Most of the cases examined into turned out wholly false or too trifling to be regarded. It also appeared by the Declaration of some of the Gentlemen that their water would be sometimes, as the Caprice of the Provost Martial led him, brought up to them in the tubs they used in their Rooms, and when the weather was so hot that they must drink or perish. On hearing a number of these instances of Cruelty, I asked who was the Author of them—they answered the provost keeper—I desired the Officer to call him up that we might have him face to face. He accordingly came in, and on being informed of what had passed, he was asked if the complaints were true. He, with great Insolence answered that every word was true—on which the British Officer, abusing him very much, asked him how he dared to treat Gentlemen in that cruel Manner. He, insolently putting his hands to his side, swore that he was as absolute there as General Howe was at the head of his Army. I observed to the Officer that now there could be no dispute about Facts, as the fellow had acknowledged every word to be true. I stated all the Facts in substance and waited again on General Robertson, who hoped I was quite satisfied with the falsity of the reports I had heard. I then stated to him the Facts and assured him that they turned out worse than anything we had heard. On his hesitating as to the truth of this assertion—I observed to him the propriety of having an Officer with me, to whom I now appealed for the truth of the Facts. He being present confirmed them—on which the General expressed great dissatisfaction, and promised that the Author of them should be punished. I insisted that the Officers should be discharged from his Power on Parole on Long Island, as other Officers were—To this after receiving from me a copy of the Facts I had taken down, he assented, &all were discharged except seven, who were detained some time before I could obtain their release. I forgot to mention that one Officer, Lieutenant—was taken Prisoner and brought in with a wound through the leg. He was sent to the Provost to be examined, next night he was put into the Dungeon and remained there ten weeks, totally forgotten by the General, and never had his wound dressed except as he washed it with a little Rum and Water given to him by the Centinels, through the—hole out of their own rations. Captain—and a Captain Chatham were confined with them and their allowance was four pounds hard spoiled Biscuit, and two pounds Pork per week, which they were obliged to eat raw. While they were thus confined for the slightest Complaints, the Provost Martial would come down and beat them unmercifully with a Rattan, and Knock them down with his fist. After this I visited two Hospitals of our Sick Prisoners, and the Sugar House:—in the two first were 211 Prisoners, and in the last about 190. They acknowledged that for about two months past they fared pretty well, being allowed two pounds of good Beef and a proportion of flour or Bread per week, by Mr. Lewis, My Agent, over and above the allowance received from the British, which was professed to be two thirds allowance; but before they had suffered much from the small allowance they had received, and and that their Bread was very bad, being mostly biscuit, but that the British soldiers made the same complaint as to the bread. From every account I received I found that their treatment had been greatly changed for the better within a few months past, except at the Provost. They all agreed that previous to the capture of General Burgoyne, and for some time after, Their treatment had been cruel beyond measure. That the Prisoners in the French church, amounting on an average to three or four hundred, could not all lay down at once, that from the 15th October to the first January they never received a single stick of wood, and that for the most part they eat their Pork Raw, when the Pews and Door, and Wood on Facings failed them for fuel.

"But as to my own personal knowledge I found General Robertson very ready to agree to every measure for alleviating the miseries of War and very candidly admitted many faults committed by the inferior Officers, and even the mistakes of the General himself, by hearkening to the representations of those around him. He showed me a letter from General Howe who was in Philadelphia, giving orders that we should not be at liberty to purchase blankets within their lines, and containing a copy of an order I had issued that they should not purchase provisions within ours, by way of retaliation, but he represented it as if my order was first. I stated the facts to General Robertson, who assured me that General Howe had been imposed upon, and requested me to state the facts by way of letter, when he immediately wrote to General Howe, urging the propriety of reversing his orders, which afterwards he did in a very hypocritical manner as will appear hereafter."

It does not seem that Cunningham was very seriously punished. It is probable that he was sent away from New York to Philadelphia, then in the hands of General Howe. Cunningham was Provost Marshal in that city during the British occupancy, where his cruelties were, if possible, more astrocious than ever before.

Dr. Albigense Waldo was a surgeon in the American army at Valley Forge, and he declares in his Journal concerning the prisoners in Philadelphia that "the British did not knock the prisoners in the head, or burn them with torches, or flay them alive, or dismember them as savages do, but they starved them slowly in a large and prosperous city. One of these unhappy men, driven to the last extreme of hunger, is said to have gnawed his own fingers to the first joint from the hand, before he expired. Others ate the mortar and stone which they chipped from the prison walls, while some were found with bits of wood and clay in their mouths, which in their death agonies they had sucked to find nourishment." [Footnote: This account is quoted by Mr. Bolton in a recent book called "The Private Soldier under Washington," a valuable contribution to American history.]

Boudinot has something to say about these wretched sufferers in the City of Brotherly Love during the months of January and February, 1778. "Various Reports having reached us with regard to the Extreme Sufferings of our Prisoners in Philadelphia, I was directed by the Commander–in–Chief to make particular inquiry into the truth. After some time I obtained full Information of their Sufferings. It was proved by some Militia of good Character that on being taken they were put under the care of the General's Guard, and kept four or five days without the least food. That on the fifth day they were taken into the Provost, where a small quantity of Raw Pork was given to them. One of their number seized and devoured it with so much eagerness that he dropped down dead:—that the Provost Martial used to sell their provisions and leave them to starve, as he did their Allowance of Wood. I received information from a British Officer who confided in my integrity, that he happened in the Provost just at the time the Provost Martial was locking up the Prisoners. He had ordered them from the Yard into the House. Some of them being ill with the Dysentery could scarcely walk, and for not coming faster he would beat them with his Rattan. One being delayed longer than the rest. On his coming up Cunningham gave him a blow with one of the large Keys of the Goal which killed him on the Spot. The Officer, exceedingly affected with the sight, went next day and lodged a formal Complaint of the Murder with General Howe's Aid. After waiting some days, and not discovering any measures taken for the tryal of Cunningham, he again went to head quarters and requested to see the General, but was refused. He repeated his Complaint to his Aid, and told him if this passed unpunished it would become disreputable to wear a British uniform. No notice being taken the Officer determined to furnish me privately with the means of proof of the Facts, so that General Washington might remonstrate to General Howe on the subject:—I reported them with the other testimony I had collected to General Washington. He accordingly wrote in pretty strong Terms to General Howe and fixed a day, when if he did not receive a satisfactory answer, he would retaliate on the prisoners in his Custody. On the day he received an answer from General Howe, acknowledging that, on Examination he found that Cunningham had sold the Prisoners' rations publicly in the Market. That he had therefor removed him from the Charge of the Prisoners and appointed Mr. Henry H. Ferguson in his place. This gave us great pleasure as we knew Mr. Ferguson to be a Gentleman of Character and great Humanity, and the issue justified our expectations. But to our great surprise Mr. Cunningham was only removed from the Charge of the Prisons in Philadelphia, and sent to that of New York. Soon after this great complaints being made of our Prisoners being likely to perish for want of Cloathing and Blankets, having been mostly stripped and robbed of their Cloaths when taken, application was made for permission to purchase (with the provisions which the British wanted,) Blankets and cloathing, which should be used only by the Prisoners while in Confinement. This was agreed to, as we were informed by our own Agent as well as by the British Commissioner. Provisions were accordingly attempted to be sent in, when General Howe pretending to ignorance in the business, forbid the provisions to be admitted, or the Blankets to be purchased. On this I gave notice to the British Commissary that after a certain day they must provide food for their prisoners south west of New Jersey, and to be sent in from their lines, as they should no longer be allowed to purchase provisions with us. The line drawn arose from our being at liberty to purchase in New York. This made a great noise, when General Howe on receiving General Robertson's letter from New York before mentioned, urging the propriety of the measures, issued an order that every Person in Philadelphia, who had a Blanket to sell or to spare should bring them into the King's Stores. When this was done he then gave my Agent permission to purchase Blankets and Cloathing, in the City of Philadelphia. On my Agent attempting it he found every Blanket in the City purchased by the Agents for the Army, so that not a Blanket could be had. My Agent knowing the necessities of our Prisoners, immediately employed persons in every part of the city and before General Howe could discover his own omission, purchased up every piece of flannel he could meet with, and made it up into a kind of Blanket, which answered our purpose."

Wherever General Howe and Cunningham were together, either in New York or in Philadelphia, the most atrocious cruelties were inflicted upon the American prisoners in their power, and yet some have endeavoured to excuse General Howe, on what grounds it is difficult to determine. It has been said that Cunningham *acted on higher authority than any in America*, and that Howe in vain endeavored to mitigate the sufferings of the prisoners. This, however, is not easy of belief. Howe must at least have wilfully blinded himself to the wicked and murderous violence of his subordinate. It was his duty to know how the prisoners at his mercy fared, and not to employ murderers to destroy them by the thousands as they were destroyed in the prisons of New York and Philadelphia.

Oliver Bunce, in His "Romance of the Revolution," thus speaks of the inhumanity of Cunningham.

"But of all atrocities those committed in the prisons and prison ships of New York are the most execrable, and indeed there is nothing in history to excel the barbarities there inflicted. Twelve thousand suffered death by their inhuman, cruel, savage, and barbarous usage on board the filthy and malignant prison ships—adding those who died and were poisoned in the infected prisons in the city a much larger number would be necessary to include all those who suffered by command of British Generals in New York. The scenes enacted in these prisons almost exceed belief. * * * Cunningham, the like of whom, for unpitying, relentless cruelty, the world has not produced, * * * thirsted for blood, and took an eager delight in murder."

He remained in New York until November, 1783, when he embarked on board a British man–of–war and America was no longer cursed with his presence. He is said to have been hung for the crime of forgery on the tenth of August, 1791. The newspapers of the day contained the accounts of his death, and his dying confession. These accounts have, however, been discredited by historians who have in vain sought the English records for the date of his death. It is said that no man of the name of Cunningham was hung in England in the year 1791. It is not possible to find any official British record of his transactions while Provost Marshal, and there seems a mystery about the disappearance of his books kept while in charge of the Provost, quite as great as the mystery which envelopes his death. But whether or no he confessed his many crimes; whether or no he received in this world a portion of the punishment he deserved, it is certain that the crimes were committed, and duly recorded in the judgment book of God, before whose awful bar he has been called to account for every one of them.

CHAPTER VI. THE CASE OF JABEZ FITCH

In presenting our gleanings from the books, papers, letters, pamphlets, and other documents that have been written on the subject of our prisoners during the Revolution, we will endeavor to follow some chronological order, so that we may carry the story on month by month and year by year until that last day of the British possession of New

York when Sergeant O'Keefe threw down upon the pavement of the Provost the keys of that prison, and made his escape on board a British man–of–war.

One of the prisoners taken on Long Island in the summer of 1776 was Captain Jabez Fitch, who was captured on the 27th of August, of that year. While a prisoner he contracted a scorbutic affection which rendered miserable thirty years of his life.

On the 29th of August he was taken to the transport Pacific. It was a very rainy day. The officers, of whom there were about twenty–five, were in one boat, and the men "being between three and four hundred in several other Boats, and had their hands tied behind them. In this Situation we were carried by several Ships, where there appeared great numbers of Women on Deck, who were very liberal of their Curses and Execrations: they were also not a little Noisy in their Insults, but clap'd their hands and used other peculiar gestures in so Extraordinary a Manner yet they were in some Danger of leaping overboard in this surprising Extacy." On arriving at the Pacific, a very large transport ship, they were told that all officers and men together were to be shut down below deck. The master of the ship was a brute named Dunn. At sundown all were driven down the hatches, with curses and execrations. "Both ye lower Decks were very full of Durt," and the rains had leaked in and made a dreadful sloppy mess of the floor, so that the mud was half over their shoes. At the same time they were so crowded that only half their number could lie down at a time.

"Some time in the Evening a number of the Infernal Savages came down with a lanthorn and loaded two small pieces or Cannon with Grape shot, which were pointed through two Ports in such a manner as to Rake ye deck where our people lay, telling us at ye same time with many Curses yt in Case of any Disturbance or the least noise in ye Night, they were to be Imediately fired on ye Damned Rebels." When allowed to come on deck "we were insulted by those Blackguard Villians in the most vulgar manner....We were allowed no water that was fit for a Beast to Drink, although they had plenty of good Water on board, which was used plentifully by the Seamen, etc.

"Lieutenant Dowdswell, with a party of Marines sent on board for our Guard; this Mr. Dowdswell treated us with considerable humanity, and appeared to be a Gentleman, nor were the Marines in General so Insolent as the Ships Crew....On the 31st the Commissary of Prisoners came on Board and took down the names, etc, of the prisoners....he told us Colonel Clark and many other Officers were confined at Flatbush. On Sunday, September

1st, we were removed to the ship Lord Rochford, commanded by one Lambert. This ship was much crowded. Most of the Officers were lodged on the quarter deck. Some nights we were considerably wet with rain."

The Lord Rochford lay off New Utrecht. On the third of September the officers that had been confined at Flatbush were brought on board the snow called the Mentor. "On the fifth," says Fitch, in his written account, of which this is an abstract, "we were removed on board this Snow, which was our prison for a long time. * * * We were about 90 in number, and ye Field Officers had Liberty of ye Cabbin, etc. * * * This Snow was commanded by one Davis, a very worthless, low–lived fellow. * * * When we first met on board the Mentor we spent a considerable time in Relating to each other ye particular Circumstances of our first being Taken, and also ye various Treatment with which we met on yt occasion, nor was this a disagreeable Entertainment in our Melancholy Situation. * * * Many of the officers and men were almost Destitute of Clothes, several having neither Britches, Stockings or Shoes, many of them when first taken were stripped entirely naked. Corporal Raymond of the 17th Regiment after being taken and Stripped was shamefully insulted and Abused by Gen'l Dehightler, seized by ye Hair of his head, thrown on the ground, etc. Some present, who had some small degree of humanity in their Composition, were so good as to favor them (the prisoners) with some old durty worn Garments, just sufficient to cover their nakedness, and in this Situation (they) were made Objects of Ridicule for ye Diversion of those Foreign Butchers.

"One Sam Talman (an Indian fellow belonging to the 17th Regiment) was Stripped and set up as a mark for them to Shoot at for Diversion or Practice, by which he Received two severe wounds, in the neck and arm * * * afterwards they destroyed him with many hundreds others by starvation in the prisons of New York.

"On October first orders came to land the prisoners in New York. This was not done until the seventh. On Monday about four o'clock Mr. Loring conducted us to a very large house on the West side of Broadway in the corner south of Warren Street near Bridewell, where we were assigned a small yard back of the house, and a Stoop in ye Front for our Walk. We were also Indulged with Liberty to pass and Repass to an adjacent pump in Ye Street."

Although paroled the officers were closely confined in this place for six weeks. Their provisions, he says: "were insufficient to preserve ye Connection between Soul and

Body, yet ye Charitable People of this City were so good as to afford us very considerable Relief on this account, but it was ye poor and those who were in low circumstances only who were thoughtful of our Necessities, and provisions were now grown scarce and Excessive dear. * * * Their unparalleled generosity was undoubtedly ye happy means of saving many Lives, notwithstanding such great numbers perished with hunger.

"Here we found a number of Officers made prisoners since we were, Colonel Selden, Colonel Moulton, etc. They were first confined in Ye City Hall. Colonel Selden died the Fryday after we arrived. He was Buried in the New Brick Churchyard, and most of the Officers were allowed to attend his Funeral. Dr. Thatcher of the British army attended him, a man of great humanity."

Captain Fitch declares that there were two thousand wounded British and Hessians in the hospitals in New York after the battle of Fort Washington, which is a much larger estimate than we have found in other accounts. He says that the day of the battle was Saturday, November 16th, and that the prisoners were not brought to New York until the Monday following. They were then confined in the Bridewell, as the City Jail was then called, and in several churches. Some of them were soon afterwards sent on board a prison ship, which was probably the Whitby. "A number of the officers were sent to our place of confinement; Colonel Rawlings, Colonel Hobby, Major (Otho) Williams, etc. Rawlings and Williams were wounded, others were also wounded, among them Lieutenant Hanson (a young Gent'n from Va.) who was Shot through ye Shoulder with a Musq't Ball of which wound he Died ye end of Dec'r.

"Many of ye charitable Inhabitants were denied admittance when they came to Visit us."

On the twentieth of November most of the officers were set at liberty on parole. "Ye first Objects of our attention were ye poor men who had been unhappily Captivated with us. They had been landed about ye same time yt we were, and confined in several Churches and other large Buildings and although we had often Received Intelligence from them with ye most Deplorable Representation of their Miserable Situation, yet when we came to visit them we found their sufferings vastly superior to what we had been able to conceive. Nor are words sufficient to convey an Adequate Idea of their Unparalled Calamity. Well might ye Prophet say, 'They yt be slain with ye sword are better than they yt be slain with hunger, for these pine away, etc.'

"Their appearance in general Rather Resembled dead Corpses than living men. Indeed great numbers had already arrived at their long home, and ye Remainder appeared far advanced on ye same Journey: their accommodations were in all respects vastly Inferior to what a New England Farmer would have provided for his Cattle, and although ye Commissary pretended to furnish them with two thirds of ye allowance of ye King's Troops, yet they were cheated out of one half of that. They were many times entirely neglected from Day to Day, and received no Provision at all; they were also frequently Imposed upon in Regard to ye Quality as well as Quantity of their provision. Especially in the Necessary article of Bread of which they often received such Rotten and mouldy stuff, as was entirely unfit for use.

"* * * A large number of ye most feeble were Removed down to ye Quaker Meeting House on Queen Street, where many hundreds of them perished in a much more miserable Situation than ye dumb Beasts, while those whose particular business it was to provide them relief, paid very little or no attention to their unparalleled sufferings. This house I understand was under ye Superintendence of one Dr. Dibuke * * * who had been at least once convicted of stealing (in Europe) and had fled to this country for protection: It was said he often made application of his Cane among ye Sick instead of other medicines. * * * I have often been in danger of being stabbed for attempting to speak to a prisoner in ye yard. * * *

"About the 24th December a large number of prisoners were embarked on a ship to be sent to New England. What privates of the 17th Regiment remained living were Included in this number, but about one half had already perished in Prison. I was afterwards informed that the Winds being unfavourable and their accommodations and provisions on board ye Ship being very similar to what they had been provided with before, a large proportion of them perished before they could reach New England, so that it is to be feared very few of them lived to see their native homes.

"Soon after there was large numbers of the prisoners sent off by land both to the Southward and Eastward so yt when ye Officers were Removed over into Long Island in the latter part of January there remained but very few of the privates in that City except those released by Death which number was supposed to be about 1800.

"General Robertson, so famous for Politeness and Humanity was commanding Officer at New York during the aforesaid treatment of the prisoners. Governor Scheene was said to have visited the prisoners at the Churches and manifested great dissatisfaction at their ill Usage, yet I was never able to learn that ye poor Sufferers Rec'd any Advantage thereby."

Captain Jabez Fitch was a prisoner eighteen months. After the Revolution he lived in Vermont, where he died in 1812.

CHAPTER VII. THE HOSPITAL DOCTOR—A TORY'S ACCOUNT OF NEW YORK IN 1777—ETHAN ALLEN'S ACCOUNT OF THE PRISONERS

The doctor spoken of by Jabez Fitch as Dr. Dibuke is perhaps the notorious character described by Mr. Elias Boudinot in the Journal from which we have already quoted. On page 35 of this book he gives us the following:

"AN ACCOUNT OF THE FRENCHMAN WHO POISONED. AMERICAN PRISONERS IN NEW YORK, AND WAS REWARDED FOR SO DOING BY GENERAL, HOWE

"When the British Army took possession of New York they found a Frenchman in Goal, under Condemnation for Burglery and Robbery. He was liberated. He was a very loos, ignorant man. Had been a Servant. This fellow was set over our Prisoners in the Hospital, as a Surgeon, though he knew not the least principle of the Art. Dr. McHenry, a Physician of note in the American Army, and then a Prisoner, finding the extreme ignorance of this man, and that he was really murdering our people, remonstrated to the British Director of the Hospital, and refused visiting our sick Prisoners if this man was not dismissed. A British Officer, convinced that he had killed several of our People, lodged a complaint against him, when he was ordered to be tryed by a Court Martial, but the morning before the Court were to set, this Officer was ordered off to St Johns, and the Criminal was discharged for want of Evidence. During this man having the Charge of our Prisoners in the Hospital, two of our Men deserted from the Hospital and came into our Army when they were ordered to me for Examination. They Joined in this story. That they were sick in the Hospital under the care of the above Frenchman. That he came and examined them, and gave to each of them a dose of Physick to be taken immediately. A Young Woman, their Nurse, made them some private signs not to take the Physick immediately. After the Doctor was gone, she told them she suspected the Powder was poison. That she had several times heard this Frenchman say that he would have ten Rebels dead in such a Room and five dead in such a Room the next morning, and it always so happened. They asked her what they should do: She told them their only chance was to get off, sick as they were, that she would help them out and they must shift for themselves. They accordingly got off safe, and brought the Physick with them. This was given to a Surgeon's Mate, who afterwards reported that he gave it to a Dog, and that he died in a very short time. I afterwards saw an account in a London Paper of this same Frenchman being taken up in England for some Crime and condemned to dye. At his Execution he acknowledged the fact of his having murdered a great number of Rebels in the Hospitals at New York by poyson. That on his reporting to General Howe the number of the Prisoners dead, he raised his pay. He further confessed that he poisoned the wells used by the American Flying Camp, which caused such an uncommon Mortality among them in the year 1776."

Jabez Fitch seems to have been mistaken in thinking that General Robertson instead of Lord Howe was commanding in New York at this time.

We will now give the account written by a Tory gentleman, who lived in New York during a part of the Revolution, of Loring, the Commissary of Prisons, appointed by General Howe in 1776. Judge Thomas Jones was a noted loyalist of the day. Finding it inconvenient to remain in this country after the war, he removed to England, where he died in 1792, having first completed his "History of New York during the Revolution." He gives a much larger number of prisoners in that city in the year 1776 than do any of the other authorities. We will, however, give his statements just as they were written.

"Upon the close of the campaign in 1776 there were not less than 10,000 prisoners (Sailors included) within the British lines in New York. A Commissary of Prisoners was therefore appointed, and one Joshua Loring, a Bostonian, was commissioned to the office with a guinea a day, and rations of all kinds for himself and family. In this appointment there was reciprocity. Loring had a handsome wife. The General, Sir William Howe, was fond of her. Joshua made no objections. He fingered the cash: the General enjoyed Madam. Everybody supposing the next campaign (should the rebels ever risk another) would put a final period to the rebellion. Loring was determined to make the most of his commission and by appropriating to his own use nearly two thirds of the rations allowed the prisoners, he actually starved to death about three hundred of the poor wretches before an exchange took place, and which was not until February, 1777, and hundreds that were alive at the time were so emaciated and enfeebled for the want of provisions, that numbers died on the road on their way home, and many lived but a few days after reaching their habitations. The war continuing, the Commissaryship of Prisoners grew so lucrative that in 1778 the Admiral thought proper to appoint one for naval prisoners. Upon the French War a Commissary was appointed for France. When Spain joined France another was appointed for Spain. When Great Britain made war upon Holland a Commissary was appointed for Dutch prisoners. Each had his guinea a day, and rations for himself and family. Besides, the prisoners were half starved, as the Commissaries filched their provisions, and disposed of them for their own use. It is a known fact, also, that whenever an exchange was to take place the preference was given to those who had, or could procure, the most money to present to the Commissaries who conducted the exchange, by which means large sums of money were unjustly extorted and demanded from the prisoners at every exchange, to the scandal and disgrace of Britons. We had five Commissaries of Prisoners, when one could have done all the business. Each Commissary had a Deputy, a Clerk, a Messenger in full pay, with rations of every kind."

As Judge Jones was an ardent Tory we would scarcely imagine that he would exaggerate in describing the corruptions of the commissaries. He greatly deplored the cruelties with which he taxed General Howe and other officials, and declared that these enormities prevented all hopes of reconciliation with Great Britain.

We will next quote from the "Life of Ethan Allen," written by himself, as he describes the condition of the prisoners in the churches in New York, more graphically than any of his contemporaries.

ETHAN ALLEN'S ACCOUNT OF THE AMERICAN PRISONERS

"Our number, about thirty–four, were all locked up in one common large room, without regard to rank, education, or any other accomplishment, where we continued from the setting to the rising sun, and as sundry of them were infected with the gaol and other distempers, the furniture of this spacious room consisted principally of excrement tubs. We petitioned for a removal of the sick into hospitals, but were denied. We remonstrated against the ungenerous usage of being confined with the privates, as being contrary to the laws and customs of nations, and particularly ungrateful in them, in consequence of the gentleman–like usage which the British imprisoned officers met with in America; and thus we wearied ourselves petitioning and remonstrating, but o no purpose at all; for

General Massey, who commanded at Halifax, was as inflexible as the d——l himself. * * * Among the prisoners were five who had a legal claim to a parole, James Lovel, Esq; Captain Francis Proctor; a Mr. Rowland, Master of a Continental armed vessel; a Mr. Taylor, his mate, and myself. * * * The prisoners were ordered to go on board of a man–of–war, which was bound for New York, but two of them were not able to go on board and were left in Halifax: one died and the other recovered. This was about the 12th of October, 1776. * * * We arrived before New York and cast an anchor the latter part of October, where we remained several days, and where Captain Smith informed me that he had recommended me to Admiral Howe, and General Sir Wm. Howe, as a gentleman of honor and veracity, and desired that I might be treated as such. Captain Burk was then ordered on board a prison ship in the harbor. I took my leave of Captain Smith, and with the other prisoners was sent on board a transport ship. * * * Some of the last days of November the prisoners were landed at New York, and I was admitted to parole with the other officers, viz: Proctor, Rowland, and Taylor. The privates were put into the filthy churches in New York, with the distressed prisoners that were taken at Fort Washington, and the second night Sergeant Roger Moore, who was bold and enterprising, found means to make his escape, with every of the remaining prisoners that were taken with me, except three who were soon after exchanged: so that out of thirty–one prisoners who went with me the round exhibited in these sheets, two only died with the enemy, and three only were exchanged, one of whom died after he came within our lines. All the rest at different times made their escape from the enemy.

"I now found myself on parole, and restricted to the limits of the city of New York, where I soon projected means to live in some measure agreeable to my rank, though I was destitute of cash. My constitution was almost worn out by such a long and barbarous captivity. * * * In consequence of a regular diet and exercise my blood recruited, and my nerves in a great measure recovered their former tone * * * in the course of six months.

"* * * Those who had the misfortune to fall into the enemy's hands at Fort Washington * * * were reserved from immediate death to famish and die with hunger: in fine the word rebel' was thought by the enemy sufficient to sanctify whatever cruelties they were pleased to inflict, death itself not excepted. * * *

"The prisoners who were brought to New York were crowded into churches, and environed with slavish Hessian guards, a people of a strange language * * * and at other times by merciless Britons, whose mode of communicating ideas being unintelligible in this country served only to tantalize and insult the helpless and perishing; but above all the hellish delight and triumph of the tories over them, as they were dying by hundreds. This was too much for me to bear as a spectator; for I saw the tories exulting over the dead bodies of their countrymen. I have gone into the churches and seen sundry of the prisoners in the agonies of death, in consequence of very hunger; and others speechless and near death, biting pieces of chips; others pleading, for God's sake for something to eat, and at the same time shivering with the cold. Hollow groans saluted my ears, and despair seemed to be imprinted on every of their countenances. The filth in these churches, in consequence of the fluxes, was almost beyond description. I have carefully sought to direct my steps so as to avoid it, but could not. They would beg for God's sake for one copper or morsel of bread. I have seen in one of the churches seven dead, at the same time, lying among the excrements of their bodies.

"It was a common practice with the enemy to convey the dead from these filthy places in carts, to be slightly buried, and I have seen whole gangs of tories making derision, and exulting over the dead, saying 'There goes another load of d———d rebels!' I have observed the British soldiers to be full of their blackguard jokes and vaunting on those occasions, but they seemed to me to be less malignant than the Tories.

"The provision dealt out to the prisoners was by no means sufficient for the support of life. It was deficient in Quantity, and much more so in Quality. The prisoners often presented me with a sample of their bread, which I certify was damaged to such a degree that it was loathsome and unfit to be eaten, and I am bold to aver it as my opinion, that it had been condemned and was of the very worst sort. I have seen and been fed upon damaged bread, in the course of my captivity, and observed the quality of such bread as has been condemned by the enemy, among which was very little so effectually spoiled as what was dealt out to these prisoners. Their allowance of meat, as they told me, was quite trifling and of the basest sort. I never saw any of it, but was informed, bad as it was, it was swallowed almost as quick as they got hold of it. I saw some of them sucking bones after they were speechless; others who could yet speak and had the use of their reason, urged me in the strongest and most pathetic manner, to use my interest in their behalf: 'For you plainly see,' said they,'that we are devoted to death and destruction,' and after I had examined more particularly into their truly deplorable condition and had become more fully apprized of the essential facts, I was persuaded that it was a premeditated and systematized plan of the British council to destroy the youths of our land, with a view thereby to deter the country and make it submit to their despotism: but as I could not do them any material service, and by any public attempt for that purpose I might endanger myself by frequenting places the most nauseous and contagious that could be conceived of, I refrained going into the churches, but frequently conversed with such of the prisoners as were admitted to come out into the yard, and found that the systematical usage still continued. The guard would often drive me away with their fixed bayonets. A Hessian one day followed me five or six rods, but by making use of my legs, I got rid of the lubber.

"Sometimes I could obtain a little conversation notwithstanding their severities.

"I was in one of the yards and it was rumoured among those in the church, and sundry of the prisoners came with their usual complaints to me, and among the rest a large–boned, tall young man, as he told me from Pennsylvania, who was reduced to a mere skeleton. He said he was glad to see me before he died, which he had expected to have done last night, but was a little revived. He further informed me that he and his brother had been urged to enlist into the British army, but had both resolved to die first; that his brother had died last night, in consequence of that resolve, and that he expected shortly to follow him; but I made the other prisoners stand a little off and told him with a low voice to enlist; he then asked whether it was right in the sight of God? I assured him that it was, and that duty to himself obliged him to deceive the British by enlisting and deserting the first opportunity; upon which he answered with transport that he would enlist. I charged him not to mention my name as his adviser, lest it should get air and I should be closely confined, in consequence of it.

"The integrity of these suffering prisoners is incredible. Many hundreds of them, I am confident, submitted to death rather than enlist in the British service, which, I am informed, they most generally were pressed to do. I was astonished at the resolution of the two brothers, particularly; it seems that they could not be stimulated to such exertions of heroism from ambition, as they were but obscure soldiers. Strong indeed must the internal principle of virtue be which supported them to brave death, and one of them went through the operation, as did many hundreds others * * * These things will have their proper effect upon the generous and brave.

"The officers on parole were most of them zealous, if possible, to afford the miserable soldiers relief, and often consulted with one another on the subject, but to no effect, being destitute of the means of subsistence which they needed, nor could they project any measure which they thought would alter their fate, or so much as be a mean of getting them out of those filthy places to the privilege of fresh air. Some projected that all the officers should go in procession to General Howe and plead the cause of the perishing soldiers, but this proposal was negatived for the following reasons: viz: because that General Howe must needs be well acquainted and have a thorough knowledge of the state and condition of the prisoners in every of their wretched apartments, and that much more particular and exact than any officer on parole could be supposed to have, as the General had a return of the circumstances of the prisoners by his own officers every morning, of the number who were alive, as also of the number who died every twenty–four hours: and consequently the bill of mortality, as collected from the daily returns, lay before him with all the material situations and circumstances of the prisoners, and provided the officers should go in procession to General Howe, according to the projection, it would give him the greatest affront, and that he would either retort upon them, that it was no part of their parole to instruct him in his conduct to prisoners; that they were mutinying against his authority, and, by affronting him, had forfeited their parole, or that, more probably, instead of saying one word to them, would order them all into as wretched a confinement as the soldiers whom they sought to relieve, for at that time the British, from the General to the private centinel, were in full confidence, nor did they so much as hesitate, but that they should conquer the country.

"Thus the consultation of the officers was confounded and broken to pieces, in consequence of the dread which at the time lay on their minds of offending General Howe; for they conceived so murderous a tryant would not be too good to destroy even the officers on the least pretence of an affront, as they were equally in his power with the soldiers; and as General Howe perfectly understood the condition of the private soldiers, it was argued that it was exactly such as he and his council had devised, and as he meant to destroy them it would be to no purpose for them to try to dissuade him from it, as they were helpless and liable to the same fate, on giving the least affront. Indeed anxious apprehensions disturbed them in their then circumstances.

"Meantime mortality raged to such an intolerable degree among the prisoners that the very school boys in the street knew the mental design of it in some measure; at least they knew that they were starved to death. Some poor women contributed to their necessity till their children were almost starved; and all persons of common understanding knew that they were devoted to the cruellest and worst of deaths.

"It was also proposed by some to make a written representation of the condition of the soldiery, and the officers to sign it, and that it should be couched in such terms, as though they were apprehensive that the General was imposed upon by his officers, in their daily returns to him of the state and condition of the prisoners, and that therefor the officers moved with compassion, were constrained to communicate to him the facts relative to them, nothing doubting but that they would meet with a speedy redress; but this proposal was most generally negatived also, and for much the same reason offered in the other case; for it was conjectured that General Howe's indignation would be moved against such officers as should attempt to whip him over his officers' backs; that he would discern that he himself was really struck at, and not the officers who made the daily returns; and therefor self preservation deterred the officers from either petitioning or remonstrating to General Howe, either verbally or in writing; as also they considered that no valuable purpose to the distressed would be obtained.

"I made several rough drafts on the subject, one of which I exhibited to the Colonels Magaw, Miles, and Atlee; and they said that they would consider the matter. Soon after I called on them, and some of the gentlemen informed me that they had written to the General on the subject, and I concluded that the gentlemen thought it best that they should write without me, as there was such spirited aversion subsisting between the British and me."

Ethan Allen goes on to say: "Our little army was retreating in New Jersey and our young men murdered by hundreds in New York." He then speaks of Washington's success at Trenton in the following terms: "This success had a mighty effect on General Howe and his council, and roused them to a sense of their own weakness. * * * Their obduracy and death–designing malevolence in some measure abated or was suspended. The prisoners, who were condemned to the most wretched and cruellest of deaths, and who survived to this period, *though most of them died before,* were immediately ordered to be sent within General Washington's lines, for an exchange, and in consequence of it were taken out of their filthy and poisonous places of confinement, and sent out of New York to their friends in haste. Several of them fell dead in the streets of New York, as they attempted to walk to the vessels in the harbor, for their intended embarkation. What number lived to reach the lines I cannot ascertain, but, from concurrent representations which I have since received from numbers of people who lived in and adjacent to such parts of the country, where they were received from the enemy, *I apprehend that most of them died in consequence of the vile usage of the enemy.* Some who were eye witnesses of the scene of mortality, more especially in that part which continued after the exchange took place, are of opinion that it was partly in consequence of a slow poison; but this I refer to the doctors who attended them, who are certainly the best judges.

"Upon the best calculation I have been able to make from personal knowledge, and the many evidences I have collected in support of the facts, I learn that, of the prisoners taken on Long Island and Fort Washington and some few others, at different times and places, about two thousand perished with hunger, cold, and sickness, occasioned by the filth of their prisons, at New York; and a number more on their passage to the continental lines; most of the residue who reached their friends having received their death wound, could not be restored by the assistance of their physicians and friends: but like their brother prisoners, fell a sacrifice to the relentless and scientific barbarity of the British. I took as much pains as the circumstances would admit of to inform myself not only of matters of fact, but likewise of the very design and aims of General Howe and his council, the latter of which I predicated on the former, and submit it to the candid public."

CHAPTER VIII. THE ACCOUNT OF ALEXANDER GRAYDON

One of the most interesting and best memoirs of revolutionary times is that written by Alexander Graydon, and as he was taken prisoner at Fort Washington, and closely connected with the events in New York during the winter of 1776–7, we will quote here his account of his captivity.

He describes the building of Fort Washington in July of 1776 by the men of Magaw's and Hand's regiments. General Putnam was the engineer. It was poorly built for defence, and not adapted for a siege.

Graydon was a captain in Colonel Shee's Regiment, but, for some reason or other, Shee went home just before the battle was fought, and his troops were commanded by Cadwallader in his stead. Graydon puts the number of privates taken prisoner at 2706 and the officers at about 210. Bedinger, as we have already seen, states that there were 2673 privates and 210 officers. He was a man of painstaking accuracy, and it is quite probable that his account is the most trustworthy. As one of the privates was Bedinger's own young brother, a boy of fifteen, whom he undoubtedly visited as often as possible, while Graydon only went once to the prisons, perhaps Bedinger had the best opportunities for computing the number of captives.

Graydon says that Colonel Rawlings was, some time late in the morning of the 16th of November, attacked by the Hessians, when he fought with great gallantry and effect as they were climbing the heights, until the arms of the riflemen became useless from the foulness they contracted from the frequent repetition of their fire.

Graydon, himself, becoming separated from his own men, mistook a party of Highlanders for them, and was obliged to surrender to them. He was put under charge of a Scotch sergeant, who said to him and his companion, Forrest: "Young men, ye should never fight against your King!"

Just then a British officer rode up at full gallop exclaiming, "What! taking prisoners! Kill them, Kill every man of them!"

"My back was towards him when he spoke," says Graydon, "and although by this time there was none of that appearance of ferocity in the guard which would induce much fear that they would execute his command, I yet thought it well enough to parry it, and turning to him, I took off my hat, saying, 'Sir, I put myself under your protection!'

"No man was ever more effectually rebuked. His manner was instantly softened; he met my salutation with an inclination of his body, and after a civil question or two, as if to make amends for his sanguinary mandate, rode off towards the fort, to which he had enquired the way.

"Though I had delivered up my arms I had not adverted to a cartouche box which I wore about my waist, and which, having once belonged to his British Majesty, presented in front the gilded letters, G. R. Exasperated at this trophy on the body of a rebel, one of the soldiers seized the belt with great violence, and in the act to unbuckle it, had nearly jerked me off my legs. To appease the offended loyalty of the honest Scot I submissively took it off and handed it to him, being conscious that I had no longer any right to it. At this moment a Hessian came up. He was not a private, neither did he look like a regular officer. He was some retainer, however, to the German troops, and as much of a brute as any one I have ever seen in human form. The wretch came near enough to elbow us, and, half unsheathing his sword, with a countenance that bespoke a most vehement desire to use it against us, he grunted out in broken English, 'Eh! you rebel! you damn rebel!'

47

"I had by this time entire confidence in our Scotchmen, and therefore regarded the caitiff with the same indifference that I should have viewed a caged wild beast, though with much greater abhorrence. * * *

"We were marched to an old stable, where we found about forty or fifty prisoners already collected, principally officers, of whom I only particularly recollect Lieutenant Brodhead of our battalion. We remained on the outside of the building; and, for nearly an hour, sustained a series of the most intolerable abuse. This was chiefly from the officers of the light infantry, for the most part young and insolent puppies, whose worthlessness was apparently their recommendation to a service, which placed them in the post of danger, and in the way of becoming food for powder, their most appropriate destination next to that of the gallows. The term 'rebel,' with the epithet 'damned' before it, was the mildest we received. We were twenty times told, sometimes with a taunting affectation of concern, that we should every man of us be hanged. * * * The indignity of being ordered about by such contemptible whipsters, for a moment unmanned me, and I was obliged to apply my handkerchief to my eyes. This was the first time in my life that I had been the victim of brutal, cowardly oppression, and I was unequal to the shock; but my elasticity of mind was soon restored, and I viewed it with the indignant contempt it deserved.

"For the greater convenience of guarding us we were now removed to the barn of Colonel Morris's house, which had been the head–quarters of our army. * * * It was a good, new building. * * * There were from a hundred and fifty to two hundred, comprising a motley group, to be sure. Men and officers of all descriptions, regulars and militia, troops continental and state, and some in hunting shirts, the mortal aversion of a red coat. Some of the officers had been plundered of their hats, and some of their coats, and upon the new society into which we were introduced, with whom a showy exterior was all in all, we were certainly not calculated to make a very favorable impression. I found Captain Tudor here, of our regiment, who, if I mistake not, had lost his hat. * * * It was announced, by an huzza, that the fort had surrendered.

"The officer who commanded the guard in whose custody we now were, was an ill–looking, low–bred fellow of this dashing corps of light infantry. * * * As I stood as near as possible to the door for the sake of air, the enclosure in which we were being extremely crowded and unpleasant, I was particularly exposed to his brutality; and repelling with some severity one of his attacks, for I was becoming desperate and careless of safety, the ruffian exclaimed, 'Not a word, sir, or damme, I'll give you my butt!' at the same time clubbing his fusee, and drawing it back as if to give the blow, I fully expected it, but he contented himself with the threat. I observed to him that I was in his power, and disposed to submit to it, though not proof against every provocation. * * * There were several British officers present, when a Serjeant—Major came to take an account of us, and particularly a list of such of us as were officers. This Serjeant, though not uncivil, had all that animated, degage impudence of air, which belongs to a self complacent, non—commissioned officer of the most arrogant army in the world; and with his pen in his hand and his paper on his knee applied to each of us in his turn for his rank. * * * The sentinels were withdrawn to the distance of about ten or twelve feet, and we were told that such of us as were officers might walk before the door. This was a great relief to us."

The officers were lodged in the barn loft quite comfortably. A young Lieutenant Beckwith had them in charge, and was a humane gentleman. In the evening he told them he would send them, if possible, a bottle of wine, but at any rate, a bottle of spirits. He kept his word as to the spirits, which was all the supper the party in the loft had. "In the morning a soldier brought me Mr. B.'s compliments, and an invitation to come down and breakfast with him. * * * I thankfully accepted his invitation, and took with me Forrest and Tudor. * * * He gave us a dish of excellent coffee, with plenty of very good toast, which was the only morsel we had eaten for the last twenty—four hours. * * * Our fellow sufferers got nothing until next morning. * * *

"All the glory that was going (in the battle of Fort Washington) had, in my idea of what had passed, been engrossed by the regiment of Rawlings, which had been actively engaged, killed a number of the enemy, and lost many themselves.

"About two o'clock Mr. B. sent me a plate amply supplied with corned beef, cabbage, and the leg and wing of a turkey, with bread in proportion."

Though Mr. Graydon calls this gentleman Mr. Becket, it seems that there was no young officer of that name at the battle of Fort Washington. Becket appears to be a mistake for Lieutenant Onslow Beckwith. The prisoners were now marched within six miles of New York and Graydon's party of officers were well quartered in a house. "Here," he continues, "for the first time we drew provisions for the famished soldiers. * * * Previously to entering the city we were drawn up for about an hour on the high ground near the East River. Here, the officers being separated from the men, we were conducted into a church, where we signed a parole."

At this place a non–commissioned British officer, who had seen him at the ordinary kept by his widowed mother in Philadelphia, when he was a boy, insisted on giving him a dollar.

"Quarters were assigned for us in the upper part of the town, in what was called 'The holy ground.' * * * I ventured to take board at four dollars per week with a Mrs. Carroll. * * * Colonel Magaw, Major West, and others, boarded with me."

He was fortunate in obtaining his trunk and mattress. Speaking of the prisons in which the privates were confined he says: "I once and once only ventured to penetrate into these abodes of human misery and despair. But to what purpose repeat my visit, when I had neither relief to administer nor comfort to bestow? * * * I endeavoured to comfort them with the hope of exchange, but humanity forbade me to counsel them to rush on sure destruction. * * * Our own condition was a paradise to theirs. * * * Thousands of my unhappy countrymen were consigned to slow, consuming tortures, equally fatal and potent to destruction."

The American officers on parole in New York prepared a memorial to Sir William Howe on the condition of these wretched sufferers, and it was signed by Colonels Magaw, Miles, and Atlee. This is, no doubt, the paper of which Colonel Ethan Allen writes. Captain Graydon was commissioned to deliver this document to Sir William Howe. He says: "The representation which had been submitted to General Howe in behalf of the suffering prisoners was more successful than had been expected. * * * The propositions had been considered by Sir William Howe, and he was disposed to accede to them. These were that the men should be sent within our lines, where they should be receipted for, and an equal number of the prisoners in our hands returned in exchange. * * * Our men, no longer soldiers (their terms for which they had enlisted having expired) and too debilitated for service, gave a claim to sound men, immediately fit to take the field, and there was moreover great danger that if they remained in New York the disease with which they were infected might be spread throughout the city. At any rate hope was admitted into the mansions of despair, the prison doors were thrown open, and the soldiers who were yet alive and capable of being moved were conveyed to our nearest posts, under the care of our regimental surgeons, to them a fortunate circumstance, since it enabled them to exchange the land of bondage for that of liberty. * * * Immediately after the release of our men a new location was assigned to us. On the 22nd of January, 1777, we were removed to Long Island."

CHAPTER IX. A FOUL PAGE OF ENGLISH HISTORY

We will not follow Mr. Graydon now to Long Island. It was then late in January, 1777. The survivors of the American prisoners were, many of them, exchanged for healthy British soldiers. The crime had been committed, one of the blackest which stains the annals of English history. By the most accurate computation at least two thousand helpless American prisoners had been slowly starved, frozen, or poisoned to death in the churches and other prisons in New York.

No excuse for this monstrous crime can be found, even by those who are anxiously in search of an adequate one.

We have endeavored to give some faint idea of the horrors of that hopeless captivity. As we have already said scarcely any one who endured imprisonment for any length of time in the churches lived to tell the tale. One of these churches was standing not many years ago, and the marks of bayonet thrusts might plainly be seen upon its pillars. What terrible deeds were enacted there we can only conjecture. We *know* that two thousand, healthy, high–spirited young men, many of them sons of gentlemen, and all patriotic, brave, and long enduring, even unto death, were foully murdered in these places of torment, compared to which ordinary captivity is described by one who endured it as paradise. We know, we say, that these young men perished awfully, rather than enlist in the British army; that posterity has almost forgotten them, and that their dreadful sufferings ought to be remembered wherever American history is read.

We have already said that it is impossible now to obtain the names of all who suffered death at the hands of their inhuman jailors during the fall and winter of 1776–7. But we have taken Captain Abraham Shepherd's company of riflemen as a sample of the prisoners, and are able, thanks to the pay roll now in our care, to indicate the fate of each man upon the list.

It is a mistake to say that no prisoners deserted to the British. After the account we have quoted from Ethan Allen's book we feel sure that no one can find the heart to blame the poor starving creatures who endeavored to preserve their remains of life in this manner.

Henry Bedinger gives the names of seven men of this company who deserted. They are

American Prisoners of the Revolution

Thomas Knox, a corporal; William Anderson, Richard Neal, George Taylor, Moses McComesky, Anthony Blackhead and Anthony Larkin. Thomas Knox did not join the British forces until the 17th of January, 1777; William Anderson on the 20th of January, 1777. Richard Neal left the American army on the tenth of August, 1776. He, therefore, was not with the regiment at Fort Washington. George Taylor deserted on the 9th of July, 1776, which was nine days after he enlisted. Moses McComesky did not desert until the 14th of June, 1777. Anthony Blackhead deserted November 15th, 1776, the day before the battle was fought; Anthony Larkin, September 15th, 1776. We cannot tell what became of any of these men. Those who died of the prisoners are no less than fifty–two in this one company of seventy–nine privates and non–commissioned officers. This may and probably does include a few who lived to be exchanged. The date of death of each man is given, but not the place in which he died.

A very singular fact about this record is that no less than *seventeen* of the prisoners of this company died on the same day, which was the fifteenth of February, 1777. Why this was so we cannot tell. We can only leave the cause of their death to the imagination of our readers. Whether they were poisoned by wholesale; whether they were murdered in attempting to escape; whether the night being extraordinarily severe, they froze to death; whether they were butchered by British bayonets, we are totally unable to tell. The record gives their names and the date of death and says that all seventeen were prisoners. That is all.

The names of these men are Jacob Wine, William Waller, Peter Snyder, Conrad Rush, David Harmon, William Moredock, William Wilson, James Wilson, Thomas Beatty, Samuel Davis, John Cassody, Peter Good, John Nixon, Christopher Peninger, Benjamin McKnight, John McSwaine, James Griffith, and Patrick Murphy.

Two or three others are mentioned as dying the day after. Is it possible that these men were on board one of the prison ships which was set on fire? If so we have been able to discover no account of such a disaster on that date.

Many of the papers of Major Henry Bedinger were destroyed. It is possible that he may have left some clue to the fate of these men, but if so it is probably not now in existence. But among the letters and memoranda written by him which have been submitted to us for inspection, is a list, written on a scrap of paper, of the men that he recruited for Captain Shepherd's Company in the summer of 1776. This paper gives the names of the men and the date on which each one died in prison. It is as follows:

LIST OF MEN RAISED BY LIEUTENANT HENRY BEDINGER, AND THAT HE BROUGHT FROM NEW TOWN, BERKELEY COUNTY, VA., AUGUST FIRST, 1776

Dennis Bush, Fourth Sergeant. (He was taken prisoner at Fort Washington, but lived to be exchanged, and was paid up to October 1st, 1778, at the end of the term for which the company enlisted.)

Conrad Cabbage, Prisoner, Died, Jan. 7th, 1777. John Cummins, Prisoner, Died, Jan. 27th, 1777. Gabriel Stevens, Prisoner, Died, March 1st, 1777. William Donally, Prisoner, Died, Jan. 10th, 1777. David Gilmer, Prisoner, Died, Jan. 26th, 1777. John Cassady, Prisoner, Died, Feb. 15th, 1777. Samuel Brown, Prisoner, Died, Feb. 26th, 1777. Peter Good, Prisoner, Died, Feb. 13th, 1777. William Boyle, Prisoner, Died, Feb. 25th, 1777. John Nixon, Prisoner, Died, Feb. 18th, 1777. Anthony Blackhead, deserted, Nov. 15th, 1776. William Case, Prisoner, Died, March 15th, 1777. Caspar Myres, Prisoner, Died, Feb. 16th, 1777. William Seaman, Prisoner, Died, July 8th, 1777. Isaac Price, Prisoner, Died, Feb. 5th, 1777. Samuel Davis, Prisoner, Died, Feb. 15th, 1777.

William Seaman was the son of Jonah Seaman, living near Darkesville. Isaac Price was an orphan, living with James' Campbell's father. Samuel Davis came from near Charlestown.

Henry Bedinger.

This is all, but it is eloquent with what it does not say. All but two of this list of seventeen young, vigorous riflemen died in prison or from the effects of confinement. One, alone had sufficient vitality to endure until the 8th of July, 1777. Perhaps he was more to be pitied than his comrades.

We now begin to understand how it happened that, out of more than 2,600 privates taken prisoner at Fort Washington, 1,900 were dead in the space of two months and four days, when the exchange of some of the survivors took place. Surely this is a lasting disgrace to one of the greatest nations of the world. If, as seems undoubtedly true, more men perished in prison than on the battle fields of the Revolution, it is difficult to see why so little is made of this fact in the many histories of that struggle that have been written. We find that the accounts of British prisons are usually dismissed in a few words, sometimes in an appendix, or a casual note. But history was ever written thus. Great victories are elaborately described; and all the pomp and circumstance of war is set down for our pleasure and instruction. But it is due to the grand solemn muse of history, who carries the torch of truth, that the other side, the horrors of war, should be as faithfully delineated. Wars will not cease until the lessons of their cruelty, their barbarity, and the dark trail of suffering they leave behind them are deeply impressed upon the mind. It is our painful task to go over the picture, putting in the shadows as we see them, however gloomy may be the effect.

CHAPTER X. A BOY IN PRISON

In the winter of 1761 a boy was born in a German settlement near Lancaster, Pennsylvania, the third son of Henry Bedinger and his wife, whose maiden name was Magdalene von Schlegel. These Germans, whom we have already mentioned, moved, in 1762, to the neighborhood of the little hamlet, then called Mecklenburg, Berkeley County, Virginia. Afterwards the name of the town was changed to Shepherdstown, in honor of its chief proprietor, Thomas Shepherd.

Daniel was a boy of fourteen when the first company of riflemen was raised at Shepherdstown by the gallant young officer, Captain Hugh Stephenson, in 1775.

The rendezvous of this company was the spring on his mother's farm, then called Bedinger's Spring, where the clear water gushes out of a great rock at the foot of an ancient oak. The son of Daniel Bedinger, Hon. Henry Bedinger, Minister to the Court of Denmark in 1853, left a short account of his father's early history, which we will quote in this place. He says: "When the war of the Revolution commenced my father's eldest brother Henry was about twenty−two years of age. His next brother, Michael, about nineteen, and he himself only in his fifteenth year. Upon the first news of hostilities his two brothers joined a volunteer company under the command of Captain Hugh Stephenson, and set off immediately to join the army at Cambridge.

"My father himself was extremely anxious to accompany them, but they and his mother, who was a widow, forbade his doing so, telling him he was entirely too young, and that he must stay at home and take care of his younger brothers and sisters. And he was thus very reluctantly compelled to remain at home. At the expiration of about twelve months his brothers returned home, and when the time for their second departure had arrived, the wonderful tales they had narrated of their life in camp had wrought so upon my father's youthful and ardent imagination that he besought them and his mother with tears in his eyes, to suffer him to accompany them. But they, regarding his youth, would not give their consent, but took their departure without him.

"However, the second night after their arrival in camp (which was at Bergen, New Jersey), they were astonished by the arrival of my father, he having run off from home and followed them all the way on foot, and now appeared before them, haggard and weary and half starved by the lengths of his march. * * * My father was taken prisoner at the battle of Fort Washington, and the privations and cruel treatment which he then underwent gave a blow to his constitution from which he never recovered. After the close of the Revolution he returned home with a constitution much shattered. * * *"

Many years after the Revolution Dr. Draper, who died in Madison, Wisconsin, and left his valuable manuscripts to the Historical Society of that State, interviewed an old veteran of the war, in Kentucky. This venerable relic of the Revolution was Major George Michael Bedinger, a brother of Daniel. Dr. Draper took down from his lips a short account of the battle of Fort Washington, where his two brothers were captured. Major G. M. Bedinger was not in service at that time, but must have received the account from one or both of his brothers. Dr. Draper says: "In the action of Fort Washington Henry Bedinger heard a Hessian captain, having been repulsed, speak to his riflemen in his own language, telling them to follow his example and reserve their fire until they were close. Bedinger, recognizing his mother tongue, watched the approach of the Hessian officer, and each levelled his unerring rifle at the other. Both fired, Bedinger was wounded in the finger: the ball passing, cut off a lock of his hair. The Hessian was shot through the head, and instantly expired. Captain Bedinger's young brother Daniel, in his company, then but a little past fifteen, shot twenty−seven rounds, and was often heard to say, after discharging his piece, 'There! take that, you ——!'

"His youthful intrepidity, and gallant conduct, so particularly attracted the attention of the officers, that, though taken prisoner, he was promoted to an ensigncy, his commission dating back six months that he might take precedence of the other ensigns of his company.

"These two brothers remained prisoners, the youngest but a few months, and the elder nearly four years, both on prison ships, with the most cruel treatment, in filthy holds, impure atmosphere, and stinted allowance of food. With such treatment it was no wonder that but eight hundred out of the 2800 prisoners taken at Fort Washington survived.

"During the captivity of his brother Henry, Major Bedinger would by labor, loans at different times, and the property sold which he inherited from his father, procure money to convey to the British Commissary of Prisoners to pay his brother Henry's board. Then he was released from the filthy prison ship, limited on his parole of honor to certain limits at Flatbush, and decently provisioned and better treated, and it is pleasant to add that the British officers having charge of these matters were faithful in the proper application of funds thus placed in their hands. Major Bedinger made many trips on this labor of fraternal affection. This, with his attention to his mother and family, kept him from regularly serving in the army. But he, never the less, would make short tours of service."

So far we have quoted Dr. Draper's recollections of an interview with George Michael Bedinger in his extreme old age. We have already given Henry Bedinger's own acount of his captivity. What we know of Daniel's far severer treatment we will give in our own words.

It was four days before the privates taken at Fort Washington had one morsel to eat. They were then given a little mouldy biscuit and raw pork. They were marched to New York, and Daniel was lodged with many others, perhaps with the whole company, in the Old Sugar House on Liberty Street. Here he very nearly died of exposure and starvation. There was no glass in the windows and scarce one of the prisoners was properly clothed. When it snowed they were drifted over as they slept.

One day Daniel discovered in some vats a deposit of sugar which he was glad to scrape to sustain life. A gentleman, confined with him in the Old Sugar House, used to tell his descendants that the most terrible fight he ever engaged in was a struggle with a comrade in prison for the carcass of a decayed rat.

It is possible that Henry Bedinger, an officer on parole in New York, may have found some means of communicating with his young brother, and even of supplying him, sometimes, with food. Daniel, however, was soon put on board a prison ship, probably the Whitby, in New York harbor.

Before the first exchange was effected the poor boy had yielded to despair, and had turned his face to the wall, to die. How bitterly he must have regretted the home he had been so ready to leave a few months before! And now the iron had eaten into his soul, and he longed for death, as the only means of release from his terrible sufferings.

Daniel's father was born in Alsace, and he himself had been brought up in a family where German was the familiar language of the household. It seems that, in some way, probably by using his mother tongue, he had touched the heart of one of the Hessian guards. When the officers in charge went among the prisoners, selecting those who were to be exchanged, they twice passed the poor boy as too far gone to be moved. But he, with a sudden revival of hope and the desire to live, begged and entreated the Hessian so pitifully not to leave him behind, that that young man, who is said to have been an officer, declared that he would be responsible for him, had him lifted and laid down in the bottom of a boat, as he was too feeble to sit or stand. In this condition he accompanied the other prisoners to a church in New York where the exchange was effected. One or more of the American surgeons accompanied the prisoners. In some way Daniel was conveyed to Philadelphia, where he completely collapsed, and was taken to one of the military hospitals.

Here, about the first of January, 1777, his devoted brother, George Michael Bedinger, found him. Major Bedinger's son, Dr. B. F. Bedinger, wrote an account of the meeting of these two brothers for Mrs. H. B. Lee, one of Daniel's daughters, which tells the rest of the story. He said:

"My father went to the hospital in search of his brother, but did not recognize him. On inquiry if there were any (that had been) prisoners there a feeble voice responded, from a little pile of straw and rags in a corner, 'Yes, Michael, there is one.'

"Overcome by his feelings my father knelt by the side of the poor emaciated boy, and took him in his arms. He then bore him to a house where he could procure some comforts in the way of food and clothing. After this he got an armchair, two pillows, and some leather straps.

"He placed his suffering and beloved charge in the chair, supported him by the pillows, swung him by the leather straps to his back, and carried him some miles into the country, where he found a friendly asylum for him in the house of some good Quakers. There he nursed him, and by the aid of the kind owners, who were farmers, gave him nourishing food, until he partially recovered strength.

"But your father was very impatient to get home, and wished to proceed before he was well able to walk, and did so leave, while my father walked by his side, with his arm around him to support him. Thus they travelled from the neighborhood of Philadelphia, to Shepherdstown (Virginia) of course by short stages, when my father restored him safe to his mother and family.

"Your father related some of the incidents of that trip to me when I last saw him at Bedford (his home) in the spring of 1817, not more than one year before his death. Our uncle, Henry Bedinger, was also a prisoner for a long time, and although he suffered greatly his suffering was not to be compared to your father's.

"After your father recovered his health he again entered the service and continued in it to the end of the war. He was made Lieutenant, and I have heard my father speak of many battles he was in, but I have forgotten the names and places." [Footnote: Letter of Dr B. F. Bedinger to Mrs H. B. Lee, written in 1871.]

After Daniel Bedinger returned home he had a relapse, and lay, for a long time, at the point of death. He, however, recovered, and re−entered the service, where the first duty assigned him was that of acting as one of the guards over the prisoners near Winchester. He afterwards fought with Morgan in the southern campaigns, was in the battle of the Cowpens, and several other engagements, serving until the army was disbanded. He was a Knight of the Order of the Cincinnati. His grandson, the Rev. Henry Bedinger, has the original parchment signed by General Washington, in his possession. This grandson is now the chaplain of the Virginia branch of the Society.

In 1791 Daniel Bedinger married Miss Sarah Rutherford, a daughter of Hon. Robert Rutherford, of Flowing Springs, in what is now Jefferson County, West Virginia, but was then part of Berkeley County, Virginia.

Lieutenant Bedinger lived in Norfolk for many years. He was first engaged in the Custom House in that city. In 1802 he accepted the position of navy agent of the Gosport Navy Yard. He died in 1818 at his home near Shepherdstown, of a malady which troubled him ever after his confinement as a prisoner in New York. He hated the British with a bitter hatred, which is not to be wondered at. He was an ardent supporter of Thomas Jefferson, and wrote much for the periodicals of the time. Withal he was a scholarly gentleman, and a warm and generous friend. He built a beautiful residence on the site of his mother's old home near Sheperdstown; where, when he died in 1818, he left a large family of children, and a wide circle of friends and admirers.

CHAPTER XI. THE NEWSPAPERS OF THE REVOLUTION

What we have been able to glean from the periodicals of the day about the state of the prisons in New York during the years 1776 and 1777 we will condense into one short chapter.

We will also give an abstract taken from a note book written by General Jeremiah Johnson, who as a boy, lived near Wallabout Bay during the Revolution and who thus describes one of the first prison ships used by the British at New York. He says: "The subject of the naval prisoners, and of the British prisons–ships, stationed at the Wallabout during the Revolution, is one which cannot be passed by in silence. From printed journals, published in New York at the close of the war, it appeared that 11,500 American prisoners had died on board the prison ships. Although this number is very great, yet if the numbers who perished had been less, the Commissary of Naval Prisoners, David Sproat, Esq., and his Deputy, had it in their power, by an official Return, to give the true number taken, exchanged, escaped, and *dead*. Such a Return has never appeared in the United States.

"David Sproat returned to America after the war, and resided in Philadelphia, where he died. [Footnote: This is, we believe, a mistake. Another account says he died at Kirkcudbright, Scotland, in 1792.] The Commissary could not have been ignorant of the statement published here on this interesting subject. We may, therefore, infer that about that number, 11,500, perished in the Prison ships.

"A large transport called the Whitby, was the first prison ship anchored in the Wallabout. She was moored near Remsen's Mill about the 20th of October, 1776, and was then crowded with prisoners. Many landsmen were prisoners on board this vessel: she was said to be the most sickly of all the prison ships. Bad provisions, bad water, and scanted rations were dealt to the prisoners. No medical men attended the sick. Disease reigned unrelieved, and hundreds died from pestilence, or were starved on board this floating Prison. I saw the sand beach, between a ravine in the hill and Mr. Remsen's dock, become filled with graves in the course of two months: and before the first of May, 1777, the ravine alluded to was itself occupied in the same way.

"In the month of May, 1777, two large ships were anchored in the Wallabout, when the prisoners were transferred from the Whitby to them. These vessels were also very sickly from the causes before stated. Although many prisoners were sent on board of them, and none exchanged, death made room for all.

"On a Sunday afternoon about the middle of October, 1777, one of these prison ships was burnt. The prisoners, except a few, who, it was said, were burnt in the vessel, were removed to the remaining ship. It was reported at the time, that the prisoners had fired their prison, which, if true, proves that they preferred death, even by fire, to the lingering sufferings of pestilence and starvation. In the month of February, 1778, the remaining prison ship was burnt, when the prisoners were removed from her to the ships then wintering in the Wallabout."

One of the first notices we have in the newspapers of the day of American prisoners is to the following effect: "London, August 5th, 1775. As every rebel, who is taken prisoner, has incurred the pain of death by the law martial, it is said that Government will charter several transports, after their arrival at Boston to carry the culprits to the East Indies for the Company's service. As it is the intention of Government only to punish the ringleaders and commanders *capitally*, and to suffer the inferior Rebels to redeem their lives by entering into the East India Company's service. This translation will only render them more useful subjects than in their native country."

This notice, copied from London papers, appeared in Holt's *New York Journal*, for October 19th, 1775. It proved to be no idle threat. How many of our brave soldiers were sent to languish out their lives in the British possessions in India, and on the coast of Africa, we have no means of knowing. Few, indeed, ever saw their homes again, but we will give, in a future chapter, the narrative of one who escaped from captivity worse than death on the island of Sumatra.

An account of the mobbing of William Cunningham and John Hill is given in both the Tory and Whig papers of the day. It occurred in March, 1775. "William Cunningham and

John Hill were mobbed by 200 men in New York, dragged through the green, Cunningham was robbed of his watch and the clothes torn off his back, etc., for being a Tory, and having made himself obnoxious to the Americans. He has often been heard blustering in behalf of the ministry, and his behavior has recommended him to the favor of several men of eminence, both in the military and civil departments. He has often been seen, on a footing of familiarity, at their houses, and parading the streets on a horse belonging to one of the gentlemen, etc., etc."

The *Virginia Gazette* in its issue for the first of July, 1775, says: "On June 6th, 1775, the prisoners taken at Lexington were exchanged. The wounded privates were soon sent on board the Levity. * * * At about three a signal was made by the Levity that they were ready to deliver up our prisoners, upon which General Putnam and Major Moncrief went to the ferry, where they received nine prisoners. The regular officers expressed themselves as highly pleased, those who had been prisoners politely acknowledged the genteel kindness they had received from their captors; the privates, who were all wounded men, expressed in the strongest terms their grateful sense of the tenderness which had been shown them in their miserable situation; some of them could do it only by their tears. It would have been to the honor of the British arms if the prisoners taken from us could with justice have made the same acknowledgement. It cannot be supposed that any officers of rank or common humanity were knowing to the repeated cruel insults that were offered them; but it may not be amiss to hint to the upstarts concerned, two truths of which they appear to be wholly ignorant, viz: That compassion is as essential a part of the character of a truly brave man as daring, and that insult offered to the person completely in the power of the insulters smells as strong of cowardice as it does of cruelty." [Footnote: The first American prisoners were taken on the 17th of June, 1775. These were thrown indiscriminately into the jail at Boston without any consideration of their rank. General Washington wrote to General Gage on this subject, to which the latter replied by asserting that the prisoners had been treated with care and kindness, though indiscriminately, as he acknowledged no rank that was not derived from the King. General Carleton during his command conducted towards the American prisoners with a degree of humanity that reflected the greatest honor on his character." From Ramsay's "History of the American Revolution"]

At the battle of the Great Bridge "the Virginia militia showed the greatest humanity and tenderness to the wounded prisoners. Several of them ran through a hot fire to lift up and bring in some that were bleeding, and whom they feared would die if not speedily assisted by the surgeon. The prisoners had been told by Lord Dunmore that the Americans would scalp them, and they cried out, 'For God's sake do not murder us!' One of them who was unable to walk calling out in this manner to one of our men, was answered by him: 'Put your arm about my neck and I'll show you what I intend to do.' Then taking him, with his arm over his neck, he walked slowly along, bearing him with great tenderness to the breastwork." *Pennsylvania Evening Post*, January 6th, 1776.

The Great Bridge was built over the southern branch of the Elizabeth River, twelve miles above Norfolk. Colonel William Woodford commanded the Virginia militia on this occasion.

"The scene closed with as much humanity as it had been conducted with bravery. The work of death being over, every one's attention was directed to the succor of the unhappy sufferers, and it is an undoubted fact that Captain Leslie was so affected with the tenderness of our troops towards those who were yet capable of assistance that he gave signs from the fort of his thankfulness for it." *Pennsylvania Evening Post*, Jan. 6th, 1776.

The first mention we can find of a British prison ship is in the *New York Packet* for the 11th of April, 1776: "Captain Hammond * * * Ordered Captain Forrester, his prisoner, who was on board the Roebuck, up to the prison ship at Norfolk in a pilot boat."

The Constitutional Gazette for the 19th of April, 1776, has this announcement, and though it does not bear directly on the subject of prisoners, it describes a set of men who were most active in taking them, and were considered by the Americans as more cruel and vindictive than even the British themselves.

"Government have sent over to Germany to engage 1,000 men called Jagers, people brought up to the use of the rifle barrel guns in boar–hunting. They are amazingly expert. Every petty prince who hath forests keeps a number of them, and they are allowed to take apprentices, by which means they are a numerous body of people. These men are intended to act in the next campaign in America, and our ministry plume themselves much in the thought of their being a complete match for the American riflemen."

From Gaine's *Mercury*, a notorious Tory paper published in New York during the British occupancy, we take the following: "November 25th, 1776. There are now 5,000 prisoners in town, many of them half naked. Congress deserts the poor wretches,—have sent them neither provisions nor clothing, nor paid attention to their distress nor that of their families. Their situation must have been doubly deplorable, but for the humanity of the King's officers. Every possible attention has been given, considering their great numbers and necessary confinement, to alleviate their distress arising from guilt, sickness, and poverty."

This needs no comment. It is too unspeakably false to be worth contradicting.

"New London, Conn., November 8th, 1776. Yesterday arrived E. Thomas, who was captured September 1st, carried to New York, and put on board the Chatham. He escaped Wednesday sennight."

"New London, Nov. 20th, 1776. American officers, prisoners on parole, are walking about the streets of New York, but soldiers are closely confined, have but half allowance, are sickly, and die fast."

"New London, Nov. 29th, 1776. A cartel arrived here for exchange of seamen only. Prisoners had miserable confinement on board of store ships and transports, where they suffered for want of the common necessaries of life."

"Exact from a letter written on board the Whitby Prison Ship. New York, Dec. 9th, 1776. Our present situation is most wretched; more than 250 prisoners, some sick and without the least assistance from physician, drug, or medicine, and fed on two–thirds allowance of salt provisions, and crowded promiscuously together without regard, to color, person or office, in the small room of a ship's between decks, allowed to walk the main deck only between sunrise and sunset. Only two at a time allowed to come on deck to do what nature requires, and sometimes denied even that, and use tubs and buckets between decks, to the great offence of every delicate, cleanly person, and prejudice of all our healths. Lord Howe has liberated all in the merchant service, but refuses to exchange those taken in arms but for like prisoners." (This is an extract from the Trumbull Papers.)

From a Connecticut paper: "This may inform those who have friends in New York, prisoners of war, that Major Wells, a prisoner, has come thence to Connecticut on parole, to collect money for the much distressed officers and soldiers there, and desires the money may be left at Landlord Betts, Norwalk; Captain Benjamin's, Stratford; Landlord Beers, New Haven; Hezekiah Wylly's, Hartford; and at said Well's, Colchester, with proper accounts from whom received, and to whom to be delivered. N. B. The letters must not be sealed, or contain anything of a political nature." Conn. Papers, Dec. 6th, 1776.

"Conn. *Gazette*, Feb. 8th, 1777. William Gamble deposes that the prisoners were huddled together with negroes, had weak grog; no swab to clean the ship; bad oil; raw pork; seamen refused them water; called them d——d rebels; the dead not buried, etc."

"Lieut. Wm. Sterrett, taken August 27, 1776, deposes that his clothing was stolen, that he was abused by the soldiers; stinted in food; etc., those who had slight wounds were allowed to perish from neglect. The recruiting officers seduced the prisoners to enlist, etc."

"March 7th, 1777. Forty–six prisoners from the Glasgow, transport ship, were landed in New Haven, where one of them, Captain Craigie, died and was buried." (Their names are published in the Connecticut *Courant*.)

Connecticut *Gazette* of April 30th, 1777, says: "The Connecticut Assembly sent to New York a sufficient supply of tow shirts and trousers for her prisoners, also L35 to Col. Ethan Allen, by his brother Levi."

"Lt. Thos. Fanning, now on parole from Long Island at Norwich, a prisoner to General Howe, will be at Hartford on his return to New York about September 8th, whence he proposes to keep the public road to King's Bridge. Letters and money left at the most noted public houses in the different towns, will be conveyed safe to the prisoners. Extraordinaries excepted." Connecticut *Gazette*, Aug. 15th, 1777.

"Jan. 8th, '77. A flag of truce vessel arrived at Milford after a tedious passage of eleven days, from New York, having above 200 prisoners, whose rueful countenances too well discovered the ill treatment they received in New York. Twenty died on the passage, and twenty since they landed." New Haven, Conn.

CHAPTER XII. THE TRUMBULL PAPERS AND OTHER SOURCES OF INFORMATION

American Prisoners of the Revolution

We will now quote from the Trumbull Papers and other productions, what is revealed to the public of the state of the prisoners in New York in 1776 and 1777. Some of our information we have obtained from a book published in 1866 called "Documents and Letters Intended to Illustrate the Revolutionary Incidents of Long Island, by Henry Onderdonk, Jr." He gives an affecting account of the wounding of General Woodhull, after his surrender, and when he had given up his sword. The British ruffians who held him insisted that he should cry, "God save the King!" whereupon, taking off his hat, he replied, reverently, "God save all of us!" At this the cruel men ran him through, giving him wounds that proved mortal, though had they been properly dressed his life might have been spared. He was mounted behind a trooper and carried to Hinchman's Tavern, Jamaica, where permission was refused to Dr. Ogden to dress his wounds. This was on the 28th of August, 1776. Next day he was taken westward and put on board an old vessel off New Utrecht. This had been a cattle ship. He was next removed to the house of Wilhelmus Van Brunt at New Utrecht. His arm mortified from neglect and it was decided to take it off. He sent express to his wife that he had no hope of recovery, and begged her to gather up what provisions she could, for he had a large farm, and hasten to his bedside. She accordingly loaded a wagon with bread, ham, crackers, butter, etc., and barely reached her husband in time to see him alive. With his dying breath he requested her to distribute the provisions she had brought to the suffering and starving American prisoners.

Elias Baylis, who was old and blind, was chairman of the Jamaica Committee of Safety. He was captured and first imprisoned in the church at New Utrecht. Afterwards he was sent to the provost prison in New York. He had a very sweet voice, and was an earnest Christian. In the prison he used to console himself and his companions in misery by singing hymns and psalms. Through the intervention of his friends, his release was obtained after two months confinement, but the rigor of prison life had been too much for his feeble frame. He died, in the arms of his daughter, as he was in a boat crossing the ferry to his home.

While in the Presbyterian church in New Utrecht used as a prison by the British, he had for companions, Daniel Duryee, William Furman, William Creed, and two others, all put into one pew. Baylis asked them to get the Bible out of the pulpit and read it to him. They feared to do this, but consented to lead the blind man to the pulpit steps. As he returned with the Bible in his hands a British guard met him, beat him violently and took away the book. They were three weeks in the church at New Utrecht. When a sufficient number of

Whig prisoners were collected there they would be marched under guard to a prison ship. One old Whig named Smith, while being conducted to his destination, appealed to an onlooker, a Tory of his acquaintance, to intercede for him. The cold reply of his neighbor was, "Ah, John, you've been a great rebel!" Smith turned to another of his acquaintances named McEvers, and said to him, "McEvers, its hard for an old man like me to have to go to a prison! Can't you do something for me?"

"What have you been doing, John?"

"Why, I've had opinions of my own!"

"Well, I'll see what I can do for you."

McEvers then went to see the officers in charge and made such representations to them that Smith was immediately released.

Adrian Onderdonk was taken to Flushing and shut up in the old Friends' Meeting House there, which is one of the oldest places of worship in America. Next day he was taken to New York. He, with other prisoners, was paraded through the streets to the provost, with a gang of loose women marching before them, to add insult to suffering.

Onderdonk says: "After awhile the rigor of the prison rules was somewhat abated." He was allowed to write home, which he did in Dutch, for provisions, such as smoked beef, butter, etc. * * * His friends procured a woman to do his washing, prepare food and bring it to him. * * * One day as he was walking through the rooms followed by his constant attendant, a negro with coils of rope around his neck, this man asked Onderdonk what he was imprisoned for.

"'I've been a Committee man,'" said he.

"'Well,' with an oath and a great deal of abuse, 'You shall be hung tomorrow.'"

This mulatto was named Richmond, and was the common hangman. He used to parade the provost with coils of ropes, requesting the prisoners to choose their own halters. He it was who hung the gallant Nathan Hale, and was Cunningham's accessory in all his brutal midnight murders. In Gaine's paper for August 4th, 1781, appears the following advertisement: "One Guinea Reward, ran away a black man named Richmond, being the common hangman, formerly the property of the rebel Colonel Patterson of Pa.

"Wm. Cunningham."

After nearly four weeks imprisonment the friends of Adrian Onderdonk procured his release. He was brought home in a wagon in the night, so pale, thin, and feeble from bodily suffering that his family scarcely recognized him. His constitution was shattered and he never recovered his former strength.

Onderdonk says that women often brought food for the prisoners in little baskets, which, after examination, were handed in. Now and then the guard might intercept what was sent, or Cunningham, if the humor took him, as he passed through the hall, might kick over vessels of soup, placed there by the charitable for the poor and friendless prisoners.

EXTRACT FROM A BETTER FROM DR. SILAS HOLMES

"The wounded prisoners taken at the battle of Brooklyn were put in the churches of Flatbush and New Utrecht, but being neglected and unattended were wallowing in their own filth, and breathed an infected and impure air. Ten days after the battle Dr. Richard Bailey was appointed to superintend the sick. He was humane, and dressed the wounded daily; got a sack bed, sheet, and blanket for each prisoner; and distributed the prisoners into the adjacent barns. When Mrs. Woodhull offered to pay Dr. Bailey for his care and attention to her husband, he said he had done no more than his duty, and if there was anything due it was to me."

Woodhull's wounds were neglected nine days before Dr. Bailey was allowed to attend them.

How long the churches were used as prisons cannot be ascertained, but we have no account of prisoners confined in any of them after the year 1777. In the North Dutch Church in New York there were, at one time, eight hundred prisoners huddled together. It was in this church that bayonet marks were discernible on its pillars, many years after the war.

The provost and old City Hall were used as prisons until Evacuation Day, when O'Keefe threw his ponderous bunch of keys on the floor and retired. The prisoners are said to have asked him where they were to go.

"To hell, for what I care," he replied.

"In the Middle Dutch Church," says Mr. John Pintard, who was a nephew of Commissary Pintard, "the prisoners taken on Long Island and at Fort Washington, sick, wounded, and well, were all indiscriminately huddled together, by hundreds and thousands, large numbers of whom died by disease, and many undoubtedly poisoned by inhuman attendants for the sake of their watches, or silver buckles."

"What was called the Brick Church was at first used as a prison, but soon it and the Presbyterian Church in Wall Street, the Scotch Church in Cedar Street, and the Friends' Meeting House were converted into hospitals."

Oliver Woodruff, who died at the age of ninety, was taken prisoner at Fort Washington, and left the following record: "We were marched to New York and went into different prisons. Eight hundred and sixteen went into the New Bridewell (between the City Hall and Broadway); some into the Sugar House; others into the Dutch Church. On Thursday morning they brought us a little provision, which was the first morsel we got to eat or drink after eating our breakfast on Saturday morning. * * * I was there (in New Bridewell) three months. In the dungeons of the old City Hall which stood on the site of what was afterwards the Custom House at first civil offenders were confined, but afterwards whale–boatmen and robbers."

Robert Troup, a young lieutenant in Colonel Lasher's battalion, testified that he and Lieut. Edward Dunscomb, Adjutant Hoogland, and two volunteers were made prisoners by a detachment of British troops at three o'clock a. m. on the 27th of August, 1776. They were carried before the generals and interrogated, with threats of hanging. Thence they were led to a house near Flatbush. At 9 a. m. they were led, in the rear of the army, to Bedford. Eighteen officers captured that morning were confined in a small soldier's tent for two nights and nearly three days. It was raining nearly all the time. Sixty privates, also, had but one tent, while at Bedford the provost marshal, Cunningham, brought with him a negro with a halter, telling them the negro had already hung several, and he imagined he would hang some more. The negro and Cunningham also heaped abuse upon the prisoners, showing them the halter, and calling them rebels, scoundrels, robbers, murderers, etc.

From Bedford they were led to Flatbush, and confined a week in a house belonging to a Mr. Leffert, on short allowance of biscuit and salt pork. Several Hessians took pity on them and gave them apples, and once some fresh beef.

From Flatbush after a week, he, with seventy or eighty other officers, were put on board a snow, lying between Gravesend and the Hook, without bedding or blankets; afflicted with vermin; soap and fresh water for washing purposes being denied them. They drank and cooked with filthy water brought from England. The captain charged a very large commission for purchasing necessaries for them with the money they procured from their friends.

After six weeks spent on the snow they were taken on the 17th of October to New York and confined in a house near Bridewell. At first they were not allowed any fuel, and afterwards only a little coal for three days in the week. Provisions were dealt out very negligently, were scanty, and of bad quality. Many were ill and most of them would have died had their wants not been supplied by poor people and loose women of the town, who took pity on them.

"Shortly after the capture of Fort Washington these officers were paroled and allowed the freedom of the town. Nearly half the prisoners taken on Long Island died. The privates were treated with great inhumanity, without fuel, or the common necessaries of life, and were obliged to obey the calls of nature in places of their confinement." It is said that the British did not hang any of the prisoners taken in August on Long Island, but "played the fool by making them ride with a rope around their necks, seated on coffins, to the gallows. Major Otho Williams was so treated."

"Adolph Myer, late of Colonel Lasher's battalion, says he was taken by the British at Montresor's Island. They threatened twice to hang him, and had a rope fixed to a tree. He was led to General Howe's quarters near Turtle Bay, who ordered him to be bound hand and foot. He was confined four days on bread and water, in the 'condemned hole' of the New Jail, without straw or bedding. He was next put into the College, and then into the New Dutch Church, whence he escaped on the twenty–fourth of January, 1777. He was treated with great inhumanity, and would have died had he not been supported by his friends. * * * Many prisoners died from want, and others were reduced to such wretchedness as to attract the attention of the loose women of the town, from whom they received considerable assistance. No care was taken of the sick, and if any died they were thrown at the door of the prison and lay there until the next day, when they were put in a cart and drawn out to the intrenchments beyond the Jews' burial ground, when they were interred by their fellow prisoners, conducted thither for that purpose. The dead were thrown into a hole promiscuously, without the usual rites of sepulchre. Myer was frequently enticed to enlist." This is one of the few accounts we have from a prisoner who was confined in one of the churches in New York, and he was so fortunate as to escape before it was too late. We wish he had given the details of his escape. In such a gloomy picture as we are obliged to present to our readers the only high lights are occasional acts of humanity, and such incidents as fortunate escapes.

It would appear, from many proofs, that the Hessian soldier was naturally a good–natured being, and he seems to have been the most humane of the prison guards. We will see, as we go on, instances of the kindness of these poor exiled mercenaries, to many of whom the war was almost as great a scene of calamity and suffering as it was to the wretched prisoners under their care.

"Lieutenant Catlin, taken September 15th, '76, was confined in prison with no sustenance for forty–eight hours; for eleven days he had only two days allowance of pork offensive to the smell, bread hard, mouldy and wormy, made of canail and dregs of flax–seed; water brackish. 'I have seen $1.50 given for a common pail full. Three or four pounds of poor Irish pork were given to three men for three days. In one church were 850 prisoners for near three months.'"

"About the 25th of December he with 225 men were put on board the Glasgow at New York to be carried to Connecticut for exchange. They were aboard eleven days, and kept on coarse broken bread, and less pork than before, and had no fire for sick or well; crowded between decks, where twenty–eight died through ill–usage and cold." (This is taken from the "History of Litchfield," page 39.)

EXTRACT FROM A LETTER DATED NEW YORK, DEC. 26, 1776

"The distress of the prisoners cannot be communicated in words. Twenty or thirty die every day; they lie in heaps unburied; what numbers of my countrymen have died by cold and hunger, perished for want of the common necessaries of life! I have seen it! This, sir, is the boasted British clemency! I myself had well nigh perished under it. The New England people can have no idea of such barbarous policy. Nothing can stop such treatment but retaliation. I ever despised private revenge, but that of the public must be in this case, both just and necessary; it is due to the manes of our murdered countrymen, and that alone can protect the survivors in the like situation. Rather than experience again their barbarity and insults, may I fall by the sword of the Hessians."

Onderdonk, who quotes this fragment, gives us no clue to the writer. A man named S. Young testifies that, "he was taken at Fort Washington and, with 500 prisoners, was kept in a barn, and had no provisions until Monday night, when the enemy threw into the stable, in a confused manner, as if to so many hogs, a quantity of biscuits in crumbs, mostly mouldy, and some crawling with maggots, which the prisoners were obliged to scramble for without any division. Next day they had a little pork which they were obliged to eat raw. Afterwards they got sometimes a bit of pork, at other times biscuits, peas, and rice. They were confined two weeks in a church, where they suffered greatly from cold, not being allowed any fire. Insulted by soldiers, women, and even negroes. Great numbers died, three, four, or more, sometimes, a day. Afterwards they were carried on board a ship, where 500 were confined below decks."

The date of this testimony is given as Dec. 15th, 1776: "W. D. says the prisoners were roughly used at Harlem on their way from Fort Washington to New York, where 800 men were stored in the New Bridewell, which was a cold, open house, the windows not glazed. They had not one mouthful from early Saturday morning until Monday. Rations per man for three days were half a pound of biscuit, half a pound of pork, half a gill of rice, half a pint of peas, and half an ounce of butter, the whole not enough for one good meal, and they were defrauded in this petty allowance. They had no straw to lie on, no fuel but one cart load per week for 800 men. At nine o'clock the Hessian guards would come and put out the fire, and lay on the poor prisoners with heavy clubs, for sitting around the fire.

"The water was very bad, as well as the bread. Prisoners died like rotten sheep, with cold, hunger, and dirt; and those who had good apparel, such as buckskin breeches, or good coats, were necessitated to sell them to purchase bread to keep them alive." Hinman, page 277.

"Mrs. White left New York Jan. 20th, 1777. She says Bridewell, the College, the New Jail, the Baptist Meeting House, and the tavern lately occupied by Mr. De la Montaigne and several other houses are filled with sick and wounded of the enemy. General Lee was under guard in a small mean house at the foot of King Street. Wm. Slade says 800 prisoners taken at Fort Washington were put into the North church. On the first of December 300 were taken from the church to the prison ship. December second he, with others, was marched to the Grosvenor transport in the North River; five hundred were crowded on board. He had to lie down before sunset to secure a place." Trumbull Papers.

"Henry Franklin affirms that about two days after the taking of Fort Washington he was in New York, and went to the North Church, in which were about 800 prisoners taken in said Fort. He inquired into their treatment, and they told him they fared hard on account both of provisions and lodging, for they were not allowed any bedding, or blankets, and the provisions had not been regularly dealt out, so that the modest or backward could get little or none, nor had they been allowed any fuel to dress their victuals. The prisoners in New York were very sickly, and died in considerable numbers."

"Feb. 11, 1777. Joshua Loring, Commissary of Prisoners, says that but little provisions had been sent in by the rebels for their prisoners." Gaine's Mercury.

Jan. 4th. 1777. "Seventy–seven prisoners went into the Sugar House. N. Murray says 800 men were in Bridewell. The doctor gave poison powders to the prisoners, who soon died. Some were sent to Honduras to cut logwood; women came to the prison–gate to sell gingerbread." Trumbull Papers.

The *New York Gazette* of May 6th, 1777, states that "of 3000 prisoners taken at Fort Washington, only 800 are living."

Mr. Onderdonk says: "There seems to have been no systematic plan adopted by the citizens of New York for the relief of the starving prisoners. We have scattering notices of a few charitable individuals, such as the following:—'Mrs. Deborah Franklin was banished from New York Nov. 21st, 1780, by the British commandant, for her unbounded liberality to the American prisoners. Mrs. Ann Mott was associated with Mrs. Todd and Mrs. Whitten in relieving the sufferings of American prisoners in New York, during the Revolution. John Fillis died at Halifax, 1792, aged 68. He was kind to American prisoners in New York. Jacob Watson, Penelope Hull, etc., are also mentioned.'"

BRITISH ACCOUNT OF MORTALITY OF PRISONERS

"P. Dobbyn, master of a transport, thus writes from New York, Jan. 15th, 1777. 'We had four or five hundred prisoners on board our ships, but they had such bad distempers that each ship buried ten or twelve a day.' Another writer, under date of Jan. 14th, '77, says, 'The Churches are full of American prisoners, who die so fast that 25 or 30 are buried at a time, in New York City. General Howe gave all who could walk their liberty, after taking their oath not to take up arms against his Majesty.'" (From a London Journal.)

CHAPTER XIII. A JOURNAL KEPT IN THE PROVOST

An old man named John Fell was taken up by the British, and confined for some months in the Provost prison. He managed to secrete writing materials and made notes of his treatment. He was imprisoned for being a Whig and one of the councilmen of Bergen, New Jersey. We will give his journal entire, as it is quoted by Mr. Onderdonk.

April 23rd, 1777. Last night I was taken prisoner from my house by 25 armed men (he lived in Bergen) who brought me down to Colonel Buskirk's at Bergen Point, and from him I was sent to Gen. Pigot, at N. Y., who sent me with Captain Van Allen to the Provost Jail.

24th. Received from Mrs. Curzon, by the hands of Mr. Amiel, $16, two shirts, two stocks, some tea, sugar, pepper, towels, tobacco, pipes, paper, and a bed and bedding.

May 1st. Dr. Lewis Antle and Capt. Thomas Golden at the door, refused admittance.

May 2nd. 6 10 P. M. died John Thomas, of smallpox, aged 70 & inoculated.

5th. Capt. Colden has brought from Mr. Curson $16.00.

11. Dr. Antle came to visit me. Nero at the door. (A dog?)

13. Cold weather.

20. Lewis Pintard came per order of Elias Boudinot to offer me money. Refused admittance. Capt. Colden came to visit me.

21. Capt and Mrs Corne came to visit me, and I was called downstairs to see them.

23. Lewis Pintard came as Commissary to take account of officers, in order to assist them with money.

24. Every person refused admittance to the Provost.

25. All prisoners paraded in the hall: supposed to look for deserters.

27. Rev. Mr. Hart and Col. Smith brought to the Provost from Long Island.

29. Stormy in Provost.

30. Not allowed to fetch good water.

31. Bad water; proposing buying tea–water, but refused. This night ten prisoners from opposite room ordered into ours, in all twenty.

June 1. Continued the same today.

2. The people ordered back to their own room.

3. Captain Van Zandt sent to the dungeon for resenting Captain Cunningham's insulting and abusing me.

4. Capt. Adams brought into our room. At 9 P.M. candles ordered out.

7. Captain Van Zandt returned from the dungeon.

8. All prisoners paraded and called over and delivered to care of Sergt. Keath. (O'Keefe, probably.) And told we are all alike, no distinction to be made.

10. Prisoners very sickly.

11. Mr Richards from Connecticut exchanged.

12. Exceeding strict and severe. "Out Lights!"

13. Melancholy scene, women refused speaking to their sick husbands, and treated cruelly by sentries.

14. Mr. James Ferris released on parole. People in jail very sickly and not allowed a doctor.

17. Capt. Corne came to speak to me; not allowed.

18. Letter from prisoners to Sergeant Keath, requesting more privileges.

19. Received six bottles claret and sundry small articles, but the note not allowed to come up.

20. Memorandum sent to Gen. Pigot with list of grievances.

21. Answered. "Grant no requests made by prisoners."

22. Mrs. Banta refused speaking to her son.

23. Mr Haight died.

24. Nineteen prisoners from Brunswick. Eighteen sent to the Sugar House.

25. Dr Bard came to visit Justice Moore, but his wife was refused, tho' her husband was dying.

26. Justice Moore died and was carried out.

27. Several sick people removed below.

30. Provost very sickly and some die.

July 3. Received from Mrs Curson per Mrs. Marriner, two half Joes.

6. Received of E. Boudinot, per Pintard, ten half Joes.

7. Capt. Thomas Golden came to the grates to see me.

9. Two men carried out to be hung for desertion, reprieved.

11. Mr Langdon brought into our room.

13. The Sergeant removed a number of prisoners from below.

14. Messrs Demarests exchanged. Dr. Romaine ordered to visit the sick.

15. A declaration of more privileges, and prisoners allowed to speak at the windows.

17. Peter Zabriskie had an order to speak with me, and let me know that all was well at home

19. Sergt. from Sugar House came to take account of officers in the Provost. Capt. Cunningham in town.

21. Sergt. took account of officers. Capt. Jas. Lowry died.

22. Mr. Miller died. Capt. Lowry buried.

Aug. 1. Very sick. Weather very hot.

5. Barry sent to the dungeon for bringing rum for Mr Phillips without leave of the Sergt. Everything looks stormy.

6. Warm weather. Growing better. Mr. Pintard came to supply prisoners of war with clothes.

10. Two prisoners from Long Island and four Lawrences from Tappan.

11. John Coven Cromwell from White Plains. Freeland from Polly (?) Fly whipped about salt.

12. Sergt. Keath took all pens and ink out of each room, and forbid the use of any on pain of the dungeon.

13. Abraham Miller discharged.

14. Jacobus Blauvelt died in the morning, buried at noon.

16. Capt. Ed. Travis brought into our room from the dungeon, where he had long been confined and cruelly treated.

17. Mr. Keath refused me liberty to send a card to Mr Amiel for a lb of tobacco.

21. Capt. Hyer discharged from the Provost.

25. Barry brought up from the dungeon, and Capt. Travis sent down again without any provocation.

26. Badcock sent to dungeon for cutting wood in the evening. Locks put on all the doors, and threatened to be locked up. Col. Ethan Allen brought to the Provost from Long Island and confined below.

27. Badcock discharged from below.

30. 5 P.M. all rooms locked up close.

31. A.M. Col Allen brought into our room.

Sep. 1. Pleasant weather. Bad water.

4. Horrid scenes of whipping.

6. Lewis Pintard brought some money for the officers. P.M. Major Otho H. Williams brought from Long Island and confined in our room. Major Wells from same place

confined below. A. M. William Lawrence of Tappan died.

8. Campbell, Taylor, John Cromwell, and Buchanan from Philadelphia discharged.

10. Provisions exceedingly ordinary,—pork very rusty, biscuit bad.

12. Capt. Travis, Capt. Chatham and others brought out of dungeon.

14. Two prisoners from Jersey, viz: Thomas Campbell of Newark and Joralemon. (Jos. Lemon?)

16. Troops returned from Jersey. Several prisoners brought to Provost viz:—Capt. Varick, Wm. Prevost Brower, etc. Seventeen prisoners from Long Island.

22. Nothing material. Major Wells brought from below upstairs.

24. Received from Mr. Curson per Mr. Amiel four guineas, six bottles of wine, and one lb tobacco.

26. Mr. Pintard carried list of prisoners and account of grievances to the General Capt. Chatham and others carried to dungeon.

28. Yesterday a number of soldiers were sent below, and several prisoners brought out of dungeon. Statement of grievances presented to General Jones which much displeased Sergt. Keath who threatened to lock up the rooms.

29. Last night Sergt. K. locked up all the rooms. Rev. Mr. Jas. Sears was admitted upstairs.

30. Sent Mr. Pintard a list of clothing wanted for continental and state prisoners in the Provost. Sergt. locks up all the rooms.

Oct. 2. Candles ordered out at eight.—Not locked up.

4. Locked up. Great numbers of ships went up North River. Received sundries from Grove Bend. Three pair ribbed hose, three towels.

5. Garret Miller, of Smith's Cove, signed his will in prison, in presence of Benjamin Goldsmith, Abr. Skinner, and myself. C. G. Miller died of small–pox—P. M. Buried.

7. Wm. Prevost discharged from Provost.

8. Capt. Chatham and Lewis Thatcher brought out of dungeon.

10. Mr. Pintard sent up blankets, shoes, and stockings for the prisoners.

12. Lt. Col. Livingstone and upwards of twenty officers from Fort Montgomery and Clinton, all below.

13. Received from Mr. Pintard a letter by flag from Peter R. Fell, A. M. Mr. Noble came to the grates to speak to me.

14. Sergt. Keath sent Lt. Mercer and Mr. Nath. Fitzrandolph to the dungeon for complaining that their room had not water sufficient.

15. Mr. Pintard brought sundry articles for the prisoners.

17. Mr. Antonio and other prisoners brought here from up North River.

19. Ben Goldsmith ill of smallpox, made his will and gave it to me. Died two A. M. Oct. 20.

21. Glorious news from the Northward.

22. Confirmation strong as Holy Writ. Beef, loaf bread, and butter drawn today.

23. Weather continues very cold. Ice in the tub in the hall. A number of vessels came down North River. Mr. Wm. Bayard at the door to take out old Mr. Morris.

24. Prisoners from the Sugar House sent on board ships.

25. Rev. Mr. Hart admitted on parole in the city. Sergt. Woolley from the Sugar House came to take names of officers, and says an exchange is expected.

28. Last night and today storm continues very severe. Provost in a terrible condition. Lt. Col. Livingston admitted upstairs a few minutes.

Nov. 1. Lt. Callender of the train ordered back on Long Island; also several officers taken at Fort Montgomery sent on parole to Long Island.

3. In the evening my daughter, Elizabeth Colden, came to see me, accompanied by Mayor Matthews.

5. Elizabeth Colden came to let me know she was going out of town. Yesterday Sergt refused her the liberty of speaking to me. Gen. Robertson's Aid—decamp came to inquire into grievances of prisoners.

16. Jail exceedingly disagreeable.—many miserable and shocking objects, nearly starved with cold and hunger,—miserable prospect before me.

18. The Town Major and Town Adjutant came with a pretence of viewing the jail.

19. Peter and Cor. Van Tassel, two prisoners from Tarrytown, in our room.

20 Mr. Pintard sent three barrels of flour to be distributed among the prisoners.

21. Mr. Pintard came for an account of what clothing the prisoners wanted.

24. Six tailors brought here from prison ship to work in making clothes for prisoners. They say the people on board are very sickly. Three hundred sent on board reduced to one hundred.

25. Mr. Dean and others brought to jail from the town.

26. Dean locked up by himself, and Mr. Forman brought upstairs attended by Rev. Mr. Inglis, and afterwards ordered downstairs. New order—one of the prisoners ordered to go to the Commissary's and see the provisions dealt out for the prisoners. Vast numbers of people assembled at the Provost in expectation of seeing an execution.

27. John, one of the milkmen, locked upstairs with a sentry at his door. A report by Mr. Webb that a prisoner, Herring, was come down to be exchanged for Mr Van Zandt or me.

30. Captain Cunningham came to the Provost.

Dec. 1. Capt. Money came down with Mr Webb to be exchanged for Major Wells.

2. Col. Butler visited the Provost and promised a doctor should attend. Received from Mr Bend cloth for a great coat, etc. Mr. Pmtard took a list of clothing wanted for the prisoners.

3. Several prisoners of war sent from here on board the prison shop, & some of the sick sent to the hospital, Dr Romaine being ordered by Sir H. Clinton to examine the sick Prisoners sickly: cause, cold. Prisoners in upper room (have) scanty clothing and only two bushels of coal for room of twenty men per week.

5. Mr. Blanch ordered out; said to be to go to Morristown to get prisoners exchanged. Cold.

7. Mr. Webb came to acquaint Major Wells his exchange was agreed to with Capt. Money.

8. Major Gen. Robertson, with Mayor came to Provost to examine prisoners. I was called and examined, and requested my parole. The General said I had made bad use of indulgence granted me, in letting my daughter come to see me. * * *

9. Major Wells exchanged.

10. Mr. Pintard sent 100 loaves for the prisoners. A. M. Walter Thurston died. Prisoners very sickly and die very fast from the hospitals and prison ships.

11. Some flags from North River.

12. Abel Wells died, a tailor from the prison ship. Mr. Pintard brought letters for sundry people.

14. Sunday. Guards more severe than ever notwithstanding General Robertson's promise of more indulgence. Capt. Van Zandt brought from Long Island.

16. Sent message to Mr Pintard for wood. Cold and entirely out of wood.

17. Commissary Winslow came and released Major Winslow on his parole on Long Island.

18. Mr Pintard sent four cords of wood for the prisoners.

19. Capt. John Paul Schoot released on parole. Mr Pintard with clothing for the people.

21. A paper found at the door of the Provost, intimating that three prisoners had a rope concealed in a bag in one of the rooms in order to make their escape. The Sergt. examined all the rooms, and at night we were all locked up.

22. Received from Mr Pintard 100 loaves and a quarter of beef.

24. Distributed clothing, etc., to the prisoners.

28. Gen. Robertson sent a doctor to examine me in consequence of the petition sent by Col. Allen for my releasement. The doctor reported to Dr. Mallet.

29. Gen. Robertson sent me word I should be liberated in town, provided I procured a gentleman in town to be responsible for my appearance. Accordingly I wrote to Hon. H. White, Esq.

30. Dr Romaine, with whom I sent the letter, said Mr White had a number of objections, but the doctor hoped to succeed in the afternoon. Mr. Winslow came and told the same story I heard the day before.

31. Sergt. Keath brought a message from the General to the same purpose as yesterday. N. B. I lost the memoranda from this date to the time of my being liberated from the Provost on Jan. 7, 1778.

New York Feb. 11. '78. Received a letter from Joshua Loring, Esq, Commissary of Prisoners, with leave from Gen. Robertson for my having the bounds of the city allowed me.

March. 23. Wrote to Major Gen. Robertson and told him this was the eleventh month of my imprisonment."

Fell's note to the general follows, in which he begs to be liberated to the house of Mrs. Marriner, who kept an ordinary in the town. A card in reply from the general states that it is impossible to comply with his request until Mr. Fell's friends give him sufficient security that he will not attempt to escape. A Mr. Langdon having broken his faith in like circumstances has given rise to a rule, which it is out of the general's power to dispense with, etc, etc.

"Feb. 4, 1778. I delivered to Mr. Pintard the wills of Garret Miller and Benjamin Goldsmith, to be forwarded to their respective families. Present E. Boudinot.

"May 20 '78, I had my parole extended by order of Gen. Daniel Jones, to my own house in Bergen County, for thirty days.

"July 2. I left town, and next day arrived safe home.

"Nov. 15, 1778 I received a certificate from A. Skinner, Deputy Com. of Prisoners of my being exchanged for Gov. Skene. Signed by Joshua Loring, Commissary General of Prisoners, dated New York, Oct 26 1778."

CHAPTER XIV. FURTHER TESTIMONY OF CRUELTIES ENDURED BY AMERICAN PRISONERS

Mr. Fell's notes on his imprisonment present the best picture we can find of the condition of the Provost Jail during the term of his captivity. We have already seen how Mr Elias Boudinot, American Commissary of Prisoners, came to that place of confinement, and what he found there. This was in February, 1778. Boudinot also describes the sufferings of the American prisoners in the early part of 1778 in Philadelphia, and Mr. Fell speaks of Cunningham's return to New York. He had, it appears, been occupied in starving prisoners in Philadelphia during his absence from the Provost, to which General Howe sent him back, after he had murdered one of his victims in Philadelphia with the great key.

It appears that the prisoners in the Provost sent an account of their treatment to General Jones, by Mr. Pintard, in September, 1777, several months before the visit of Mr. Elias Boudinot. They complained that they were closely confined in the jail without distinction of rank or character, amongst felons, a number of whom were under sentence of death: that their friends were not allowed to speak to them, even through the grates: that they were put on the scanty allowance of two pounds hard biscuit, and two pounds of raw pork per week, without fuel to dress it. That they were frequently supplied with water from a pump where all kinds of filth was thrown, by which it was rendered obnoxious and unwholesome, the effects of which were to cause much sickness. That good water could have been as easily obtained. That they were denied the benefit of a hospital; not permitted to send for medicine, nor to have the services of a doctor, even when in the greatest distress. That married men and others who lay at the point of death were refused permission to have their wives or other relations admitted to see them. And that these poor women, for attempting to gain admittance, were often beaten from the prison door. That commissioned officers, and others, persons of character and reputation, were frequently, without a cause, thrown into a loathsome dungeon, insulted in a gross manner, and vilely abused by a Provost Marshal, who was allowed to be one of the basest characters in the British Army, and whose power was so unlimited, that he had caned an officer, on a trivial occasion; and frequently beaten the sick privates when unable to stand, "many of whom are daily obliged to enlist in the New Corps to prevent perishing for want of the necessaries of life.

"Neither pen, ink, or paper allowed (to prevent their treatment being made public) the consequence of which indeed, the prisoners themselves dread, knowing the malignant disposition of their keeper."

The Board of War reported on the 21 of January, 1778, that there were 900 privates and 300 officers in New York, prisoners, and that "the privates have been crowded all summer in sugar houses, and the officers boarded on Long Island, except about thirty, who have been confined in the Provost–Guard, and in most loathsome jails, and that since Oct. 1st, all those prisoners, both officers and privates, have been confined in prisons, prison ships, or the Provost." Lists of prisoners in the Provost; those taken by the

Falcon, Dec. 1777, and those belonging to Connecticut who were in the Quaker and Brick Meeting House hospitals in Jan. 1778, may be found in the Trumbull Papers, VII, 62.

It seems that General Lee, while a prisoner in New York, in 1778, drew a prize of $500 in the New York Lottery, and immediately distributed it among the prisoners in that city. A New London, Connecticut, paper, dated Feb. 20, 1778, states that "it is said that the American prisoners, since we have had a Commissary in New York, are well served with good provisions, which are furnished at the expense of the States, and they are in general very healthy."

We fear this was a rose–colored view of the matter, though there is no doubt that our commissaries did what they could to alleviate the miseries of captivity.

Onderdonk quotes from Gaine's *Mercury* an advertisement for nurses in the hospital, but it is undated. "Nurses wanted immediately to attend the prison hospitals in this city. Good recommendations required, signed by two respectable inhabitants. Lewis Pintard."

From the New York *Gazette*, May 6, 1778, we take the following: "Colonel Miles, Irvin, and fifty more exchanged."

"Conn. *Gazette*. July 10, '78. About three weeks ago Robert Shefield, of Stonington, made his escape from New York after confinement in a prison ship. After he was taken he, with his crew of ten, were thrust into the fore–peak, and put in irons. On their arrival at New York they were carried on board a prison ship, and to the hatchways, on opening which, tell not of Pandora's box, for that must be an alabaster box in comparison to the opening of these hatches. True there were gratings (to let in air) but they kept their boats upon them. The steam of the hold was enough to scald the skin, and take away the breath, the stench enough to poison the air all around.

"On his descending these dreary mansions of woe, and beholding the numerous spectacles of wretchedness and despair, his soul fainted within him. A little epitome of hell,—about 300 men confined between decks, half Frenchmen. He was informed there were three more of these vehicles of contagion, which contained a like number of miserable Frenchmen also, who were treated worse, if possible, than Americans.

"The heat was so intense that (the hot sun shining all day on deck) they were all naked, which also served the well to get rid of vermin, but the sick were eaten up alive. Their sickly countenances, and ghastly looks were truly horrible; some swearing and blaspheming; others crying, praying, and wringing their hands; and stalking about like ghosts; others delirious, raving and storming,—all panting for breath; some dead, and corrupting. The air was so foul that at times a lamp could not be kept burning, by reason of which the bodies were not missed until they had been dead ten days.

"One person alone was admitted on deck at a time, after sunset, which occasioned much filth to run into the hold, and mingle with the bilge water, which was not pumped out while he was aboard, notwithstanding the decks were leaky, and the prisoners begged permission to let in water and pump it out again.

"While Mr. Sheffield was on board, which was six days, five or six died daily, and three of his people. He was sent for on shore as evidence in a Court of Admiralty for condemning his own vessel, and happily escaped.

"He was informed in New York that the fresh meat sent in to our prisoners by our Commissary was taken by the men–of–war for their own use. This he can say: he did not see any aboard the ship he was in, but they were well supplied with soft bread from our Commissaries on shore. But the provision (be it what it will) is not the complaint. Fresh air and fresh water, God's free gift, is all their cry."

"New London, Conn. July 31. 78. Last week 500 or 600 prisoners were released from confinement at New York and sent out chiefly by way of New Jersey, being exchanged."

"New London Conn. Sep. 26, 78. All American prisoners are nearly sent out of New York, but there are 615 French prisoners still there."

"Oct 18, 78. The Ship, Good Hope, lies in the North River."

"New London Dec. 18, 78. A Flag with 70 men from the horrible prison ships of New York arrived: 30 very sickly, 2 died since they arrived."

"N. London. Dec. 25, 78. A cartel arived here from New York with 172 American prisoners. They were landed here and in Groton, the greater part are sickly and in most deplorable condition, owing chiefly to the ill usage in the prison ships, where numbers had their feet and legs frozen"

CHAPTER XV. THE OLD SUGAR HOUSE—TRINTY CHURCHYARD

We will now take our readers with us to the Sugar House on Liberty Street, long called the Old Sugar House, and the only one of the three Sugar Houses which appear to have been used as a place of confinement for American prisoners of war after the year 1777.

We have already mentioned this dreary abode of wretchedness, but it deserves a more elaborate description.

From Valentine's Manual of the Common Council of New York for 1844 we will copy the following brief sketch of the British Prisons in New York during the Revolution.

"The British took possession of New York Sep. 15, '76, and the capture of Ft. Washington, Nov. 16, threw 2700 prisoners into their power. To these must be added 1000 taken at the battle of Brooklyn, and such private citizens as were arrested for their political principles, in New York City and on Long Island, and we may safely conclude that Sir William Howe had at least 5000 prisoners to provide for.

"The sudden influx of so many prisoners; the recent capture of the city, and the unlooked–for conflagration of a fourth part of it, threw his affairs into such confusion that, from these circumstances alone, the prisoners must have suffered much, from want of food and other bodily comforts, but there was superadded the studied cruelty of Captain Cunningham, the Provost Marshal, and his deputies, and the criminal negligence of Sir Wm. Howe.

"To contain such a vast number of prisoners the ordinary places of confinement were insufficient. Accordingly the Brick Church, the Middle Church, the North Church, and the French Church were appropriated to their use. Beside these, Columbia College, the Sugar House, the New Gaol, the new Bridewell, and the old City Hall were filled to their utmost capacity.

American Prisoners of the Revolution

"Till within a few years there stood on Liberty Street, south of the Middle Dutch Church, a dark, stone building, with small, deep porthole looking windows, rising tier above tier; exhibiting a dungeon–like aspect. It was five stories high, and each story was divided into two dreary apartments.

"On the stones and bricks in the wall were to be seen names and dates, as if done with a prisoner's penknife, or nail. There was a strong, gaol–like door opening on Liberty St., and another on the southeast, descending into a dismal cellar, also used as a prison. There was a walk nearly broad enough for a cart to travel around it, where night and day, two British or Hessian guards walked their weary rounds. The yard was surrounded by a close board fence, nine feet high. 'In the suffocating heat of summer,' says Wm. Dunlap, 'I saw every narrow aperture of these stone walls filled with human heads, face above face, seeking a portion of the external air.'

"While the gaol fever was raging in the summer of 1777, the prisoners were let out in companies of twenty, for half an hour at a time, to breathe fresh air, and inside they were so crowded, that they divided their numbers into squads of six each. No. 1 stood for ten minutes as close to the windows as they could, and then No. 2 took their places, and so on.

"Seats there were none, and their beds were but straw, intermixed with vermin.

"For many days the dead–cart visited the prison every morning, into which eight or ten corpses were flung or piled up, like sticks of wood, and dumped into ditches in the outskirts of the city."

Silas Talbot says: "A New York gentleman keeps a window shutter that was used as a checkerboard in the Sugar House. The prisoners daily unhinged it, and played on it."

Many years ago a small pamphlet was printed in New York to prove that some of the American prisoners who died in the Old Sugar House were buried in Trinity church–yard. Andrew S. Norwood, who was a boy during the Revolution, deposed that he used to carry food to John Van Dyke, in this prison. The other prisoners would try to wrest away the food, as they were driven mad by hunger. They were frequently fed with bread made from old, worm–eaten ship biscuits, reground into meal and offensive to the smell. Many of the prisoners died, and some were put into oblong boxes, sometimes two in a box, and buried in Trinity church–yard, and the boy, himself, witnessed some of the interments. A part of Trinity church–yard was used as a common burying–ground,—as was also the yard of St. George's Church, and what was called the Swamp Burying–Ground.

This boy also deposed that his uncle Clifford was murdered during the Revolution, it was supposed by foreign soldiers, and he was buried in Trinity church–yard.

Jacob Freeman, also a boy during the Revolution, deposed that his father and several other inhabitants of Woodbridge were arrested and sent to New York. His grandfather was sixty years old, and when he was arrested, his son, who was concealed and could have escaped, came out of his hiding–place and surrendered himself for the purpose of accompanying his father to prison. The son was a Lieutenant. They were confined in the Sugar House several months. Every day some of the prisoners died and were buried in Old Trinity church–yard. Ensign Jacob Barnitz was wounded in both legs at the battle of Fort Washington. He was conveyed to New York and there thrown into the Sugar House, and suffered to lie on the damp ground. A kind friend had him conveyed to more comfortable quarters. Barnitz came from York, or Lancaster, Pa.

Little John Pennell was a cabin boy, bound to Captain White of the sloop of war, Nancy, in 1776. He testified that the prisoners of the Sugar House, which was very damp, were buried on the hill called "The Holy Ground." "I saw where they were buried. The graves were long and six feet wide. Five or six were buried in one grave." It was Trinity Church ground.

We will now give an account of Levi Hanford, who was imprisoned in the Sugar House in 1777. Levi Hanford was a son of Levi Hanford, and was born in Connecticut, in the town of Norwalk, on the 19th of Feb., 1759. In 1775 he enlisted in a militia company. In 1776 he was in service in New York. In March 1777, being then a member of a company commanded by Captain Seth Seymour, he was captured with twelve others under Lieut. J. B. Eels, at the "Old Well" in South Norwalk, Conn. While a prisoner in the Old Sugar House he sent the following letter to his father. A friend wrote the first part for him, and he appears to have finished it in his own handwriting.

New York June 7. 1777

American Prisoners of the Revolution

Loving Father:—

I take the opportunity to let you know I am alive, and in reasonable health, since I had the small−pox.—thanks be to the Lord for it. * * * I received the things you sent me. * * * I wish you would go and see if you can't get us exchanged—if you please. Matthias Comstock is dead. Sam. Hasted, Ebenezer Hoyt, Jonathan Kellog has gone to the hospital to be inoculated today. We want money very much. I have been sick but hope I am better. There is a doctor here that has helpt me. * * * I would not go to the Hospital, for all manner of disease prevail there. * * * If you can possibly help us send to the Governor and try to help us. * * * Remember my kind love to all my friends. I am

Your Obedient son, Levi Hanford.

Poor Levi Hanford was sent to the prison ship, Good Intent, and was not exchanged until the 8th of May, 1778.

In the "Journal of American History," the third number of the second volume, on page 527, are the recollections of Thomas Stone, a soldier of the Revolution, who was born in Guilford, Conn., in 1755. In April, 1777, he enlisted under Capt. James Watson in Colonel Samuel Webb's Regiment, Connecticut line. He spent the following campaign near the Hudson. The 9th of December following Stone and his comrades under Gen. Parsons, embarked on board some small vessel at Norwalk, Conn, with a view to take a small fort on Long Island. "We left the shore," he says, "about six o'clock, P. M. The night was very dark, the sloop which I was aboard of parted from the other vessels, and at daybreak found ourselves alongside a British frigate. Our sloop grounded, we struck our colors−fatal hour! We were conducted to New York, introduced to the Jersey Prison Ship. We were all destitute of any clothing except what we had on; we now began to taste the vials of Monarchial tender mercy.

"About the 25th of Jan. 1778, we were taken from the ships to the Sugar House, which during the inclement season was more intolerable than the Ships.

"We left the floating Hell with joy, but alas, our joy was of short duration. Cold and famine were now our destiny. Not a pane of glass, nor even a board to a single window in the house, and no fire but once in three days to cook our small allowance of provision. There was a scene that truly tried body and soul. Old shoes were bought and eaten with as much relish as a pig or a turkey; a beef bone of four or five ounces, after it was picked clean, was sold by the British guard for as many coppers.

"In the spring our misery increased; frozen feet began to mortify; by the first of April, death took from our numbers, and, I hope, from their misery, from seven to ten a day; and by the first of May out of sixty–nine taken with me only fifteen were alive, and eight out of that number unable to work.

"Death stared the living in the face: we were now attacked by a fever which threatened to clear our walls of its miserable inhabitants.

"About the 20th of July I made my escape from the prison–yard. Just before the lamps were lighted. I got safely out of the city, passed all the guards, was often fired at, but still safe as to any injury done me; arrived at Harlem River eastward of King's Bridge.

"Hope and fear were now in full exercise. The alarm was struck by the sentinels keeping firing at me. I arrived at the banks of Harlem,—five men met me with their bayonets at my heart; to resist was instant death, and to give up, little better.

"I was conducted to the main guard, kept there until morning then started for New York with waiters with bayonets at my back, arrived at my old habitation about 1 o'clock, P. M.; was introduced to the Prison keeper who threatened me with instant death, gave me two heavy blows with his cane; I caught his arm and the guard interfered. Was driven to the provost, thrust into a dungeon, a stone floor, not a blanket, not a board, not a straw to rest on. Next day was visited by a Refugee Lieutenant, offered to enlist me, offered a bounty, I declined. Next day renewed the visit, made further offers, told me the General was determined I should starve to death where I was unless I would enter their service. I told him his General dare not do it. (I shall here omit the imprecations I gave him in charge.)

"The third day I was visited by two British officers, offered me a sergeant's post, threatened me with death as before, in case I refused. I replied, 'Death if they dare!'

"In about ten minutes the door was opened, a guard took me to my old habitation the Sugar House, it being about the same time of day I left my cell that I entered it, being three days and nights without a morsel of food or a drop of water,—all this for the crime of getting out of prison. When in the dungeon reflecting upon my situation I thought if ever mortal could be justified in praying for the destruction of his enemies, I am the man.

"After my escape the guard was augmented, and about this time a new prison keeper was appointed, our situation became more tolerable.

"The 16th of July was exchanged. Language would fail me to describe the joy of that hour; but it was transitory. On the morning of the 16th, some friends, or what is still more odious, some Refugees, cast into the Prison yard a quantity of warm bread, and it was devoured with greediness. The prison gate was opened, we marched out about the number of 250. Those belonging to the North and Eastern States were conducted to the North River and driven on board the flag ship, and landed at Elizabethtown, New Jersey. Those who ate of the bread soon sickened; there was death in the bread they had eaten. Some began to complain in about half an hour after eating the bread, one was taken sick after another in quick succession and the cry was, 'Poison, poison!' I was taken sick about an hour after eating. When we landed, some could walk, and some could not. I walked to town about two miles, being led most of the way by two men. About one half of our number did not eat of the bread, as a report had been brought into the prison *that the prisoners taken at Fort Washington had been poisoned in the same way.*

"The sick were conveyed in wagons to White Plains, where I expected to meet my regiment, but they had been on the march to Rhode Island I believe, about a week. I was now in a real dilemma; I had not the vestige of a shirt to my body, was moneyless and friendless. What to do I knew not. Unable to walk, a gentleman, I think his name was Allen, offered to carry me to New Haven, which he did. The next day I was conveyed to Guilford, the place of my birth, but no near relative to help me. Here I learned that my father had died in the service the Spring before. I was taken in by a hospitable uncle, but in moderate circumstances. Dr. Readfield attended me for about four months I was salivated twice, but it had no good effect. They sent me 30 miles to Dr Little of East Haddam, who under kind Providence restored me to such state of health that I joined my Regiment in the Spring following.

"In the year 1780, I think in the month of June, General Green met the enemy at Springfield, New Jersey, and in the engagement I had my left elbow dislocated in the afternoon. The British fired the village and retreated. We pursued until dark. The next morning my arm was so swollen that it *could* not, or at least was not put right, and it has been ever since a weak, feeble joint, which has disabled me from most kinds of manual labor."

To this account the grandson of Thomas Stone, the Rev. Hiram Stone, adds some notes, in one of which he says, speaking of the Sugar House: "I have repeatedly heard my grandfather relate that there were no windows left in the building, and that during the winter season the snow would be driven entirely across the great rooms in the different stories, and in the morning lie in drifts upon our poor, hungry, unprotected prisoners. Of a morning several frozen corpses would be dragged out, thrown into wagons like logs, then driven away and pitched into a large hole or trench, and covered up like dead brutes."

Speaking of the custom of sending the exchanged prisoners as far as possible from their own homes, he says: "I well remember hearing my grandfather explain this strange conduct of the enemy in the following way. Alter the poison was thus perfidiously administered, the prisoners belonging at the North were sent across to the Jersey side, while those of the South were sent in an opposite direction, the intention of the enemy evidently being to send the exchanged prisoners as far from home as possible, that most of them might die of the effect of the poison before reaching their friends. Grandfather used to speak of the treatment of our prisoners as most cruel and murderous, though charging it more to the Tories or Refugees than to the British.

"The effects of the poison taken into his system were never eradicated in the life–time of my grandfather, a 'breaking out,' or rash, appearing every spring, greatly to his annoyance and discomfort."

CHAPTER XVI. THE CASE OF JOHN BLATCHFORD

In our attempt to describe the sufferings of American prisoners taken during the Revolution, we have, for the most part, confined ourselves to New York, only because we have been unable to make extensive research into the records of the British prisons in other places. But what little we have been able to gather on the subject of the prisoners sent out of America we will also lay before our readers.

We have already stated the fact that some of our prisoners were sent to India and some to Africa. They seem to have been sold into slavery, and purchased by the East India

Company, and the African Company as well.

It is doubtful if any of the poor prisoners sent to the unwholesome climate of Africa ever returned to tell the story of British cruelties inflicted upon them there,—where hard work in the burning sun,—scanty fare,—and jungle fever soon ended their miseries. But one American prisoner escaped from the Island of Sumatra, where he had been employed in the pepperfields belonging to the East India Company. His story is eventful, and we will give the reader an abridgement of it, as it was told by himself, in his narrative, first published in a New England newspaper.

John Blatchford was born at Cape Ann, Mass., in the year 1762. In June, 1777, he went as a cabin boy on board the Hancock, a continental ship commanded by Capt. John Manly. On the 8th of July the Hancock was captured by the Rainbow, under Sir George Collier, and her crew was taken to Halifax.

John Blatchford was, at this time, in his sixteenth year. He was of medium height, with broad shoulders, full chest, and well proportioned figure. His complexion was sallow, his eyes dark, and his hair black and curly. He united great strength with remarkable endurance, else he could not have survived the rough treatment he experienced at the hands of fate. It is said that as a man he was temperate, grave, and dignified, and although his strength was so great, and his courage most undaunted, yet he was peaceable and slow to anger. His narrative appears to have been dictated by himself to some better educated person. It was first published in New London, Conn., in the year 1788. In the year 1797 an abstract of it appeared in Philip Freneau's *Time Piece*, a paper published in New York. In July, 1860, the entire production was published in the *Cape Ann Gazette*. We will now continue the narrative in Blatchford's own words:

"On our arrival at Halifax we were taken on shore and confined in a prison which had formerly been a sugar–house.

"The large number of prisoners confined in this house, near 300, together with a scanty allowance of provisions, occasioned it to be very sickly. * * * George Barnard, who had been a midshipman on the Hancock, and who was confined in the same room as myself, concerted a plan to release us, which was to be effected by digging a small passage under ground, to extend to a garden that was behind the prison, and without the prison wall, where we might make a breach in the night with safety, and probably all obtain our

94

liberty. This plan greatly elated our spirits, and we were anxious to proceed immediately in executing it.

"Our cabins were built one above another, from the floor to the height of a man's head; and mine was pitched upon to be taken up; and six of us agreed to do the work, whose names were George Barnard, William Atkins, late midshipmen in the Hancock; Lemuel Towle of Cape Ann, Isaiah Churchill of Plymouth; Asa Cole of Weathersfield, and myself.

"We took up the cabin and cut a hole in the plank underneath. The sugar house stood on a foundation of stone which raised the floor four feet above the ground, and gave us sufficient room to work, and to convey away the dirt that we dug up.

"The instruments that we had to work with were one scraper, one long spike, and some sharp sticks; with these we proceeded in our difficult undertaking. As the hole was too small to admit of more than one person to work at a time we dug by turns during ten or twelve days, and carried the dirt in our bosoms to another part of the cellar. By this time we supposed we had dug far enough, and word was given out among the prisoners to prepare themselves for flight.

"But while we were in the midst of our gayety, congratulating ourselves upon our prospects, we were basely betrayed by one of our own countrymen, whose name was Knowles. He had been a midshipman on board the Boston frigate, and was put on board the Fox when she was taken by the Hancock and Boston. What could have induced him to commit so vile an action cannot be conceived, as no advantage could accrue to him from our detection, and death was the certain consequence to many of his miserable countrymen. That it was so is all that I can say. A few hours before we were to have attempted our escape Knowles informed the Sergeant of the guard of our design, and by his treachery cost his country the lives of more than one hundred valuable citizens,—fathers, and husbands, whose return would have rejoiced the hearts of now weeping, fatherless children, and called forth tears of joy from wives, now helpless and disconsolate widows.

"When we were discovered the whole guard were ordered into the room and being informed by Knowles who it was that performed the work we were all six confined in irons; the hole was filled up and a sentinel constantly placed in the room, to prevent any further attempt.

"We were all placed in close confinement, until two of my fellow−sufferers, Barnard and Cole, died; one of which was put into the ground with his irons on his hands.

"I was afterwards permitted to walk the yard. But as my irons were too small, and caused my hands to swell, and made them very sore, I asked the Sergeant to take them off and give me larger ones. He being a person of humanity, and compassionating my sufferings, changed my irons for others that were larger, and more easy to my hands.

"Knowles, who was also permitted to walk the yard, for his perfidy, would take every opportunity to insult and mortify me, by asking me whether I wanted to run away again, and when I was going home, etc?

"His daily affronts, together with his conduct in betraying, his countrymen, so exasperated me that I wished for nothing more than an opportunity to convince him that I did not love him.

"One day as he was tantalizing over me as usual, I suddenly drew my one hand out of my irons, flew at him and struck him in the face, knocked out two or three of his teeth, and bruised his mouth very much. He cried out that the prisoner had got loose, but before any assistance came, I had put my hand again into the hand−cuff, and was walking about the yard as usual. When the guard came they demanded of me in what manner I struck him. I replied with both my hands.

"They then tried to pull my hands out, but could not, and concluded it must be as I said. Some laughed and some were angry, but in the end I was ordered again into prison.

"The next day I was sent on board the Greyhound, frigate, Capt. Dickson, bound on a cruise in Boston Bay.

"After being out a few days we met with a severe gale of wind, in which we sprung our main−mast, and received considerable other damage. We were then obliged to bear away for the West Indies, and on our passage fell in with and took a brig from Norwich, laden with stock.

"The Captain and hands were put on board a Danish vessel the same day. We carried the brig into Antigua, where we immediately repaired, and were ordered in company of the Vulture, sloop of war, to convoy a sloop of merchantmen into New York.

"We left the fleet off Sandy Hook, and sailed for Philadelphia, where we lay until we were made a packet, and ordered for Halifax with dispatches. We had a quick passage, and arrived safe.

"While we lay in the road Admiral Byron arrived, in the Princess Royal from England, who, being short of men, and we having a surplusage for a packet, many of our men were ordered on board the Princess Royal, and among them most of our boat's crew.

"Soon after, some of the officers going on shore, I was ordered into the boat. We landed at the Governor's slip—it being then near night. This was the first time since I had been on board the Greyhound that I had had an opportunity to escape from her, as they were before this particularly careful of me; therefore I was determined to get away if possible, and to effect it I waded round a wharf and went up a byway, fearing I should meet the officers. I soon got into the street, and made the best of my way towards Irishtown (the southern suburbs of Halifax) where I expected to be safe, but unfortunately while running I was met and stopped by an emissary, who demanded of me my business, and where I was going? I tried to deceive him, that he might let me pass, but it was in vain, he ordered me to follow him.

"I offered him what money I had, about seven shillings, sixpence, to let me go, this too was in vain. I then told him I was an American, making my escape, from a long confinement, and was determined to pass, and took up a stone. He immediately drew his bayonet, and ordered me to go back with him. I refused and told him to keep his distance. He then run upon me and pushed his bayonet into my side. It come out near my navel; but the wound was not very deep; he then made a second pass at me, and stabbed me through my arm; he was about to stab me a third time, when I struck him with the stone and knocked him down. I then run, but the guard who had been alarmed, immediately took me and carried me before the Governor, where I understood the man was dead.

"I was threatened with every kind of death, and ordered out of the Governor's presence. * * * Next day I was sent on board the Greyhound, the ship I had run from, and we sailed for England. Our captain being a humane man ordered my irons off, a few days after we

97

sailed, and permitted me to do duty as formerly. Being out thirteen days we spoke the Hazard sloop of war, who informed that the French fleet was then cruising in the English Channel. For this reason we put into Cork, and the dispatches were forwarded to England.

"While we lay in the Cove of Cork I jumped overboard with the intention of getting away; unfortunately I was discovered and fired at by the marines; the boat was immediately sent after me, took me up, and carried me on board again. At this time almost all the officers were on shore, and the ship was left in charge of the sailing–master, one Drummond, who beat me most cruelly. To get out of his way I run forward, he followed me, and as I was running back he came up with me and threw me down the main–hold. The fall, together with the beating was so severe that I was deprived of my senses for a considerable time. When I recovered them I found myself in the carpenter's berth, placed upon some old canvas between two chests, having my right thigh, leg and arm broken, and several parts of my body severely bruised. In this situation I lay eighteen days till our officers, who had been on business to Dublin, came on board. The captain inquired for the prisoners, and on being informed of my situation came down with the doctor to set my bones, but finding them callussed they concluded not to meddle with me.

"The ship lay at Cork until the French fleet left the Channel, and then sailed for Spithead. On our arrival there I was sent in irons on board the Princess Amelia, and the next day was carried on board the Brittania, in Portsmouth Harbor, to be tried before Sir Thomas Pye, lord high admiral of England, and President of the court martial.

"Before the officers had collected I was put under the care of a sentinel, and the seamen and women who came on board compassionated my sufferings, which rather heightened than diminished my distress.

"I was sitting under the awning, almost overpowered by the reflection of my unhappy situation, every morning expecting to be summoned for my trial, when I heard somebody enquire for the prisoner, and supposing it to be an officer I rose up and answered that I was there.

"The gentleman came to me, told me to be of good chear, and taking out a bottle of cordial, bade me drink, which I did. He then enquired where I belonged. I informed him.

He asked me if I had parents living, and if I had any friends in England? I answered I had neither. He then assured me he was my friend, and would render me all the assistance in his power. He then enquired of me every circumstance relative to my fray with the man at Halifax, for whose death I was now to be tried and instructed me what to say on my trial, etc."

Whether this man was a philanthropist, or an agent for the East India Company, we do not know. He instructed Blatchford to plead guilty, and then defended him from the charge of murder, no doubt on the plea of self–defence. Blatchford was therefore acquitted of murder, but apparently sold to the East India Company as a slave. How this was condoned we do not know, but will let the poor sailor continue his narrative in his own words.

"I was carried on board an Indiaman, and immediately put down into the run, where I was confined ten days. * * * On the seventh day I heard the boatswain pipe all hands, and about noon I was called up on board, where I found myself on board the Princess Royal, Captain Robert Kerr, bound to the East Indies, with six others, all large ships belonging to the East India Company." He had been told that he was to be sent back to America to be exchanged, and his disappointment amounted almost to despair.

"Our captain told me if I behaved well and did my duty I should receive as good usage as any man on board; this gave me great encouragement. I now found my destiny fixed, that whatever I could do would not in the least alter my situation, and therefor was determined to do the best I could, and make myself as contented as my unfortunate situation would admit.

"After being on board seven days I found there were in the Princess Royal 82 Americans, all destined to the East Indies, for being what they called 'Rebels.'

"We had a passage of seventeen weeks to St Helena, where we put in and landed part of our cargo, which consisted wholly of provisions. * * * The ship lay here about three weeks. We then sailed for Batavia, and on the passage touched at the Cape of Good Hope, where we found the whole of the fleet that sailed with us from England. We took in some provisions and necessaries, and set sail for Batavia, where we arrived in ten weeks. Here we purchased a large quantity of arrack, and remained a considerable time.

"We then sailed for Bencoulen in the Island of Sumatria, and after a passage of about six weeks arrived there. This was in June, 1780.

"At this place the Americans were all carried on shore, and I found that I was no longer to remain on board the ship, but condemned to serve as a soldier for five years. I offered to bind myself to the captain for five years, or any longer term if I might serve on board the ship. He told me it was impossible for me to be released from acting as a soldier, unless I could pay L50, sterling. As I was unable to do this I was obliged to go through the manual exercise with the other prisoners; among whom was Wm. Randall of Boston, and Josiah Folgier of Nantucket, both young men, and one of them an old ship–mate of mine.

"These two and myself agreed to behave as ignorant and awkward as possible, and what motions we learned one day we were to forget the next. We pursued this conduct nearly a fortnight, and were beaten every day by the drill–sergeant who exercised us, and when he found we were determined, in our obstinacy, and that it was not possible for him to learn us anything, we were all three sent into the pepper gardens belonging to the East India Company; and continued picking peppers from morning till night, and allowed but two scanty meals a day. This, together with the amazing heat of the sun, the island lying under the equator, was too much for an American constitution, unused to a hot climate, and we expected that we should soon end our misery and our lives; but Providence still preserved us for greater hardships.

"The Americans died daily with heat and hard fare, which determined my two comrades and myself in an endeavor to make our escape. We had been in the pepper–gardens four months when an opportunity offered, and we resolved upon trying our fortune. Folgier, Randall and myself sat out with an intention of reaching Croy (a small harbor where the Dutch often touched at to water, on the opposite side of the island). Folgier had by some means got a bayonet, which he fixed in the end of a stick. Randall and myself had nothing but staves, which were all the weapons we carried with us. We provided ourselves with fireworks [he means flints to strike fire] for our journey, which we pursued unmolested till the fourth day just at night, when we heard a rustle in the bushes and discovered nine sepoys, who rushed out upon us.

"Folgier being the most resolute of us run at one of them, and pushed his bayonet through his body into a tree. Randall knocked down another; but they overpowered us, bound us, and carried us back to the fort, which we reached in a day and a half, though we had been four days travelling from it, owing to the circle we made by going round the shore, and they came across the woods being acquainted with the way.

"Immediately on our arrival at the fort the Governor called a court martial, to have us tried. We were soon all condemned to be shot next morning at seven o'clock, and ordered to be sent into the dungeon and confined in irons, where we were attended by an adjutant who brought a priest with him to pray and converse with us, but Folgier, who hated the sight of an Englishman, desired that we might be left alone. * * * the clergyman reprimanded him, and told him he made very light of his situation on the supposition that he would be reprieved; but if he expected it he deceived himself. Folgier still persisted in the clergyman's leaving us, if he would have us make our peace with God, 'for,' said he, 'the sight of Englishmen, from whom we have received such treatment, is more disagreeable than the evil spirits of which you have spoken;' that, if he could have his choice, he would choose death in preference to life, if he must have it on the condition of such barbarous usage as he had received from their hands; and the thoughts of death did not seem so hideous to him as his past sufferings.

"He visited us again about midnight, but finding his company was not acceptable, he soon left us to our melancholy reflections.

"Before sunrise we heard the drums beat, and soon after heard the direful noise of the door grating on its iron hinges. We were all taken out, our irons taken off, and we conducted by a strong guard of soldiers to the parade, surrounded by a circle of armed men, and led into the midst of them, where three white officers were placed by our side;—silence was then commanded, and the adjutant taking a paper out of his pocket read our sentence;—and now I cannot describe my feelings upon this occasion, nor can it be felt by any one but those who have experienced some remarkable deliverance from the grim hand of death, when surrounded on all sides, and nothing but death expected from every quarter, and by Divine Providence there is some way found out for escape—so it seemed to me when the adjutant pulled out another paper from his pocket and read: 'That the Governor and Council, in consideration of the youth of Randall and myself, supposing us to be led on by Folgier, who was the oldest, thought proper to pardon us from death, and that instead we were to receive 800 lashes each.'

"Although this last sentence seemed terrible to me, yet in comparison with death, it seemed to be light. Poor Folgier was shot in our presence,—previous to which we were told we might go and converse with him. Randall went and talked with him first, and after him I went up to take my leave, but my feelings were such at the time I had not power to utter a single word to my departing friend, who seemed as undaunted and seemingly as willing to die as I was to be released, and told me not to forget the promises we had formerly made to each other, which was to embrace the first opportunity to escape.

"We parted, and he was immediately after shot dead. We were next taken and tied, and the adjutant brought a small whip made of cotton, which consisted of a number of strands and knotted at the ends; but these knots were all cut off by the adjutant before the drummer took it, which made it not worse than to have been whipped with cotton yarn.

"After being whipped 800 lashes we were sent to the Company's hospital, where we had been about three weeks when Randall told me he intended very soon to make his escape:—This somewhat surprised me, as I had lost all hopes of regaining my liberty, and supposed he had. I told him I had hoped he would never mention it again; but however, if that was his design, I would accompany him. He advised me, if I was fearful, to tarry behind; but finding he was determined on going, I resolved to run the risque once more; and as we were then in a hospital we were not suspected of such a design.

"Having provided ourselves with fire—works, and knives, about the first of December, 1780, we sat out, with the intent to reach the Dutch settlement of Croy, which is about two or three hundred miles distance upon a direct line, but as we were obliged to travel along the coast (fearing to risque the nearest way), it was a journey of 800 miles.

"We took each a stick and hung it around our neck, and every day cut a notch, which was the method we took to keep time.

"In this manner we travelled, living upon fruit, turtle eggs, and sometimes turtle, which we cooked every night with the fire we built to secure us from wild beasts, they being in great plenty,—such as buffaloes, tigers, jackanapes, leopards, lions, and baboons and monkies.

"On the 30th day of our traveling we met with nothing we could eat and found no water. At night we found some fruit which appeared to the eyes to be very delicious, different from any we had seen in our travels. It resembled a fruit which grows in the West Indies, called a Jack, about the size of an orange. We being very dry and hungry immediately gathered some of this fruit, but finding it of a sweet, sickish taste, I eat but two. Randall eat freely. In the evening we found we were poisoned: I was sick and puked considerably, Randall was sick and began to swell all round his body. He grew worse all night, but continued to have his senses till the next day, when he died, and left me to mourn my greater wretchedness,—more than 400 miles from any settlement, no companion, the wide ocean on one side, and a prowling wilderness on the other, liable to many kinds of death, more terrible than being shot.

"I laid down by Randall's body, wishing, if possible, that he might return and tell me what course to take. My thoughts almost distracted me, so that I was unable to do anything untill the next day, during all which time I continued by the side of Randall. I then got up and made a hole in the sand and buried him.

"I now continued my journey as well as the weak state of my body would permit,—the weather being at the time extremely hot and rainy. I frequently lay down and would wish that I might never rise again;—despair had almost wholly possessed me; and sometimes in a kind of delirium I would fancy I heard my mother's voice, and my father calling me, and I would answer them. At other times my wild imagination would paint to my view scenes which I was acquainted with. Then supposing myself near home I would run as fast as my legs could carry me. Frequently I fancied that I heard dogs bark, men cutting wood, and every noise which I have heard in my native country.

"One day as I was travelling a small dog, as I thought it to be, came fawning round me and followed me, but I soon discovered it to be a young lion. I supposed that its dam must be nigh, and therefore run. It followed me some time and then left me. I proceeded on, but had not got far from it before it began to cry. I looked round and saw a lioness making towards it. She yelled most frightfully, which greatly terrified me; but she laid down something from her mouth for her young one, and then with another yell turned and went off from me.

"Some days after I was travelling by the edge of a woods, which from its appearance had felt severely the effects of a tornado or hurricane, the trees being all torn up by the roots, and I heard a crackling noise in the bushes. Looking about I saw a monstrous large tiger making slowly towards me, which frightened me exceedingly. When he had approached within a few rods of me, in my surprise I lifted up my hands and hollowed very loud. The sudden noise frightened him, seemingly as much as I had been, and he immediately turned and run into the woods, and I saw him no more.

"After this I continued to travel on without molestation, only from the monkies who were here so plentiful that oftentimes I saw them in large droves; sometimes I run from them, as if afraid of them, they would then follow, grin, and chatter at me, and when they got near I would turn, and they would run from me back into the woods, and climb the trees to get out of my way.

"It was now 15 weeks since I had left the hospital. I had travelled most all of the day without any water and began to be very thirsty, when I heard the sound of running water, as it were down a fall of rocks. I had heard it a considerable time and at last began to suspect it was nothing, but imaginary, as many other noises I had before thought to have heard. I however went on as fast as I could, and at length discovered a brook. On approaching it I was not a little surprised and rejoiced by the sight of a Female Indian, who was fishing at the brook. She had no other dress on than that which mother nature affords impartially to all her children, except a small cloth which she wore round her waist.

"I knew not how to address myself to her. I was afraid if I spoke she would run, and therefore I made a small noise; upon which she looked round, and seeing me, run across the brook, seemingly much frightened, leaving her fishing line. I went up to her basket which contained five or six fish which looked much like our trout. I took up the basket and attempted to wade across where she had passed, but was too weak to wade across in that place, and went further up the stream, where I passed over, and then looking for the Indian woman I saw her at some distance behind a large cocoa–nut tree. I walked towards her but dared not keep my eyes steadily upon her lest she would run as she did before. I called to her in English, and she answered in her own tongue, which I could not understand. I then called to her in the Malaysian, which I understood a little of; she answered me in a kind of surprise and asked me in the name of Okrum Footee (the name of their God) from whence I came, and where I was going. I answered her as well as I could in the Melais, that I was from Fort Marlborough, and going to Croy—that I was making my escape from the English, by whom I had been taken in war. She told me that she had been taken by the Malays some years before, for that the two nations were always at war, and that she had been kept as a slave among them three years and was then retaken by her countrymen. While we were talking together she appeared to be very shy, and I durst not come nearer than a rod to her, lest she should run from me. She said that Croy, the place I was bound to, was about three miles distant: That if I would follow her she would conduct me to her countrymen, who were but a small distance off. I begged her to plead with her countrymen to spare my life. She said she would, and assured me that if I behaved well I should not be hurt. She then conducted me to a small village, consisting of huts or wigwams. When we arrived at the village the children that saw me were frightened and run away from me, and the women exhibited a great deal of fear and kept at a distance. But my guide called to them and told them not to be afraid, for that I was not come to hurt them, and then informed them from whence I came, and that I was going to Croy.

"I told my guide I was very hungry, and she sent the children for something for me to eat. They came and brought me little round balls of rice, and they, not daring to come nigh, threw them at me. These I picked up and eat. Afterwards a woman brought some rice and goat's milk in a copper bason, and setting it on the ground made signs for me to take it up and eat it, which I did, and then put the bason down again. They then poked away the bason with a stick, battered it with stones, and making a hole in the ground, buried it.

"After that they conducted me to a small hut, and told me to tarry there until the morning, when they would conduct me to the harbor. I had but little sleep that night, and was up several time to look out, and saw two or three Indians at a little distance from the hut, who I supposed were placed there to watch me.

"Early in the morning numbers came around the hut, and the female who was my guide asked me where my country was? I could not make her understand, only that it was at a great distance. She then asked me if my countrymen eat men? I told her, no, and seeing some goats pointed at them, and told her we eat such as them. She then asked me what made me white, and if it was not the white rain that come upon us when we were small * * * as I wished to please them I told her that I supposed it was, for it was only in certain seasons of the year that it fell, and in hot weather when it did not fall the people grew darker until it returned, and then the people all grew white again. This seemed to please them very much.

105

"My protectress then brought a young man to me who she said was her brother, and who would show me the way to the harbour. She then cut a stick about eight feet long, and he took hold of one end and gave me the other. She told me that she had instructed her brother what to say at the harbour. He then led off, and I followed. During our walk I put out my hand to him several times, and made signs of friendship, but he seemed to be afraid of me, and would look upwards and then fall flat on the ground and kiss it: this he repeated as often as I made any sign or token of friendship to him.

"When we had got near the harbor he made a sign for me to sit down upon a rock, which I did. He then left me and went, as I supposed, to talk to the people at the water concerning me; but I had not sat long before I saw a vessel coming round the point into the harbor.

"They soon came on shore in the boat. I went down to them and made my case known and when the boat returned on board they took me with them. It was a Dutch snow bound from China to Batavia. After they had wooded and watered they set sail for Batavia:—being out about three weeks we arrived there: I tarried on board her about three weeks longer, and then got on board a Spanish ship which was from Rio de la Plate bound to Spain, but by stress of weather was obliged to put into this port. After the vessel had repaired we sailed for Spain. When we made the Cape of Good Hope we fell in with two British cruisers of twenty guns each, who engaged us and did the vessel considerable damage, but at length we beat them off, and then run for the coast of Brazil, where we arrived safe, and began to work at repairing our ship, but upon examination she was found to be not fit to proceed on her voyage. She was therefore condemned. I then left her and got on board a Portuguese snow bound up to St. Helena, and we arrived safe at that place.

"I then went on shore and quitted her and engaged in the garrison there to do duty as a soldier for my provisions till some ship should arrive there bound for England. After serving there a month I entered on board a ship called the Stormont, but orders were soon after received that no Indiaman should sail without convoy; and we lay here six months, during which time the Captain died.

"While I was in St. Helena the vessel in which I came out from England arrived here, homeward bound; she being on the return from her second voyage since I came from England. And now I made known my case to Captain Kerr, who readily took me on board the Princess Royal, and used me kindly and those of my old ship–mates on board were glad to see me again. Captain Kerr on first seeing me asked me if I was not afraid to let him know who I was, and endeavored to frighten me; yet his conduct towards me was humane and kind.

"It had been very sickly on board the Princess Royal, and the greater part of the hands who came out of England in her had died, and she was now manned chiefly with lascars. Among those who had died was the boatswain, and boatswain's mate, and Captain Kerr made me boatswain of the ship, in which office I continued until we arrived in London, and it protected me from being impressed upon our arrival in England.

"We sailed from St. Helena about the first of November, 1781, under convoy of the Experiment of fifty guns, commanded by Captain Henry, and the Shark sloop of war of 18 guns, and we arrived in London about the first of March, 1782, it having been about two years and a half from the time I had left it.

"In about a fortnight after our arrival in London I entered on board the King George, a store–ship bound to Antigua, and after four weeks passage arrived there.

"The second night after we came to anchor in Antigua I took the ship's boat and escaped in her to Montserrat (in the West Indies) which place had but just before been taken by the French.

"Here I did not meet with the treatment which I expected; for on my arrival at Montserrat I was immediately taken up and put in prison, where I continued twenty–four hours, and my boat taken from me. I was then sent to Guadaloupe, and examined by the Governor. I made known my case to him, by acquainting him with the misfortunes I had gone through in my captivity, and in making my escape. He seemed to commiserate me, gave me ten dollars for the boat that I escaped in, and provided a passage for me on board a French brigantine that was bound from Gaudaloupe to Philadelphia.

"The vessel sailed in a few days, and now my prospects were favorable, but my misfortunes were not to end here, for after being out twenty–one days we fell in with the Anphitrite and Amphene, two British cruizers, off the Capes of Delaware, by which we were taken, carried in to New York and put on board the Jersey prison ship. After being on board about a week a cartel was fitted out for France, and I was sent on board as a

French prisoner. The cartel was ordered for St. Maloes, and after a passage of thirty–two days we arrived safe at that place.

"Finding no American vessel at St. Male's, I went to the Commandant, and procured a pass to go by land to Port l'Orient. On my arrival there I found three American privateers belonging to Beverley in the Massachusetts. I was much elated at seeing so many of my countrymen, some of whom I was well acquainted with. I immediately entered on board the Buccaneer, Captain Pheirson. We sailed on a cruise, and after being out eighteen days we returned to L'Orient with six prizes. Three days after our arrival in port we heard the joyful news of peace; on which the privateer was dismantled, the people discharged, and Captain P sailed on a merchant voyage to Norway.

"I then entered on board a brig bound to Lisbon (Captain Ellenwood of Beverley) and arrived at Lisbon in eight days. We took in a cargo of salt, and sailed for Beverley, where we arrived the ninth of May, 1783. Being now only fifteen miles from home, I immediately set out for Cape Ann, went to my father's house, and had an agreeable meeting with my friends, after an absence of almost six years.

"John Blatchford

"New London, May 10th, 1788.

"N. B. Those who are acquainted with the narrator will not scruple to give full credence to the foregoing account, and others may satisfy themselves by conversing with him. The scars he carries are a proof of his narrative, and a gentleman of New London who was several months with him, was acquainted with part of his sufferings, though it was out of his power to relieve him. He is a poor man with a wife and two children. His employment is fishing and coasting. *Editor*."

Our readers may be interested to know what became of John Blatchford, who wrote, or dictated, the narrative we have given, in the year 1788. He was, at that time, a married man. He had married a young woman named Ann Grover. He entered the merchant marine, and died at Port au Prince about the year 1794, when nearly thirty–three years of age. Thus early closed the career of a brave man, who had experienced much hardship, and had suffered greatly from man's inhumanity to man, and who is, as far as we know, the only American prisoner sent to the East Indies who ever returned to tell the story of the barbarities inflicted upon him.

CHAPTER XVII. BENJAMIN FRANKLIN AND OTHERS ON THE SUBJECT OF AMERICAN PRISONERS

When Benjamin Franklin and Silas Deane were in Paris they wrote the following letter to Lord Stormont, the English Ambassador to France.

Paris, April 2nd, 1777.

My Lord:—

We did ourselves the honor of writing some time since to your Lordship on the subject of exchanging prisoners: you did not condescend to give us any answer, and therefore we expect none to this. We, however, take the liberty of sending you copies of certain depositions which we shall transmit to Congress, whereby it will be known to your Court, that the United States are not unacquainted with the barbarous treatment their people receive when they have the misfortune to be your prisoners here in Europe, and that if your conduct towards us is not altered, it is not unlikely that severe reprisals may be thought justifiable from a necessity of putting some check to such abominable practices. For the sake of humanity it is to be wished that men would endeavor to alleviate the unavoidable miseries attending a state of war. It has been said that among the civilized nations of Europe the ancient horrors of that state are much diminished; but the compelling men by chains, stripes, and famine to fight against their friends and relatives, is a new mode of barbarity, which your nation alone has the honor of inventing, and the sending American prisoners of war to Africa and Asia, remote from all probability of exchange, and where they can scarce hope ever to hear from their families, even if the unwholesomeness of the climate does not put a speedy end to their lives, is a manner of treating captives that you can justify by no other precedent or custom except that of the black savages of Guinea. We are your Lordship's most obedient, humble servants, Benjamin Franklin, Silas Deane.

The reply to this letter was laconic.

"The King's Ambassador recognizes no letters from Rebels, except when they come to ask mercy."

Inclosed in the letter from our representatives were the following depositions.

THE DEPOSITION OF ELIPHALET DOWNER

Eliphalet Downer, Surgeon, taken in the Yankee privateer, testifies that after he was made prisoner by Captains Ross and Hodge, who took advantage of the generous conduct of Captain Johnson of the Yankee to them his prisoners, and of the confidence he placed in them in consequence of that conduct and their assurances; he and his countrymen were closely confined, yet assured that on their arrival in port they should be set at liberty, and these assurances were repeated in the most solemn manner, instead of which they were, on their approach to land, in the hot weather of August, shut up in a small cabin; the windows of which were spiked down and no air admitted, insomuch that they were all in danger of suffocation from the excessive heat.

Three or four days after their arrival in the river Thames they were relieved from this situation in the middle of the night, hurried on board a tender and sent down to Sheerness, where the deponent was put into the Ardent, and there falling sick of a violent fever in consequence of such treatment, and languishing in that situation for some time, he was removed, still sick, to the Mars, and notwithstanding repeated petitions to be suffered to be sent to prison on shore, he was detained until having the appearance of a mortification in his legs, he was sent to Haslar hospital, from whence after recovering his health, he had the good fortune to make his escape.

While on board those ships and in the hospital he was informed and believes that many of his countrymen, after experiencing even worse treatment than he, were sent to the East Indies, and many of those taken at Quebec were sent to the coast of Africa, as soldiers.

THE DEPOSITION OF CAPTAIN SETH CLARK OF NEWBURY PORT IN THE STATE OF MASSACHUSETTS BAY IN AMERICA

"This deponent saith that on his return from Cape Nichola Mole to Newbury Port, he was taken on the 17th of September last by an armed schooner in his British Majesty's service, ——Coats, Esquire, Commander, and carried down to Jamaica, on his arrival at which place he was sent on board the Squirrel, another armed vessel, ——Douglas, Esquire, Commander, where, although master and half owner of the vessel in which he was taken, he was returned as a common sailor before the mast, and in that situation sailed for England in the month of November, on the twenty–fifth of which month they took a schooner from Port a Pie to Charlestown, S. C., to which place she belonged, when the owner, Mr. Burt, and the master, Mr. Bean, were brought on board. On the latter's denying he had any ship papers Captain Douglas ordered him to be stripped and tied up and then whipped with a wire cat of nine tails that drew blood every stroke and then on his saying that he had thrown his papers overboard he was untied and ordered to his duty as a common sailor, with no place for himself or his people to lay on but the decks. On their arrival at Spithead, the deponent was removed to the Monarch, and there ordered to do duty as a fore–mast–man, and on his refusing on account of inability to do it, he was threatened by the Lieutenant, a Mr. Stoney, that if he spoke one word to the contrary he should be brought to the gangway, and there severely flogged.

"After this he was again removed and put on board the Bar–fleur, where he remained until the tenth of February. On board this ship the deponent saw several American prisoners, who were closely confined and ironed, with only four men's allowance to six. These prisoners and others informed this deponent that a number of American prisoners had been taken out of the ship and sent to the East Indies and the coast of Africa, which he has told would have been his fate, had he arrived sooner.

"This deponent further saith, That in Haslar hospital, to which place on account of sickness he was removed from the Bar–fleur, he saw a Captain Chase of Providence, New England, who told him he had been taken in a sloop of which he was half owner and master, on his passage from Providence to South Carolina, by an English transport, and turned over to a ship of war, where he was confined in irons thirteen weeks, insulted, beat, and abused by the petty officers and common sailors, and on being released from irons was ordered to do duty as a foremost man until his arrival in England, when being dangerously ill he was sent to said hospital."

Paris March 30th. 1777.

Benjamin Franklin, in a letter written in 1780, to a Mr. Hartley, an English gentleman who was opposed to the war, said that Congress had investigated the cruelties perpetrated by the English upon their defenceless prisoners, and had instructed him to prepare a *school book* for the use of American children, to be illustrated by thirty–five good engravings, each to picture some scene of horror, some enormity of suffering, such as should indelibly impress upon the minds of the school children a dread of British rule, and a hatred of British malice and wickedness!

The old philosopher did not accomplish this task: had he done so it is improbable that we would have so long remained in ignorance of some of the facts which we are now endeavoring to collect. It will be pleasant to glance, for a moment, on the other side the subject. It is well known that there was a large party in England, who, like Benjamin Franklin's correspondent, were opposed to the war; men of humanity, fair–minded enough to sympathize with the struggles of an oppressed people, of the same blood as themselves.

"The Prisoners of 1776, A Relic of the Revolution," is a little book edited by the Rev. R. Livesey, and published in Boston, in 1854. The facts in this volume were complied from the journal of Charles Herbert of Newburyport, Mass. This young man was taken prisoner in December, 1776. He was a sailor on board the brigantine Dolton. He and his companions were confined in the Old Mill Prison in Plymouth, England.

Herbert, who was in his nineteenth year, was a prisoner more than two years. He managed to keep a journal during his captivity, and has left us an account of his treatment by the English which is a pleasant relief in its contrast to the dark pictures that we have drawn of the wretchedness of American prisoners elsewhere. A collection of upwards of $30,000 was taken up in England for the relief of our prisoners confined in English jails.

Herbert secreted his journal in a chest which had a false bottom. It is too long to give in its entirety, but we have made a few extracts which will describe the treatment the men received in England, where all that was done was open to public inspection, and where no such inhuman monsters as Cunningham were suffered to work their evil will upon their victims.

"Dec. 24th, 1776. We were taken by the Reasonable, man–of–war of 64 guns. I put on two shirts, pair of drawers and breeches, and trousers over them, two or three jackets, and a pair of new shoes, and then filled my bosom and pockets as full as I could carry. Nothing but a few old rags and twelve old blankets were sent to us. Ordered down to the cable tier. Almost suffocated. Nothing but the bare cable to lie on, and that very uneven.

"Jan. 15, 1777. We hear that the British forces have taken Fort Washington with a loss of 800."

After several changes Herbert was put on board the Tarbay, a ship of 74 guns, and confined between decks, with not room for all to lie down at once.

"Very cold. Have to lie on a wet deck without blankets. Some obliged to sit up all night."

On the 18th of February they received flock beds and pillows, rugs, and blankets. "Ours are a great comfort to us after laying fifty–five nights without any, all the time since we were taken. * * *

"We are told that the Captain of this ship, whose name is Royer, gave us these clothes and beds out of his own pocket."

On the twelfth of April he was carried on shore to the hospital, where his daily allowance was a pound of beef, a pound of potatoes, and three pints of beer.

On the 7th of May he writes: "I now have a pound of bread, half a pound of mutton and a quart of beer daily. The doctor is very kind. Three of our company have died."

On the fifth of June he was committed to the Old Mill Prison at Plymouth. Many entries in his journal record the escapes of his companions. "Captain Brown made his escape." "William Woodward of the charming Sallie escaped, etc., etc."

June 6th he records: "Our allowance here in prison is a pound of beef, a pound of greens, and a quart of beer, and a little pot liquor that the greens and beef were boiled in, without any thickening." Still he declares that he has "a continued gnawing in his stomach." The people of the neighborhood came to see them daily when they were exercising in the prison yard, and sometimes gave them money and provisions through the pickets of the high fence that surrounded the prison grounds. Herbert had a mechanical turn, and made boxes which he sold to these visitors, procuring himself many comforts in this manner.

About ten prisoners were brought in daily. They were constantly digging their way out and were sometimes recaptured, but a great number made their escape. On the twentieth of July he records that they begin to make a breach in the prison wall. "Their intention is to dig eighteen feet underground to get into a field on the other side of the wall.

"We put all the dirt in our chests."

August third he says: "There are 173 prisoners in the wards. On the fifth thirty−two escaped, but three were brought back. These were confined in the Black Hole forty days on half allowance, and obliged to lie on the bare floor.

"September 12th. We had a paper wherein was a melancholy account of the barbarous treatment of American prisoners, taken at Ticonderoga.

"Sept. 16th. Today about twenty old countrymen petitioned the Board for permission to go on board His Majesty's ships.

"Jan. 7th. 1778. 289 prisoners here in Plymouth. In Portsmouth there are 140 prisoners. Today the prison was smoked with charcoal and brim−stone."

He records the gift of clothes, blankets, and all sorts of provisions. They were allowed to wash at the pump in relays of six. Tobacco and everything necessary was freely given them.

"Jan. 27th. The officers in a separate prison are allowed to burn candles in the evening until gun−fire, which is eight o'clock.

"28th. Today some new washing troughs were brought up for us to wash our clothes in; and now we have plenty of clothes, soap, water, and tubs to wash in. In general we are tolerably clean.

"Feb. 1st. Sunday. Last evening between 7 and 9 o'clock five of the officers in a separate prison, who had agreed with the sentry to let them go, made their escape and took two sentries with them. The five officers were Captain Henry Johnston, Captain Eleazar Johnston, Offin Boardman, Samuel Treadwell, and one Mr. Deal.

"Feb. 8th. Sunday. We have the paper wherein is an account of a letter from Dr. Franklin, Dean, and Lee, to Lord North, and to the ministry, putting them in mind of the abuse which the prisoners have had from time to time, and giving them to know that it is in the power of the Americans to make ample retaliation. * * * We learn that their answer was that in America there was an exchange."

On the 9th of March he writes: "We are all strong, fat and hearty.

"March 12th. Today our two fathers came to see us as they generally do once or twice a week. They are Mr. Heath, and Mr. Sorry, the former a Presbyterian minister, in Dock, the latter a merchant in Plymouth. They are the two agents appointed by the Committee in London to supply us with necessaries. A smile from them seems like a smile from a father. They tell us that everything goes well on our side.

"April 7th. Today the latter (Mr. Sorry) came to see us, and we desired him, for the future, to send us a four penny white loaf instead of a six–penny one to each mess, per day, for we have more provision than many of us want to eat, and any person can easily conjecture that prisoners, in our situation, who have suffered so much for the want of provisions would abhor such an act as to waste what we have suffered so much for the want of."

Herbert was liberated at the end of two years. Enough has been quoted to prove the humanity with which the prisoners at Plymouth were treated. He gives a valuable list of crews in Old Mill Prison, Plymouth, during the time of his incarceration, with the names of captains, number that escaped, those who died, and those who joined the English.

Joined NAMES OF SHIPS AND CAPTAINS No. of British
Men Escaped Died Ships Brig Dolton, Capt. Johnston 120 21 8 7 Sloop Charming Sally, Capt. Brown. 52 6 7 16 Brig Fancy, Capt. Lee 56 11 2 0 Brig Lexington, Capt. Johnston 51 6 1 26 Schooner Warren, Capt. Ravel 40 2 0 6

PARTS OF CREWS TAKEN INTO PLYMOUTH

Brig Freedom, Capt. Euston 11 3 1 0 Ship Reprisal, Capt. Weeks 10 2 0 3 Sloop Hawk 6 0 0 0 Schooner Hawk, Capt. Hibbert 6 0 0 0 Schooner Black Snake, Capt. Lucran 3 1 0 0 Ship Oliver Cromwell 7 1 0 4 Letter of Marque Janey, Capt. Rollo 2 1 0 0 Brig Cabot 3 0 0 0 True Blue, Capt. Furlong 1 0 0 0 Ranger 1 0 0 0 Sloop Lucretia 2 0 0 0 Musquito Tender 1 0 0 1 Schooner, Capt. Burnell 2 1 0 1 Sturdy Beggar 3 0 0 0 Revenge, Capt Cunningham 3 0 0 0

Total 380 55 19 62
Remained in Prison until exchanged, 244

Before we leave the subject of Plymouth we must record the fact that some time in the year 1779 a prize was brought into the harbor captured from the French with 80 French prisoners. The English crew put in charge of the prize procured liquor, and, in company of some of the loose women of the town, went below to make a night of it. In the dead of night the Frenchmen seized the ship, secured the hatches, cut the cable, took her out of port, homeward bound, and escaped.

A writer in the London *Gazette* in a letter to the Lord Mayor, dated August 6th, 1776, says: "I was last week on board the American privateer called the Yankee, commanded by Captain Johnson, and lately brought into this port by Captain Ross, who commanded one of the West India sugar ships, taken by the privateer in July last: and as an Englishman I earnestly wish your Lordship, who is so happily placed at the head of this great city (justly famed for its great humanity even to its enemies), would be pleased to go likewise, or send proper persons, to see the truly shocking and I may say barbarous and miserable condition of the unfortunate American prisoners, who, however criminal they may be thought to have been, are deserving of pity, and entitled to common humanity.

"They are twenty–five in number, and all inhumanly shut close down, like wild beasts, in a small stinking apartment, in the hold of a sloop, about seventy tons burden, without a breath of air, in this sultry season, but what they receive from a small grating overhead, the openings in which are not more than two inches square in any part, and through which the sun beats intensely hot all day, only two or three being permitted to come on deck at a time; and then they are exposed in the open sun, which is reflected from the decks like a burning glass.

"I do not at all exaggerate, my lord, I speak the truth, and the resemblance that this barbarity bears to the memorable Black Hole at Calcutta, as a gentleman present on Saturday observed, strikes every eye at the sight. All England ought to know that the same game is now acting upon the Thames on board this privateer, that all the world cried out against, and shuddered at the mention of in India, some years ago, as practised on Captain Hollowell and other of the King's good subjects. The putrid steams issuing from the hold are so hot and offensive that one cannot, without the utmost danger, breathe over it, and I should not be at all surprised if it should cause a plague to spread.

"The miserable wretches below look like persons in a hot bath, panting, sweating, and fainting, for want of air; and the surgeon declares that they must all soon perish in this situation, especially as they are almost all in a sickly state from bilious disorders.

"The captain and surgeon, it is true, have the liberty of the cabin (if it deserves the name of a cabin), and make no complaints on their own account. They are both sensible and well behaved young men, and can give a very good account of themselves, having no signs of fear, and being supported by a consciousness of the justice of their cause.

"They are men of character, of good families in New England, and highly respected in their different occupations; but being stripped of their all by the burning of towns, and other destructive measures of the present unnatural war, were forced to take the disagreeable method of making reprisals to maintain themselves and their children rather than starve. * * * English prisoners taken by the Americans have been treated with the most remarkable tenderness and generosity, as numbers who are safely returned to England most freely confess, to the honor of our brethern in the colonies, and it is a fact, which can be well attested in London, that this very surgeon on board the privateer, after the battle of Lexington, April 19th, 1775, for many days voluntarily and generously without fee or reward employed himself in dressing the King's wounded soldiers, who but an hour before would have shot him if they could have come at him, and in making a collection for their refreshment, of wine, linen, money, etc., in the town where he lived. * * * The capture of the privateer was, solely owing to the ill–judged lenity and brotherly kindness of Captain Johnson, who not considering his English prisoners in the same light that he would French or Spanish, put them under no sort of confinement, but permitted them to walk the decks as freely as his own people at all times. Taking advantage of this indulgence the prisoners one day watched their opportunity when most of the privateer's people were below, and asleep, shut down the hatches, and making all fast, had immediate possession of the vessel without using any force."

What the effect of this generous letter was we have no means of discovering. It displays the sentiments of a large party in England, who bitterly condemned the "unnatural war against the Colonies."

CHAPTER XVIII. THE ADVENTURES OF ANDREW SHERBURNE

While we are on the subject of the treatment of American prisoners in England, which forms a most grateful contrast to that which they received in New York, Philadelphia, and other parts of America, we will give an abstract of the adventures of another young man who was confined in the Old Mill Prison at Plymouth, England. This young man was named Andrew Sherburne. He was born at Rye, New Hampshire, on the 3oth of September, 1765.

He first served on the continental ship of war, Ranger, which shipped a crew at Portsmouth, N. H. His father consented that he should go with her, and his two half uncles, Timothy and James Weymouth, were on board. There were about forty boys in the crew. Andrew was then in his fourteenth year, and was employed as waiter to the boatswain. The vessel sailed in the month of June, 1779. She took ten prizes and sailed for home, where she arrived in August, 1779. Next year she sailed again on another cruise, but was taken prisoner by the British at Charleston, S. C., on the 12th of May, 1780.

"Our officers," says Sherburne, "were paroled and allowed to retain their waiters. We were for several days entirely destitute of provisions except muscles, which we gathered from the muscle beds. I was at this time waiter to Captain Pierce Powers, master's mate of the Ranger. He treated me with the kindness of a father."

"At this time," he continues, "Captain Simpson and the other officers procured a small vessel which was employed as a cartel, to transport the officers, their boys and baggage, agreeably to the terms of capitulation, to Newport, R. I. It being difficult to obtain suitable casks for water they procured such as they could. These proved to be foul, and after we got to sea our water became filthy and extremely noxious. Very few if any on board escaped an attack of the diarrhoea."

After his return he next shipped under Captain Wilds on the Greyhound, from Portsmouth, N. H., and at last, after many adventures, was taken prisoner by Newfoundlanders, off Newfoundland. He was then put on board the Fairy, a British sloop of war, commanded by Captain Yeo, "a complete tyrant" "Wilds and myself," he continues, "were called to the quarter deck, and after having been asked a few questions by Captain Yeo, he turned to his officers and said: 'They are a couple of fine lads for his Majesty's service. Mr. Gray, see that they do their duty.'"

When the sloop arrived in England the boys complained that they were prisoners of war, in consequence of which they were sent to the Old Mill Prison at Plymouth, accused of "rebellion, piracy, and high treason."

Here they found acquaintances from Portsmouth, N. H. The other prisoners were very kind to young Sherburne, gave him clothing and sent him to a school which was kept in the prison. Ship building and other arts were carried on in this place, and he learned navigation, which was of great service to him in after life.

The fare, he declared, was tolerably good, but there was not enough of it. He amused himself by making little toy ships. He became ill and delirious, but recovered in time to be sent to America when a general exchange of prisoners was effected in 1781. The rest of his adventures has nothing to do with prisons, in England, and shall not now be detailed.

Although the accounts of the English prisons left by Herbert, Sherburne and others are so favorable, yet it seems that, after the year 1780, there was some cause of complaint even there. We will quote a passage from the British Annual Register to prove this statement. This passage we take from the Register for 1781, page 152.

"A petition was presented to the House the same day (June 20th) by Mr. Fox, from the American prisoners in Mill Prison, Plymouth, setting forth that they were treated with less humanity than the French and Spanish, though by reason that they had no Agent established in this country for their protection, they were entitled to expect a larger share of indulgence than others. They had not a sufficient allowance of *bread*, and were very scantily furnished with clothing.

"A similar petition was presented to the House of Peers by the Duke of Richmond, and these petitions occasioned considerable debate in both Houses. Several motions were grounded on these petitions, but to those proposed by the Lords and gentlemen in the opposition, were determined in the negative, and others to *exculpate* the Government in this business were resolved in the affirmative. It appeared upon inquiry, that the

American prisoners were allowed a half pound of bread less per day than the French and Spanish prisoners. But the petitions of the Americans produced no alterations in their favor, and the conduct of the Administration was equally unpolitic and illiberal. The additional allowance, which was solicited on behalf of the prisoners, could be no object, either to Government or to the Nation, and it was certainly unwise, by treating American prisoners worse than those of France or Spain, to increase the fatal animosity which had unhappily taken place between the mother country and the Colonies, and this, too, at a period when the subjugation of the latter had become hopeless."

CHAPTER XIX. MORE ABOUT THE ENGLISH PRISONS—MEMOIR OF ELI BICKFORD—CAPTAIN FANNING

Eli Bickford, who was born on the 29th of September, 1754, in the town of Durham, N. H., and enlisted on a privateer, was taken prisoner by the British, confined at first on the Old Jersey, and afterwards sent to England with many others, in a vessel commanded by Captain Smallcorn, whom he called "a sample of the smallest corn he had ever met." While on board this vessel he was taken down with the smallpox. No beds or bedding were provided for the prisoners and a plank on deck was his only pillow. He and his fellow sufferers were treated with great severity, and insulted at every turn. When they reached England they were sent to prison, where he remained in close confinement for four years and six months.

Finding a piece of a door hinge, he and some of the others endeavored to make their escape by digging a passage under the walls. A report of their proceedings reached the jailer, but, secure in the strength of the walls he did not believe it. This jailor would frequently jest with Bickford on the subject, asking him when he intended to make his escape. His answers were so truthful and accurate that they served to blind the jailor still further. One morning as this official entered the prison he said: "Well, Bickford, how soon will you be ready to go out?"

"Tomorrow night!" answered Bickford.

"O, that's only some of your nonsense," he replied.

However, it was true.

After digging a passage for some days underground, the prisoners found themselves under an adjoining house. They proceeded to take up the brick floor, unlocked the door and passed out, without disturbing the inmates, who were all asleep. Unable to escape they concealed themselves for awhile, and then tamely gave themselves up. Such a vigilant watch was kept upon the house after they were missed from the prison, that they had no other choice. So they made a contract with a man who was to return them to the prison, and then give them half of the reward of forty shillings which was offered for their re−capture. So successful was this expedient that it was often put into operation when they needed money.

As a punishment for endeavoring to escape they were confined in the Black Hole for a week on bread and water.

Bickford describes the prison regulations for preserving order which were made and carried out by the prisoners themselves. If a difficulty arose between two of them it was settled in the following manner. The prisoners formed a circle in the centre of which the disputants took their stand, and exchanged a few rounds of well−directed blows, after which they shook hands, and were better friends than before.

Bickford was not released until peace was declared. He then returned to his family, who had long thought him dead. It was on Sunday morning that he reached his native town. As he passed the meeting house he was recognized, and the whole congregation ran out to see and greet him.

He had but seven dollars as his whole capital when he married. He moved to Vermont, where he farmed a small place, and succeeded in making a comfortable livelihood. He attained the great age of 101, and was one of the last surviving prisoners of the Revolution.

THE ADVENTURES OF A NAVAL OFFICER

In the year 1806 a little book with this title was published in New York, by Captain Nathaniel Fanning. It was dedicated to John Jackson, Esquire, the man who did so much to interest the public in the preservation and interment of the remains of the martyrs of the prisonships in the Wallabout.

Fanning was born in Connecticut, in the year 1755. On the 26th of May, 1778, he went on board the brig Angelica, commanded by Captain William Dennis, which was about to sail on a six months cruise. There were 98 men and boys in the crew, and Fanning was prize–master on board the privateer. She was captured by the Andromeda, a frigate of 28 guns, five days from Philadelphia, with General Howe on board on his way back to England.

All the prisoners were paraded on deck and asked if they were willing to engage in his British Majesty's service. Nearly all answered in the negative. They were then told that they were "a set of rebels," and that it was more than probable that they would all be hung at Portsmouth.

Their baggage was then taken away, and they were confined in the hold of the ship. Their clothes were stolen by the sailors, and a frock and cheap trousers dealt out to each man in their place.

The heat was intolerable in the hold, although they went naked. In this condition they plotted to seize the vessel, and procured some weapons through the agency of their surgeon. Spencer, the captain's clerk, betrayed them to the captain of the Andromeda, and, after that, the hatches were barred down, and they began to think that they would all die of suffocation. The sentence pronounced upon them was that they should be allowed only half a pint of water a day for each man, and barely food enough to sustain life.

Their condition would have been terrible, but, fortunately for them, they were lodged upon the water casks, over which was constructed a temporary deck. By boring holes in the planks they managed, by means of a proof glass, to obtain all the water they needed.

Between them and the general's store room was nothing but a partition of plank. They went to work to make an aperture through which a man could pass into this store room. A young man named Howard from Rhode Island was their instigator in all these operations. They discovered that one of the shifting boards abaft the pump room was loose, and that they could ship and unship it as they pleased. When it was unshipped there was just room for a man to crawl into the store room. "Howard first went in," writes Captain Fanning, "and presently desired me to hand him a mug or can with a proof glass. A few minutes after he handed me back the same full, saying 'My friends, as good Madeira wine as ever was drank at the table of an Emperor!'

"I took it from his hands and drank about half a pint.

"Thus we lived like hearty fellows, taking care every night to secure provisions, dried fruit, and wines for the day following * * * and all without our enemies' knowledge."

Scurvy broke out among the crew, and some of the British sailors died, but the Americans were all "brave and hearty."

"The Captain would say, 'What! are none of them damned Yankees sick? Damn them, there's nothing but thunder and lightning will kill 'em.'" On the thirtieth of June the vessel arrived at Portsmouth. The prisoners were sent to Hazel hospital, to be examined by the Commissioners of the Admiralty, and then marched to Forton prison, where they were committed under the charges of piracy and high treason. This prison was about two miles from Portsmouth harbor, and consisted of two commodious buildings, with a yard between them large enough to parade a guard of 100 men, which was the number required to maintain law and order at the station.

They also had a spacious lot of about three quarters of an acre in extent, adjoining the houses, in which they took their daily exercise. In the middle of this lot was a shed with seats. It was open on all sides. The lot was surrounded by a wall of iron pickets, eight feet in height. The agent for American prisoners was nicknamed by them "the old crab." He was very old and ugly.

Only three-fourths of the usual allowance to prisoners of war was dealt out to them, and they seem to have fared much worse than the inmates of the Old Mill Prison at Plymouth.

Captain Fanning declares that they were half starved, and would sometimes beg bones from the people who came to look at them. When they obtained bones they would dig out the marrow, and devour it. The guard was cruel and spiteful. One day they heated some pokers red hot and began to burn the prisoners' shirts that were hung up to dry. These men begged the guard, in a very civil manner, not to burn all their shirts, as they had only one apiece. This remonstrance producing no effect they then ran to the pickets and snatched away their shirts. At this the officer on command ordered a sentinel to fire on them. This he did, killing one prisoner, and wounding several. There were three hundred American prisoners in the yard at this time.

These prisons appear to have been very imperfectly guarded, and the regular occupation of the captives, whenever their guards were asleep or absent, was to make excavations for the purpose of escaping. A great many regained their freedom in this manner, though some were occasionally brought back and punished by being shut up for forty days in the Black Hole on bread and water. Some, less fortunate, remained three or four years in the prison.

There was always digging going on in some part of the prison and as soon as one hole was discovered and plastered up, another would be begun. For a long time they concealed the dirt that they took out of these excavations in an old stack of disused chimneys. The hours for performing the work were between eleven and three o'clock at night. Early in the morning they ceased from their labors, concealing the hole they had made by pasting white paper over it.

There was a school kept constantly in the prison, where many of them had the first opportunity that had ever been granted them of receiving an education. Many learned to read and write, and became proficient in French.

At one time there were 367 officers confined in this place. In the course of twelve months 138 of them escaped and got safely to France. While some of the men were digging at night, others would be dancing to drown the noise. They had several violins, and seem to have been a reckless and jovial set.

The officers bunked on the second floor over the guard room of the English officers. At times they would make so much noise that the guard would rush up the stairs, only to find all lights out and every man *asleep and snoring* in his hammock. They would relieve their feelings by a volley of abusive language and go down stairs again, when instantly the whole company would be on their feet, the violins would strike up, and the fun be more fast and furious than ever. These rushes of the guard would sometimes be repeated several times a night, when they would always find the prisoners in their hammocks. Each hammock had what was called a "king's rug," a straw bed, and pillow.

At one time several men were suddenly taken sick, with strong symptoms of poison. They were removed to the hospital, and for a time, there was great alarm. The prisoners feared that "the same game was playing here as had been done on the Old Jersey, where we had heard that thousands of our countrymen had died." The poison employed in this instance was glass pounded fine and cooked with their bread.

An English clergyman named Wren sympathized strongly with the prisoners and assisted them to escape. He lived at Gosport, and if any of the captives were so fortunate as to dig themselves out and succeed in reaching his house, they were safe. This good man begged money and food for "his children," as he called them.

On the second of June, 1779, 120 of them were exchanged. There were then 600 confined in that prison. On the 6th of June they sailed for Nantes in France. The French treated them with great kindness, made up a purse for them, and gave them decent clothing.

Fanning next went to L'Orient, and there met John Paul Jones, who invited him to go on board the Bon Homme Richard as a midshipman. They sailed on the 14th of August on the memorable expedition to the British Channel.

After being with Jones for some time Fanning, on the 23rd of March, 1781, sailed for home in a privateer from Morlaix, France. This privateer was captured by the English frigate, Aurora.

"Captain Anthon and myself and crew," writes Mr. Fanning, "were all ordered to a prison at about two miles from Falmouth. The very dirtiest and most loathsome building I ever saw. Swarms of lice, remarkably fat and full grown; bed bugs, and fleas. I believe the former were of Dutch extraction, as there were confined here a number of Dutch prisoners of war, and such a company of dirty fellows I never saw before or since."

Yet these same poor fellows ceded to Captain Anthon and Mr. Fanning a corner of the prison for their private use. This they managed to get thoroughly cleansed, screened themselves off with some sheets, provided themselves with large swinging cots, and were tolerably comfortable. They were paroled and allowed full liberty within bounds, which were a mile and a half from the prison. In about six weeks Fanning was again exchanged, and went to Cherbourg in France, where he met Captain Manly, who had just escaped from the Mill prison after three years confinment.

CHAPTER XX. SOME SOUTHERN NAVAL PRISONERS

Very little is known of the State navies of the south during the Revolution. Each State had her own small navy, and many were the interesting adventures, some successful, and others unfortunate, that the hardy sailors encountered. The story of each one of these little vessels would be as interesting as a romance, but we are here only concerned with the meagre accounts that have reached us of the sufferings of some of the crews of the privateers who were so unlucky as to fall into the hands of the enemy.

In the infant navy of Virginia were many small, extremely fleet vessels. The names of some of the Virginia ships, built at Gosport, Fredericksburg, and other Virginia towns, were the Tartar, Oxford, Thetis, Virginia, Industry, Cormorant, Loyalist (which appears to have been captured from the British), Pocohontas, Dragon, Washington, Tempest, Defiance, Oliver Cromwell, Renown, Apollo, and the Marquis Lafayette. Virginia also owned a prisonship called the Gloucester. Brigs and brigantines owned by the State were called the Raleigh, Jefferson, Sallie Norton, Northampton, Hampton, Greyhound, Dolphin, Liberty, Mosquito, Rochester, Willing Lass, Wilkes, American Fabius, Morning Star, and Mars. Schooners were the Adventure, Hornet, Speedwell, Lewis, Nicholson, Experiment, Harrison, Mayflower, Revenge, Peace and Plenty, Patriot, Liberty, and the Betsy. Sloops were the Virginia, Rattlesnake, Scorpion, Congress, Liberty, Eminence, Game–Cock, and the American Congress. Some of the galleys were the Accomac, Diligence, Hero, Gloucester, Safeguard, Manly, Henry, Norfolk, Revenge, Caswell, Protector, Washington, Page, Lewis, Dragon, and Dasher. There were two armed pilot boats named Molly and Fly. Barges were the York and Richmond. The Oxford, Cormorant, and Loyalist were prizes. The two latter were taken from the English by the French and sold to Virginia.

What an interesting book might be written about this little navy! Nearly all were destined to fall at last into the hands of the enemy; their crews to languish out the remainder of their days in foul dungeons, where famine and disease made short work of them. Little remains to us now except the names of these vessels.

The Virginia was built at Gosport. The Dragon and some others were built at Fredericksburg. Many were built at Norfolk.

The Hermit was early captured by the British. The gallant little Mosquito was taken by the Ariadne. Her crew was confined in a loathsome jail at Barbadoes. But her officers were sent to England, and confined in Fortune jail at Gosport. They succeeded in escaping and made their way to France. The names of these officers were Captain John Harris; Lieutenant Chamberlayne; Midshipman Alexander Moore; Alexander Dock, Captain of Marines; and George Catlett, Lieutenant of Marines.

The Raleigh was captured by the British frigate Thames. Her crew was so shamefully maltreated that upon representations made to the Council of State upon their condition, it was recommended that by way of retaliation the crew of the Solebay, a sloop of war which had fallen into the hands of the Americans, should be visited with the like severe treatment. To what extent this was carried out we cannot discover.

The Scorpion was taken by the British in the year 1781, a fatal year for the navy of Virginia.

In the year 1857 an unsigned article on the subject of the Virginia Navy was published in the *Southern Literary Messenger*, which goes on to say: "But of all the sufferings in these troublous times none endured such horrors as did those Americans who were so unfortunate as to become prisoners of war to the British. They were treated more as felons than as honorable enemies. It can scarcely be credited that an enlightened people would thus have been so lost to the common instincts of humanity, as were they in their conduct towards men of the same blood, and speaking the same language with themselves. True it is they sometimes excused the cruelty of their procedures by avowing in many instances their prisoners were deserters from the English flag, and were to be dealt with accordingly. Be this as it may, no instance is on record where a Tory whom the Americans had good cause to regard as a traitor, was visited with the severities which characterized the treatment of the ordinary military captives, on the part of the English authorities. * * * The patriotic seamen of the Virginia navy were no exceptions to the rule when they fell into the hands of the more powerful lords of the ocean. They were carried in numbers to Bermuda, and to the West Indies, and cast into loathsome and pestilential prisons, from which a few sometimes managed to escape, at the peril of their lives. Respect of position and rank found no favor in the eyes of their ungenerous captors, and no appeal could reach their hearts except through the promises of bribes. Many languished and died in those places, away from country and friends, whose fate was not known until long after they had passed away. But it was not altogether abroad that they were so cruelly maltreated. The record of their sufferings in the prisons of the enemy, in our own country, is left to testify against these relentless persecutors.

"In New York and Halifax many of the Virginian officers and seamen were relieved of their pains, alone by the hand of death; and in their own State, at Portsmouth, the like fate overtook many more, who had endured horrors rivalled only by the terrors of the Black Hole of Calcutta. * * * The reader will agree that we do not exaggerate when he shall have seen the case as given under oath by one who was in every respect a competent witness.

"It will be remembered that, in another part of this narrative, mention was made of the loss in Lynhaven Bay of the galley Dasher, and the capture of the officers and the crew. Captain Willis Wilson was her unfortunate commander on that occasion. He and his men were confined in the Provost Jail at Portsmouth, Virginia, and after his release he made public the 'secrets' of that 'Prison House,' by the following deposition, which is copied from the original document.

"'The deposition of Willis Wilson, being first sworn deposes and sayeth: That about the 23rd July last the deponent was taken a prisoner of war; was conducted to Portsmouth (Virginia) after having been plundered of all his clothing, etc., and there lodged with about 190 other prisoners, in the Provost. This deponent during twenty odd days was a spectator to the most savage cruelty with which the unhappy prisoners were treated by the English. The deponent has every reason to believe there was a premeditated scheme to infect all the prisoners who had not been infected with the smallpox. There were upwards of 100 prisoners who never had the disorder, notwithstanding which negroes, with the infection upon them, were lodged under the same roof of the Provost. Others were sent in to attend upon the prisoners, with the scabs of that disorder upon them.

"'Some of the prisoners soon caught the disorder, others were down with the flux, and some from fevers. From such a complication of disorders 'twas thought expedient to petition General O'Hara who was then commanding officer, for a removal of the sick, or those who were not, as yet, infected with the smallpox. Accordingly a petition was sent by Dr. Smith who shortly returned with a verbal answer, as he said, from the General. He said the General desired him to inform the prisoners that the *law of nations was annihilated*, that he had nothing then to bind them but bolts and bars, and they were to continue where they were, but that they were free agents to inoculate if they chose.

"'About thirty agreed with the same Smith to inoculate them at a guinea a man; he performed the operation, received his guinea from many, and then left them to shift for themselves, though he had agreed to attend them through the disorder. Many of them, as well as those who took it in the natural way, died. Colonel Gee, with many respectable characters, fell victims to the unrelenting cruelty of O'Hara, who would admit of no discrimination between the officers, privates, negroes, and felons; but promiscuously confined the whole in one house. * * * They also suffered often from want of water, and such as they got was very muddy and unfit to drink.

"'Willis Wilson.

"'This day came before me Captain Willis Wilson and made oath that the above is true.

"'Samuel Thorogood.'"

There is much of great interest in this article on the Virginia Navy which is not to our present purpose. The writer goes on to tell how, on one occasion, the ship Favorite, bearing a flag of truce, was returning to Virginia, with a number of Americans who had just been liberated or exchanged in Bermuda, when she was overhauled by a British man-of-war, and both her crew and passengers robbed of all they had. The British ships which committed this dastardly deed were the Tiger, of 14 guns, and the schooner Surprise, of 10 guns.

Captain James Barron, afterwards Commodore Barren, was the master spirit of the service in Virginia. One of the Virginian vessels, very appropriately named the Victory, was commanded by him, and was never defeated.

In 1781 Joseph Galloway wrote a letter to Lord Howe in which he says: "The rebel navy has been in a great measure destroyed by the small British force remaining in America, and the privateers sent out from New York. Their navy, which consisted, at the time of your departure, of about thirty vessels, is now reduced to eight, and the number of privateers fitted out in New England amounting to an hundred and upwards is now less than forty."

CHAPTER XXI. EXTRACTS FROM NEWSPAPERS—SOME OF THE PRISON SHIPS—CASE OF CAPTAIN BIRDSALL

At the risk of repetition of some facts that have already been given, we must again refer the reader to some extracts from the newspapers of the day. In this instance the truth can best be established by the mouths of many witnesses, and we do not hesitate to give the English side whenever we have been able to discover anything bearing on the subject in the so–called loyal periodicals of the time.

From Freeman's *Journal,* date of Jan. 19th, 1777, we take the following:

"General Howe has discharged all the privates who were prisoners in New York. Half he sent to the world of spirits for want of food: the others he hath sent to warn their countrymen of the danger of falling into his hands, and to convince them by ocular demonstration, that it is infinitely better to be slain in battle, than to be taken prisoner by British brutes, whose tender mercies are cruelties."

In the *Connecticut Journal* of Jan. 30th, 1777, is the following:

"This account of the sufferings of these unfortunate men was obtained from the prisoners themselves. As soon as they were taken they were robbed of all their baggage; of whatever money they had, though it were of paper; of their silver shoe buckles and knee buckles, etc.; and many were stripped almost of their clothes. Especially those who had good clothes were stripped at once, being told that such were 'too good for rebels.'

"Thus deprived of their clothes and baggage, they were unable to shift even their linen, and were obliged to wear the same shirts for even three or four months together, whereby they became extremely nasty; and this of itself was sufficient to bring on them many mortal diseases.

"After they were taken they were in the first place put on board the ships, and thrust down into the hold, where not a breath of fresh air could be obtained, and they were nearly suffocated for want of air.

"Some who were taken at Fort Washington were first in this manner thrust down into the holds of vessels in such numbers that even in the cold season of November they could scarcely bear any clothes on them, being kept in a constant sweat. Yet these same persons, after lying in this situation awhile, till the pores of their bodies were as perfectly open as possible, were of a sudden taken out and put into some of the churches of New York, without covering, or a spark of fire, where they suffered as much by the cold as they did by the sweating stagnation of the air in the other situation; and the consequence was that they took such colds as brought on the most fatal diseases, and swept them off almost beyond conception.

"Besides these things they suffered severely for want of provisions. The commissioners pretended to allow a half a pound of bread, and four ounces of pork per day; but of this pittance they were much cut short. What was given them for three days was not enough for one day and, in some instances, they went for three days without a single mouthful of food of any kind. They were pinched to such an extent that some on board the ships would pick up and eat the salt that happened to be scattered there; others gathered up the bran which the light horse wasted, and eat it, mixed with dirt and filth as it was.

"Nor was this all, both the bread and pork which they did allow them was extremely bad. For the bread, some of it was made out of the bran which they brought over to feed their light horse, and the rest of it was so muddy, and the pork so damnified, being so soaked in bilge water during the transportation from Europe, that they were not fit to be eaten by human creatures, and when they were eaten were very unwholesome. Such bread and pork as they would not pretend to give to their own countrymen they gave to our poor sick dying prisoners.

"Nor were they in this doleful condition allowed a sufficiency of water. One would have thought that water was so cheap and plentiful an element, that they would not have grudged them that. But there are, it seems, no bounds to their cruelty. The water allowed them was so brackish, and withal nasty, that they could not drink it until reduced to extremity. Nor did they let them have a sufficiency of even such water as this.

"When winter came on, our people suffered extremely for want of fire and clothes to keep them warm. They were confined in churches where there were no fireplaces that they could make fires, even if they had wood. But wood was only allowed them for cooking their pittance of victuals; and for that purpose very sparingly. They had none to keep them warm even in the extremest of weather, although they were almost naked, and the few clothes they had were their summer clothes. Nor had they a single blanket, nor any bedding, not even straw allowed them until a little before Christmas.

"At the time those were taken on Long Island a considerable part of them were sick of the dysentery; and with this distemper on them were first crowded on board the ships, afterwards in the churches in New York, three, four or five hundred together, without any blankets, or anything for even the sick to lie upon, but the bare floors or pavements.

"In this situation that contagious distemper soon communicated from the sick to the well, who would probably have remained so, had they not in this manner been thrust in together without regard to sick or well, or to the sultry, unwholesome season, it being then the heat of summer. Of this distemper numbers died daily, and many others by their confinement and the sultry season contracted fevers and died of them. During their sickness, with these and other diseases, they had no medicines, nothing soothing or comfortable for sick people, and were not so much as visited by the physician for months together.

"Nor ought we to omit the insults which the humane Britons offered to our people, nor the artifices which they used to enlist them in their service to fight against their country. It seems that one end of their starving our people was to bring them, by dint of necessity, to turn rebels to their own country, their own consciences, and their God. For while thus famishing they would come and say to them: 'This is the just punishment of your rebellion. Nay, you are treated too well for rebels; you have not received half you deserve or half you shall receive. But if you will enlist into his Majesty's service, you shall have victuals and clothes enough.'

"As to insults, the British officers, besides continually cursing and swearing at them as rebels, often threatened to hang them all; and, on a particular time, ordered a number, each man to choose his halter out of a parcel offered, wherewith to be hanged; and even went so far as to cause a gallows to be erected before the prison, as if they were to be immediately executed.

"They further threatened to send them all into the East Indies, and sell them there for slaves.

"In these and numberless other ways did the British officers seem to rack their inventions to insult, terrify, and vex the poor prisoners. The meanest, upstart officers among them would insult and abuse our colonels and chief officers.

"In this situation, without clothes, without victuals or drink, or even water, or with those which were base and unwholesome; without fire, a number of them sick, first with a contagious and nauseous distemper; these, with others, crowded by hundreds into close confinement, at the most unwholesome season of the year, and continued there for four months without blankets, bedding, or straw; without linen to shift or clothes to cover their bodies;—No wonder they all became sickly, and having at the same time no medicine, no help of physicians, nothing to refresh or support nature, died by scores in a night, and those who were so far gone as to be unable to help themselves lay uncared for, till death, more kind than Britons, put an end to their misery.

"By these means, and in this way, 1,500 brave Americans, who had nobly gone forth in defence of their injured, oppressed country, but whom the chance at war had cast into the hands of our enemies, died in New York, many of whom were very amiable, promising youths, of good families, the very flower of our land; and of those who lived to come out of prison, the greater part, as far as I can learn, are dead or dying. Their constitutions are broken; the stamina of nature worn out; they cannot recover—they die. Even the few that might have survived are dying of the smallpox. For it seems that our enemies determining that even these, whom a good constitution and a kind Providence had carried through unexampled sufferings, should not at last escape death, just before their release from imprisonment infected them with that fatal distemper.

"To these circumstances we subjoin the manner in which they buried those of our people who died. They dragged them out of the prison by one leg or one arm, piled them up without doors, there let them lie until a sufficient number were dead to make a cart load, then loaded them up in a cart, drove the cart thus loaded out to the ditches made by our people when fortifying New York; there they would tip the cart, tumble the corpses together into the ditch, and afterwards slightly cover them with earth. * * * While our poor prisoners have been thus treated by our foes, the prisoners we have taken have enjoyed the liberty of walking and riding about within large limits at their pleasure; have been freely supplied with every necessary, and have even lived on the fat of the land. None have been so well fed, so plump, and so merry as they; and this generous treatment, it is said, they could not but remember. For when they were returned in the exchange of prisoners, and saw the miserable, famished, dying state of our prisoners, conscious of the treatment they had received, they could not refrain from tears." *Connecticut Journal,* Jan. 30th, 1777.

In April of the year 1777 a committee that was appointed by Congress to inquire into the doings of the British on their different marches through New York and New Jersey reported that "The prisoners, instead of that humane treatment which those taken by the United States experienced, were in general treated with the greatest barbarity. Many of them were kept near four days without food altogether. * * * Freemen and men of substance suffered all that generous minds could suffer from the contempt and mockery of British and foreign mercenaries. Multitudes died in prison. When they were sent out several died in being carried from the boats on shore, or upon the road attempting to go home. The committee, in the course of their inquiry, learned that sometimes the common soldiers expressed sympathy with the prisoners, and the foreigners (did this) more than the English. But this was seldom or never the case with the officers, nor have they been able to hear of any charitable assistance given them by the inhabitants who remained in, or resorted to the city of New York, which neglect, if universal, they believe was never known to happen in any similar case in a Christian country."

We have already shown that some of the citizens of New York, even a number of the profligate women of the town, did their best to relieve the wants of the perishing prisoners. But the guards were very strict, and what they could do was inadequate to remove the distresses under which these victims of cruelty and oppression died. As we are attempting to make this work a compendium of all the facts that can be gathered upon the subject, we must beg the reader's indulgence if we continue to give corroborating testimony of the same character, from the periodicals of the day. We will next quote from the *New Hampshire Gazette,* date of February 4th, 1779.

"It is painful to repeat the indubitable accounts we are constantly receiving, of the cruel and inhuman treatment of the subjects of these States from the British in New York and other places. They who hear our countrymen who have been so unfortunate as to fall into the hands of those unrelenting tyrants, relate the sad story of their captivity, the insults they have received, and the slow, cool, systematic manner in which great numbers of those who could not be prevailed on to enter their service have been murdered, must have hearts of stone not to melt with pity for the sufferers, and burn with indignation at their tormentors. As we have daily fresh instances to prove the truth of such a representation, public justice requires that repeated public mention should be made of them. A cartel vessel lately arrived at New London in Connecticut, carrying about 130 American prisoners from the prison ships in New York. Such was the condition in which these poor creatures were put on board the cartel, that in the short run, 16 died on board; upwards of sixty when they were landed, were scarcely able to move, and the remainder greatly emaciated and enfeebled; and many who continue alive are never likely to recover their former health. The greatest inhumanity was experienced by the prisoners in a ship of which one Nelson, a Scotchman, had the superintendence. Upwards of 300 American prisoners were confined at a time, on board this ship. There was but one small fire–place allowed to cook the food of such a number. The allowance of the prisoners was, moreover, frequently delayed, insomuch that, in the short days of November and December, it was not begun to be delivered out until 11 o'clock in the forenoon so that the whole could not be served until three. At sunset the fire was ordered to be quenched; no plea from the many sick, from their absolute necessity, the shortness of the time or the smallness of the hearth, was allowed to avail. The known consequence was that some had not their food dressed at all; many were obliged to eat it half raw. On board the ship no flour, oatmeal, and things of like nature, suited to the condition of infirm people, were allowed to the many sick, nothing but ship–bread, beef, and pork. This is the account given by a number of prisoners, who are credible persons, and this is but a part of their sufferings; so that the excuse made by the enemy that the prisoners were emaciated and died by contagious sickness, which no one could prevent, is futile. It requires no great sagacity to know that crowding people together without fresh air, and feeding, or rather starving them in such a manner as the prisoners have been, must unavoidably produce a contagion. Nor is it a want of candor to suppose that many of our enemies saw with pleasure this contagion, which might have been so easily prevented, among the prisoners who could not be persuaded to enter the service."

THE CASE OF CAPTAIN BIRDSALL

Soon after the battle of Long Island Captain Birdsall, a Whig officer, made a successful attempt to release an American vessel laden with flour for the army, which had been captured in the Sound by the British. Captain Birdsall offered, if the undertaking was approved of by his superior officer, to superintend the enterprise himself. The proposal was accepted, when Birdsall, with a few picked men, made the experiment, and succeeded in sending the vessel to her original destination. But he and one of his men fell into the hands of the enemy. He was sent to the Provost Jail under surveillance of "that monster in human shape, the infamous Cunningham." He requested the use of pen, ink, and paper, for the purpose of acquainting his family of his situation. On being refused he made a reply which drew from the keeper some opprobious epithets, accompanied by a thrust from his sword, which penetrated the shoulder of his victim, and caused the blood to flow freely. Being locked up alone in a filthy apartment, and denied any assistance whatever, he was obliged to dress the wound with his own linen, and then to endure, in solitude and misery, every indignity which the malice of the Provost Master urged him to inflict upon a *damned rebel*, who, he declared, ought to be hung. "After several months of confinement and starvation he was exchanged."

Two Whig gentlemen of Long Island were imprisoned in the Provost Prison some time in the year 1777. Two English Quakers named Jacob Watson and Robert Murray at last procured their release. Their names were George Townsend and John Kirk. Kirk caught the smallpox while in prison. He was sent home in a covered wagon. His wife met him at the door, and tenderly nursed him through the disorder. He recovered in due time, but she and her infant daughter died of the malady. There were hundreds of such cases: indeed throughout the war contagion was carried into every part of the country by soldiers and former prisoners. In some instances the British were accused of selling inoculated clothing to the prisoners. Let us hope that some, at least, of these reports are unfounded.

The North Dutch Church was the last of the churches used as prisons to be torn down. As late as 1850 it was still standing, and marks of bayonet thrusts were plainly to be discerned upon its pillars. How many of the wretched sufferers were in this manner done to death we have no means of discovering, but it must have been easier to die in that manner than to have endured the protracted agonies of death by starvation.

John Pintard, who assisted his uncle, Lewis Pintard, Commissioner for American prisoners in New York, thus wrote of their sufferings. It must be remembered that the prisoners taken in 1776 died, for the most part, before our struggling nation was able to protect them, before Commissioners had been appointed, and when, in her feeble infancy, the Republic was powerless to aid them.

"The prisoners taken on Long Island and at Fort Washington, sick, wounded, and well, were all indiscriminately huddled together, by hundreds and thousands, large numbers of whom died by disease, and many undoubtedly poisoned by inhuman attendants, for the sake of their watches or silver buckles."

American Prisoners of the Revolution

It was on the 20th of January, 1777, that Washington proposed to Mr. Lewis Pintard, a merchant of New York, that he should accept the position as resident agent for American prisoners. In May of that year General Parsons sent to Washington a plan for making a raid upon Long Island, and bringing off the American officers, prisoners of war on parole. Washington, however, disapproved of the plan, and it was not executed.

No one sympathized with the unfortunate victims of British cruelty more deeply than the Commander–in–chief. But he keenly felt the injustice of exchanging sound, healthy, British soldiers, for starved and dying wretches, for the most part unable even to reach their homes. In a letter written by him on the 28th of May, 1777, to General Howe, he declared that a great proportion of prisoners sent out by the British were not fit subjects for exchange, and that, being made so unfit by the severity of their treatment, a deduction should be made. It is needless to say that the British General refused this proposition.

On the 10th of June, 1777, Washington, in a long letter to General Howe, states that he gave clothing to the British prisoners in his care. He also declares that he was not informed of the sufferings of the Americans in New York until too late, and that he was refused permission to establish an agency in that city to purchase what was necessary to supply the wants of the prisoners.

It was not until after the battle of Trenton that anything could be done to relieve these poor men. Washington, by his heroism, when he led his little band across the half frozen Delaware, saved the lives of the small remnant of prisoners in New York. After the battle he had so many British and Hessian prisoners in his power, that he was able to impress upon the British general the fact that American prisoners were too valuable to be murdered outright, and that it was more expedient to keep them alive for purposes of exchange.

Rivington's *Gazette* of Jan. 15th, 1779, contains this notice: "Privateers arriving in New York Harbor are to put their prisoners on board the Good Hope or Prince of Wales prison ships.

"James Dick."

If the Jersey were in use at that time it must have been too crowded for further occupancy. But although there is frequent mention in the periodicals of the day of the prison ships of New York the Jersey did not become notorious until later.

On the 29th of June, 1779, Sir George Collier, in a notice in Rivington's *Gazette*, forbids "privateers landing prisoners on Long Island to the damage and annoyance of His Majesty's faithful servants."

This order was no doubt issued, in fear of contagion, which fear led the British to remove their prison ships out of New York Harbor to the retired waters of Wallabout Bay, where the work of destruction could go on with less fear of producing a general pestilence.

In the issue for the 23rd of August, 1779, we read: "To be sold, The sails and rigging of the ship Good Hope. Masts, spars, and yards as good as new."

Among the accounts of cruelty to the prisoners it is refreshing to come upon such a paragraph as this, from a New London, Conn. paper, dated August 18th, 1779. "Last week five or six hundred American prisoners were exchanged. A flag returned here with 47 American prisoners, and though taken out of the Good Hope prison ship, it must (for once) be acknowledged that all were very well and healthy. Only 150 left."

The next quotation that we will give contains one of the first mentions of the Jersey as a prison ship, that we have been able to find.

"New London, Sept. 1st, 1779. D. Stanton testifies that he was taken June 5th and put in the Jersey prison ship. An allowance from Congress was sent on board. About three or four weeks past we were removed on board the Good Hope, where we found many sick. There is now a hospital ship provided, to which they are removed, and good attention paid."

A Boston paper dated September 2nd, 1779, has the following: "Returned to this port Alexander Dickey, Commissary of Prisoners, from New York, with a cartel, having on board 180 American prisoners. Their countenances indicate that they have undergone every conceivable inhumanity."

"New London, Sep. 29th 1779. A Flag arrived here from New York with 117 prisoners, chiefly from New England."

American Prisoners of the Revolution

From Rivington's *Gazette,* March 1st, 1780. "Last Saturday afternoon the Good Hope prison ship, lying in the Wallebocht Bay was entirely consumed after having been wilfully set on fire by a Connecticut man named Woodbury, who confessed to the fact. He with others of the incendiaries are removed to the Provost. The prisoners let each other down from the port holes and decks into the water."

So that was the end of the Good Hope. She seems to have been burned by some of the prisoners in utter desperation, probably with some hope that, in the confusion, they might be enabled to escape, though we do not learn that any of them were so fortunate, and the only consequence of the deed appears to have been that the remaining ships were crowded to suffocation.

A writer in the Connecticut *Gazette,* whose name is not given, says: "May 25th, 1780. I am now a prisoner on board the Falmouth, a place the most dreadful; we are confined so that we have not room even to lie down all at once to sleep. It is the most horrible, cursed, hole that can be thought of. I was sick and longed for some small beer, while I lay unpitied at death's door, with a putrid fever, and though I had money I was not permitted to send for it. I offered repeatedly a hard dollar for a pint. The wretch who went forward and backward would not oblige me. I am just able to creep about. Four prisoners have escaped from this ship. One having, as by accident, thrown his hat overboard, begged leave to go after it in a small boat, which lay alongside. Having reached the hat they secured the sentinel and made for the Jersey shore, though several armed boats pursued, and shot was fired from the shipping."

The New Jersey *Gazette* of June 4th, 1780, says: "Thirty–five Americans, including five officers, made their escape from the prison ship at New York and got safely off."

"For Sale. The remains of the hospital ship Kitty, as they now lie at the Wallebocht, with launch, anchors, and cables." Gaine's *Mercury,* July 1st, 1780.

New Jersey *Gazette*, August 23, 1780. "Captain Grumet, who made his escape from the Scorpion prison ship, at New York, on the evening of the 15th, says more lenity is shown the prisoners. There are 200 in the Strombolo, and 120 in the Scorpion."

It was in 1780 that the poet Freneau was a prisoner on the Scorpion, which, at that time, was anchored in the East River. In Rivington's *Gazette*, at the end of that year, the "hulks of his Majesty's sloops Scorpion and Hunter" are advertised for sale. Also "the Strombolo fire–ship, now lying in North River." It appears, however, that there were no purchasers, and they remained unsold. They were still in use until the end of the year 1781. Gaine's *Mercury* declares that "the Strombolo, from August 21st to December 10th, 1781, had never less than 150 prisoners on board, oftener over 200."

"Captain Cahoon with four others escaped from a prison ship to Long Island in a boat, March 8, notwithstanding they were fired on from the prison and hospital ships, and pursued by guard boats from three in the afternoon to seven in the evening. He left 200 prisoners in New York." *Connecticut Journal*, March 22, 1781.

The *Connecticut Gazette*, in May, 1781, stated that 1100 French and American prisoners had died during the winter in the prison ships. "New London, November 17th, 1781. A Flag of truce returned here from New York with 132 prisoners, with the rest of those carried off by Arnold. They are chiefly from the prison ships, and some from the Sugar House, and are mostly sick."

"New London, Jan. 4th, 1782. 130 prisoners landed here from New York December third, in most deplorable condition. A great part are since dead, and the survivors so debilitated that they will drag out a miserable existence. It is enough to melt the most obdurate heart to see these miserable objects landed at our wharves sick and dying, and the few rags they have on covered with vermin and their own excrements."

CHAPTER XXII. THE JOURNAL OF DR. ELIAS CORNELIUS—BRITISH PRISONS IN THE SOUTH

We must now conduct our readers back to the Provost Prison in New York, where, for some time, Colonel Ethan Allen was incarcerated. Dr. Elias Cornelius, a surgeon's mate, was taken prisoner by the British on the 22nd of August, 1777. On that day he had ridden to the enemy's advanced post to make observations, voluntarily accompanying a scouting party. On his way back he was surprised, over–powered, and captured by a party of British soldiers.

This was at East Chester. He seems to have lagged behind the rest of the party, and thus describes the occurrence: "On riding into town (East Chester) four men started from behind a shed and took me prisoner. They immediately began robbing me of everything I had, horse and harness, pistols, Great Coat, shoe−buckles, pocket book, which contained over thirty pounds, and other things. The leader of the guard abused me very much. * * * When we arrived at King's Bridge I was put under the Provost Guard, with a man named Prichard and several other prisoners." They were kept at the guard house there for some time, and regaled with mouldy bread, rum and water, and sour apples, which were thrown down for them to scramble for, as if they were so many pigs. They were at last marched to New York. Just before reaching that city they were carried before a Hessian general to be "made a show of." The Hessians mocked them, told them they were all to be hung, and even went so far as to draw their swords across their throats. But a Hessian surgeon's mate took pity on Cornelius, and gave him a glass of wine.

On the march to New York in the hot summer afternoon they were not allowed to stop even for a drink of water. Cornelius was in a fainting condition, when a poor woman, compassionating his sad plight, asked to be allowed to give them some water. They were then about four miles from New York. She ran into her house and brought out several pails of beer, three or four loaves of bread, two or three pounds of cheese, and besides all this, she gave money to some of the prisoners. Her name was Mrs. Clemons. She was from Boston and kept a small store along the road to New York.

Cornelius says: "We marched till we come to the Bowery, three quarters of a mile from New York. * * * As we come into town, Hessians, Negroes, and children insulted, stoned, and abused us. * * * In this way we were led through half the streets as a show. * * * At last we were ordered to the Sugar House, which formerly went by the name of Livingstone's Sugar House. Here one Walley, a Sergeant of the 20th Regiment of Irish traitors in the British service, had the charge of the prisoners. This man was the most barbarous, cruel man that ever I saw. He drove us into the yard like so many hogs. From there he ordered us into the Sugar House, which was the dirtiest and most disagreeable place that I ever saw, and the water in the pump was not better than that in the docks. The top of the house was open * * * to the weather, so that when it rained the water ran through every floor, and it was impossible for us to keep dry. Mr. Walley gave thirteen of us four pounds of mouldy bread and four pounds of poor Irish pork for four days. I asked Mr Walley if I was not to have my parole. He answered 'No!' When I asked for pen and ink to write a few lines to my father, he struck me across the face with a staff which I have seen him beat the prisoners." (with)

On the next morning Cornelius was conveyed to the Provost Guard. "I was then taken down to a Dungeon. The provost marshal was Sergeant Keith" (Cunningham appears to have been, at this time, murdering the unfortunate prisoners in his power at Philadelphia).

"There was in this place a Captain Travis of Virginia, and Captain of a sloop of war. There were also in this dismal place nine thieves, murderers, etc. A Captain Chatham was taken sick with nervous fever. I requested the Sergeant to suffer me to send for some medicine, or I believed he might die, to which he replied he might die, and if he did he would bury him.

"All the provisions each man had was but two pounds meat and two pounds bread for a week, always one and sometimes both was not fit to eat. * * * I had no change of linen from the 25th of August to the 12th of September."

It seems that the father of Cornelius, who lived on Long Island, was an ardent Tory. Cornelius asked Sergeant O'Keefe to be allowed to send to his father for money and clothing. But this was refused. "In this hideous place," he continues, "I was kept until the 20th of September; when Sergeant Keath took Captains C., and Travis, and myself, and led us to the upper part of the prison, where were Ethan Allen, Major Williams, Paine and Wells and others. Major Williams belonged at Maryland and was taken prisoner at Fort Washington. * * *

"While at this place we were not allowed to speak to any friend, not even out of the window. I have frequently seen women beaten with canes and ram–rods who have come to the prisons' windows to speak to their Husbands, Sons, or Brothers, and officers put in the dungeon just for asking for cold water."

Dried peas were given out to the prisoners, without the means of cooking them.

When Fort Montgomery was taken by the British the American officers who had been in command at that post were brought to the Provost and put into two small rooms on the lower floor. Some of them were badly wounded, but no surgeon was allowed to dress their wounds. Cornelius asked permission to do so, but this was refused. "All of us in the upper prison," he continues, "were sometimes allowed to go on top of the house. I took this opportunity to throw some Ointment and Lint down the chimney to the wounded in the lower rooms with directions how to use it. I knew only one of them—Lt. Col.

Livingstone."

At the time of Burgoyne's surrender a rumor of the event reached the prisoners, and women passing along the street made signs to assure them that that general was really a captive. Colonel Livingstone received a letter from his father giving an account of Burgoyne's surrender. "Soon we heard hollooing and other expressions of joy from him and others in the (lower) rooms. * * * He put the letter up through a crack in the floor for us to read. * * * The whole prison was filled with joy inexpressible. * * * From this time we were better treated, although the provision was bad, but we drew rather larger quantities of it. Some butter, and about a gill of rice and some cole were dealt out to us, which we never drew before.

"About this time my father came to see me. I was called down to the grates. My heart at first was troubled within me; I burst into tears, and did not speak for some minutes. I put my hand through the grates, and took my father's and held it fast. The poor old gentleman shed many tears, and seemed much troubled to see me in so woeful a place. * * * He asked me what I thought of myself now, and why I could not have been ruled by him. * * * Soon the Provost Marshal came and said he could not allow my father to stay longer.

"* * * Toward the latter part of December we had Continental bread and beef sent us, and as much wood as we wished to burn. A friend gave me some money which was very useful.

"Jan. 9th, 1778. This day Mr. Walley came and took from the prison myself and six others under guard to the Sugar House. * * * At this time my health was bad, being troubled with the scurvy, and my prospects for the winter were dark."

He describes the Sugar House as a dreadful place of torment, and says that thirty disorderly men were allowed to steal from the other prisoners the few comforts they possessed. They would even take the sick out of their beds, steal their bedding, and beat and kick the wretched sufferers. The articles thus procured they would sell to Mr. Walley (or Woolley) for rum.

On the 13th of January Cornelius was sent to the hospital. The Brick Meeting House was used for the sick among the prisoners.

"Here," he continues, "I stayed until the 16th. I was not much better than I was in the Sugar House, no medicine was given me, though I had a cough and a fever. The Surgeon wished me as soon as I got better to take the care of the sick, provided I could get my parole.

"Jan. 16th. On coming next morning he (the surgeon) said he could get my parole. I was now determined to make my escape, though hardly able to undertake it. Just at dusk, having made the Sentinel intoxicated, I with others, went out into the backyard to endeavor to escape over the fence. The others being backward about going first, I climbed upon a tombstone and gave a spring, and went over safe, and then gave orders for the others to do so also. A little Irish lad undertook to leap over, and caught his clothes in the spikes on the wall, and made something of a noise. The sentinel being aroused called out 'Rouse!' which is the same as to command the guards to turn out. They were soon out and surrounded the prison. In the mean time I had made my way to St. Paul's Church, which was the wrong way to get out of town.

"The guards, expecting that I had gone towards North River, went in that direction. On arriving at the Church I turned into the street to go by the College and thus go out of town by the side of the river. Soon after I was out of town I heard the eight o'clock gun, which * * * was the signal for the sentinels to hail every man that came by. I wished much to cross the river, but could not find any boat suitable. While going along up the side of the river at 9 P.M., I was challenged by a sentinel with the usual word (Burdon), upon which I answered nothing, and on being challenged the second time I answered 'Friend.' He bade me advance and give the countersign, upon which I fancied (pretended) I was drunk, and advanced in a staggering manner, and after falling to the ground he asked me where I was going. I told him 'Home,' but that I had got lost, and having been to New York had taken rather too much liquor, and become somewhat intoxicated. He then asked me my name which I told him was Matthew Hoppen. Mr. Hoppen lived not far distant. I solicited him to put me in the right direction, but he told me I must not go until the Sergeant of the guard dismissed me from him, unless I could give him the countersign. I still entreated him to let me go. Soon he consented and directed my course, which I thanked him for. Soon the moon arose and made it very light, and there being snow on the ground, crusted over, and no wind, therefore a person walking could be heard a great distance.

"At this time the tumor in my lungs broke, and being afraid to cough for fear of being heard, prevented me from relieving myself of the pus that was lodged there.

144

"I had now to cross lots that were cleared and covered with snow, the houses being thick on the road which I was to cross, and for fear of being heard I lay myself flat on my stomach and crept along on the frozen snow. When I come to the fence I climbed over, and walked down the road, near a house where there was music and dancing. At this time one of the guards came out. I immediately fell down upon my face. Soon the man went into the house. I rose again, and crossed the fence into the field, and proceeded towards the river. There being no trees or rocks to prevent my being seen, and not being able to walk without being heard, and the dogs beginning to bark, I lay myself down flat again, and crept across the field, which took me half an hour. I at length reached the river and walked by the side of it some distance, and saw a small creek which ran up into the island, and by the side of it a small house, and two Sentinels one on each side of it. Not knowing what to do I crept into a hole in the bank which led in between two rocks. Here I heard them talk. I concluded to endeavor to go around the head of the creek, which was about half a mile, but on getting out of the hole I took hold of the limb of a tree which gave way, and made a great noise. The sentinel, on hearing it said, 'Did you not hear a person on the creek?'

"I waited some minutes and then went around the head of the creek and came down the river on the other side to see if I could not find a boat to cross to Long Island. But on finding sentinels near by I retreated a short distance back, and went up the river. I had not gone more than thirty rods when I saw another sentinel posted on the bank of the river where I must pass. * * * I stood some time thinking what course to pursue, but on looking at the man found he did not move and was leaning on his gun. I succeeded in passing by without waking him up. After this I found a Sentinel every fifteen or twenty rods until I came within two miles of Hell Gate. Here I stayed until my feet began to freeze, and having nothing to eat I went a mile further up the river. It now being late I crept into the bushes and lay down to think what to do next. I concluded to remain where I was during the night, and early in the morning to go down to New York and endeavor to find some house to conceal myself in.

"In the morning as soon as the Revelry Beating commenced I went on my way to New York which was eight miles from this place. After proceeding awhile I heard the morning guns fired from New York, though I was four miles from it. I passed the sentinels unmolested down the middle of the road, and arrived there before many were up. I met many British and Hessian soldiers whom I knew very well, but they did not know me.

"I went to a house, and found them friends of America, and was kindly received of them, and (they) promised to keep me a few days.

"I had not been here but three quarters of an hour when I was obliged to call for a bed. After being in bed two or three hours I was taken with a stoppage in my breast, and made my resperation difficult, and still being afraid to cough loud for fear of being heard. The good lady of the house gave me some medicine of my own prescribing, which soon gave me relief. Soon after a rumor spread about town among the friends of America of my confinement, and expecting soon to be retaken, they took measures to have me conveyed to Long Island, which was accordingly done.

"Feb. 18th, 1778. The same day I was landed I walked nine miles, and put up at a friend's house, during my walk I passed my Grandfather's house, and dare not go in for fear he would deliver me up to the British. Next morning I started on my journey again, and reached the place I intended at 12 o'clock, and put up with two friends. The next morning I and two companions started from our friends with four days provisions, and shovels and axes to build us a hut in the woods. We each of us had a musket, powder, and balls. After going two miles in the woods we dug away the snow and made us a fire. After warming ourselves we set to work to build ourselves a hut; and got one side of it done the first day, and the next we finished it. It was tolerably comfortable. We kept large fires, and cooked our meat on the coals. In eight or ten days we had some provisions brought us by our friends. At this time we heard that Captain Rogers was cast away on Long Island, and concealed by some of his friends. We went to see him, and found him. We attempted to stay in the house in a back room. At about ten A. M. there came in a Tory, he knowing some of us seemed much troubled. We made him promise that he would not make known our escape. The next day our two comrades went back to their old quarters, and Captain Rogers and myself and a friend went into the woods and built us a hut, about ten miles from my former companions, with whom we kept up a constant correspondence. Soon a man was brought to us by our friends, whom we found to be John Rolston, a man who was confined in the Provost Jail with us, and was carried to the Hospital about three weeks after I was, and made his escape the same way, and by friends was brought to Long Island.

"March 19th, 1778. About 5 o'clock a friend came to us and and said we had an opportunity to go over to New England in a boat that had just landed with four Tories, that had stolen the boat at Fairfield, Conn. We immediately sent word to our two friends with whom I first helped to build a hut, but they could not be found. At sunset those that came in the boat went off, and some of our friends guided us through the woods to the boat, taking two oars with us, for fear we should not find any in the boat. On arrival at the place our kind friends helped us off. We rowed very fast till we were a great distance from land. The moon rose soon, and the wind being fair we arrived we knew not where, about a half hour before day. We went on shore, and soon found it was Norwalk, Conn. We had bade farewell to Long Island, for the present, upon which I composed the following lines:—

"O fair you well, once happy land,
  Where peace and plenty dwelt,
But now oppressed by tyrants' hands,
  Where naught but fury's felt

"Behold I leave you for awhile,
  To mourn for all your sons,
Who daily bleed that you may smile
  When we've your freedom won

"After being rested, just as the day began to dawn, we walked to a place called the Old Mill, where we found a guard (American) who hailed us at a distance, and on coming up to him kindly received us, and invited us to his house to warm us. This being done we went home with Captain Rodgers, for he lived in Norwalk. Here we went to bed at sunrise, and stayed till 10 o'clock. After dinner we took leave of Captain Rodgers and started for head–quarters in Pennsylvania, where the grand Army was at that time. In seven days we arrived at Valley Forge.

"Elias Cornelius."

This portion of the journal of Dr. Cornelius was published in the *Putnam County Republican*, in 1895, with a short account of the author.

Dr. Cornelius was born on Long Island in 1758, and was just twenty at the time of his capture. His ancestors came from Holland. They were of good birth, and brought a seal bearing their coat of arms to this country. On the 15th of April, 1777, he was appointed surgeon's mate to the Second Regiment of Rhode Island troops under Colonel Israel

147

Angell.

The article in the *Republican* gives a description of Cunningham and the Provost which we do not quote in full, as it contains little that is new. It says, however that "While Cunningham's victims were dying off from cold and starvation like cattle, he is said to have actually mingled an arsenical preparation with the food to make them die the quicker. It is recorded that he boasted that he had killed more rebels with his own hand than had been slain by all the King's forces in America."

Cornelius continued in the Continental service until January 1st, 1781, and received an honorable discharge. After the war he settled at Yorktown, Westchester County, and came to be known as the "beloved physician." He was very gentle and kind, and a great Presbyterian. He died in 1823, and left descendants, one of whom is Judge C. M. Tompkins, of Washington, D. C.

As we have seen, Cunningham was not always in charge of the Provost. It appears that, during his absence in Philadelphia and other places, where he spread death and destruction, he left Sergeant O'Keefe, almost as great a villian as himself, in charge of the hapless prisoners in New York. It is to be hoped that his boast that he had killed more Americans than all the King's forces is an exaggeration. It may, however, be true that in the years 1776 and 1777 he destroyed more American soldiers than had, at that time, fallen on the field of battle.

When an old building that had been used as a prison near the City Hall was torn down a few years ago to make way for the Subway Station of the Brooklyn Bridge, a great number of skeletons were found *in its cellars*. That these men starved to death or came to their end by violence cannot be doubted. New York, at the time of the Revolution, extended to about three–quarters of a mile from the Battery, its suburbs lying around what is now Fulton Street. Cornelius speaks of the Bowery as about three–quarters of a mile from New York! "St. Paul's Church," says Mr. Haltigan, in his very readable book called "The Irish in the American Revolution," "where Washington attended divine service, is now the only building standing that existed in those days, and that is a veritable monument to Irish and American patriotism. * * * On the Boston Post Road, where it crossed a brook in the vicinity of Fifty–Second street and Second avenue, then called Beekman's Hill, William Beekman had an extensive country house. During the Revolution this house was the British headquarters, and residence of Sir William Howe, where Nathan Hale was condemned to death, and where Major Andre received his last instructions before going on his ill–fated mission to the traitor Arnold."

Lossing tells us of the imprisonment of one of the signers of the Declaration of Independence, in the following language: "Suffering and woe held terrible sway after Cornwallis and his army swept over the plains of New Jersey. Like others of the signers of the great Declaration, Richard Stockton was marked for peculiar vengeance by the enemy. So suddenly did the flying Americans pass by in the autumn of 1776, and so soon were the Hessian vultures and their British companions on the trail, that he had barely time to remove his family to a place of safety before his beautiful mansion was filled with rude soldiery. The house was pillaged, the horses and stock were driven away, the furniture was converted into fuel, the choice old wines in the cellar were drunk, the valuable library, and all the papers of Mr. Stockton were committed to the flames, and the estate was laid waste. Mr. Stockton's place of concealment was discovered by a party of loyalists, who entered the house at night, dragged him from his bed, and treating him with every indignity that malice could invent, hurried him to New York, where he was confined in the loathsome Provost Jail and treated with the utmost cruelty. When, through the interposition of Congress he was released, his constitution was hopelessly shattered, and he did not live to see the independence of his country achieved. He died at his home at Princeton, in February, 1781, blessed to the last with the tender and affectionate attentions of his noble wife."

We have gathered very little information about the British prisons in the south, but that little shall be laid before the reader. It repeats the same sad story of suffering and death of hundreds of martyrs to the cause of liberty, and of terrible cruelty on the part of the English as long as they were victorious.

Mr. Haltigan tells of the "tender mercies" of Cornwallis at the south in the following words: "Cornwallis was even more cruel than Clinton, and more flagrant in his violations of the conditions of capitulation. After the fall of Charleston the real misery of the inhabitants began. Every stipulation made by Sir Henry Clinton for their welfare was not only grossly violated, but he sent out expeditions in various sections to plunder and kill the inhabitants, and scourge the country generally. One of these under Tarleton surprised Colonel Buford and his Virginia regiment at Waxhaw, N. C., and while negotiations were pending for a surrender, the Americans, without notice, were suddenly attacked and massacred in cold blood. Colonel Buford and one hundred of his men saved themselves only by flight. Though the rest sued for quarter, one hundred and thirteen of them were killed on the spot, and one hundred and fifty more were so badly hacked by Tarleton's dragoons that they could not be removed. Only fifty–three out of the entire regiment were spared and taken prisoners. 'Tarleton's quarter' thereafter became the synonym for barbarity. * * * Feeling the silent influence of the eminent citizens under parole in Charleston, Cornwallis resolved to expatriate them to Florida.

"Lieutenant Governor Gadsden and seventy–seven other public and influential men were taken from their beds by armed parties, before dawn on the morning of the 27th of August, 1780, hurried on board the Sandwich prison ship, without being allowed to bid adieu to their families, and were conveyed to St. Augustine.

"The pretence for this measure, by which the British authorities attempted to justify it, was the false accusation that these men were concerting a scheme for burning the town and massacring the loyal inhabitants. Nobody believed the tale, and the act was made more flagrant by this wicked calumny. Arrived at St. Augustine the prisoners were offered paroles to enjoy liberty within the precincts of the town. Gadsden, the sturdy patriot, refused acquiescence, for he disdained making further terms with a power that did not regard the sanctity of a solemn treaty. He was determined not to be deceived the second time.

"'Had the British commanders,' he said, 'regarded the terms of capitulation at Charleston I might now, although a prisoner, enjoy the smiles and consolations of my family under my own roof; but even without a shadow of accusation preferred against me, for any act inconsistent with my plighted faith, I am torn from them, and here, in a distant land, invited to enter into new engagements. I will give no parole.'

"'Think better of it,' said Governor Tonyn, who was in command, 'a second refusal of it will fix your destiny,—a dungeon will be your future habitation.'

"'Prepare it then,' replied the inflexible patriot, 'I will give no parole, so help me God!'

"And the petty tyrant did prepare it, and for forty–two weeks that patriot, of almost threescore years of age, never saw the light of the blessed sun, but lay incarcerated in the dungeon of the castle of St Augustine. All the other prisoners accepted paroles, but they were exposed to indignities more harrowing to the sensitive soul than close confinement.

When they were exchanged, in June, 1781, they were not allowed even to touch at Charleston, but were sent to Philadelphia, whither their families had been banished when the prisoners were taken to the Sandwich. More than a thousand persons were thus exiled, and husbands and wives, fathers and children, first met in a distant State after a separation of ten months.

"Nearly all the soldiers taken prisoners at Charleston were confined in prison ships in the harbor, where foul air, bad food, filth, and disease killed hundreds of them. Those confined at Haddrell's Point also suffered terribly. Many of them had been nurtured in affluence; now far from friends and entirely without means, they were reduced to the greatest straits. They were not even allowed to fish for their support, but were obliged to perform the most menial services. After thirteen months captivity, Cornwallis ordered them to be sent to the West Indies, and this cruel order would have been carried out, but for the general exchange of prisoners which took place soon afterwards.

"Governor Rutledge, in speaking before the South Carolina Assembly at Jacksonboro, thus eloquently referred to the rigorous and unjustifiable conduct of the British authorities:

"'Regardless of the sacred ties of honor, destitute of the feelings of humanity, and determined to extinguish, if possible, every spark of freedom in this country, the enemy, with the insolent pride of conquerors, gave unbounded scope to the exercise of their tyrannical disposition, infringed their public engagements, and violated their most solemn treaties. Many of our worthiest citizens, without cause, were long and closely confined, some on board prison ships, and others in the town and castle of St. Augustine. Their properties were disposed of at the will and caprice of the enemy, and their families sent to a different and distant part of the continent without the means of support. Many who had surrendered prisoners of war were killed in cold blood. Several suffered death in the most ignominious manner, and others were delivered up to savages and put to tortures, under which they expired. Thus the lives, liberties, and properties of the people were dependent solely on the pleasure of the British officers, who deprived them of either or all on the most frivolous pretenses. Indians, slaves, and a desperate banditti of the most profligate characters were caressed and employed by the enemy to execute their infamous purposes. Devastation and ruin marked their progress and that of their adherents; nor were their violences restrained by the charms or influence of beauty and innocence; even the fair sex, whom it is the duty of all, and the pleasure and pride of the brave to protect, they and their tender offspring, were victims to the inveterate malice of an unrelenting foe. Neither the tears of mothers, nor the cries of infants could excite pity or compassion. Not only the peaceful habitation of the widow, the aged and the infirm, but the holy temples of the Most High were consumed in flames, kindled by their sacrilegious hands. They have tarnished the glory of the British army, disgraced the profession of a British soldiery, and fixed indelible stigmas of rapine, cruelty and peridy, and profaneness on the British name.'"

When in 1808 the Tammany Society of New York laid the cornerstone of a vault in which the bones of many of the prison ship martyrs were laid Joseph D. Fay, Esq., made an oration in which he said:

"But the suffering of those unfortunate Americans whom the dreadful chances of war had destined for the prison–ships, were far greater than any which have been told. In that deadly season of the year, when the dog–star rages with relentless fury, when a pure air is especially necessary to health, the British locked their prisoner, after long marches, in the dungeons of ships affected with contagion, and reeking with the filth of crowded captives, dead and dying. * * * No reasoning, no praying could obtain from his stern tyrants the smallest alleviation of his fate.

"In South Carolina the British officer called Fraser, after trying in every manner to induce the prisoners to enlist, said to them: 'Go to your dungeons in the prison ships, where you shall perish and rot, but first let me tell you that the rations which have been hitherto allowed for your wives and children shall, from this moment, cease forever; and you shall die assured that they are starving in the public streets, and that *you* are the authors of their fate.'

"A sentence so terribly awful appalled the firm soul of every listening hero. A solemn silence followed the declaration; they cast their wondering eyes one upon the other, and valor, for a moment, hung suspended between love of family, and love of country. Love of country at length rose superior to every other consideration, and moved by one impulse, this glorious band of patriots thundered into the astonished ears of their persecutors, 'The prison–ships and Death, or Washington and our country!'

"Meagre famine shook hands with haggard pestilence, joining a league to appall, conquer, and destroy the glorious spirit of liberty."

CHAPTER XXIII. A POET ON A PRISON SHIP

Philip Freneau, the poet of the Revolution, as he has been called, was of French Huguenot ancestry. The Freneaus came to New York in 1685. His mother was Agnes Watson, a resident of New York, and the poet was born on the second of January, 1752.

In the year 1780 a vessel of which he was the owner, called the Aurora, was taken by the British. Freneau was on board, though he was not the captain of the ship. The British man–of–war, Iris, made the Aurora her prize, after a fight in which the sailing master and many of the crew were killed. This was in May, 1780. The survivors were brought to New York, and confined on board the prison ship, Scorpion. Freneau has left a poem describing the horrors of his captivity in very strong language, and it is easy to conceive that his suffering must have been intense to have aroused such bitter feelings. We give a part of his poem, as it contains the best description of the indignities inflicted upon the prisoners, and their mental and physical sufferings that we have found in any work on the subject.

PART OF PHILIP FRENEAU'S POEM ON THE PRISON SHIPS

Conveyed to York we found, at length, too late,
That Death was better than the prisoner's fate
There doomed to famine, shackles, and despair,
Condemned to breathe a foul, infected air,
In sickly hulks, devoted while we lay,—
Successive funerals gloomed each dismal day

The various horrors of these hulks to tell—
These prison ships where Pain and Penance dwell,
Where Death in ten–fold vengeance holds his reign,
And injured ghosts, yet unavenged, complain:
This be my task—ungenerous Britons, you
Conspire to murder whom you can't subdue

* * * * *

So much we suffered from the tribe I hate,
So near they shoved us to the brink of fate,
When two long months in these dark hulks we lay,
Barred down by night, and fainting all the day,
In the fierce fervors of the solar beam
Cooled by no breeze on Hudson's mountain stream,
That not unsung these threescore days shall fall
To black oblivion that would cover all.

No masts or sails these crowded ships adorn,
Dismal to view, neglected and forlorn;
Here mighty ills oppressed the imprisoned throng;
Dull were our slumbers, and our nights were long.
From morn to eve along the decks we lay,
Scorched into fevers by the solar ray;
No friendly awning cast a welcome shade,
Once was it promised, and was never made;
No favors could these sons of Death bestow,
'Twas endless vengeance, and unceasing woe.
Immortal hatred doth their breasts engage,
And this lost empire swells their souls with rage.

Two hulks on Hudson's stormy bosom lie,
Two, on the east, alarm the pitying eye,
There, the black Scorpion at her mooring rides,
And there Strombolo, swinging, yields the tides;
Here bulky Jersey fills a larger space,
And Hunter, to all hospitals disgrace.
Thou Scorpion, fatal to thy crowded throng,
Dire theme of horror to Plutonian song,
Requir'st my lay,—thy sultry decks I know,
And all the torments that exist below!
The briny wave that Hudson's bosom fills
Drained through her bottom in a thousand rills;
Rotten and old, replete with sighs and groans,
Scarce on the water she sustained her bones:

Here, doomed to toil, or founder in the tide,
At the moist pumps incessantly we plied;
Here, doomed to starve, like famished dogs we tore
The scant allowance that our tyrants bore.
Remembrance shudders at this scene of fears,
Still in my view, some tyrant chief appears,
Some base–born Hessian slave walks threatening by,
Some servile Scot with murder in his eye,
Still haunts my sight, as vainly they bemoan
Rebellions managed so unlike their own.
O may I never feel the poignant pain
To live subjected to such fiends again!
Stewards and mates that hostile Britain bore,
Cut from the gallows on their native shore;
Their ghastly looks and vengeance beaming eyes
Still to my view in dismal visions rise,—
O may I ne'er review these dire abodes,
These piles for slaughter floating on the floods!
And you that o'er the troubled ocean go
Strike not your standards to this venomed foe,
Better the greedy wave should swallow all,
Better to meet the death–conducting ball,
Better to sleep on ocean's oozy bed,
At once destroyed and numbered with the dead,
Than thus to perish in the face of day
Where twice ten thousand deaths one death delay.
When to the ocean sinks the western sun,
And the scorched tories fire their evening gun,
"Down, rebels, down!" the angry Scotchmen cry,
"Base dogs, descend, or by our broadswords die!"

Hail, dark abode! What can with thee compare?
Heat, sickness, famine, death, and stagnant air,—

* * * * *

American Prisoners of the Revolution

Swift from the guarded decks we rushed along,
And vainly sought repose, so vast our throng.
Three hundred wretches here, denied all light,
In crowded quarters pass the infernal night.
Some for a bed their tattered vestments join,
And some on chest, and some on floors recline;
Shut from the blessings of the evening air
Pensive we lay with mingled corpses there:
Meagre and wan, and scorched with heat below,
We looked like ghosts ere death had made us so:
How could we else, where heat and hunger joined
Thus to debase the body and the mind?
Where cruel thirst the parching throat invades,
Dries up the man and fits him for the shades?
No waters laded from the bubbling spring
To these dire ships these little tyrants bring—
By plank and ponderous beams completely walled
In vain for water, still in vain we called.
No drop was granted to the midnight prayer
To rebels in these regions of despair!
The loathsome cask a deadly dose contains,
Its poison circles through the languid veins.
"Here, generous Briton, generous, as you say,
To my parched tongue one cooling drop convey—
Hell has no mischief like a thirsty throat,
Nor one tormentor like your David Sproat!"

Dull flew the hours till, from the East displayed,
Sweet morn dispelled the horrors of the shade:
On every side dire objects met the sight,
And pallid forms, and murders of the night:
The dead were past their pains, the living groan,
Nor dare to hope another morn their own.

* * * * *

American Prisoners of the Revolution

O'er distant streams appears the living green,
And leafy trees on mountain tops are seen:
But they no grove or grassy mountain tread,
Marked for a longer journey to the dead.

Black as the clouds that shade St. Kilda's shore,
Wild as the winds that round her mountains roar,
At every post some surly vagrant stands,
Culled from the English, or the Scottish bands.
Dispensing death triumphantly they stand,
Their musquets ready to obey command;
Wounds are their sport, and ruin is their aim;
On their dark souls compassion has no claim,
And discord only can their spirits please,
Such were our tyrants here, such foes as these.

* * * * *

But such a train of endless woes abound
So many mischiefs in these hulks are found
That on them all a poem to prolong
Would swell too high the horrors of our song.
Hunger and thirst to work our woe combine,
And mouldy bread, and flesh of rotten swine;
The mangled carcase and the battered brain;
The doctor's poison, and the captain's cane;
The soldier's musquet, and the steward's debt:
The evening shackle, and the noonday threat.

* * * * *

That charm whose virtue warms the world beside,
Was by these tyrants to our use denied.
While yet they deigned that healthsome balm to lade,
The putrid water felt its powerful aid;
But when refused, to aggravate our pains,

Then fevers raged and revelled through our veins;
Throughout my frame I felt its deadly heat;
I felt my pulse with quicker motions beat;
A pallid hue o'er every face was spread,
Unusual pains attacked the fainting head:
No physic here, no doctor to assist,
With oaths they placed me on the sick man's list:
Twelve wretches more the same dark symptoms took,
And these were entered on the doctor's book.
The loathsome Hunter was our destined place,
The Hunter, to all hospitals disgrace.
With soldiers sent to guard us on the road,
Joyful we left the Scorpion's dire abode:
Some tears we shed for the remaining crew,
Then cursed the hulk, and from her sides withdrew.

THE HOSPITAL PRISON SHIP

Now towards the Hunter's gloomy decks we came,
A slaughter house, yet hospital in name;
For none came there till ruined with their fees,
And half consumed, and dying of disease:—

But when too near, with laboring oar, we plied,
The Mate, with curses, drove us from the side:—
That wretch, who banished from the navy crew,
Grown old in blood did here his trade renew.
His rancorous tongue, when on his charge let loose,
Uttered reproaches, scandal, and abuse;
Gave all to hell who dared his king disown,
And swore mankind were made for George alone.
A thousand times, to irritate our woe,
He wished us foundered in the gulph below:
A thousand times he brandished high his stick,
And swore as often, that we were not sick:—
And yet so pale! that we were thought by some

A freight of ghosts from Death's dominions come.
But, calmed at length, for who can always rage?
Or the fierce war of boundless passion wage?
He pointed to the stairs that led below
To damps, disease, and varied forms of woe:—
Down to the gloom I took my pensive way,
Along the decks the dying captives lay,
Some struck with madness, some with scurvy pained,
But still of putrid fevers most complained.
On the hard floors the wasted objects laid
There tossed and tumbled in the dismal shade:
There no soft voice their bitter fate bemoaned,
But Death strode stately, while his victims groaned.
Of leaky decks I heard them long complain,
Drowned as they were in deluges of rain:
Denied the comforts of a dying bed,
And not a pillow to support the head:
How could they else but pine, and grieve and sigh,
Detest a wretched life, and wish to die?

Scarce had I mingled with this wretched band,
When a thin victim seized me by the hand:—
"And art thou come?"—death heavy on his eyes—
"And art thou come to these abodes?" he cries,
"Why didst thou leave the Scorpion's dark retreat?
And hither haste, a surer death to meet?
Why didst thou leave thy damp, infected cell?
If that was purgatory, this is hell.
We too, grown weary of that horrid shade,
Petitioned early for the Doctor's aid;
His aid denied, more deadly symptoms came,
Weak and yet weaker, glowed the vital flame;
And when disease had worn us down so low
That few could tell if we were ghosts or no,
And all asserted death would be our fate,
Then to the Doctor we were sent, too late"

Ah! rest in peace, each injured, parted shade,
By cruel hands in death's dark weeds arrayed,
The days to come shall to your memory raise
Piles on these shores, to spread through earth your praise.

THE HESSIAN DOCTOR

From Brooklyn heights a Hessian doctor came,
Nor great his skill, nor greater much his fame:
Fair Science never called the wretch her son,
And Art disdained the stupid man to own.

He on his charge the healing work begun
With antmomial mixtures by the tun:
Ten minutes was the time he deigned to stay,
The time of grace allotted once a day:
He drenched us well with bitter draughts, tis true,
Nostrums from hell, and cortex from Peru:
Some with his pills he sent to Pluto's reign,
And some he blistered with his flies of Spain.
His Tartar doses walked their deadly round,
Till the lean patient at the potion frowned,
And swore that hemlock, death, or what you will,
Were nonsense to the drugs that stuffed his bill.
On those refusing he bestowed a kick,
Or menaced vengeance with his walking stick:
Here uncontrolled he exercised his trade,
And grew experienced by the deaths he made.

Knave though he was, yet candor must confess
Not chief physician was this man of Hesse:
One master o'er the murdering tribe was placed,
By him the rest were honored or disgraced
Once, and but once, by some strange fortune led,
He came to see the dying and the dead.
He came, but anger so inflamed his eye,

And such a faulchion glittered on his thigh,
And such a gloom his visage darkened o'er,
And two such pistols in his hands he bore,
That, by the gods, with such a load of steel,
We thought he came to murder, not to heal.
Rage in his heart, and mischief in his head,
He gloomed destruction, and had smote us dead
Had he so dared, but fear withheld his hand,
He came, blasphemed, and turned again to land

THE BENEVOLENT CAPTAIN

From this poor vessel, and her sickly crew
A british seaman all his titles drew,
Captain, Esquire, Commander, too, in chief,
And hence he gained his bread and hence his beef:
But sir, you might have searched creation round,
And such another ruffian not have found
Though unprovoked an angry face he bore,—
All were astonished at the oaths he swore
He swore, till every prisoner stood aghast,
And thought him Satan in a brimstone blast
He wished us banished from the public light;
He wished us shrouded in perpetual night;

    * * * * *

He swore, besides, that should the ship take fire
We, too, must in the pitchy flames expire—
That if we wretches did not scrub the decks
His staff should break our base, rebellious necks;

    * * * * *

If, where he walked, a murdered carcase lay,
Still dreadful was the language of the day;

161

He called us dogs, and would have held us so,
But terror checked the meditated blow
Of vengeance, from our injured nation due,
To him, and all the base, unmanly crew
Such food they sent to make complete our woes
It looked like carrion torn from hungry crows
Such vermin vile on every joint were seen,
So black, corrupted, mortified, and lean,
That once we tried to move our flinty chief,
And thus addressed him, holding up the beef—
"See, Captain, see, what rotten bones we pick,
What kills the healthy cannot cure the sick,
Not dogs on such by Christian men are fed,
And see, good master, see, what lousy bread!"
"Your meat or bread," this man of death replied,
"Tis not my care to manage or provide
But this, base rebel dogs I'd have you know,
That better than you merit we bestow—
Out of my sight!" nor more he deigned to say,
But whisked about, and frowning, strode away

CONCLUSION

Each day at least six carcases we bore
And scratched them graves along the sandy shore
By feeble hands the shallow graves were made,
No stone memorial o'er the corpses laid
In barren sands and far from home they lie,
No friend to shed a tear when passing by
O'er the mean tombs insulting Britons tread,
Spurn at the sand, and curse the rebel dead.
When to your arms these fatal islands fall—
For first or last, they must be conquered, all,
Americans! to rites sepulchral just
With gentlest footstep press this kindred dust,
And o'er the tombs, if tombs can then be found,

162

Place the green turf, and plant the myrtle round

This poem was written in 1780, the year that Freneau was captured. He was on board the Scorpion and Hunter about two months, and was then exchanged. We fear that he has not in the least exaggerated the horrors of his situation. In fact there seem to have been many bloody pages torn from the book of history, that can never be perused. Many dark deeds were done in these foul prisons, of which we can only give hints, and the details of many crimes committed against the helpless prisoners are left to our imaginations. But enough and more than enough is known to make us fear that *inhumanity*, a species of cruelty unknown to the lower animals, is really one of the most prominent characteristics of men. History is a long and bloody record of battles, massacres, torture chambers; greed and violence; bigotry and sin. The root of all crimes is selfishness. What we call inhumanity is we fear not *inhuman*, but *human nature unrestrained*. It is true that some progress is made, and it is no longer the custom to kill all captives, at least not in civilized countries. But war will always be "*horrida bella*," chiefly because war means license, when the unrestrained, wolfish passions of man get for the time the upper hand. Our task, however, is not that of a moralist, but of a narrator of facts, from which all who read can draw the obvious moral for themselves.

CHAPTER XXIV. "THERE WAS A SHIP"

Of all the ships that were ever launched the "Old Jersey" is the most notorious. Never before or since, in the dark annals of human sufferings, has so small a space enclosed such a heavy weight of misery. No other prison has destroyed so many human beings in so short a space of time. And yet the Jersey was once as staunch and beautiful a vessel as ever formed a part of the Royal Navy of one of the proudest nations of the world. How little did her builders imagine that she would go down to history accompanied by the execrations of all who are acquainted with her terrible record!

It is said that it was in the late spring of 1780 that the Old Jersey, as she was then called, was first moored in Wallabout Bay, off the coast of Long Island. We can find no record to prove that she was used as a prison ship until the winter of that year. She was, at first, a hospital ship for British soldiers.

The reason for the removal of the unfortunate prisoners from the ships in New York

Harbor was that pestilential sickness was fast destroying them, and it was feared that the inhabitants of New York would suffer from the prevailing epidemics. They were therefore placed in rotten hulks off the quiet shores of Long Island, where, secluded from the public eye, they were allowed to perish by the thousands from cruel and criminal neglect.

"The Old Jersey and the two hospital ships," says General J. Johnson, "remained in the Wallabout until New York was evacuated by the British. The Jersey was the receiving ship: the others, truly, the ships of death!

"It has been generally thought that all the prisoners died on board the Jersey. This is not true. Many may have died on board of her who were not reported as sick, but all who were placed on the sick list were removed to the hospital ships, from which they were usually taken, sewed up in a blanket, to their graves.

"After the hospital ships were brought into the Wallabout, it was reported that the sick were attended by physicians. Few indeed were those who recovered, or came back to tell the tale of their sufferings in those horrible places. It was no uncommon sight to see five or six dead bodies brought on shore in a single morning, when a small excavation would be dug at the foot of the hill, the bodies cast into it, and then a man with a shovel would quickly cover them by shovelling sand down the hill upon them.

"Many were buried in a ravine of this hill and many on Mr. Remsen's farm. The whole shore, from Rennie's Point, to Mr. Remsen's dooryard, was a place of graves; as were also the slope of the hill near the house; the shore, from Mr. Remsen's barn along the mill–pond to Rappelye's farm; and the sandy island between the flood–gates and the mill–dam, while a few were buried on the shore on the east side of the Wallabout.

"Thus did Death reign here, from 1776 (when the Whitby prison ship was first moored in the Wallabout) until the peace. The whole Wallabout was a sickly place during the war. The atmosphere seemed to be charged with foul air: from the prison ships; and with the effluvia of dead bodies washed out of their graves by the tides. * * * More than half of the dead buried on the outer side of the mill–pond, were washed out by the waves at high tide, during northeasterly winds.

"The bodies of the dead lay exposed along the beach, drying and bleaching in the sun, and whitening the shores, till reached by the power of a succeeding storm, as the agitated waves receded, the bones receded with them into the deep, where they remain, unseen by man, awaiting the resurrection morn, when, again joined to the spirits to which they belong, they will meet their persecuting murderers at the bar of the Supreme Judge of the quick and the dead.

"We have ourselves," General Johnson continues, "examined many of the skulls lying on the shore. From the teeth they appeared to be the remains of men in the prime of life."

We will quote more of this interesting account written by an eyewitness of the horrors he records, in a later chapter. At present we will endeavor to give the reader a short history of the Jersey, from the day of her launching to her degradation, when she was devoted to the foul usages of a prison ship.

She was a fourth rate ship of the line, mounting sixty guns, and carrying a crew of four hundred men. She was built in 1736, having succeeded to the name of a celebrated 50–gun ship, which was then withdrawn from the service, and with which she must not be confounded. In 1737 she was fitted for sea as one of the Channel Fleet, commanded by Sir John Norris.

In the fall of 1738 the command of the Jersey was given to Captain Edmund Williams, and in July, 1739, she was one of the vessels which were sent to the Mediterranean under Rear Admiral Chaloner Ogle, when a threatened rupture with Spain rendered it necessary to strengthen the naval force in that quarter.

The trouble in the Mediterranean having been quieted by the appearance of so strong a fleet, in 1740 the Jersey returned home; but she was again sent out, under the command of Captain Peter Lawrence, and was one of the vessels forming the fleet of Sir John Norris, when, in the fall of that year and in the spring of 1741, that gentleman made his fruitless demonstrations against the Spanish coast. Soon afterwards the Jersey, still forming one of the fleet commanded by Sir Chaloner Ogle, was sent to the West Indies, to strengthen the forces at that station, commanded by Vice–Admiral Vernon, and she was with that distinguished officer when he made his well–known, unsuccessful attack on Carthagena, and the Spanish dominions in America in that year.

In March, 1743, Captain Lawrence was succeeded m the command of the Jersey by Captain Harry Norris, youngest son of Admiral Sir John Norris: and the Jersey formed one of the fleet commanded by Sir John Norris, which was designed to watch the enemy's Brest fleet; but having suffered severely from a storm while on that station, she was obliged to return to the Downs.

Captain Harry Norris having been promoted to a heavier ship, the command of the Jersey was given soon afterwards to Captain Charles Hardy subsequently well known as Governor of the Colony of New York; and in June, 1744, that officer having been appointed to the command of the Newfoundland Station, she sailed for North America, and bore his flag in those waters during the remainder of the year. In 1745, still under the immediate command of Captain Hardy, the Jersey was one of the ships which, under Vice–Admiral Medley, were sent to the Mediterranean, where Vice–Admiral Sir William Rowley then commanded; and as she continued on that station during the following year there is little doubt that Captain Hardy remained there, during the remainder of his term of service on that vessel.

It was while under the command of Captain Hardy in July, 1745, that the Jersey was engaged with the French ship, St. Esprit, of 74 guns, in one of the most desperate engagements on record. The action continued during two hours and a half, when the St. Esprit was compelled to bear away for Cadiz, where she was repaired and refitted for sea. At the close of Sir Charles Hardy's term of service in 1747, the Jersey was laid up, evidently unfit for active service; and in October, 1748, she was reported among the "hulks" in port.

On the renewal of hostilities with France in 1756 the Jersey was refitted for service, and the command given to Captain John Barker, and in May, 1757, she was sent to the Mediterranean, where, under the orders of Admiral Henry Osbourne, she continued upwards of two years, having been present, on the 28th of February, 1758, when M. du Quesne made his ineffectual attempt to reinforce M. De la Clue, who was then closely confined, with the fleet under his command, in the harbor of Carthagena.

On the 18th of August, 1759, while commanded by Captain Barker, the Jersey, with the Culloden and the Conqueror, were ordered by Admiral Boscowan, the commander of the fleet, to proceed to the mouth of the harbor of Toulon, for the purpose of cutting out or destroying two French ships which were moored there under cover of the batteries with the hope of forcing the French Admiral, De la Clue, to an engagement. The three ships approached the harbour, as directed, with great firmness; but they were assailed by so heavy a fire, not only from the enemy's ships and fortifications, but from several masked batteries, that, after an unequal but desperate contest of upwards of three hours, they were compelled to retire without having succeeded in their object; and to repair to Gibraltar to be refitted.

In the course of the year 1759 Captain Barker was succeeded in the command of the Jersey by Captain Andrew Wilkinson, under whom, forming one of the Mediterranean fleet, commanded by Sir Charles Saunders, she continued in active service until 1763.

In 1763 peace was established, and the Jersey returned to England and was laid up; but in May, 1766, she was again commissioned, and under the command of Captain William Dickson, and bearing the flag of Admiral Spry, she was ordered to her former station in the Mediterranean, where she remained three years.

In the spring of 1769, bearing the flag of Commodore Sir John Byron, the Jersey sailed for America. She seems to have returned home at the close of the summer, and her active duties appear to have been brought to an end.

She remained out of commission until 1776, when, without armament, and under the command of Captain Anthony Halstead, she was ordered to New York as a hospital ship.

Captain Halstead died on the 17th of May, 1778, and, in July following, he was succeeded by Commander David Laird, under whom, either as a hospital, or a prison ship, she remained in Wallabout bay, until she was abandoned at the close of the war, to her fate, which was to rot in the mud at her moorings, until, at last, she sank, and for many years her wretched worm–eaten old hulk could be seen at low tide, shunned by all, a sorry spectacle, the ghost of what had once been a gallant man–of–war.

This short history of the Jersey has been condensed from the account written in 1865 by Mr. Henry B. Dawson and published at Morrisania, New York, in that year.

In an oration delivered by Mr. Jonathan Russel, in Providence, R. I., on the 4th of July 1800, he thus speaks of this ill–fated vessel and of her victims: "But it was not in the ardent conflicts of the field only, that our countrymen fell; it was not the ordinary chances of war alone which they had to encounter. Happy indeed, thrice happy were Warren, Montgomery, and Mercer; happy those other gallant spirits who fell with glory in the heat of the battle, distinguished by their country and covered with her applause. Every soul sensible to honor, envies rather than compassionates their fate. It was in the dungeons of our inhuman invaders; it was in the loathsome and pestiferous prisons, that the wretchedness of our countrymen still makes the heart bleed. It was there that hunger, and thirst, and disease, and all the contumely that cold–hearted cruelty could bestow, sharpened every pang of death. Misery there wrung every fibre that could feel, before she gave the Blow of Grace which sent the sufferer to eternity. It is said that poison was employed. No, there was no such mercy there. There, nothing was employed which could blunt the susceptibility to anguish, or which, by hastening death, could rob its agonies of a single pang. On board one only of these Prison ships above 11,000 of our brave countrymen are said to have perished. She was called the Jersey. Her wreck still remains, and at low ebb, presents to the world its accursed and blighted fragments. Twice in twenty–four hours the winds of Heaven sigh through it, and repeat the groans of our expiring countrymen; and twice the ocean hides in her bosom those deadly and polluted ruins, which all her waters cannot purify. Every rain that descends washes from the unconsecrated bank the bones of those intrepid sufferers. They lie, naked on the shore, accusing the neglect of their countrymen. How long shall gratitude, and even piety deny them burial? They ought to be collected in one vast ossory, which shall stand a monument to future ages, of the two extremes of human character: of that depravity which, trampling on the rights of misfortune, perpetrated cold and calculating murder on a wretched and defenceless prisoner; and that virtue which animated this prisoner to die a willing martyr to his country. Or rather, were it possible, there ought to be raised a Colossal Column whose base sinking to Hell, should let the murderers read their infamy inscribed upon it; and whose capital of Corinthian laurel ascending to Heaven, should show the sainted Patriots that they have triumphed.

"Deep and dreadful as the coloring of this picture may appear, it is but a taint and imperfect sketch of the original. You must remember a thousand unutterable calamities; a thousand instances of domestic as well as national anxiety and distress; which mock description. You ought to remember them; you ought to hand them down in tradition to your posterity, that they may know the awful price their fathers paid for freedom."

CHAPTER XXV. A DESCRIPTION OF THE JERSEY

SONNET

SUGGESTED BY A VISION OF THE JERSEY PRISON SHIP

BY W P P

O Sea! in whose unfathomable gloom
A world forlorn of wreck and ruin lies,
In thy avenging majesty arise,
And with a sound as of the trump of doom
Whelm from all eyes for aye yon living tomb,
Wherein the martyr patriots groaned for years,
A prey to hunger and the bitter jeers
Of foes in whose relentless breasts no room
Was ever found for pity or remorse;
But haunting anger and a savage hate,
That spared not e'en their victim's very corse,
But left it, outcast, to its carrion fate
Wherefore, arise, O Sea! and sternly sweep
This floating dungeon to thy lowest deep

It was stated in the portion of the eloquent oration given in our last chapter that more than 11,000 prisoners perished on board the Jersey alone, during the space of three years and a half that she was moored in the waters of Wallabout Bay. This statement has never been contradicted, as far as we know, by British authority. Yet we trust that it is exaggerated. It would give an average of more than three thousand deaths a year. The whole number of names copied from the English War Records of prisoners on board the Jersey is about 8,000. This, however, is an incomplete list. You will in vain search through its pages to find the recorded names of many prisoners who have left well attested accounts of their captivity on board that fatal vessel. All that we can say now is that the number who perished there is very great.

As late as 1841 the bones of many of these victims were still to be found on the shores of

Walabout Bay, in and around the Navy Yard. On the 4th of February of that year some workmen, while engaged in digging away an embankment in Jackson Street, Brooklyn, near the Navy Yard, accidentally uncovered a quantity of human bones, among which was a skeleton having a pair of iron manacles still upon the wrists. (See Thompson's History of Long Island, Vol. 1, page 247.)

In a paper published at Fishkill on the 18th of May, 1783, is the following card: "To All Printers, of Public Newspapers:—Tell it to the world, and let it be published in every Newspaper throughout America, Europe, Asia, and Africa, to the everlasting disgrace and infamy of the British King's commanders at New York: That during the late war it is said that 11,644 American prisoners have suffered death by their inhuman, cruel, savage, and barbarous usage on board the filthy and malignant British prison ship called the Jersey, lying at New York. Britons tremble, lest the vengeance of Heaven fall on your isle, for the blood of these unfortunate victims!

"An American"

"They died, the young, the loved, the brave,
  The death barge came for them,
And where the seas yon black rocks lave
  Is heard their requiem
They buried them and threw the sand
Unhallowed o'er that patriot band

The black ship like a demon sate
  Upon the prowling deep,
From her came fearful sounds of hate,
  Till pain stilled all in sleep
It was the sleep that victims take,
Tied, tortured, dying, at the stake.

Yet some the deep has now updug,
  Their bones are in the sun,
Whether by sword or deadly drug
  They perished, one by one,
Was it not dread for mortal eye

To see them all so strangely die?

Are there those murdered men who died
　For freedom and for me?
They seem to point, in martyred pride
　To that spot upon the sea
From whence came once the frenzied yell,
From out that wreck, that prison hell"

This rough but strong old poem was written many years ago by a Mr. Whitman We have taken the liberty of retouching it to a slight degree.

It is well known that *twenty hogsheads* of bones were collected in 1808 from the shores of the Wallabout, and buried under the auspices of the Tammany Society in a vault prepared for the purpose. These were but a small part of the remains of the victims of the prison ships. Many were, as we have seen, washed into the sea, and many more were interred on the shores of New York Harbor, before the prison ships were removed to the Wallabout. It will be better that we should give the accounts left to us by eye witnesses of the sufferings on board these prison ships, and we will therefore quote from the narrative of John Van Dyke, who was confined on board the Jersey before her removal to the Wallabout.

Captain John Van Dyke was taken prisoner in May, 1780, at which time he says: "We were put on board the prison ship Jersey, anchored off Fly Market. (New York City) This ship had been a hospital ship. When I came on board her stench was so great, and my breathing this putrid air—I thought it would kill me, but after being on board some days I got used to it, and as though all was a common smell. * * *

"On board the Jersey prison ship it was short allowance, so short a person would think it was not possible for a man to live on. They starved the American prisoners to make them enlist in their service. I will now relate a fact. Every man in a mess of six took his daily turn to get the mess's provisions. One day I went to the galley and drew a piece of salt, boiled pork. I went to our mess to divide it. * * * I cut each one his share, and each one eat our day's allowance in one mouthful of this salt pork and nothing else. One day called peaday I took the drawer of our doctor's chest (Dr. Hodges of Philadelphia) and went to the galley, which was the cooking place, with my drawer for a soup dish. I held it under a large brass cock, the cook turned it. I received the allowance of my mess, and behold! Brown water, and fifteen floating peas—no peas on the bottom of my drawer, and this for six men's allowance for 24 hours. The peas were all in the bottom of the kettle. Those left would be taken to New York and, I suppose, sold.

"One day in the week, called pudding day, we would receive three pounds of damaged flour, in it would be green lumps such as their men would not eat, and one pound of very bad raisins, one third raisin sticks. We would pick out the sticks, mash the lumps of flour, put all with some water into our drawer, mix our pudding and put it into a bag and boil it with a tally tied to it with the number of our mess. This was a day's allowance. We, for some time, drew a half pint of rum for each man. One day Captain Lard (Laird) who commanded the ship Jersey, came on board. As soon as he was on the main deck of the ship he cried out for the boatswain. The boatswain arrived and in a very quick motion, took off his hat. There being on deck two half hogshead tubs where our allowance of rum was mixed into grog, Captain L., said, 'Have the prisoners had their allowance of rum today?' 'No, sir' answered the boatswain. Captain L. replied, 'Damn your soul, you rascal, heave it overboard.'

"The boatswain, with help, upset the tubs of rum on the middle deck. The grog rum run out of the scuppers of the ship into the river. I saw no more grog on board. * * * Every fair day a number of British officers and sergeants would come on board, form in two ranks on the quarter deck, facing inwards, the prisoners in the after part of the quarter deck. As the boatswain would call a name, the word would be 'Pass!' As the prisoners passed between the ranks officers and sergeants stared them in the face. This was done to catch deserters, and if they caught nothing the sergeants would come on the middle deck and cry out 'Five guineas bounty to any man that will enter his Majesty's service!'

"Shortly after this party left the ship a Hessian party would come on board, and the prisoners had to go through the same routine of duty again.

"From the Jersey prison ship eighty of us were taken to the pink stern sloop−of−war Hunter, Captain Thomas Henderson, Commander. We were taken there in a large ship's long boat, towed by a ten−oar barge, and one other barge with a guard of soldiers in the rear.

"On board the ship Hunter we drew one third allowance, and every Monday we received a loaf of wet bread, weighing seven pounds for each mess. This loaf was from Mr. John Pintard's father, of New York, the American Commissary, and this bread, with the allowance of provisions, we found sufficient to live on.

"After we had been on board some time Mr. David Sproat, the British Commissary of prisoners, came on board; all the prisoners were ordered aft; the roll was called and as each man passed him Mr. Sproat would ask, 'Are you a seaman?' The answer was 'Landsman, landsman.' There were ten landsmen to one answer of half seaman. When the roll was finished Mr. Sproat said to our sea officers, 'Gentlemen, how do you make out at sea, for the most part of you are landsmen?'

"Our officers answered: 'You hear often how we make out. When we meet our force, or rather more than our force we give a good account of them.'

"Mr. Sproat asked, 'And are not your vessels better manned than these. Our officers replied, 'Mr Sproat, we are the best manned out of the port of Philadelphia.' Mr. Sproat shrugged his shoulders saying, 'I cannot see how you do it.'"

We do not understand what John Van Dyke meant by his expression "half seaman." It is probable that the sailors among the prisoners pretended to be soldiers in order to be exchanged. There was much more difficulty in exchanging sailors than soldiers, as we shall see. David Sproat was the British Commissary for Naval Prisoners alone. In a paper published in New York in April 28th, 1780, appears the following notice:—"I do hereby direct all Captains, Commanders, Masters, and Prize Masters of ships and other vessels, who bring naval prisoners into this port, immediately to send a list of their names to this office, No. 33 Maiden Lane, where they will receive an order how to dispose of them.

"(Signed) David Sproat."

The Jersey and some of the other prison ships often had landsmen among their prisoners, at least until the last years of the war, when they were so overcrowded with sailors, that there must have been scant room for any one else.

The next prisoner whose recollections we will consider is Captain Silas Talbot, who was confined on board the Jersey in the fall of 1780. He says: "All her port holes were closed.

173

* * * There were about 1,100 prisoners on board. There were no berths or seats, to lie down on, not a bench to sit on. Many were almost without cloaths. The dysentery, fever, phrenzy and despair prevailed among them, and filled the place with filth, disgust and horror. The scantiness of the allowance, the bad quality of the provisions, the brutality of the guards, and the sick, pining for comforts they could not obtain, altogether furnished continually one of the greatest scenes of human distress and misery ever beheld. It was now the middle of October, the weather was cool and clear, with frosty nights, so that the number of deaths per day was *reduced to an average of ten*, and this number was considered by the survivors a small one, when compared with the terrible mortality that had prevailed for three months before. The human bones and skulls, yet bleaching on the shore of Long Island, and daily exposed, by the falling down of the high bank on which the prisoners were buried, is a shocking sight, and manifestly demonstrates that the Jersey prison ship had been as destructive as a field of battle."

CHAPTER XXVI. THE EXPERIENCE OF EBENEZER FOX

Ebenezer Fox, a prisoner on board the Jersey, wrote a little book about his dreadful experiences when he was a very old man. The book was written in 1838, and published by Charles Fox in Boston in 1848. Ebenezer Fox was born in the East Parish of Roxbury, Mass., in 1763. In the spring of 1775 he and another boy named Kelly ran away to sea. Fox shipped as a cabin boy in a vessel commanded by Captain Joseph Manchester.

He made several cruises and returned home. In 1779 he enlisted, going as a substitute for the barber to whom he was apprenticed. His company was commanded by Captain William Bird of Boston in a regiment under Colonel Proctor. Afterwards he signed ship's papers and entered the naval service on a twenty gun ship called the Protector, Captain John F. Williams of Massachusetts. On the lst of April, 1780, they sailed for a six months cruise, and on the ninth of June, 1780, fought the Admiral Duff until she took fire and blew up. A short time afterwards the Protector was captured by two English ships called the Roebuck and Mayday.

Fox concealed fifteen dollars in the crown of his hat, and fifteen more in the soles of his shoes.

All the prisoners were sent into the hold. One third of the crew of the Protector were pressed into the British service. The others were sent to the Jersey. Evidently this prison ship had already become notorious, for Fox writes: "The idea of being incarcerated in this floating pandemonium filled us with horror, but the ideas we had formed of its horror fell far short of the reality. * * * The Jersey was removed from the East River, and moored with chain cables at the Wallabout in consequence of the fears entertained that the sickness which prevailed among the prisoners might spread to the shore. * * * I now found myself in a loathsome prison, among a collection of the most wretched and disgusting looking objects that I ever beheld in human form.

"Here was a motley crew, covered with rags and filth; visages pallid with disease; emaciated with hunger and anxiety; and hardly retaining a trace of their original appearance. Here were men, who had once enjoyed life while riding over the mountain wave or roaming through pleasant fields, full of health and vigor, now shrivelled by a scanty and unwholesome diet, ghastly with inhaling an impure atmosphere, exposed to contagion; in contact with disease, and surrounded with the horrors of sickness, and death. Here, thought I, must I linger out the morning of my life" (he was seventeen) "in tedious days and sleepless nights, enduring a weary and degrading captivity, till death should terminate my sufferings, and no friend will know of my departure.

"A prisoner on board the 'Old Jersey!' The very thought was appalling. I could hardly realize my situation.

"The first thing we found it necessary to do after our capture was to form ourselves into small parties called messes, consisting of six in each, as previous to doing this, we could obtain no food. All the prisoners were obliged to fast on the first day of their arrival, and seldom on the second could they obtain any food in season for cooking it. * * * All the prisoners fared alike; officers and sailors received the same treatment on board of this old hulk. * * * We were all 'rebels.' The only distinction known among us was made by the prisoners themselves, which was shown in allowing those who had been officers previous to their captivity, to congregate in the extreme afterpart of the ship, and to keep it exclusively to themselves as their place of abode. * * * The prisoners were confined in the two main decks below. The lowest dungeon was inhabited by those prisoners who were foreigners, and whose treatment was more severe than that of the Americans.

"The inhabitants of this lower region were the most miserable and disgusting looking objects that can be conceived. Daily washing in salt water, together with their extreme emaciation, caused the skin to appear like dried parchment. Many of them remained unwashed for weeks; their hair long, and matted, and filled with vermin; their beards never cut except occasionally with a pair of shears, which did not improve their comeliness, though it might add to their comfort. Their clothes were mere rags, secured to their bodies in every way that ingenuity could devise.

"Many of these men had been in this lamentable condition for two years, part of the time on board other prison ships; and having given up all hope of ever being exchanged, had become resigned to their situation. These men were foreigners whose whole lives had been one continual scene of toil, hardship, and suffering. Their feelings were blunted; their dispositions soured; they had no sympathies for the world; no home to mourn for; no friends to lament for their fate. But far different was the condition of the most numerous class of prisoners, composed mostly of young men from New England, fresh from home.

"They had reason to deplore the sudden change in their condition. * * * The thoughts of home, of parents, brothers, sisters, and friends, would crowd upon their minds, and brooding on what they had been, and what they were, their desire for home became a madness. The dismal and disgusting scene around; the wretched objects continually in sight; and 'hope deferred which maketh the heart sick', produced a state of melancholy that often ended in death,—the death of a broken heart."

Fox describes the food and drink, the prison regulations, deaths, and burials, just as they were described by Captain Dring, who wrote the fullest account of the Jersey, and from whose memoirs we shall quote further on. He says of their shallow graves in the sand of the Wallabout: "This was the last resting place of many a son and a brother,—young and noble−spirited men, who had left their happy homes and kind friends to offer their lives in the service of their country. * * * Poor fellows! They suffered more than their older companions in misery. They could not endure their hopeless and wearisome captivity:—to live on from day to day, denied the power of doing anything; condemned to that most irksome and heart−sickening of all situations, utter inactivity; their restless and impetuous spirits, like caged lions, panted to be free, and the conflict was too much for endurance, enfeebled and worn out as they were with suffering and confinement. * * * The fate of many of these unhappy victims must have remained forever unknown to their friends; for in so large a number, no exact account could be kept of those who died, and they rested in a nameless grave; while those who performed the last sad rites were hurried away before their task was half completed, and forbid to express their horror and indignation at this insulting negligence towards the dead. * * *

"The regular crew of the Jersey consisted of a Captain, two Mates, a steward, a cook, and about twelve sailors. There was likewise on board a guard of about thirty soldiers, from the different regiments quartered on Long Island, who were relieved by a fresh party every week.

"The physical force of the prisoners was sufficient at any time to take possession of the ship, but the difficulty was to dispose of themselves after a successful attempt. Long Island was in possession of the British, and the inhabitants were favorable to the British cause. To leave the ship and land on the island, would be followed by almost certain detection; and the miseries of our captivity would be increased by additional cruelties heaped upon us from the vindictive feelings of our oppressors.

"Yet, small as was the chance for succeeding in the undertaking, the attempt to escape was often made, and in not a few instances with success.

"Our sufferings were so intolerable, that we felt it to be our duty to expose ourselves to almost any risk to obtain our liberty. To remain on board of the prison ship seemed to be certain death, and in its most horrid form; to be killed, while endeavoring to get away, could be no worse.

"American prisoners are proverbial for their ingenuity in devising ways and means to accomplish their plans, whether they be devised for their own comfort and benefit, or for the purpose of annoying and tormenting their keepers.

"Although we were guarded with vigilance yet there did not appear much system in the management of the prisoners; for we frequently missed a whole mess from our number, while their disappearance was not noticed by our keepers. Occasionally a few would be brought back who had been found in the woods upon Long Island, and taken up by the Tories.

"Our mess one day noticed that the mess that occupied the place next to them were among the missing. This circumstance led to much conjecture and inquiry respecting the manner in which they had effected their escape. By watching the movements of our neighbors we soon found out the process necessary to be adopted.

"Any plan which a mess had formed they kept a secret among their number, in order to insure a greater prospect of success. * * * For the convenience of the officers of the ship a closet, called the "round house", had been constructed under the forecastle, the door of which was kept locked. This room was seldom used, there being other conveniences in the ship preferable to it.

"Some of the prisoners had contrived to pick the lock of the door; and as it was not discovered the door remained unfastened.

"After we had missed our neighbor prisoners, and had ascertained to our satisfaction their mode of operation, the members of our mess determined to seize the first opportunity that offered to attempt our escape. We selected a day, about the 15th of August, and made all the preparations in our power for ensuring us success in our undertaking. At sunset, when the usual cry from the officer of the guard, 'Down, rebels, down!' was heard, instead of following the multitude down the hatchways, our mess, consisting of six, all Americans, succeeded in getting into the 'round house', except one. The round house was found too small to contain more than five; and the sixth man, whose name, I think, was Putnam of Boston, concealed himself under a large tub, which happened to be lying near the place of our confinement. The situation of the five, as closely packed in the round house as we could stand and breathe, was so uncomfortable as to make us very desirous of vacating it as soon as possible.

"We remained thus cooped up, hardly daring to breathe, for fear we should be heard by the guard. The prisoners were all below, and no noise was heard above, saving the tramp of the guard as he paced the deck. It was customary, after the prisoners were secured below, for the ship's mate every night to search above; this, however, was considered a mere formality, and the duty was very imperfectly executed. While we were anxiously awaiting the completion of this service, an event transpired, that we little anticipated, and which led to our detection.

"One of the prisoners, an Irishman, had made his arrangements to escape the same evening, and had not communicated with any one on the subject except a countryman of his, whom he persuaded to bury him up in the coal hole, near the forecastle.

"Whether his friend covered him faithfully or not, or whether the Irishman thought that if he could not see anybody, nobody could see him, or whether, feeling uncomfortable in his position, he turned over to relieve himself, I know not; but when the mate looked in the coal hole he espied something rather whiter than the coal, which he soon ascertained to be the Irishman's shoulder. This discovery made the officer suspicious, and induced him to make a more thorough search than usual.

"We heard the uproar that followed the discovery, and the threats of the mate that he would search every damned corner. He soon arrived at the round house, and we heard him ask a soldier for the key. Our hopes and expectations were a little raised when we heard the soldier reply, 'There is no need of searching this place, for the door is kept constantly locked.'

"But the mate was not to be diverted from his purpose, and ordered the soldier to get the key.

"During the absence of the soldier, we had a little time to reflect upon the dangers of our situation; crowded together in a space so small as not to admit of motion; with no other protection than the thickness of a board; guarded on the outside by about twelve soldiers, armed with cutlasses, and the mate, considerably drunk, with a pistol in each hand, threatening every moment to fire through;—our feelings may be more easily conceived than described. There was but little time for deliberation; something must be immediately done. * * * In a whispered consultation of some moments, we conceived that the safest course we could pursue would be to break out with all the violence we could exercise, overcome every obstacle, and reach the quarter–deck. By this time the soldier had arrived with the key, and upon applying it, the door was found to be unlocked. We now heard our last summons from the mate, with imprecations too horrible to be repeated, and threatening us with instant destruction if we did not immediately come out.

"To remain any longer where we were would have been certain death to some of us; we therefore carried our hastily formed plan into execution. The door opened outwards, and forming ourselves into a solid body, we burst open the door, rushed out pellmell, and making a brisk use of our fists, knocked the guard heels over head in all directions, at the same time running with all possible speed for the quarter–deck. As I rushed out, being in the rear, I received a wound from a cutlass on my side, the scar of which remains to this day.

"As nearly all the guards were prostrated by our unexpected sally, we arrived at our destined place, without being pursued by anything but curses and threats.

"The mate exercised his authority to protect us from the rage of the soldiers, who were in pursuit of us, as soon as they had recovered from the prostration into which they had been thrown; and, with the assistance of the Captain's mistress, whom the noise had brought upon deck, and whose sympathy was excited when she saw we were about to be murdered: she placed herself between us and the enraged guard, and made such an outcry as to bring the Captain" (Laird) "up, who ordered the guard to take their station at a little distance and to watch us narrowly. We were all put in irons, our feet being fastened to a long bar, a guard placed over us, and in this situation we were left to pass the night.

"During the time of the transactions related, our fellow prisoner, Putnam, remained quietly under the tub, and heard the noise from his hiding place. He was not suffered to remain long in suspense. A soldier lifted up the tub, and seeing the poor prisoner, thrust his bayonet into his body, just above his hip, and then drove him to the quarter–deck, to take his place in irons among us. The blood flowed profusely from his wound, and he was soon after sent on board the hospital ship, and we never heard anything respecting him afterwards.

"With disappointed expectations we passed a dreary night. A cold fog, followed by rain, came on; to which we were exposed, without any blankets or covering to protect us from the inclemency of the weather. Our sufferings of mind and body during that horrible night, exceeded any that I have ever experienced.

"We were chilled almost to death, and the only way we could preserve heat enough in our bodies to prevent our perishing, was to lie upon each other by turns.

"Morning at last came, and we were released from our fetters. Our limbs were so stiff that we could hardly stand. Our fellow prisoners assisted us below, and wrapping us in blankets, we were at last restored to a state of comparative comfort.

"For attempting to escape we were punished by having our miserable allowance reduced one third in quantity for a month; and we had found the whole of it hardly sufficient to sustain life. * * *

"One day a boat came alongside containing about sixty firkins of grease, which they called butter. The prisoners were always ready to assist in the performance of any labor necessary to be done on board of the ship, as it afforded some little relief to the tedious monotony of their lives. On this occasion they were ready to assist in hoisting the butter on board. The firkins were first deposited upon the deck, and then lowered down the main hatchway. Some of the prisoners, who were the most officious in giving their assistance, contrived to secrete a firkin, by rolling it forward under the forecastle, and afterwards carrying it below in their bedding.

"This was considered as quite a windfall; and being divided among a few of us, proved a considerable luxury. It helped to fill up the pores in our mouldy bread, when the worms were dislodged, and gave to the crumbling particles a little more consistency.

"Several weeks after our unsuccessful attempt to escape, another one attended with better success, was made by a number of the prisoners. At sunset the prisoners were driven below, and the main hatchway was closed. In this there was a trap–door, large enough for a man to pass through, and a sentinel was placed over it with orders to permit one prisoner at a time to come up during the night.

"The plan that had been formed was this:—one of the prisoners should ascend, and dispose of the sentinel in such a manner that he should be no obstacle in the way of those who were to follow.

"Among the soldiers was an Irishman who, in consequence of having a head of hair remarkable for its curly appearance, and withal a very crabbed disposition, had been nicknamed 'Billy the Ram'. He was the sentinel on duty this night, for one was deemed sufficient, as the prisoners were considered secure when they were below, having no other place of egress saving the trap–door, over which the sentinel was stationed.

"Late in the night one of the prisoners, a bold, athletic fellow, ascended upon deck, and in an artful manner engaged the attention of Billy the Ram, in conversation respecting the war; lamenting that he had engaged in so unnatural a contest, expressing his intention of enlisting in the British service, and requesting Billy's advice respecting the course necessary to be pursued to obtain the confidence of the officers.

"Billy happened to be in a mood to take some interest in his views, and showed an inclination, quite uncommon for him, to prolong the conversation. Unsuspicious of any evil design on the part of the prisoner, and while leaning carelessly on his gun, Billy received a tremendous blow from the fist of his entertainer on the back of his head, which brought him to the deck in a state of insensibility.

"As soon as he was heard to fall by those below, who were anxiously awaiting the result of the friendly conversation of their pioneer with Billy, and were satisfied that the final knock−out argument had been given, they began to ascend, and, one after another, to jump overboard, to the number of about thirty.

"The noise aroused the guard, who came upon deck, where they found Billy not sufficiently recovered from the stunning effects of the blow he had received to give any account of the transaction. A noise was heard in the water; but it was so dark that no object could be distinguished. The attention of the guard, however, was directed to certain spots which exhibited a luminous appearance, which salt water is known to assume in the night when it is agitated, and to these appearances they directed their fire, and getting out the boats, picked out about half the number that attempted to escape, many of whom were wounded, though not one was killed. The rest escaped.

"During the uproar overhead the prisoners below encouraged the fugitives, and expressed their approbation of their proceedings in three hearty cheers; for which gratification we suffered our usual punishment—a short allowance of our already short and miserable fare.

"For about a fortnight after this transaction it would have been a hazardous experiment to approach near to 'Billy the Ram', and it was a long time before we ventured to speak to him, and finally to obtain from him an account of the events of the evening.

"Not long after this another successful attempt to escape was made, which for its boldness is perhaps unparalleled in the history of such transactions.

"One pleasant morning about ten o'clock a boat came alongside, containing a number of gentlemen from New York, who came for the purpose of gratifying themselves with a sight of the miserable tenants of the prison−ship, influenced by the same kind of curiosity that induces some people to travel a great distance to witness an execution.

"The boat, which was a beautiful yawl, and sat like a swan upon the water, was manned by four oarsmen, with a man at the helm. Considerable attention and respect was shown the visitors, the ship's side being manned when they showed their intention of coming on board, and the usual naval courtesies extended. The gentlemen were soon on board; and the crew of the yawl, having secured her to the forechains on the larboard side of the ship, were permitted to ascend the deck.

"A soldier as usual was pacing with a slow and measured tread the whole length of the deck, wheeling round with measured precision, when he arrived at the end of his walk; and whether upon this occasion, any one interested in his movements had secretly slipped a guinea into his hand, not to quicken but to retard his progress, was never known; but it was evident to the prisoners that he had never occupied so much time before in measuring the distance with his back to the place where the yawl was fastened.

"At this time there were sitting in the forecastle, apparently admiring the beautiful appearance of the yawl, four mates and a captain, who had been brought on board as prisoners a few days previous, taken in some vessel from a southern port.

"As soon as the sentry had passed these men, in his straightforward march, they, in a very quiet manner, lowered themselves down into the yawl, cut the rope, and the four mates taking in hand the oars, while the captain managed the helm, in less time than I have taken to describe it, they were under full sweep from the ship. They plied the oars with such vigor that every stroke they took seemed to take the boat out of the water. In the meantime the sentry heard nothing and saw nothing of this transaction, till he had arrived at the end of his march, when, in wheeling slowly round, he could no longer affect ignorance, or avoid seeing that the boat was several times its length from the ship. He immediately fired; but, whether he exercised his best skill as a marksman, or whether it was on account of the boat's going ahead its whole length at every pull of the rowers, I could never exactly ascertain, but the ball fell harmlessly into the water. The report of the gun brought the whole guard out, who blazed away at the fugitives, without producing any dimunition in the rapidity of their progress.

"By this time the officers of the ship were on deck with their visitors; and while all were gazing with astonishment at the boldness and effrontery of the achievement, the guard were firing as fast as they could load their guns. When the prisoners gave three cheers to the yawl's crew, as an expression of their joy at their success, the Captain ordered all of us to be driven below at the point of the bayonet, and there we were confined the remainder of the day.

"These five men escaped, greatly to the mortification of the captain and officers of the prison−ship. After this, as long as I remained a prisoner, whenever any visitors came on board, all the prisoners were driven below, where they were obliged to remain till the company had departed."

CHAPTER XXVII. THE EXPERIENCE OF EBENEZER FOX (CONTINUED)

The miseries of our condition were continually increasing. The pestilence on board spread rapidly; and every day added to our bill of mortality. The young were its most frequent victims. The number of the prisoners was constantly augmenting, notwithstanding the frequent and successful attempts to escape. When we were mustered and called upon to answer to our names, and it was ascertained that nearly two hundred had mysteriously disappeared, without leaving any information of their departure, the officers of the ship endeavored to make amends for their past remissness by increasing the rigor of our confinement, and depriving us of all hope of adopting any of the means for liberating ourselves from our cruel thralldom, so successfully practiced by many of our comrades.

"With the hope that some relief might be obtained to meliorate the wretchedness of our situation, the prisoners petitioned General Clinton, commanding the British forces in New York, for permission to send a memorial to General Washington, describing our condition, and requesting his influence in our behalf, that some exchange of prisoners might be effected.

"Permission was obtained, and the memorial was sent. * * * General Washington wrote to Congress, and also to the British Commissary of Naval prisoners, remonstrating with him, deprecating the cruel treatment of the Americans, and threatening retaliation.

"The long detention of American sailors on board of British prison−ships was to be attributed to the little pains taken by our countrymen to retain British subjects who were taken prisoner on the ocean during the war. Our privateers captured many British seamen, who, when willing to enlist in our service, as was generally the case, were received on board of our ships. Those who were brought into port were suffered to go at large; for in the impoverished condition of the country, no state or town was willing to subject itself to the expence of maintaining prisoners in a state of confinement; they were permitted to provide for themselves. In this way the number of British seamen was too small for a regular and equal exchange. Thus the British seamen, after their capture, enjoyed the blessings of liberty, the light of the sun, and the purity of the atmosphere, while the poor American sailors were compelled to drag out a miserable existence amid want and distress, famine and pestilence. As every principle of justice and humanity was disregarded by the British in their treatment of the prisoners, so likewise was every moral and legal right violated in compelling them to enter into their service.

"We had obtained some information in relation to an expected draught that would soon be made upon the prisoners to fill up a complement of men that were wanted for the service of his Majesty's fleet.

"One day in the last part of August our fears for the dreaded event were realized. A British officer with a number of soldiers came on board. The prisoners were all ordered on deck, placed on the larboard gangway, and marched in single file round to the quarter–deck, where the officers stood to inspect them, and select such ones as suited their fancies without any reference to the rights of the prisoners. * * * We continued to march round in solemn and melancholy processsion, till they had selected from among our number about three hundred of the ablest, nearly all of whom were Americans, and they were directed to go below under a guard, to collect together whatever things they wished to take belonging to them. They were then driven into the boats, waiting alongside, and left the prison ship, not to enjoy their freedom, but to be subjected to the iron despotism, and galling slavery of a British man–of–war; to waste their lives in a foreign service; and toil for masters whom they hated. Such, however, were the horrors of our situation as prisoners, and so small was the prospect of relief, that we almost envied the lot of those who left the ship to go into the service of the enemy.

"That the reader may not think I have given an exaggerated account of our sufferings on board the Jersey, I will here introduce some facts related in the histories of the Revolutionary War. I introduce them as an apology for the course that I and many of my fellow citizens adopted to obtain temporary relief from our sufferings.

American Prisoners of the Revolution

"The prisoners captured by Sir William Howe in 1776 amounted to several thousands. *
* * The privates were confined in prisons, deserted churches, and other large open
buildings, entirely unfit for the habitations of human beings, in severe winter weather,
without any of the most ordinary comforts of life.

"To the indelible and everlasting disgrace of the British name, these unfortunate victims
of a barbarity more befitting savages than gentlemen belonging to a nation boasting itself
to be the most enlightened and civilized of the world,—many hundreds of them, perished
from want of proper food and attention.

"The cruelty of their inhuman jailors was not terminated by the death of these wretched
men, as so little care was taken to remove the corpses that seven dead bodies have been
seen at one time lying in one of the buildings in the midst of their living
fellow–prisoners, who were perhaps envying them their release from misery. Their food
* * * was generally that which was rejected by the British ships as unfit to be eaten by the
sailors, and unwholesome in the highest degree, as well as disgusting in taste and
appearance.

"In December, 1776, the American board of war, after procuring such evidence as
convinced them of the truth of their statements, reported that: 'There were 900 privates
and 300 officers of the American army, prisoners in the city of New York, and 500
privates and 50 officers in Philadelphia. That since the beginning of October, all these
officers and privates had been confined in prisons or in the provost. That, from the best
evidence the subject could admit of, the general allowance of the prisoners did not exceed
four ounces of meat a day, and that often so damaged as to be uneatable. That it had been
a common practice of the British to keep their prisoners four or five days without a
morsel of meat and thus tempt them to enlist to save their lives.'

"Many were actually starved to death, in hope of making them enroll themselves in the
British army. The American sailors when captured suffered even more than the soldiers,
for they were confined on board prison ships in great numbers, and in a manner which
showed that the British officers were willing to treat fellow beings, whose only crime was
love of liberty, worse than the vilest animals; and indeed in every respect, with as much
cruelty as is endured by the miserable inhabitants of the worst class of slave ships. * * *
In the course of the war it has been asserted on good evidence, that 11,000 prisoners died
on board the Jersey. * * * These unfortunate beings died in agony in the midst of their

186

fellow sufferers, who were obliged to witness their tortures, without the power of relieving their dying countrymen, even by cooling their parched lips with a drop of cold water, or a breath of fresh air; and, when the last breath had left the emaciated body, they sometimes remained for hours in close contact with the corpse, without room to shrink from companions that Death had made so horrible, and when at last the dead were removed, they were sent in boats to the shore, and so imperfectly buried that long after the war was ended, their bones lay whitening in the sun on the beach of Long Island, a lasting memorial of British cruelty, so entirely unwarranted by all the laws of war or even common humanity.

"They could not even pretend that they were retaliating, for the Americans invariably treated their prisoners with kindness, and as though they were fellow men. All the time that these cruelties were performed those who were deprived of every comfort and necessary were constantly entreated to leave the American service, and induced to believe, while kept from all knowledge of public affairs, that the republican cause was hopeless; that all engaged in it would meet the punishment of traitors to the king, and that all their prospect of saving their lives, or escaping from an imprisonment worse than death to young and high–spirited men, as most of them were, would be in joining the British army, where they would be sure of good pay and quick promotion.

"These were the means employed by our enemies to increase their own forces, and discourage the patriots, and it is not strange they were successful in many instances. High sentiments of honor could not well exist in the poor, half–famished prisoners, who were denied even water to quench their thirst, or the privilege of breathing fresh, pure air, and cramped, day after day, in a space too small to admit of exercising their weary limbs, with the fear of wasting their lives in a captivity, which could not serve their country, nor gain honor to themselves.

"But worse than all was the mortifying consideration that, after they had suffered for the love of their country, more than sailors in active service, they might die in these horrible places, and be laid with their countrymen on the shores of Long Island, or some equally exposed spot, without the rites of burial, and their names never be heard of by those who, in future ages, would look back to the roll of patriots, who died in defence of liberty, with admiration and respect, while, on the contrary, by dissembling for a time, they might be able to regain a place in the service so dear to them, and in which they were ready to endure any hardship or encounter any danger.

American Prisoners of the Revolution

"Of all the prisons, on land or water, for the confinement of the Americans, during the Revolutionary War, the Old Jersey was acknowledged to be the worst; such an accumulation of horrors was not to be found in any other one, or perhaps in all collectively.

"The very name of it struck terror into the sailor's heart, and caused him to fight more desperately, to avoid being made a captive. Suffering as we did, day after day, with no prospect of relief, our numbers continually augmenting, * * * can it be thought strange that the younger part of the prisoners, to whom confinement seemed worse than death, should be tempted to enlist into the British service; especially when, by so doing, it was probable that some opportunity would be offered to desert? We were satisfied that death would soon put an end to our sufferings if we remained prisoners much longer, yet when we discussed the expediency of seeking a change in our condition, which we were satisfied could not be worse under any circumstances, and it was proposed that we should enter the service of King George, our minds revolted at the idea, and we abandoned the intention.

"In the midst of our distresses, perplexities, and troubles of this period, we were not a little puzzled to know how to dispose of the vermin that would accumulate upon our persons, notwithstanding all our attempts at cleanliness. To catch them was a very easy task, but to undertake to deprive each individual captive of life, as rapidly as they could have been taken, would have been a more herculean task for each individual daily, than the destruction of 3000 Philistines by Sampson of old. To throw them overboard would have been but a small relief, as they would probably add to the impurities of the boiler, by being deposited in it the first time it was filled up for cooking our unsavory mess. What then was to be done with them? A general consultation was held, and it was determined to deprive them of their liberty. This being agreed upon, the prisoners immediately went to work, for their comfort and amusement, to make a liberal contribution of those migratory creatures, who were compelled to colonize for a time within the boundaries of a large snuff box appropriated for the purpose. There they lay, snugly ensconced, of all colors, ages, and sizes, to the amount of some hundreds, waiting for orders.

"British recruiting officers frequently came on board, and held out to the prisoners tempting offers to enlist in his Majesty's service; not to fight against their own country, but to perform garrison duty in the island of Jamaica.

"One day an Irish officer came on board for this purpose, and not meeting with much success among the prisoners who happened to be on deck, he descended below to repeat his offers. He was a remarkably tall man, and was obliged to stoop as he passed along between decks. The prisoners were disposed for a frolic, and kept the officer in their company for some time, flattering him with expectations, till he discovered their insincerity, and left them in no very pleasant humor. As he passed along, bending his body and bringing his broad shoulders to nearly a horizontal position, the idea occurred to our minds to furnish him with some recruits from the colony in the snuff box. A favorable opportunity presented, the cover of the box was removed, and the whole contents discharged upon the red-coated back of the officer. Three cheers from the prisoners followed the migration, and the officer ascended to the deck, unconscious of the number and variety of the recruits he had obtained without the formality of an enlistment. The captain of the ship, suspecting that some joke had been practised, or some mischief perpetrated, from the noise below, met the officer at the head of the gangway, and seeing the vermin crawling up his shoulders, and aiming at his head, with the instinct peculiar to them, exclaimed, 'Hoot mon! what's the maitter wi' your back!' * * * By this time many of them in their wanderings, had travelled from the rear to the front, and showed themselves, to the astonishment of the officer. He flung off his coat, in a paroxysm of rage, which was not allayed by three cheers from the prisoners on deck. Confinement below, with a short allowance, was our punishment for this gratification.

"From some information we had obtained we were in daily expectation of a visit from the British recruiting officers, and from the summary method of their procedure, no one felt safe from the danger of being forced into their service. Many of the prisoners thought it would be better to enlist voluntarily, as it was probable that afterwards they would be permitted to remain on Long Island, preparatory to their departure to the West Indies, and during that time some opportunity would be offered for their escape to the Jersey shore. * * * Soon after we had formed this desperate resolve a recruiting officer came on board to enlist men for the 88th Regiment to be stationed at Kingston, in the island of Jamaica. * * * The recruiting officer presented his papers for our signature. We hesitated, we stared at each other, and felt we were about to do a deed of which we were ashamed, and which we might regret. Again we heard the tempting offers, and again the assurance that we should not be called upon to fight against our government or country, and with the hope that we should find an opportunity to desert, of which it was our firm intention to avail ourselves when offered,—with such hopes, expectations, and motives, we signed the papers, and became soldiers in his Majesty's service,

"How often did we afterwards lament that we had ever lived to see this hour? How often did we regret that we were not in our wretched prison ship again, or buried in the sand at the Wallabout!"

There were twelve of the prisoners who left the Jersey with Ebenezer Fox. They were at first taken to Long Island and lodged in barns, but so vigilantly were they guarded that they found it impossible to escape. They were all sent to Kingston, and Fox was allowed to resume his occupation as a barber, much patronized by the officers stationed at that post. He was soon allowed the freedom of the city, and furnished with a pass to go about it as much as he wished. At last, in company with four other Americans, he escaped, and after many adventures the party succeeded in reaching Cuba, by means of a small sailing boat which they pressed into service for that purpose. From Cuba they took passage in a small vessel for St. Domingo, and dropped anchor at Cape Francois, afterwards called Cape Henri. There they went on board the American frigate, Flora, of 32 guns, commanded by Captain Henry Johnson, of Boston.

The vessel soon sailed for France and took several prizes. It finally went up the Garonne to Bordeaux, where it remained nine months. In the harbor of Bordeaux were about six hundred vessels bearing the flags of various nations. Here they remained until peace was proclaimed, when Fox procured service on board an American brig lying at Nantes, and set sail for home in April, 1783.

At length he again reached his mother's house at Roxbury, after an absence of about three years. His mother, at first, did not recognize him. She entertained him as a stranger, until he made himself known, and then her joy was great, for she had long mourned him as lost.

CHAPTER XXVIII. THE CASE OF CHRISTOPHER HAWKINS

Christopher Hawkins was born in Providence, Rhode Island, in 1764. When he was in his thirteenth year he sailed on board an American privateer as a cabin boy. The privateer was a schooner, called the Eagle, commanded by Captain Potter. Taken prisoner by the British, Hawkins was sent on board the Asia, an old transport ship, but was soon taken off this vessel, then used for the confinement of American prisoners, and sent on board a frigate, the Maidstone, to serve as a waiter to the British officers on board. He remained on board the Maidstone a year. At the end of that time he was allowed a good deal of liberty. He and another boy were sent on shore to New York with a message, managed to elude the sentinels, and escaped first to Long Island, and afterwards returned home to Providence.

About 1781 he again went on board a privateer under Captain Whipple, was again captured, and this time he was sent to the Jersey. He describes the condition of the prisoners on their way in a transport to this fearful prison ship. They were so crowded together that they could scarcely move, yet they all joined in singing a patriotic song every stanza of which ended with the words:

"For America and all her sons forever will shine!"

They were on board this transport three or four days unable to sit or lie down for want of room. When at last they reached the Jersey they found 800 prisoners on board. Many of these poor wretches would become sick in the night and die before day. Hawkins was obliged to lie down to rest only twenty feet from the gangway, and in the path of the prisoners who would run over him to get on the upper deck. He describes the condition of these men as appalling.

"Near us," he writes, "was a guard ship and hospital ship, and along the shore a line of sentinels at regular intervals."

Yet he determined to escape. Many did so; and many were murdered in the attempt. A mess of six had just met a dreadful fate. One of them became terrified and exclaimed as soon as he touched the water, "O Lord, I shall be drowned!" The guard turned out, and murdered five of the poor wretches. The sixth managed to hide, and held on by the flukes of the anchor with nothing but his nose above water. Early in the morning he climbed up the anchor over the bow of the ship to the forecastle, and fled below. A boy named Waterman and Hawkins determined to drop through a port–hole, and endeavor to reach Long Island by swimming. He thus describes the adventure:

"The thunder–storm was opportune to our design, for having previously obtained from the cook's room an old axe and crow–bar from the upper deck for the purpose, we concealed them till an opportunity should offer for their use. We took advantage of the peals of thunder in a storm that came over us in the afternoon to break one of the gun ports on the lower deck, which was strongly barred with iron and bolts. * * * When a peal of thunder roared we worked with all our might with the axe and crow–bar against the bars and bolts. When the peals subsided we ceased, without our blows being heard by the British, until another peal commenced. We then went to work again, and so on, until our work was completed to our liking. The bars and bolts, after we had knocked them loose, were replaced so as not to draw the attention of our British gentry if they should happen to visit the lower deck before our departure. We also hung some old apparel over and around the shattered gunport to conceal any marks.

"Being thus and otherwise prepared for our escape, the ship was visited by our Captain Whipple the next day after we had broken the gun–port. To him we communicated our intention and contemplated means of escape. He strongly remonstrated against the design. We told him we should start the ensuing evening. Captain Whipple answered:

"'How do you think of escaping?'

"I answered, 'By swimming to that point,' at the same time pointing to a place then in our view on Long Island, in a northeasterly direction from the prison ship. We must do this to avoid the sentinels who were stationed in the neighborhood of the ship.

"'What!' said Captain Whipple, 'Do you think of swimming to that point?'

"'Yes, we must, to avoid the sentinels,' I answered.

"'Well,' said Captain Whipple, 'Give it up, It is only throwing your lives away, for there is not a man on earth who can swim from this ship to that point as cold as the water is now. Why, how far do you think it is?'

"'Why,' I answered, 'Waterman and myself have estimated the distance at a mile and a half.'

"'Yes,' said he, 'It's all of two and a half miles. You cannot measure across as well as I can. So you had better give it up, for I have encouragement of getting home next week, and if I do, I will make it my whole business to get you all exchanged immediately.'

"Altho' Waterman was several years my senior in age, the conversation was carried on between Captain Whipple and myself for the reason that Captain W. was more acquainted with me than with Waterman, but Waterman was present." (Captain Whipple was captured five times during the Revolution, each time on his own vessel.)

"His advice had great weight on our minds, but did not shake our purpose. We had not been on board the Old Jersey more than one hour before we began to plot our escape. We had been only three days on board when we left it forever. We had been on board long enough to discover the awful scenes which took place daily in this 'floating hell.'

"Our preparations for leaving were completed by procuring a piece of rope from an old cable that was stretched under the fo'castle of the ship, * * * and wound around the cable to preserve it. We had each of us packed our wearing apparel in a knapsack for each, made on board the Old Jersey. I gave some of my apparel to the two Smiths. I stowed in my knapsack a thick woolen sailor jacket, well lined, a pair of thick pantaloons, one vest, a pair of heavy silver shoe buckles, two silk handkerchiefs, four silver dollars, not forgetting a junk bottle of rum, which we had purchased on board at a dear rate. Waterman had stowed his apparel and other articles in his knapsack. Mine was very heavy. It was fastened to my back with two very strong garters, passing over my shoulders, and under each arm, and fastened with a string to my breast, bringing my right and left garter in contact near the centre.

"Thus equipt we were ready to commit ourselves to the watery element, and to our graves, as many of our hardy fellow prisoners predicted. The evening was as good an one as we could desire at that season of the year, the weather was mild and hazy, and the night extremely dark.

"It was arranged between Waterman and myself that after leaving the ship we should be governed in our course by the lights on board the ships and the responses of the sentinels on shore, and after arriving on shore to repair near a dwelling house which we could see from the Old Jersey in the day time, and spend the balance of the night in a barn, but a few rods from the dwelling.

"Waterman was the first to leave the ship through the broken—open gun—port, and suspended to the rope by his hands, and at the end behind him (it was held) by several of our fellow prisoners whom we were leaving behind us, and with whom we affectionately parted with reciprocal good wishes. He succeeded in gaining the water and in leaving the ship without discovery from the British. It had been agreed, if detection was about to take place, that he should be received again into the ship. I had agreed to follow him in one minute in the same manner. I left and followed in half that time, and succeeded in leaving the ship without giving the least alarm to those who had held us in captivity.

"I kept along close to the side of the ship until I gained the stern, and then left the ship. This was all done very slowly, sinking my body as deep in the water as possible, without stopping my course, until I was at such a distance from her that my motions in the water would not create attention from those on board. After gaining a suitable distance from the ship, I hailed Waterman three times. He did not answer me. * * * I have never seen him since he left the Old Jersey to this day. His fate and success I have since learned from James Waterman, one of his brothers.

"In the meantime I kept on my course without thinking that any accident would befall him, as I knew him to be an excellent swimmer, and no fainthearted or timid fellow.

"I could take my course very well from the light reflected from the stern lanthorns of the prison, guards, and hospital ships, and also from the responses of the sentinels on shore; in the words, 'All's well.' These responses were repeated every half hour on board the guard ship, and by the sentinels. * * * These repetitions served me to keep the time I was employed in reaching the shore;—no object occupied my mind during this time so much as my friend Waterman, if I may except my own success in getting to land in safety.

"I flattered myself I should find him on shore or at the barn we had agreed to occupy after we might gain it. After I had been swimming nearly or quite two hours my knapsack had broken loose from my back, from the wearing off of the garters under my arms, in consequence of the friction in swimming. * * * This occurrence did not please me much. I endeavored to retain my knapsack by putting it under one arm, * * * but soon found that this impeded my progress, and led me from my true course. * * * By this time I had become much chilled, and benumbed from cold, but could swim tolerably well. * * * I hesitated whether or not to retain my knapsack longer in my possession, or part from it forever, I soon determined on the latter, and sent it adrift. In this balancing state of mind and subsequent decision I was cool and self collected as perhaps at any time in my life. * * * I now soon found I was close in with the shore. * * * I swam within twelve feet of the shore before I could touch bottom, and in so doing I found I could not stand, I was so cold * * * but I moved around in shoal water until I found I could stand, then stept on shore. * * * I had not sent my clothes adrift more than twenty–five minutes or so before striking the shore. I was completely naked except for a small hat on my head which I had brought from the Old Jersey. What a situation was this, without covering to hide my naked body, in an enemy's country, without food or means to obtain any, and among Tories more unrelenting than the devil,—more perils to encounter and nothing to aid me but the interposition of heaven! Yet I had gained an important portion of my enterprise: I had got on land, after swimming in the water two hours and a half, and a distance of perhaps two miles and a half."

Hawkins at last found the barn and slept in it the rest of the night, but not before falling over a rock in the darkness, and bruising his naked body severely. Next morning a black girl came into the barn, apparently hunting for eggs, but he did not dare reveal himself to her. He remained there all day, and endeavored to milk the cows, but they were afraid of a naked stranger. He left the place in the night and travelled east. In a field he found some overripe water melons, but they were neither wholesome nor palatable. After wandering a long time in the rain he came to another barn, and in it he slept soundly until late the next day. Nearly famished he again wandered on and found in an orchard a few half rotten pears. Near by was a potato patch which he entered hoping to get some of them. Here a young woman, who had been stooping down digging potatoes, started up. "I was, of course," he continues, "naked, my head excepted. She was, or appeared to be, excessively frightened, and ran towards a house, screeching and screaming at every step." Hawkins ran in the other direction, and got safely away. At last the poor boy found another barn, and lay, that night, upon a heap of flax. After sunrise next morning he concluded to go on his way. "I could see the farmers at their labor in the fields. I then concluded to still keep on my course, and go to some of these people then in sight. I was, by this time, almost worn out with hunger. I slowly approached two tall young men who were gathering garden sauce. They soon discovered me and appeared astonished at my appearance, and began to draw away from me, but I spoke to them in the following words:—'Don't be afraid of me: I am a human being!' They then made a halt and inquired of me, 'Are you scared?' 'No,' said I. They then advanced slowly towards me, and inquired, 'How came you here naked?'

"I seated myself on the ground and told them the truth."

One of the young men told him to conceal himself from the sight of the neighbors, and he would go and consult with his mother what had best be done. He soon returned, bringing two large pieces of bread and butter and a decent pair of pantaloons. He then told him to go to the side of the barn and wait there for his mother, but not to allow himself to be seen. The boys' mother came out to speak to him with a shirt on her arm. As he incautiously moved around the side of the barn to meet her, she exclaimed, "For God's sake don't let that black woman see you!" A slave was washing clothes near the back door of the farm house. The poor woman explained to Hawkins that this negress would betray him, "For she is as big a devil as any of the king's folks, and she will bring me out, and then we should all be put in the provost and die there, for my husband was put there more than two years ago, and rotted and died there not more than two weeks since."

The poor woman wept as she told her story, and the escaped prisoner wept with her. This woman and her two sons were Dutch, and their house was only nine miles from Brooklyn ferry. She now directed the boy to a house at Oyster Bay where she said there was a man who would assist him to escape.

After running many risks he found the house at last, but the woman who answered his knock told him that her husband was away and when he explained who he was she became very angry, and said that it was her duty to give him up. So he ran away from her, and at last fell into the hands of a party of British, who recaptured him, and declared that they would send him immediately back to the prison ship. They were quartered in a house near Oyster Bay, and here they locked him in a room, and he was told to lie down on some straw to sleep, as it was now night. In the night the fleas troubled him so much that he was very restless. A sentinel had been placed to guard him, and when this wretch heard him moving in the dark he exclaimed, "Lie still, G—d—– you," and pricked him several times with his bayonet, so that the poor boy felt the fresh blood running down his body. He begged the sentinel to spare his life, declaring that it was hard he should be killed merely because the fleas had made him restless. He now did not dare to move, and was obliged to endure the attacks the fleas and the stiffness of his wounds in perfect silence until the sentinel was relieved. The next sentinel was kind and humane and seemed to compassionate his sufferings. He said that some men were natural brutes, and seemed to take an interest in the boy, but could do little for him. At daylight he was sent to the quarters of a Tory colonel a mile from the guard room. The colonel was a tall man of fine appearance, who examined him, and then said he must be sent back to the Jersey. The poor lad was now left in an unlocked room on the ground floor of the colonel's house. He was given his breakfast, and a mulatto man was set to guard him. Now there was a pantry opening into this room, and a negro girl, who appeared very friendly with the mulatto, called him to eat his breakfast in this pantry. The mulatto, while eating, would look out every few minutes. Just after one of these inspections the boy got up softly, with his shoes in his hands, stepped across the room, out at the back door, and concealed himself in a patch of standing hemp. From thence he made his way into an orchard, and out into a wood lot. Here he hid himself and remained quiet for several hours, and although he heard several persons talking near him, he was not pursued. At last he stole out, walked about six miles, and at night fall entered a barn and slept there. He was in rather better case than before his recapture, for a doctor belonging to the British service had taken pity on him the night before, and had furnished him with warm clothes, shoes, and a little money.

Next morning a woman who lived in a small house near the road gave him some bread and milk. The time of the year was autumn, it was a day or two before Cornwallis's surrender at Yorktown. He now very fortunately met an acquaintance named Captain Daniel Havens. He was an uncle of a boy named John Sawyer, with whom young Hawkins had run away from New York some years before. Through the agency of this old friend Hawkins got on board a smuggler in the night and finally reached home in safety.

Christopher Hawkins's account of the Old Jersey is not so reliable as that of some others who were among her inmates. He was only on board that vessel three days, but in that time he saw enough to decide him to risk death in the attempt to escape rather than remain any longer on board of her. He declares that: "The cruel and unjustifiable treatment of the prisoners by the British soon produced the most demoralizing effects upon them. Boxing was tolerated without stint.... After I left the ship an American vessel came into the port of New York as a cartel for the exchange of prisoners.... A ship's mate was so fortunate as to be one of the exchanged. He had a large chest on board, and, as privately as he could, he put the cabin boy into the chest, locked him in, and carried him on board the cartel. A prisoner named Spicer had seen the boy put into the chest, and after he had been conveyed on board the cartel, Spicer communicated the affair to the commanding officer on board the Jersey. The cartel was immediately boarded, as she had not yet left the port, and the boy was found and brought back. Spicer paid for his treachery with his life. The prisoners knocked him down the hatchway, when they were going down for the night; they then fell upon him, cut off his ears, and mangled him in a shocking manner, so that he died in a day or two."

This event occured after he left the ship, according to his own narrative. The same story is told in a different way by an eye witness of undoubted veracity. He says that the prisoners were so incensed against Spicer that they determined to kill him. For this purpose some of them held him, while another was about to cut his throat, when the guards, hearing the uproar, rushed down the hatchway, and rescued him.

Hawkins also says: "I one day observed a prisoner on the forecastle of the ship, with his shirt in his hands, having stripped it from his body, deliberately picking the vermin from the pleats and putting them in his mouth. * * * I stepped very near the man and commenced a conversation with him. He said he had been on board two years and a half, or eighteen months. He had completely lost count of time, was a skeleton and nearly naked. This was only one case from perhaps a hundred similar. This man appeared in tolerable health as to body, his emaciation excepted. * * * The discipline of the prisoners by the British was in many respects of the most shocking and appalling character. The roll of the prisoners, as I was informed, was called every three months, unless a large acquisiton of prisoners should render it necessary more often. The next day after our crew were put on board the roll was called, and the police regulations of the ship were read. I heard this. One of the new regulations was to the effect that every captive trying to get away should suffer instant death, and should not even be taken on board alive."

It appears that David Laird commanded the Old Jersey from 1778 until early in the year 1781. He was then relieved of the command, and this office was given to a man named John Sporne, or Spohn, until the 9th of April, 1783, when all the prisoners remaining in her were released, and she was abandoned. The dread of contagion kept visitors aloof. She was still moored in the mud of the Wallabout by chain cables, and gradually sank lower and lower. There is a beam of her preserved as a curiosity at the Naval Museum at Brooklyn.

David Laird, the Scotchman who commanded her until the early part of 1781, returned to New York after the peace of 1783 as captain of a merchant ship, and moored his vessel at or near Peck's Slip. A number of persons who had been prisoners on board the Jersey, and had suffered by his cruelty, assembled on the wharf to receive him, but he deemed it prudent to remain on ship–board during the short time his vessel was there.

It is in the recollections of Ebenezer Fox that we have the only mention ever made of a woman on board that dreadful place, the Old Jersey, and although she may have been and probably was an abandoned character, yet she seems to have been merciful, and unwilling to see the prisoners who were attempting to escape, butchered before her eyes. It is indeed to be hoped that no other woman ever set foot in that terrible place to suffer with the prisoners, and yet there are a few women's names in the list of these wretched creatures given in the appendix to this book. It is most likely, however, that these were men, and that their feminine appellations were nicknames. [Footnote: One is named Nancy and one Bella, etc.]

CHAPTER XXIX. TESTIMONY OF PRISONERS ON BOARD THE JERSEY

We must again quote from Ebenezer Fox, whose description of the provisions dealt out to the prisoners on board the prison ships shall now be given.

"The prisoners received their mess rations at nine in the morning. * * * All our food appeared to be damaged. The bread was mostly mouldy, and filled with worms. It required considerable rapping upon the deck, before these worms could be dislodged from their lurking places in a biscuit. As for the pork, we were cheated out of it more than half the time, and when it was obtained one would have judged from its motley hues, exhibiting the consistence and appearance of variegated soap, that it was the flesh of the porpoise or sea hog, and had been an inhabitant of the ocean, rather than a sty. * * * The flavor was so unsavory that it would have been rejected as unfit for the stuffing of even Bologna sausages. The provisions were generally damaged, and from the imperfect manner in which they were cooked were about as indigestible as grape shot. The flour and oatmeal was often sour, and when the suet was mixed with the flour it might be nosed half the length of the ship. The first view of the beef would excite an idea of veneration for its antiquity, * * * its color was a dark mahogany, and its solidity would have set the keenest edge of a broad axe at defiance to cut across the grain, though like oakum it could be pulled to pieces, one way, in strings, like rope yarn. * * * It was so completely saturated with salt that after having been boiled in water taken from the sea, it was found to be considerably freshened by the process. * * * Such was our food, but the quality was not all of which we had to complain. * * * The cooking was done in a great copper vessel. * * * The Jersey, from her size, and lying near the shore, was embedded in the mud, and I don't recollect seeing her afloat the whole time I was a prisoner. All the filth that accumulated among upwards of a thousand men was daily thrown overboard, and would remain there until carried away by the tide. The impurity of the water may be easily conceived, and in that water our meat was boiled. It will be recollected, too, that the water was salt, which caused the inside of the copper to be corroded to such a degree that it was lined with a coat of verdigris. Meat thus cooked must, in some degree, be poisoned, and the effects of it were manifest in the cadaverous countenances of the emaciated beings who had remained on board for any length of time.

"* * * We passed the night amid the accumulated horrors of sighs and groans; of foul vapor; a nauseous and putrid atmosphere, in a stifling and almost suffocating heat. * * * Little sleep could be enjoyed, for the vermin were so horribly abundant that all the personal cleanliness we could practice would not protect us from their attacks."

The public papers of the day often contained accounts of the cruelties practiced upon the prisoners on the ships. In the *Pennsylvania Packet* of Sept. 4th, 1781, there is an extract from a letter written by a prisoner whose name is not given.

"EXTRACT FROM A LETTER DATED ON BOARD THE JERSEY (VULGARLY CALLED HELL) PRISON SHIP

"New York August 10th 1781

"There is nothing but death or entering into the British service before me. Our ship's company is reduced by death and entering into the British service to the small number of 19. * * * I am not able to give you even the outlines of my exile; but this much I will inform you, that we bury 6, 7, 8, 9, 10, and 11 in a day. We have 200 more sick and falling sick every day; the sickness is the yellow fever, small pox, and in short everything else that can be mentioned."

"New London. Conn. March 3rd. 1782. Sunday last a flag ship returned from New York which brought twenty Americans who had been a long time on board a prison ship. About 1,000 of our countrymen remain in the prison ships at New York, great part of whom have been in close confinement for more than six months, and in the most deplorable condition: many of them seeing no prospect of release are entering into the British service to elude the contagion with which the ships are fraught."

EXTRACT OF A LETTER WRITTEN ON BOARD THE PRISON SHIP JERSEY, APRIL 26TH, 1782.

"I am sorry to write you from this miserable place. I can assure you that since I have been here we have had only twenty men exchanged, although we are in number upwards of 700, exclusive of the sick in the Hospital ships, who died like sheep; therefore my intention is, if possible, to enter on board some merchant or transport vessel, as it is impossible for so many men to keep alive in one vessel."

"Providence. May 25th 1782. Sunday last a flag of truce returned here from New York and brought a few prisoners. We learn that 1100 Americans were on board the prison and hospital ships at New York, when the flag sailed from thence, and that from six to seven were generally buried every day."

"Salem. Mass. Extract from a letter of an officer on board the Jersey.—'The deplorable situation I am in cannot be expressed. The captains, lieutenants, and sailing masters have gone to the Provost, but they have only gotten out of the frying pan into the fire. I am left here with about 700 miserable objects, eaten up by lice, and daily taking fevers, which carry them off fast. Nov 9th 1782."

By repeated acts of cruelty on the part of the British the Americans were, at last, stung to attempt something like retaliation. In 1782 a prison ship, given that name, was fitted up and stationed in the Thames near New London, as we learn from the following extract:

"New London, Conn. May 24th 1782. Last Saturday the Retaliation prison ship was safely moored in the river Thames, about a mile from the ferry, for the receipt of such British prisoners as may fall into our hands, since which about 100 prisoners have been put on board."

It is said that this ship was in use but a short time, and we have been unable to learn anything further of her history.

Thomas Philbrook, who was a prisoner on board the Jersey for several months was one of the "working–party," whose duty it was to scrub the decks, attend to the sick, and bring up the dead. He says: "As the morning dawned there would be heard the loud, unfeeling, and horrid cry, 'Rebels! Bring up your dead!'

"Staggering under the weight of some stark, still form, I would at length gain the upper deck, when I would be met with the salutation: 'What! *you alive yet?* Well, you are a tough one!'"

CHAPTER XXX. RECOLLECTIONS OF ANDREW SHERBURNE

Andrew Sherburne, a lad of seventeen, shipped on the Scorpion, Captain R. Salter, a small vessel, with a crew of eighteen men. This vessel was captured by the Amphion, about the middle of November, 1782. Sherburne says that the sailors plundered them of everything they possessed, and that thirteen of them were put on board the Amphion, and sent down to the cable tiers between the two decks, where they found nearly a hundred of their countrymen, who were prisoners of war.

"We were very much crowded, and having nothing but the cables to lay on, our beds were as hard and unpleasant as though they were made of cord wood, and indeed we had not sufficient room for each to stretch himself at the same time.

"After about two weeks we arrived at New York, and were put on board that wretched ship the Jersey. The New York prison ships had been the terror of American tars for years. The Old Jersey had become notorious in consequence of the unparallelled mortality on board her. * * *

"I entered the Jersey towards the last of November, I had just entered the eighteenth year of my age, and had now to commence a scene of suffering almost without a parallel. * * * A large proportion of the prisoners had been robbed of their clothing. * * * Early in the winter the British took the Chesapeake frigate of about thirty guns, and 300 hands. All were sent on board the Jersey, which so overcrowded her, that she was very sickly. This crew died exceedingly fast, for a large proportion were fresh hands, unused to the sea."

Sherburne says that boats from the city brought provisions to sell to such of the prisoners as were so fortunate as to be possessed of money, and that most of them were able to make purchases from them. A piece of sausage from seven to nine inches long sold for sixpence.

In January, 1783, Sherburne became ill and was sent to the Frederick, a hospital ship. In this two men shared every bunk, and the conditions were wretchedly unsanitary. He was placed in a bunk with a man named Wills from Massachusetts, a very gentle and patient sufferer, who soon died.

"I have seen seven men drawn out and piled together on the lower hatchway, who had died in one night on board the Frederick.

"There were ten or twelve nurses, and about a hundred sick. Some, if not all of the nurses, were prisoners. * * * They would indulge in playing cards and drinking, while their fellows were thirsting for water and some dying. At night the hatches were shut down and locked, and the nurses lived in the steerage, and there was not the least attention paid to the sick except by the convalescent, who were so frequently called upon that, in many cases, they overdid themselves, relapsed, and died."

Sherburne suffered extremely from the cold. "I have often," he says "toiled the greatest part of the night, in rubbing my feet and legs to keep them from freezing. * * * In consequence of these chills I have been obliged to wear a laced stocking upon my left leg for nearly thirty years past. My bunk was directly against the ballast–port; and the port not being caulked, when there came a snow–storm the snow would blow through the seams in my bed, but in those cases there was one advantage to me, when I could not otherwise procure water to quench my thirst. The provision allowed the sick was a gill of wine, and twelve ounces of bread per day. The wine was of an ordinary quality, and the bread made of sour or musty flour, and sometimes poorly baked. There was a small sheet iron stove between decks, but the fuel was green, and not plenty, and there were some peevish and surly fellows generally about it. I never got an opportunity to sit by it, but I could generally get the favor of some one near it to lay a slice of bread upon it, to warm or toast it a little, to put into my wine and water. We sometimes failed in getting our wine for several days together; we had the promise of its being made up to us, but this promise was seldom performed. * * * Water was brought on board in casks by the working party, and when it was very cold it would freeze in the casks, and it would be difficult to get it out. * * * I was frequently under the necessity of pleading hard to get my cup filled. I could not eat my bread, but gave it to those who brought me water. I have given three days allowance to have a tin cup of water brought me. * * * A company of the good citizens of New York supplied all the sick with a pint of good Bohea tea, well sweetened with molasses a day; and this was constant. I believe this tea saved my life, and the lives of hundreds of others. * * * The physicians used to visit the sick once in several days: their stay was short, nor did they administer much medicine. Were I able to give a full description of our wretched and filthy condition I should almost question whether it would be credited. * * * It was God's good pleasure to raise me up once more so that I could just make out to walk, and I was again returned to the Jersey prison ship."

Here he received sad news. One of his uncles was a prisoner on board the Jersey, and had been very kind to him, giving him a share of his money with which to purchase necessaries. Now he found his uncle about to take his place in the hospital ship. A boy named Stephen Nichols also informed him of the death in his absence of the gunner of their ship, whose name was Daniel Davis. This poor man had his feet and legs frozen, from which he died.

"Nichols and myself were quite attached to each other. * * * We stalked about the decks together, lamenting our forlorn condition. In a few days there came orders to remove all the prisoners from the Jersey in order to cleanse the ship. We were removed on board of transports, and directly there came on a heavy storm. The ship on which I was was exceedingly crowded, so that there was not room enough for each man to lay down under deck, and the passing and repassing by day had made the lower deck entirely wet. Our condition was distressing. After a few days we were all put on board the Jersey again. A large number had taken violent colds, myself among the rest. The hospital ships were soon crowded, and even the Jersey herself shortly became about as much of a hospital ship as the others."

Sherburne was again sent to a hospital ship, where he was rejoiced to find his uncle convalescing. A man who lay next him had been a nurse, but had had his feet and legs frozen, the toes and bottom of his feet fell off.

Two brothers shared a bunk near him. Their names were John and Abraham Falls. John was twenty–three, and Abraham only sixteen. Both were very sick. One night Abraham was heard imploring John not to lie on him, and the other invalids reproached him for his cruelty in thus treating his young brother. But John was deaf to their reproaches, for he was dead. Abraham was too ill to move from under him. Next day the dead brother was removed from the living one, but it was too late to save him, and the poor boy died that morning.

Sherburne says that only five of his crew of thirteen survived, and that in many instances a much larger proportion died.

"At length came news of peace. It was exceedingly trying to our feelings to see our ship mates daily leaving us, until our ship was almost deserted. We were, however, convalescent, but we gained exceedingly slowly. * * * I think there were but seven or eight left on board the hospital ship when we left it, in a small schooner sent from R. I., for the purpose of taking home some who belonged to that place, and the commander of the hospital ship had the humanity to use his influence with the master of the cartel to take us on board, and to our unspeakable joy he consented."

When at last he reached home he says: "My brother Sam took me into another room to divest me of my filthy garments and to wash and dress me. He having taken off my clothes and seen my bones projecting here and there, was so astonished that his strength left him. He sat down on the point of fainting, and could render me no further service. I was able to wash myself and put on my clothes."

After this he was obliged to spend twenty days in bed. Poor Mrs. Falls, the mother of the two young men who had died on the hospital ship, called on him and heard the fate of her sons. She was in an agony, and almost fainted, and kept asking if it was not a mistake that *both* were dead.

CHAPTER XXXI. CAPTAIN ROSWELL PALMER

In the year 1865 a son of Captain Roswell Palmer, of Connecticut, wrote a letter to Mr. Henry Drowne, in which he narrates the story of his father's captivity, which we will condense in these pages. He says that his father was born in Stonington, Conn., in August, 1764, and was about seventeen at the time of his capture by the British, which must have been in 1781.

Palmer had several relations in the army, and was anxious to enlist, but was rejected as too young. His uncle, however, received him as an assistant in the Commissary Department, and when the brig Pilgrim, of Stonington, was commissioned to make war on the public enemy, the rejected volunteer was warmly welcomed on board by his kinsman, Captain Humphrey Crary.

American Prisoners of the Revolution

The first night after putting to sea, the Pilgrim encountered a British fleet just entering the Vineyard Sound. A chase and running fight of several hours ensued, but at length the vessel was crippled and compelled to surrender. The prize was taken into Holmes' Hole, and the crew subsequently brought to New York. Mr. Henry Palmer thus describes the Jersey, which was his father's destination.

"The Jersey never left her anchorage at the Wallabout, whether from decrepitude, or the intolerable burden of woes and wrongs accumulated in her wretched hulk,—but sank slowly down at last into the subjacent ooze, as if to hide her shame from human sight, and more than forty years after my father pointed out to me at low tide huge remnants of her unburied skeleton.

"On board of this dread Bastile were crowded year after year, some 1,400 prisoners, mostly Americans. The discipline was very strict, while the smallest possible attention was paid by their warders to the sufferings of the captives. Cleanliness was simply an impossibility, where the quarters were so narrow, the occupants so numerous, and little opportunity afforded for washing the person or the tatters that sought to hide its nakedness. Fortunate was the wretch who possessed a clean linen rag, for this, placed in his bosom, seemed to attract to it crowds of his crawling tormentors, whose squatter sovereignty could be disposed of by the wholesale at his pleasure.

"The food of the prisoners consisted mainly of spoiled sea biscuit, and of navy beef, which had become worthless from long voyaging in many climes years before. These biscuits were so worm−eaten that a slight pressure of the hand reduced them to dust, which rose up in little clouds of insubstantial aliment, as if in mockery of the half famished expectants. For variety a ration called 'Burgoo,' was prepared several times a week, consisting of mouldy oatmeal and water, boiled in two great Coppers, and served out in tubs, like swill to swine.

"By degrees they grew callous to each other's miseries, and alert to seize any advantage over their fellow sufferers. Many played cards day and night, regardless of the scenes of woe and despair around them. * * * The remains (of those who died) were huddled into blankets, and so slightly interred on the neighboring slope that scores of them, bared by the rains, were always visible to their less fortunate comrades left to pine in hopeless captivity. * * * After having been imprisoned about a year and a half my father, one night, during a paroxysm of fever, rushed on board, and jumped overboard.

"The shock restored him to consciousness, he was soon rescued, and the next morning was taken by the Surgeon–General's orders to his quarters in Cherry St., near Pearl, where he remained until the close of the war. The kind doctor had taken a fancy to the handsome Yankee patient, whom he treated with fatherly kindness; giving him books to read; and having him present at his operations and dissections; and finally urged him to seek his fortune in Europe, where he should receive a good surgical education free of charge.

"The temptation was very great, but the rememberance of a nearer home and dearer friends, unseen for years, was greater, and to them the long lost returned at last, as one from the dead."

Captain Palmer commanded a merchant ship after the war, retired and bought a farm near Stockbridge, Mass. He followed the sea over forty years. In appearance he was very tall, erect, robust, and of rare physical power and endurance. He had remarkably small hands and feet, a high and fair forehead, his hair was very black, a tangle of luxuriant curls, and his eyes were clear hazel. He died in his 79th year, in 1844, leaving a large family of children. In his own memoranda he writes: "Four or five hundred Frenchmen were transferred as prisoners to the orlop deck of the Jersey. They were much better treated than we Americans on the deck above them. All, however, suffered very much for the want of water, crowding around two half hogsheads when they were brought on board, and often fighting for the first drink. On one of these occasions a Virginian near me was elbowed by a Spaniard and thrust him back. The Spaniard drew a sheath knife, when the Virginian knocked him headlong backwards, down two hatches, which had just been opened for heaving up a hogshead of stale water from the hold, for the prisoners' drink. This water had probably been there for years, and was as ropy as molasses.

"There was a deal of trouble between the American and the French and Spanish prisoners. The latter slept in hammocks, we, on the *floor* of the deck next above them. One night our boys went down * * * and, at a given signal, cut the hammock lashings of the French and Spanish prisoners at the head, and let them all down by the run on the dirty floor. In the midst of the row that followed this deed of darkness, the Americans stole back to their quarters, and were all fast asleep when the English guard came down.

"No lights were permitted after ten o'clock. We used, however, to hide our candles occasionally under our hats, when the order came to 'Douse the glim!' One night the officer of the guard discovered our disobedience, and came storming down the hatchway with a file of soldiers. Our lights were all extinguished in a moment, and we on the alert for our tyrants, whom we seized with a will, and hustled to and fro in the darkness, till their cries aroused the whole ship."

An uncle of Roswell Palmer's named Eliakim Palmer, a man named Thomas Hitchcock, and John Searles were prisoners on board the Scorpion, a British 74, anchored off the Battery, New York. They were about to be transferred to the Old Jersey, when Hitchcock went into the chains and dropped his hat into the water. On his return he begged for a boat to recover it, and being earnestly seconded by Lieutenant Palmer, the officer of the deck finally consented, ordering a guard to accompany the "damned rebels." They were a long time in getting the boat off. The hat, in the mean time, floated away from the ship. They rowed very awkwardly, of course got jeered at uproariously for "Yankee land lubbers," and were presently ordered to return. Being then nearly out of musket range, Lieutenant Palmer suddenly seized and disarmed the astonished guard, while his comrades were not slow in manifesting their latent adroitness in the use of the oar, to the no less astonishment of their deriders. In a moment the Bay was alive with excitement; many shots, big and little, were fired at the audacious fugitives from all the fleet; boats put off in hot pursuit; but the Stonington boys reached the Jersey shore in safety, and escaped with their prisoner to Washington's headquarters, where the tact and bravery they had displayed received the approval of the great commander.

Lieutenant Eliakim Palmer was again taken prisoner later in the war and again escaped. This time he was on board the Jersey. He cut away three iron bars let into an aperture on the side of the ship on the orlop deck, formerly a part of her hold. He swam ashore with his shirt and trousers tied to his head. Having lost his trousers he was obliged to make his way down Long Island for nearly its whole length, in his shirt only. He hid in ditches during the day, subsisting on berries, and the bounty of cows, milked directly into his mouth. He crawled by the sentries stationed at different parts of the island, and at length, after many days, reached Oyster Pond Point, whence he was smuggled by friends to his home in Stonington, Conn.

CHAPTER XXXII. THE NARRATIVE OF CAPTAIN ALEXANDER COFFIN

American Prisoners of the Revolution

In 1807 Dr. Mitchell, of New York published a small volume entitled: "The Destructive Operation of Foul Air, Tainted Provisions, Bad Water, and Personal Filthiness, Upon Human Constitutions, Exemplified in the Unparallelled Cruelty of the British to the American Captives at New York During the Revolutionary War, on Board their Prison and Hospital ships. By Captain Alexander Coffin, Junior, One of the Surviving Sufferers. In a Communication to Dr. Mitchell, dated September 4th, 1807."

Truly our ancestors were long–winded! A part of this narrative is as follows: "I shall furnish you with an account of the treatment that I, with other of my fellow citizens, received on board the Jersey and John prison ships, those monuments of British barbarity and infamy. I shall give you nothing but a plain simple statement of facts that cannot be controverted. And I begin my narrative from the time of my leaving the South Carolina frigate.

"In June, 1782, I left the above–mentioned frigate in the Havana, on board of which I had long served as a mid–ship–man, and made several trading voyages. I sailed early in September, from Baltimore, for the Havana, in a fleet of about forty sail, most of which were captured, and we among the rest, by the British frigate, Ceres, Captain Hawkins, a man in every sense of the word a perfect brute.

"Though our commander, Captain Hughes, was a very gentlemanly man, he was treated in the most shameful and abusive manner by said Hawkins, and ordered below to mess with the petty officers. Our officers were put into the cable tier, with the crew, and a guard placed at the hatchway to prevent more than two going on deck at a time. The provisions were of the very worst kind, and very short allowance even of them. They frequently gave us pea–soup, that is pea–water, for the pease and the soup, all but about a gallon or two, were taken for the ship's company, and the coppers filled up with water, and brought down to us in a strap–tub. And Sir, I might have defied any person on earth, possessing the most acute olfactory powers and the most refined taste to decide, either by one or the other or both of these senses, whether it was pease and water, slush and water, or swill.

"After living and being treated in this way, subject to every insult and abuse for ten or twelve days, we fell in with the Champion, a British twenty gun ship, which was bound to New York to refit, and were all sent on board of her The Captain was a true seaman and a gentleman, and our treatment was so different from what we had experienced on board the Ceres, that it was like being removed from Purgatory to Paradise. His name, I think, was Edwards.

"We arrived about the beginning of October in New York and were immediately sent on board the prison–ship in a small schooner, called, ironically enough, the Relief, commanded by one Gardner, an Irishman.

"This schooner Relief plied between the prison ship and New York, and carried the water and provisions from that city to the ship. In fact the said schooner might emphatically be called the Relief, for the execrable water and provisions she carried relieved many of my brave but unfortunate countrymen by death, from the misery and savage treatment they daily endured.

"Before I go on to relate the treatment we experienced on board the Jersey, I will make one remark, and that is if you were to rake the infernal regions, I doubt whether you could find such another set of demons as the officers and men who had charge of the Old Jersey Prison–ship, and, Sir, I shall not be surprised if you, possessing the finer feelings which I believe to be interwoven in the composition of men, and which are not totally torn from the *piece*, till by a long and obstinate perseverance in the meanest, the basest, and cruellest of all human acts, a man becomes lost to every sense of honor, of justice, of humanity, and common honesty; I shall not be surprised, I say, if you, possessing these finer feelings, should doubt whether men could be so lost to their sacred obligations to their God; and the moral ties which ought to bind them to their duty toward their fellow men, as those men were, who had the charge, and also who had any agency in the affairs of the Jersey prison–ship.

"On my arrival on board the Old Jersey, I found there about 1,100 prisoners; many of them had been there from three to six months, but few lived over that time if they did not get away by some means or other. They were generally in the most deplorable situation, mere walking skeletons, without money, and scarcely clothes to cover their nakedness, and overrun with lice from head to feet.

"The provisions, Sir, that were served out to us, was not more than four or five ounces of meat, and about as much bread, all condemned provisions from the ships of war, which, no doubt, were supplied with new in their stead, and the new, in all probability, charged by the commissaries to the Jersey. They, however, know best about that; and however secure they may now feel, they will have to render an account of that business to a Judge who cannot be deceived. This fact, however, I can safely aver, that both the times I was confined on board the prison ships, there never were provisions served out to the prisoners that would have been eatable by men that were not literally in a starving situation.

"The water that we were forced to use was carried from the city, and I postively assert that I never after having followed the sea thirty years, had on board of any ship, (and I have been three years on some of my voyages,) water so bad as that we were obliged to use on board the Old Jersey; when there was, as it were to tantalize us, as pure water, not more than three cables length from us, at the Mill in the Wallabout, as was perhaps ever drank.

"There were hogs kept in pens on the Gun—deck for their own use; and I have seen the prisoners watch an opportunity, and with a tin pot steal the bran from the hogs' trough, and go into the Galley and when they could get an opportunity, boil it over the fire, and eat it, as you, Sir, would eat of good soup when hungry. This I have seen more than once, and there are now living besides me, who can bear testimony to the same fact. There are many other facts equally abominable that I could mention, but the very thought of those things brings to my recollection scenes the most distressing.

"When I reflect how many hundreds of my brave and intrepid countrymen I have seen, in all the bloom of health, brought on board of that ship, and in a few days numbered with the dead, in consequence of the savage treatment they there received, I can but adore my Creator that He suffered me to escape; but I did not escape, Sir, without being brought to the very verge of the grave.

"This was the second time I was on board, which I shall mention more particularly hereafter. Those of us who had money fared much better than those who had none. I had made out to save, when taken, about twenty dollars, and with that I could buy from the bumboats, that were permitted to come alongside, bread, fruit, etc.; but, Sir, the bumboatmen were of the same kidney as the officers of the Jersey and we got nothing from them without paying through the nose for it, and I soon found the bottom of my purse; after which I fared no better than the rest. I was, however, fortunate in one respect; for after having been there about six weeks, two of my countrymen, (I am a Nantucket man) happened to come to New York to endeavor to recover a whaling sloop that had been captured, with a whaling license from Admiral Digby; and they found means to procure my release, passing me for a Quaker, to which I confess I had no pretensions further than my mother being a member of that respectable society. Thus, Sir, I returned to my friends, fit for the newest fashion, after an absence of three years.

"For my whole wardrobe I carried on my back, which consisted of a jacket, shirt, and trousers, a pair of old shoes and a handkerchief, which served me for a hat, and had more than two months, for I lost my hat the day we were taken, from the maintop–gallant yard, furling the top–gallant sail.

"My clothing, I forgot to mention, was completed laced with locomotive tinsel, and moved as by instinct, in all directions; but as my mother was not fond of such company, she furnished me with a suit of my father's, who was absent at sea, and condemned my laced suit for the benefit of all concerned.

"Being then in the prime of youth, about eighteen years of age, and naturally of a roving disposition; I could not bear the idea of being idle at home. I therefore proceeded to Providence, R. I., and shipped on board the brig Betsy and Polly, Captain Robert Folger, bound for Virginia and Amsterdam. We sailed from Newport early in February, 1783; and were taken five days after, off the capes of Virginia, by the Fair American privateer, of those parts, mounting sixteen six–pounders, and having 85 men, commanded by one Burton, a refugee, most of whose officers were of the same stamp. We were immediately handcuffed two and two, and ordered into the hold in the cable–tier. Having been plundered of our beds and bedding, the softest bed we had was the soft side of a water cask, and the coils of a cable.

"The Fair American, after having been handsomely dressed by an United States vessel of half of her force, was obliged to put into New York, then in possession of the British army, to refit, and we arrived within the Hook about the beginning of March, and were put on board a pilot boat, and brought up to this city. The boat hauled up alongside the Crane–wharf, where we had our irons knocked off, the mark of which I carry to this day; and were put on board the same schooner, Relief, mentioned in a former part of this narrative, and sent up once more to the prison–ship.

"It was just three months from my leaving the Old Jersey to my being again a prisoner on board of her, and on my return I found but very few of the men I had left three months before. Some had made their escape; some had been exchanged; but the greater part had taken up their abode under the surface of the hill, which you can see from your windows, where their bones are mouldering to dust, mingled with mother earth; a lesson to Americans, written *in capitals, on British cruelty and injustice.*

"I found, on my return on board the Jersey, more prisoners than when I left her; and she being so crowded, they were obliged to send about 200 of us on board the John, a transport–ship of about 300 tons.

"There we were treated worse, if possible, than on board the Jersey, and our accommodations were infinitely worse, for the Jersey, being an old, condemned 64 gun ship had two tiers of ports fore and aft, air–ports, and large hatchways, which gave a pretty free circulation of air through the ship; whereas the John, being a merchant–ship, and with small hatchways, and the hatchways being laid down every night, and no man being allowed to go on deck * * * the effluvia arising from these, together with the already contaminated air, occasioned by the breath of so many people so pent up together, was enough to destroy men of the most healthy and robust constitutions. All the time I was on board this ship, not a prisoner eat his allowance, bad as it was, cooked, more than three or four times; but eat it raw as it came out of the barrel. * * * In the middle of the ship, between decks, was raised a platform of boards about two and a half feet high, for those prisoners to sleep on who had no hammocks. On this they used frequently to sit and play at cards to pass the time. One night in particular, several of us sat to see them play until about ten o'clock, and then retired to our hammocks. About one A. M, we were called and told that one Bird was dying; we turned out and went to where he lay, and found him just expiring. Thus, at 10 P. M, the young man was apparently as well as any of us, and at one A. M. had paid the debt to nature. Many others went off in the same way. It will perhaps be said that men die suddenly anywhere. True, but do they die suddenly anywhere from the same cause? After all these things it is, I think, impossible for the mind to form any other conclusion than that there was a premeditated design to destroy as many Americans as they could on board the prison–ships; the treatment of the prisoners warrants the conclusion; but it is mean, base, and cowardly, to endeavor to conquer an enemy by such infamous means, and truly characteristic of base and cowardly wretches. The truly brave will always treat their prisoners well.

"There were two or three hospital–ships near the prison–ships; and so soon as any of the prisoners complained of being sick, they were sent on board of one of them; and I verily believe that not one out of a hundred ever returned or recovered. I am sure I never knew but one to recover. Almost, and in fact I believe I may say every morning, a large boat from each of the hospital ships went loaded with dead bodies, which were all tumbled together into a hole dug for the purpose, on the hill where the national navy–yard now is.

"A singular affair happened on board of one of the hospital–ships, and no less true than singular. All the prisoners that died after the boat with the load had gone ashore were sewed up in hammocks, and left on deck till next morning. As usual, a great number had thus been disposed of. In the morning, while employed in loading the boat, one of the seamen perceived motion in one of the hammocks, just as they were about launching it down the board placel for that purpose from the gunwale of the ship into the boat, and exclaimed, 'Damn my eyes! That fellow isn't dead!' and if I have been rightly informed, and I believe I have, there was quite a dispute between the man and the others about it. They swore he was dead enough, and should go into the boat; he swore he should not be launched, as they termed it, and took his knife and ripped open the hammock, and behold, the man was really alive. There had been a heavy rain during the night; and as the vital functions had not totally ceased, but were merely suspended in consequence of the main–spring being out of order, this seasonable moistening must have given tone and elasticity to the great spring, which must have communicated to the lesser ones, and put the whole machinery again into motion. You know better about this than I do, and can better judge of the cause of the re–animation of the man. * * * He was a native of Rhode Island; his name was Gavot. He went to Rhode Island in the same flag of truce as myself, about a month afterwards. I felt extremely ill, but made out to keep about until I got home. My parents then lived on the island of Nantucket. I was then taken down, and lay in my bed six weeks in the most deplorable situation; my body was swelled to a great degree, and my legs were as big round as my body now is, and affected with the most excruciating pains. What my disorder was I will not pretend to say; but Dr. Tupper, quite an eminent physician, and a noted tory, who attended me, declared to my mother that he knew of nothing that would operate in the manner that my disorder did, but poison. For the truth of that I refer to my father and brothers, and to Mr. Henry Coffin, father to Captain Peter Coffin, of the Manchester Packet of this point.

"Thus, Sir, in some haste, without much attention to order or diction, I have given you part of the history of my life and sufferings, but I endeavored to bear them as became an American. And I must mention before I close, to the everlasting honor of those unfortunate Americans who were on board the Jersey, that notwithstanding the savage treatment they received, and death staring them in the face, every attempt which was made by the British to persuade them to enter their ships of war or in their army, was treated with the utmost contempt; and I saw only one instance of defection while I was on board, and that person was hooted at and abused by the prisoners till the boat was out of hearing. Their patriotism in preferring such treatment, and even death in its most frightful shapes, to the service of the British, and fighting against their own country has seldom been equalled, certainly never excelled, and if there be no monument raised with hands to commemorate the virtue of those men, it is stamped in capitals on the heart of every American acquainted with their merit and sufferings, and will there remain as long as the blood flows from its fountains."

We have already seen that many of the prisoners on board the Jersey were impressed into the service of British men–of–war, and that others voluntarily enlisted for garrison duty in the West Indies. It seems probable, however, that, as Captain Coffin asserts, few enlisted in the service to fight against their own countrymen, and those few were probably actuated by the hope of deserting. It is certain that thousands preferred death to such a method of escaping from prison, as is proved by the multitudes of corpses interred in the sand of the Wallabout, all of whom could, in this way, have saved their lives. Conditions changed on board the Jersey, from time to time. Thus, the water supply that was at one time brought by the schooner Relief from New York, was, at other times, procured from a beautiful spring on Long Island, as we will see in our next chapter.

Some of the prisoners speak of the foul air on board the prison ship caused by the fact that all her port holes were closed, and a few openings cut in her sides, which were insufficient to ventilate her. Coffin says there was a good passage of air through the vessel from her port holes. It is probable that the Jersey became so notorious as a death trap that at last, for very shame, some attempt was made to secure more sanitary conditions. Thus, just before peace was established, she was, for the first time, overhauled and cleaned, the wretched occupants being sent away for the purpose. The port holes were very probably opened, and this is the more likely as we read of some of the prisoners freezing to death during the last year of the war. From that calamity, at least, they were safe as long as they were deprived of outer air.

CHAPTER XXXIII. A WONDERFUL DELIVERANCE

There are few records of religious feeling on board the "Jersey, vulgarly called 'Hell.'" No clergyman was ever known to set foot on board of her, although a city of churches was so near. The fear of contagion may have kept ministers of the gospel away. Visitors came, as we have seen, but not to soothe the sufferings of the prisoners, or to comfort those who were dying. It is said that a young doctor, named George Vandewater attended the sick, until he took a fatal disease and died. He was a resident of Brooklyn, and seems to have been actuated by motives of humanity, and therefore his name deserves a place in this record.

But although the rough seamen who left narratives of their experiences in that fearful place have told us little or nothing about the inner feelings of those poor sufferers, yet it must be presumed that many a silent prayer went up to the Judge and Father of all men, from the depths of that foul prison ship. There was one boy on board the Jersey, one at least, and we hope that there were many more, who trusted in God that He could deliver him, even "from the nethermost hell."

A large proportion of the prisoners were young men in their teens, who had been attracted by the mysterious fascination of the sea; many of them had run away from good homes, and had left sorrowing parents and friends to mourn their loss. The feelings of these young men, full of eager hopes, and as yet unsoured by too rough handling in their wrestle with the world, suddenly transferred to the deck of the Jersey, has been well described by Fox and other captives, whose adventures we have transcribed in these pages.

We have now to tell the experience of a youth on the Jersey who lived to be a minister, and for many years was in charge of a church at Berkeley. This youth was sensitive, delicate, and far from strong. His faith in human nature received a shock, and his disposition was warped at the most receptive and formative period of his life, by the terrible scenes of suffering on the one hand, and relentless cruelty on the other, that he witnessed in that fatal place. He wrote, in his memoir many years after: *"I have since found that the whole world is but one great prison−house of guilty, sorrowful, and dying men, who live in pride, envy, and malice, hateful, and hating one another."*

American Prisoners of the Revolution

This is one of the most terrible indictments of the human race that was ever written. Let us hope that it is not wholly true.

In 1833 the Rev. Thomas Andros published his recollections under the title, "The Old Jersey Captive." We will give an abstract of them. He begins by saying: "I was but in my seventeenth year when the struggle commenced. In the summer of 1781 the ship Hannah, a very rich prize, was captured and brought into the port of New London. It infatuated great numbers of our young men who flocked on board our private armed ships in hopes of as great a prize. * * * I entered on board a new Brig called the 'Fair American.' She carried sixteen guns. * * * We were captured on the 27th of August, by the Solebay frigate, and safely stowed away in the Old Jersey prison ship at New York, an old, unsightly, rotten hulk.

"Her dark and filthy appearance perfectly corresponded with the death and despair that reigned within. She was moored three quarters of a mile to the eastward of Brooklyn ferry, near a tide–mill on the Long Island shore. The nearest distance to land was about twenty rods. No other British ship ever proved the means of the destruction of so many human beings."

Andros puts the number of men who perished on board the Jersey as 11,000, and continues: "After it was known that it was next to certain death to confine a prisoner here, the inhumanity and wickedness of doing it was about the same as if he had been taken into the city and deliberately shot on some public square. * * * Never did any Howard or angel of pity appear to inquire into or alleviate our woes. Once or twice a bag of apples was hurled into the midst of hundreds of prisoners, crowded together as thick as they could stand, and life and limbs were endangered by the scramble. This was a cruel sport. When I saw it about to commence I fled to the most distant part of the ship."

At night, he says, the prisoners were driven down to darkness between decks, secured by iron gratings and an armed soldiery. He thus speaks of the tasks imposed upon the prisoners: "Around the well–room an armed guard were forcing up the prisoners to the winches to clear the ship of water, and prevent her sinking; and little could be heard but a roar of mutual execrations, reproaches and insults.

"Sights of woe, regions of sorrow, doleful shades;
Where peace and rest can never dwell

"When I became an inmate of this abode of suffering, despair, and death, there were about 400 on board, but in a short time they were increased to 1,200.

"All the most deadly diseases were pressed into the service of the king of terrors, but his prime ministers were dysentery, small pox, and yellow fever. The healthy and the diseased were mingled together in the main ship."

He says that the two hospital ships were soon overcrowded, and that two hundred or more of the prisoners, who soon became sick in consequence of the want of room, were lodged in the fore–part of the lower gun–deck, where all the prisoners were confined at night.

"Utter derangement was a common sympton of yellow fever, and to increase the horror of darkness which enshrouded us, for we were allowed no light, the voice of warning would be heard, 'Take care! There's a madman stalking through the ship with a knife in his hand!'"

Andros says that he sometimes found the man by whose side he had lain all night a corpse in the morning. There were many sick with raging fever, and their loud cries for water, which could only be obtained on the upper deck, mingled with the groans of the dying, and the execrations of the tormented sufferers. If they attempted to get water from the upper deck, the sentry would push them back with his bayonet. Andros, at one time, had a narrow escape with his life, from one of these bayonet thrusts.

"In the morning the hatches were thrown open and we were allowed to ascend. The first object we saw was a boat loaded with dead bodies conveying them to the Long Island shore, where they were very slightly covered with sand. * * * Let our disease be what it would we were abandoned to our fate. No English physician ever came near us."

Thirteen of the crew to which Andros belonged were on the Jersey. In a short time all but three or four were dead. The healthiest died first. They were seized vith yellow fever, which was an epidemic on the ship, and died in a few hours. Andros escaped contagion longer than any of his companions, with one exception. He says that the prisoners were furnished with buckets and brushes to cleanse the ship, and vinegar to sprinkle the floors, but that most of them had fallen into a condition of apathy and despair, and that they seldom exerted themselves to improve their condition.

"The encouragement to do so was small. The whole ship was equally affected, and contained pestilence enough to desolate a world; disease and death were wrought into her very timbers. At the time I left it is to be supposed a more filthy, contagious, and deadly abode never existed among a Christianized people.

"The lower hold and the orlop deck were such a terror that no man would venture down into them. * * * Our water was good could we have had enough of it: the bread was superlatively bad. I do not recollect seeing any which was not full of living vermin, but eat it, worms and all, we must, or starve. * * * A secret, prejudicial to a prisoner, revealed to the guard, was death. Captain Young of Boston concealed himself in a large chest belonging to a sailor going to be exchanged, and was carried on board the cartel, and we considered his escape as certain, but the secret leaked out, and he was brought back and one Spicer of Providence being suspected as the traitor the enraged prisoners were about to cut his throat. The guard rushed down and rescued him.

"I knew no one to be seduced into the British service. They tried to force one of our crew into the navy, but he chose rather to die than perform any duty, and he was again restored to the prison−ship."

Andros declares that there was no trace of religion exhibited on board the Jersey. He also says that the prisoners made a set of rules for themselves by which they regulated their conduct towards each other. No one was allowed to tyrannize over the weak, and morality was enforced by rules, and any infraction of these regulations was severely punished.

He speaks of scenes of dreadful suffering which he witnessed:

"Which things, most worthy of pity, I myself saw,
And of them was a part."

"The prison ship is a blot which a thousand ages cannot eradicate from the name of Britian. * * * While on board almost every thought was occupied to invent some plan of escape. The time now came when I must be delivered from the ship or die. I was seized with yellow fever, and should certainly take the small−pox with it, and who does not know that I could not survive the operation of both of these diseases at once. * * * I assisted in nursing those who had the pox most violently.

"The arrival of a cartel and my being exchanged would but render my death the more sure."

Yet he endeavored to promote his exchange by stepping up and giving in his name among the first, when a list of the prisoners was taken. Andros was not strong, and as he himself says, disease often seemed to pass over the weak and sickly, and to attack, with deadly result, the prisoners who were the healthiest and most vigorous.

"It was the policy of the English to return for sound and healthy men sent from our prisons, such Americans as had but just the breath of life in them, sure to die before they reached home. The guard would tell a man while in health, 'You haven't been here long enough, you are too well to be exchanged.'

"There was one more method of getting from the ship," Andros continues, "and that was at night to steal down through a gun–port which we had managed to open unbeknown to the guard, and swim ashore." This, he declared, was for him a forlorn hope. Already under the influence of yellow fever, and barely able to walk, he was, even when well, unable to swim ten rods. Discovery was almost certain, for the guards now kept vigilant watch to prevent any one escaping in this manner, and they shot all whom they detected in the act of escaping. Yet this poor young man trusted in God. He writes: "God, who had something more for me to do, undertook for me." Mr. Emery, the sailing master, was going ashore for water. Andros stepped up to him and asked: "Mr. Emery, may I go on shore with you after water?"

No such favor had ever been granted a prisoner, and Andros scarcely knew what prompted him to prefer such a request. To his immense surprise, the sailing master, who must have had a heart after all, replied, "Yes, with all my heart." He was evidently struck with compassion for the poor, apparently dying, young man.

Andros, to the astonishment of his companions, immediately descended into the boat. Some of them asked: "What is that sick man going on shore for?"

The British sailors endeavored to dissuade him, thinking that he would probably die on the excursion.

"'So, to put them all to silence, I again ascended on board, for I had neglected to take my great–coat. But I put it on, and waited for the sailing–master. The boat was pushed off, I attempted to row, but an English sailor said, very kindly, 'Give me the oar. You are too unwell.' * * * I looked back to the black and unsightly old ship as to an object of the greatest horror. * * * We ascended the creek and arrived at the spring, and I proposed to the sailors to go in quest of apples."

The sailing–master said to him, "This fresh air will be of service to you." This emboldened him to ask leave to ascend a bank about thirty feet high, and to call at a house near the spring to ask for refreshment. "Go," said Mr. Emery, "but take care not to be out of the way." He replied that his state of health was such that nothing was to be feared from him on that account. He managed to get into a small orchard that belonged to the farmhouse. There he saw a sentinel, who was placed on guard over a pile of apples. He soon convinced himself that this man was indifferent to his movements, and, watching his opportunity, when the man's back was turned, he slipped beyond the orchard, into a dense swamp, covered with a thick undergrowth of saplings and bushes. Here there was a huge prostrate log twenty feet in length, curtained with a dense tangle of green briar.

"Lifting up this covering I crept in, close by the log, and rested comfortably, defended from the northeast storm which soon commenced."

He heard the boat's crew making inquiries for him but no one discovered his hiding–place. One of them declared that he was safe enough, and would never live to go a mile. In the middle of the night he left his hiding place, and fell into a road which he pursued some distance. When he heard approaching footsteps he would creep off the path, roll himself up into a ball to look like a bush, and remain perfectly still until the coast was clear. He now felt that a wonderful Providence was watching over him. His forethought in returning for his overcoat was the means of saving his life, as he would undoubtedly have perished from exposure without it. Next night he hid in a high stack of hay, suffering greatly. When the storm was over he left this hiding place, and entered a deep hollow in the woods near by, where he felt secure from observation. Here he took off his clothes and spread them in the sun to dry.

Returning to the road he was proceeding on his way, when at a bend in the road, he came upon two light dragoons, evidently looking for him. What was he to do? His mind acted quickly, and, as they approached, he leisurely got over a fence into a small corn field, near a cottage by the way–side. Here he busied himself as if he were the owner of the cottage, going about the field; deliberately picking up ears of corn; righting up the cap sheaf of a stack of stalks, and examining each one. He had lost his hat, and had a handkerchief around his head, which helped to deceive the dragoons, who supposed that he had just come out of the cottage. They eyed him sharply, but passed on.

After this he dared not show himself, and wandered about, living on apples and water. He would lie concealed all day, in barns or hollows of the woods. At night he travelled as far as his weakened condition would allow He often found unfermented cider at the presses, for it was cider–making time.

After several days of this wandering life he sought refuge in a barn, where he was found by a cross old man, who refused to do anything for him. He says that in the course of his wanderings he uniformly found women kind and helpful. They gave him food and kept his secret. One night, feeling utterly spent, he came to the poor dwelling of an old man and his wife, on the east side of Long Island. These good people assisted him by every means in their power, as if he were their own son. They took off his clothes, giving him another suit until they had baked all his garments in the oven to destroy the vermin which tormented him day and night. They insisted upon his occupying a clean bed. That night he slept sweetly, rid of the intolerable torture of being eaten up alive. He managed to reach Sag Harbor, where he found two other escaped prisoners. Soon he was smuggled to Connecticut in a whale–boat, and restored to his mother. It was late in October when he reached home. He was very ill and delirious for a long time, but finally recovered, taught school for some time, and finally became a minister of the gospel.

CHAPTER XXXIV. THE NARRATIVE OF CAPTAIN DRING

By far the most complete account of life on board the Old Jersey is contained in Captain Dring's Recollections. His nature was hopeful, and his constitution strong and enduring. He attempted to make the best of his situation, and succeeded in leading as nearly a tolerable life on board the prison–ship as was possible. His book is too long for insertion in these pages, but we will endeavor to give the reader an abstract of it.

This book was published in 1865, having been prepared for the press and annotated by

Mr. Albert G. Greene, who speaks of Captain Dring as "a frank, outspoken, and honest seaman." His original manuscript was first published in 1829.

Dring describes the prison ships as leaky old hulks, condemned as unfit for hospitals or store ships, but considered good enough for prisoners doomed to speedy annihilation. He says:

"There is little doubt that the superior officers of the Royal Navy under whose exclusive jurisdiction were these ships, intended to insure, as far as possible, the good health of those who were confined on board of them; there is just as little doubt, however, that the inferior officers, under whose control those prisoners were more immediately placed, * * * too often frustrated the purposes of their superior officers, and too often disgraced humanity, by their wilful disregard of the policy of their Government, and of the orders of their superiors, by the uncalled–for severity of their treatment of those who were placed in their custody, and by their shameless malappropriation of the means of support which were placed in their hands for the sustenance of the prisoners."

However that may be, the superior officers must have known that the prison ships were unfit for human habitation; that they were fearfully overcrowded; and that the mortality on board of them was unprecedented in the annals of prison life.

The introduction to Captain Drings's recollections declares, what is well known, that General Washington possessed but limited authority; he was the Commander–in–Chief of the army, but had nothing to do with the American Navy, and still less with the crews of privateers, who made up a very large portion of the men on board the Jersey. Yet he did all he could, actuated, as he always was, by the purest motives of benevolence and humanity.

"The authority to exchange naval prisoners," to quote from this introduction, "was not invested in Washington, but in the Financier, and as the prisoners on the Jersey freely set forth in their petition, the former was comparatively helpless in the premises, although he earnestly desired to relieve them from their sufferings.

"It will be seen from these circumstances that no blame could properly attach to General Washington, or the Continental Congress, or the Commissary of Prisoners; the blame belonged to those who were engaged in privateering, all of whom had been accustomed to release, without parole, the crews of the vessels which they captured, or enlist them on other privateers; in both cases removing the very means by which alone the release of their captive fellow seamen could be properly and safely effected.

"From the careful perusal of all the information we possess on this interesting subject, the reader will arise with the conviction that, by unwarrantable abuses of authority; and unprincipled disregard of the purposes of the British Government in some of its agents, great numbers of helpless American prisoners were wantonly plunged into the deepest distress; exposed to the most severe sufferings, and carried to unhonored graves. * * * Enough will remain uncontradicted by competent testimony to brand with everlasting infamy all who were immediately concerned in the business; and to bring a blush of shame on the cheek of every one who feels the least interest in the memory of any one who, no matter how remotely, was a party to so mean and yet so horrible an outrage. * * * The authors and abettors of the outrages to which reference has been made will stand convicted not only of the most heartless criminality against the laws of humanity and the laws of God, but of the most flagrant violation of the Laws of Nations, and the Law of the Land."

These extracts are all taken from the Introduction to Captain Dring's Recollections, written by Mr. H. B. Dawson, in June, 1865.

Captain Dring was born in Newport, R. I., on the third of August, 1758. He died in August, 1825, in Providence, R. I., and was about 67 years of age at the time of his death. He was many years in the merchant service, and wrote his recollections in 1824.

"I was first confined on the Good Hope, in the year 1779, then lying in the North River opposite the city of New York, but after a confinement of more than four months, I succeeded in making my escape to the Jersey shore."

Captain Dring is said to have been one of the party who escaped from the Good Hope in October, 1779. The New Jersey papers thus described the escape.

"Chatham, N. J. Last Wednesday morning about one o'clock made their escape from the Good Hope prison ship in the North River, nine Captains and two privates. Among the number was Captain James Prince, who has been confined four months, and having no prospect of being exchanged, concerted a plan in conjunction with the other gentlemen to make their escape, which they effected in the following manner: They confined the Mate, disarmed the sentinels, and hoisted out the boat which was on deck; they brought off nine stands of arms, one pair of pistols, and a sufficient quantity of ammunition, being determined not to be taken alive. They had scarce got clear of the ship before the alarm was given, when they were fired on by three different ships, but fortunately no person was hurt. Captain Prince speaks in the highest terms of Captain Charles Nelson, who commanded the prison-ship, using the prisoners with a great deal of humanity, particularly himself.

"I was again captured in 1782," Dring continues, "and conveyed on board the Jersey, where * * * I was a witness and partaker of the unspeakable sufferings of that wretched class of American prisoners who were there taught the utmost extreme of human misery. I am now far advanced in years, and am the only survivor, with the exception of two, of a crew of 65 men. I often pass the descendant of one of my old companions in captivity, and the recollection comes fresh to my mind that his father was my comrade and fellow sufferer in prison; that I saw him breathe his last upon the deck of the Jersey, and assisted at his interment at the Waleboght; * * *

"In May, 1782, I sailed from Providence, R. I., as Master's-mate, on board a privateer called the Chance, commanded by Captain Daniel Aborn, mounting 12 six-pound cannon, and having a crew of 65 men."

This vessel was captured in a few days by the Belisarius, of 26 guns, commanded by Captain Graves. The prisoners were brought to New York and the Belisarius dropped her anchor abreast of the city. A large gondola soon came alongside, in which was seated David Sproat, the much-hated British Commissary of Naval Prisoners. He was an American refugee, universally detested for the insolence of his manners, and the cruelty of his conduct. The prisoners were ordered into the boats, and told to apply themselves to the oars, but declined to exert themselves in that manner, whereupon he scowled at them and remarked, "I'll soon fix you, my lads!"

David Sproat found America too hot for him after the war and died at Kirkcudbright, Scotland, in 1799.

Dring says: "My station in the boat as we hauled alongside, was exactly opposite one of the air-ports in the side of the ship. From this aperture proceeded a strong current of foul vapor of a kind to which I had been before accustomed while confined on board the Good Hope, the peculiar disgusting smell of which I then recollected, after a lapse of three years. This was, however, far more foul and loathsome than anything which I had ever met with on board that ship, and it produced a sensation of nausea far beyond my powers of description.

"Here, while waiting for orders to ascend on board, we were addressed by some of the prisoners from the air–ports * * * after some questions whence we came, and respecting the manner of our capture, one of the prisoners said that it was a lamentable thing to see so many young men in the prime of health and vigor condemned to a living grave." He went on to say that Death passed over such human skeletons as himself as unworthy of his powers, but that he delighted in making the strong, the youthful, and the vigorous, his prey.

After the prisoners had been made to descend the hatchways, these were then fastened down for the night. Dring says it was impossible for him to find one of his companions in the darkness.

"Surrounded by I knew not whom, except that they were beings as wretched as myself; with dismal sounds meeting my ears from every direction; a nauseous and putrid atmosphere filling my lungs at every breath; and a stifling and suffocating heat which almost deprived me of sense, even of life. Previous to leaving the boat I had put on several articles of clothing, for the purpose of security, but I was soon compelled to disencumber myself of these. * * * Thoughts of sleep did not enter into my mind."

He discovered a gleam of light from one of the port–holes and keeping hold of his bag endeavored to make his way to it, but was greeted by curses and imprecations from those who were lying on the deck, and whom he disturbed. At length he arrived at the desired spot, but found it occupied. In the morning he saw himself surrounded by a crowd of forms, with the hues of death and famine upon their faces. At eight o'clock they were permitted to ascend on deck, and he found some of his friends.

"Pale and meagre, the throng came on deck, to view for a few moments the morning sun, and then to descend again, to pass another day of misery and wretchedness. I found myself surrounded by a motley crew of wretches, with tattered garments and pallid visages. * * * Among them I saw one ruddy and heathful countenance, and recognized the features of one of my late companions on the Belisarius. But how different did he appear from the group around him * * * men who, now shrunken and decayed, had but a short time before been as strong, as healthful, and as vigorous as himself. * * * During the night I had, in addition to my other sufferings, been tormented with what I supposed to be vermin, and on coming upon deck, I found that a black silk handkerchief, which I wore around my neck, was completely spotted with them. Although this had often been mentioned as one of the nuisances of the place, yet as I had never before been in a situation to witness anything of the kind, the sight made me shudder, as I knew at once that as long as I should remain on board, these loathsome creatures would be my constant companions and unceasing tormentors.

"The next disgusting object which met my sight was a man suffering from small–pox, and in a few minutes I found myself surrounded by many others laboring under the same disease in every stage of its progress."

Dring was obliged to inoculate himself, as that was thought to be the safest way of taking the disease. He borrowed some virus from a sufferer, and scarified the skin of his hand with a pin. He then bound up his hand. Next morning he found that it had festered. He took the disease lightly, and soon recovered, while a very large proportion of those who contracted smallpox in the natural manner died of it.

All the prisoners from the Belisarius were obliged to fast for twenty–four hours. Dring had some ship biscuit with him, in his bag. These he distributed to his companions. They then formed themselves into messes of six each, and next morning drew their scanty pittance of food.

We have said that Dring and the other officers on board solved the problem of living with *comparative* comfort on board the Jersey. As they were officers, the gun–room was given up to their use, and they were not so terribly crowded as the common sailors. Also the officers had money to supply many of their wants, but all this will appear in the course of the narrative.

He says that, even on the second day of their confinement, they could not obtain their allowance of food in time to cook it. No distinction of rank was made by the jailors on the Jersey, but the prisoners themselves agreed to allow the officers to occupy the extreme afterpart of the ship, between decks, called the gun–room. Dring soon became an inmate of this place, in company with the other officers who were already in possession, and these tendered him all the little services in their power.

The different messes were all numbered. At nine o'clock the steward and his assistants would take their places at the window in the bulk head in the steward's room, and ring a bell. A man from each mess stood ready to be in time to answer when his number was called. The rations were all prepared ready for delivery. They were on two–thirds allowance. This is the full allowance for a British seaman:

Sunday—1 lb. biscuit, 1 lb. pork, and half a pint of peas.
Monday—1 lb. biscuit, 1 pint oatmeal, 2 oz. butter.
Tuesday–1 lb. biscuit, and 2 lbs. beef.
Wednesday—1–1/2 lbs. flour, and 2 ounces suet.
Thursday—Same as Sunday.
Friday—Same as Monday.
Saturday—Same as Tuesday.

Two thirds of this allowance for each man would have been sufficient to sustain life, had it been of moderately good quality. They never received butter, but a rancid and ill–smelling substance called sweet oil. "The smell of it, accustomed as we were to everything foul and nauseous, was more than we could endure. We, however, always received it, and gave it to the poor, half–starved Frenchmen who were on board, who took it gratefully, and swallowed it with a little salt and their wormy bread."

Oil had been dealt out to the prisoners on the Good Hope, but there it was hoarded carefully, for they were allowed lights until nine P.M., so they used it in their lamps. But on the Jersey, Dring declares that neither light nor fire was ever allowed.

Often their provisions were not dealt out in time to be cooked that day, and then they had to fast or eat them raw. The cooking was done in the "Great Copper" under the forecastle. This was a boiler enclosed in brick–work about eight feet square. It was large enough to contain two or three hogsheads of water. It was square, and divided into two portions. In one side peas and oatmeal were boiled in fresh water. On the other side the meat was boiled in salt water, and as we have already stated the food was poisoned by copperas. This was the cause, it is believed, of many deaths, especially as the water was obtained from alongside the ship, and was extremely unwholesome.

The portion of each mess was designated by a tally fastened to it by a string. Hundreds of tallies were to be seen hanging over the sides of the brick—work by their strings, each eagerly watched by some member of the mess, who waited to receive it.

The meat was suffered to remain in the boiler a certain time, then the cook's bell was rung, and the pittance of food must be immediately removed, whether sufficiently cooked or not. The proportion of peas and oatmeal belonging to each mess was measured out of the copper after it was boiled.

The cook alone seemed to have much flesh on his bones. He had been a prisoner, but seeing no prospect of ever being liberated he had offered his services, and his mates and scullions were also prisoners who had followed his example. The cook was not ill—natured, and although often cursed by the prisoners when out of hearing, he really displayed fortitude and forbearance far beyond what most men would have been capable of showing. "At times, when his patience was exhausted, he did, indeed, make the hot water fly among us, but a reconciliation was usually effected with little difficulty.

"Many of the different messes had obtained leave from His Majesty the Cook to prepare their own rations, separate from the general mess in the great boiler. For this purpose a great many spikes and hooks had been driven into the brick—work by which the boiler was enclosed, on which to suspend their tin kettles. As soon as we were permitted to go on deck in the morning, some one took the tin kettle belonging to the mess, with as much water and as many splinters of wood as we had been able to procure during the previous day, and carried them to the Galley; and there having suspended his kettle on one of the hooks or spikes stood ready to kindle his little fire as soon as the Cook or his mates would permit. It required but little fire to boil our food in these kettles, for their bottoms were made concave, and the fire was applied directly in the centre, and let the remaining brands be ever so small they were all carefully quenched; and having been conveyed below were kept for use on a future occasion.

"Much contention often arose through our endeavors to obtain places around the brick—work, but these disputes were always promptly decided by the Cook, from whose mandate there was no appeal. No sooner had one prisoner completed the cooking for his mess, than another supplicant stood ready to take his place; and they thus continued to throng the galley, during the whole time that the fire was allowed to remain under the Great Copper, unless it happened to be the pleasure of the Cook to drive them away. *[...]

Each man in the mess procured and saved as much water as possible during the previous day; as no person was ever allowed to take more than a pint at a time from the scuttle–cask in which it was kept. Every individual was therefor obliged each day to save a little for the common use of the mess on the next morning. By this arrangement the mess to which I belonged had always a small quantity of fresh water in store, which we carefully kept, with a few other necessaries, in a chest which we used in common.

"During the whole period of my confinement I never partook of any food which had been prepared in the Great Copper. It is to this fact that I have always attributed, under Divine Providence, the degree of health which I preserved on board. I was thereby also, at times, enabled to procure several necessary and comfortable things, such as tea, sugar, etc. so that, wretchedly as I was situated, my condition was far preferable to that of most of my fellow sufferers, which has ever been to me a theme of sincere and lasting gratitude to Heaven.

"But terrible indeed was the condition of most of my fellow captives. Memory still brings before me those emaciated beings, moving from the Galley with their wretched pittance of meat; each creeping to the spot where his mess was assembled, to divide it with a group of haggard and sickly creatures, their garments hanging in tatters round their meagre limbs, and the hue of death upon their careworn faces. By these it was consumed with the scanty remnants of bread, which was often mouldy and filled with worms. And even from this vile fare they would rise up in torments from the cravings of unsatisfied hunger and thirst.

"No vegetables of any description were ever afforded us by our inhuman keepers. Good Heaven! what a luxury to us would then have been even a few potatoes!—if but the very leavings of swine. * * *

> "Oh my heart sinks, my pitying eyes o'erflow,
> When memory paints the picture of their woe
> Where my poor countrymen in bondage wait
> The slow enfranchisement of lingering fate,
> Greeting with groans the unwelcome night's return,
> While rage and shame their gloomy bosoms burn,
> And chiding, every hour, the slow–paced sun,
> Endure their woes till all his race was run

No one to mark the sufferers with a tear
No friend to comfort, and no hope to cheer,
And like the dull, unpitied brutes repair
To stalls as wretched, and as coarse a fare;
Thank Heaven one day of misery was o'er,
And sink to sleep, and wish to wake no more."

CHAPTER XXXV. THE NARRATIVE OF CAPTAIN DRING (CONTINUED)

"The quarter–deck of the Jersey covered about one–fourth of the upper deck, and the forecastle extended from the stern, about one–eighth part of the length of the upper deck. Sentinels were stationed on the gangways on each side of the upper deck, leading from the quarter–deck to the forecastle. These gangways were about five feet wide; and here the prisoners were allowed to pass and repass. The intermediate space from the bulkhead of the quarter–deck to the forecastle was filled with long spars and booms, and called the spar–deck. The temporary covering afforded by the spar–deck was of the greatest benefit to the prisoners, as it served to shield us from the rain and the scorching rays of the sun. It was here, therefore, that our movables were placed when we were engaged in cleaning the lower decks. The spar–deck was also the only place where we were allowed to walk, and was crowded through the day by the prisoners on deck. Owing to the great number of prisoners, and the small space allowed us by the spar–deck, it was our custom to walk in platoons, each facing the same way, and turning at the same time. The Derrick for taking in wood, water, etc., stood on the starboard side of the spar–deck. On the larboard side of the ship was placed the accommodation ladder, leading from the gangway to the water. At the head of the ladder a sentinel was also stationed.

"The head of the accommodation ladder was near the door of the barricade, which extended across the front of the quarter–deck, and projected a few feet beyond the sides of the ship. The barricade was about ten feet high, and was pierced with loop–holes for musketry in order that the prisoners might be fired on from behind it, if occasion should require.

"The regular crew of the ship consisted of a Captain, two Mates, a Steward, a Corporal, and about 12 sailors. The crew of the ship had no communication whatever with the prisoners. No person was ever permitted to pass through the barricade door, except when it was required that the messes should be examined and regulated, in which case each man had to pass through, and go between decks, and there remain until the examination was completed. None of the guard or of the ship's crew ever came among the prisoners while I was on board. I never saw one of her officers or men except when there were passengers going in the boat, to or from the stern–ladder.

"On the two decks below, where we were confined at night, our chests, boxes, and bags were arranged in two lines along the decks, about ten feet distant from the sides of the ship; thus leaving as wide a space unencumbered in the middle of each deck, fore and aft, as our crowded situation would admit. Between these tiers of chests, etc., and the sides of the ship, was the place where the different messes assembled; and some of the messes were also separated from their neighbors by a temporary partition of chests, etc. Some individuals of the different messes usually slept on the chests, in order to preserve their contents from being plundered in the night.

"At night the spaces in the middle of the decks were much encumbered with hammocks, but these were always removed in the morning. * * * My usual place of abode being in the Gunroom, I was never under the necessity of descending to the lower dungeon; and during my confinement I had no disposition to visit it. It was inhabited by the most wretched in appearance of all our miserable company. From the disgusting and squalid appearance of the groups which I saw ascending the stairs which led to it, it must have been more dismal, if possible, than that part of the hulk where I resided. Its occupants appeared to be mostly foreigners, who had seen and survived every variety of human suffering. The faces of many of them were covered with dirt and filth; their long hair and beards matted and foul; clothed in rags, and with scarcely a sufficient supply of these to cover their disgusting bodies. Many among them possessed no clothing except the remnant of those garments which they wore when first brought on board; and were unable to procure even any material for patching these together, when they had been worn to tatters by constant use. * * * Some, and indeed many of them, had not the means of procuring a razor, or an ounce of soap.

"Their beards were occasionally reduced by each other with a pair of shears or scissors. * * * Their skins were discoloured by continual washing in salt water, added to the circumstance that it was impossible for them to wash their linen in any other manner than by laying it on the deck and stamping on it with their feet, after it had been immersed in salt water, their bodies remaining naked during the process.

"To men in this situation everything like ordinary cleanliness was impossible. Much that was disgusting in their appearance undoubtedly originated from neglect, which long confinement had rendered habitual, until it created a confirmed indifference to personal appearance.

"As soon as the gratings had been fastened over the hatchways for the night, we usually went to our sleeping places. It was, of course, always desirable to obtain a station as near as possible to the side of the ship, and, if practicable, in the immediate vicinity of one of the air–ports, as this not only afforded us a better air, but also rendered us less liable to be trodden upon by those who were moving about the decks during the night.

"But silence was a stranger to our dark abode. There were continual noises during the night. The groans of the sick and the dying; the curses poured out by the weary and exhausted upon our inhuman keepers; the restlessness caused by the suffocating heat, and the confined and poisonous air, mingled with the wild and incoherent ravings of delirium, were the sounds which every night were raised around us in every direction. Such was our ordinary situation, but at times the consequences of our crowded condition were still more terrible, and proved fatal to many of our number in a single night.

"But, strange as it may appear, notwithstanding all the * * * suffering which was there endured I knew many who had been inmates of that abode for two years, who were apparently perfectly well. They had, as they expressed it, 'been through the furnace and become seasoned.' Most of these, however, were foreigners, who appeared to have abandoned all hope of ever being exchanged, and had become quite indifferent with regard to the place of their abode.

"But far different was the condition of that portion of our number who were natives of the United States. These formed by far the most numerous class of the prisoners. Most of these were young men, * * * who had been captured soon after leaving their homes, and during their first voyage. After they had been here immured the sudden change in their situation was like a sentence of death. Many a one was crushed down beneath the sickness of the heart, so well described by the poet:—

"'Night and day,
Brooding on what he had been, what he was,
'Twas more than he could bear, his longing fits
Thickened upon him. *His desire for Home
Became a madness*'

"These poor creatures had, in many instances, been plundered of their wearing apparel by their captors, and here, the dismal and disgusting objects by which they were surrounded, the vermin which infested them, the vile and loathsome food, and what with *them* was far from being the lightest of their trials, their ceaseless longing after their *homes*, * * * all combined, had a wonderful effect on them. Dejection and anguish were soon visible on their countenances. They became dismayed and terror–stricken; and many of them absolutely died that most awful of all human deaths, the effects of a *broken heart*.

"A custom had long been established that certain labor which it was necessary should be performed daily, should be done by a company, usually called the 'Working party.' This consisted of about twenty able–bodied men chosen from among the prisoners, and was commanded, in daily rotation, by those of our number who had formerly been officers of vessels. The commander of the party for the day bore the title of Boatswain. The members of the Working–party received, as a compensation for their services, a full allowance of provisions, and half a pint of rum each, with the privilege of going on deck early in the morning, to breathe the pure air.

"This privilege alone was a sufficient compensation for all the duty which was required of them.

"Their routine of service was to wash down that part of the upper deck and gangways where the prisoners were permitted to walk; to spread the awning, or to hoist on board the wood, water, and other supplies, from the boats in which the same were brought alongside the ship.

"When the prisoners ascended to the upper deck in the morning, if the day was fair, each carried up his hammock and bedding, which were all placed upon the spar–deck, or booms. The Working–party then took the sick and disabled who remained below, and placed them in the bunks prepared for them upon the centre–deck; they then, if any of the prisoners had died during the night, carried up the dead bodies, and laid them upon the

234

booms; after which it was their duty to wash down the main decks below; during which operation the prisoners remained on the upper deck, except such as chose to go below and volunteer their services in the performance of this duty.

"Around the railing of the hatchway leading from the centre to the lower decks, were placed a number of large tubs for the occasional use of the prisoners during the night, and as general receptacles of filth. Although these were indispensably necessary to us, yet they were highly offensive. It was a part of the duty of the Working–party to carry these on deck, at the time when the prisoners ascended in the morning, and to return them between decks in the afternoon.

"Our beds and clothing were kept on deck until nearly the hour when we were to be ordered below for the night. During this interval * * * the decks washed and cleared of all incumbrance, except the poor wretches who lay in the bunks, it was quite refreshing after the suffocating heat and foul vapors of the night to walk between decks. There was then some circulation of air through the ship, and, for a few hours, our existence was, in some degree, tolerable.

"About two hours before sunset the order was usually issued for the prisoners to carry their hammocks, etc., below. After this had been done we were all either to retire between decks, or to remain above until sunset according to our own pleasure. Everything which we could do conducive to cleanliness having then been performed, if we ever felt anything like enjoyment in this wretched abode, it was during this brief interval, when we breathed the cool air of the approaching night, and felt the luxury of our evening pipe. But short indeed was this interval of repose. The Working–party was soon ordered to carry the tubs below, and we prepared to descend to our gloomy and crowded dungeons. This was no sooner done than the gratings were closed over the hatchways, the sentinels stationed, and we left to sicken and pine beneath our accumulated torments; with our guards above crying aloud, through the long night, 'All's well!'"

Captain Dring says that at that time the Jersey was used for seamen alone. The average number on board was one thousand. It consisted of the crews of vessels of all the nations with which the English were at war. But the greater number had been captured on board American vessels.

There were three hospital ships in the Wallabout; the Stromboli, the Hunter, and the Scorpion. [Footnote: At one time as we have seen, the Scorpion was a prison ship, from which Freneau was sent to the Hunter hospital ship.] There was not room enough on board these ships for all the sick, and a part of the upper deck of the Jersey was therefore prepared for their accommodation. These were on the after part of the upper deck, on the larboard side, where those who felt the symptoms of approaching sickness could lie down, in order to be found by the nurses as soon as possible.

Few ever returned from the hospital ships to the Jersey. Dring knew but three such instances during his imprisonment. He says that "the outward appearance of these hospitals was disgusting in the highest degree. The sight of them was terrible to us. Their appearance was even more shocking than that of our own miserable hulk.

"On board the Jersey among the prisoners were about half a dozen men known by the appellation of nurses. I never learned by whom they were appointed, or whether they had any regular appointment at all. But one fact I knew well; they were all thieves. They were, however, sometimes useful in assisting the sick to ascend from below to the gangway on the upper deck, to be examined by the visiting Surgeon who attended from the Hunter every day, when the weather was good. If a sick man was pronounced by the Surgeon to be a proper subject for one of the hospital ships, he was put into the boat waiting alongside; but not without the loss or detention of his effects, if he had any, as these were at once taken by the nurses, as their own property. * * * I had found Mr. Robert Carver, our Gunner while on board the Chance, sick in one of the bunks where those retired who wished to be removed. He was without a bed or pillow, and had put on all the wearing apparel which he possessed, wishing to preserve it, and being sensible of his situation. I found him sitting upright in the bunk, with his great–coat on over the rest of his garments, and his hat between his knees. The weather was excessively hot, and, in the place where he lay, the heat was overpowering. I at once saw that he was delirious, a sure presage that the end was near. I took off his great–coat, and having folded and placed it under his head for a pillow, I laid him upon it, and went immediately to prepare him some tea. I was absent but a few minutes, and, on returning, met one of the thievish Nurses with Carver's great–coat in his hand. On ordering him to return it his reply was that it was a perquisite of the Nurses, and the only one they had; that the man was dying, and the great–coat could be of no further use to him. I however, took possession of the coat, and on my liberation, returned it to the family of the owner. Mr Carver soon after expired where he lay. We procured a blanket in which to wrap his body, which was thus prepared for interment. Others of the crew of the Chance had died before that time. Mr Carver was a man of strong and robust constitution. Such men were subject to the most violent attacks of the fever, and were also its most certain victims."

CHAPTER XXXVI. THE INTERMENT OF THE DEAD

Captain Dring continues his narrative by describing the manner in which the dead were interred in the sand of the Wallabout. Every morning, he says, the dead bodies were carried to the upper deck and there laid upon the gratings. Any person who could procure, and chose to furnish, a blanket, was allowed to sew it around the remains of his departed companion.

"The signal being made, a boat was soon seen approaching from the Hunter, and if there were any dead on board the other ships, the boat received them, on her way to the Jersey.

"The corpse was laid upon a board, to which some ropes were attached as straps; as it was often the case that bodies were sent on shore for interment before they had become sufficiently stiff to be lowered into the boat by a single strap. Thus prepared a tackle was attached to the board, and the remains * * * were hoisted over the side of the ship into the boat, without further ceremony. If several bodies were waiting for interment, but one of them was lowered into the boat at a time, for the sake of decency. The prisoners were always very anxious to be engaged in the duty of interment, not so much from a feeling of humanity, or from a wish to pay respect to the remains of the dead, for to these feelings they had almost become strangers, as from the desire of once more placing their feet on the land, if but for a few minutes. A sufficient number of prisoners having received permission to assist in this duty, they entered the boat accompanied by a guard of soldiers, and put off from the ship.

"I obtained leave to assist in the burial of the body of Mr. Carver, * * * and after landing at a low wharf which had been built from the shore, we first went to a small hut, which stood near the wharf, and was used as a place of deposit for the handbarrows and shovels provided for these occasions. Having placed the corpses on the barrows, and received our hoes and shovels, we proceeded to the side of the bank near the Waleboght. Here a vacant space having been selected, we were directed to dig a trench in the sand, of a proper length for the reception of the bodies. We continued our labor until the guards considered that a sufficient space had been excavated. The corpses were then laid in the trench without ceremony, and we threw the sand over them. The whole appeared to produce no more effect upon our guards than if they were burying the bodies of dead animals, instead of men. They scarcely allowed us time to look about us; for no sooner had we heaped the earth upon the trench, than we were ordered to march. But a single glance was sufficient to show us parts of many bodies which were exposed to view, although they had probably been placed there with the same mockery of interment but a few days before.

"Having thus performed, as well as we were permitted to do it, the last duty to the dead, and the guards having stationed themselves on each side of us, we began reluctantly to retrace our steps to the boat. We had enjoyed the pleasure of breathing for a few minutes the air of our native soil; and the thought of return to the crowded prison–ship was terrible in the extreme. As we passed by the waterside we implored our guards to allow us to bathe, or even to wash ourselves for a few minutes, but this was refused us.

"I was the only person of our party who wore a pair of shoes, and well recollect that I took them off for the pleasure of feeling the earth, or rather the sand, as we went along. * * * We went by a small patch of turf, some pieces of which we tore up from the earth, and obtained permission to carry them on board for our comrades to smell them. Circumstances like these may appear trifling to the careless reader; but let him be assured that they were far from being trifles to men situated as we had been. The inflictions which we had endured; the duty which we had just performed; the feeling that we must, in a few minutes, re–enter the place of suffering, from which, in all probability, we should never return alive; all tended to render everything connected with the firm land beneath, and the sweet air above us, objects of deep and thrilling interest.

"Having arrived at the hut we there deposited our implements, and walked to the landing–place, where we prevailed on our guards, who were Hessians, to allow us the gratification of remaining nearly half an hour before we returned to the boat.

"Near us stood a house occupied by a miller, and we had been told that a tide–mill which he attended was in the immediate vicinity, as a landing–place for which the wharf where we stood had been erected. * * * It was designated by the prisoners by the appellation of the 'Old Dutchman's,' and its very walls were viewed by us with feelings of veneration, as we had been told that the amiable daughter of its owner had kept an accurate account of the number of bodies that had been brought on shore for interment from the Jersey and hospital ships. This could easily be done in the house, as its windows commanded a fair view of the landing place. We were not, however, gratified by a sight of herself, or of any other inmate of the house.

"Sadly did we approach and re–enter our foul and disgusting place of confinement. The pieces of turf which we carried on board were sought for by our fellow prisoners, with the greatest avidity, every fragment being passed by them from hand to hand, and its smell inhaled as if it had been a fragrant rose. * * * The first of the crew of the Chance to die was a lad named Palmer, about twelve years of age, and the youngest of our crew. When on board the Chance he was a waiter to the officers, and he continued in this duty after we were placed on board the Jersey. He had, with many others of our crew, been inoculated for the small–pox, immediately after our arrival on board. The usual symptoms appeared at the proper time, and we supposed the appearance of his disorder favorable, but these soon changed, and the yellow hue of his features declared the approach of death. * * * The night he died was truly a wretched one for me. I spent most of it in total darkness, holding him during his convulsions. * * * I had done everything in my power for this poor boy, during his sickness, and could render him but one more kind office (after his death). I assisted to sew a blanket around his body, which was, with others who had died, during the night, conveyed upon deck in the morning, to be at the usual hour hurried to the bank at the Walebocht. I regretted that I could not assist at his interment, as I was then suffering with the small–pox myself, neither am I certain that permission would have been granted me, if I had sought it. Our keepers appeared to have no idea that the prisoners could feel any regard for each other, but appeared to think us as cold–hearted as themselves. If anything like sympathy was ever shown us by any of them it was done by the Hessians. * * * The next deaths among our company were those of Thomas Mitchell and his son–in–law, Thomas Sturmey. It is a singular fact that both of these men died at the same time."

THE GUARDS ON BOARD THE JERSEY

"In addition to the regular officers and seamen of the Jersey, there were stationed on board about a dozen old invalid Marines, but our actual guard was composed of soldiers from the different regiments quartered on Long Island. The number usually on duty on board was about thirty. Each week they were relieved by a fresh party. They were English, Hessian, and Refugees. We always preferred the Hessians, from whom we received better treatment than from the others. As to the English, we did not complain, being aware that they merely obeyed their orders, in regard to us; but the Refugees * * * were viewed by us with scorn and hatred. I do not recollect, however, that a guard of these miscreants was placed over us more than three times, during which their presence occasioned much tumult and confusion; for the prisoners could not endure the sight of these men, and occasionally assailed them with abusive language, while they, in turn, treated us with all the severity in their power. We dared not approach near them, for fear of their bayonets, and of course could not pass along the gangways where they were stationed; but were obliged to crawl along upon the booms, in order to get fore and aft, or to go up and down the hatchways. They never answered any of our remarks respecting them, but would merely point to their uniforms, as much as to say, 'We are clothed by our Sovereign, while you are naked.' They were as much gratified by the idea of leaving us as we were at seeing them depart.

"Many provoking gestures were made by the prisoners as they left the ship, and our curses followed them as far as we could make ourselves heard.

"A regiment of Refugees, with a green uniform, were then quartered at Brooklyn. We were invited to join this Royal band, and to partake of his Majesty's pardon and bounty. But the prisoners, in the midst of their unbounded sufferings, of their dreadful privations, and consuming anguish, spurned the insulting offer. They preferred to linger and to die rather than desert their country's cause. During the whole period of my confinement I never knew a single instance of enlistment among the prisoners of the Jersey.

"The only duty, to my knowledge, ever performed by the old Marines was to guard the water−butt, near which one of them was stationed with a drawn cutlass. They were ordered to allow no prisoner to carry away more than one pint at once, but we were allowed to drink at the butt as much as we pleased, for which purpose two or three copper ladles were chained to the cask. Having been long on board and regular in performance of this duty, they had become familiar with the faces of the prisoners, and could, in many instances, detect the frauds which we practiced upon them in order to obtain more fresh water for our cooking than was allowed us by the regulations of the ship. Over the water the sailors had no control. The daily consumption of water on board was at least equal to 700 gallons. I know not whence it was brought, but presume it was from Brooklyn. One large gondola, or boat, was kept in constant employment to furnish the necessary supply.

"So much of the water as was not required on deck for immediate use was conducted into butts, placed in the lower hold of the hulk, through a leather hose, passing through her side, near the bends. To this water we had recourse, when we could procure no other.

"When water in any degree fit for use was brought on board, it is impossible to describe the struggle which ensued, in consequence of our haste and exertions to procure a draught of it. The best which was ever afforded us was very brackish, but that from the ship's hold was nauseous in the highest degree. This must be evident when the fact is stated that the butts for receiving it had never been cleaned since they were put in the hold. The quantity of foul sediment which they contained was therefore very great, and was disturbed and mixed with the water as often as a new supply was poured into them, thereby rendering their whole contents a substance of the most disgusting and poisonous nature. I have not the least doubt that the use of this vile compound caused the death of hundreds of the prisoners, when, to allay their tormenting thirst, they were driven by desperation to drink this liquid poison, and to abide the consequences."

CHAPTER XXXVII. DAME GRANT AND HER BOAT

"One indulgence was allowed us by our keepers, if indulgence it can be called. They had given permission for a boat to come alongside the ship, with a supply of a few necessary articles, to be sold to such of the prisoners as possessed the means of paying for them. This trade was carried on by a very corpulent old woman, known among us by the name of Dame Grant. Her visits, which were made every other day, were of much benefit to us, and, I presume, a source of profit to herself. She brought us soft bread and fruit, with various other articles, such as tea, sugar, etc., all of which she previously put up into small paper parcels, from one ounce to a pound in weight, with the price affixed to each, from which she would never deviate. The bulk of the old lady completely filled the stern sheets of the boat, where she sat, with her box of goods before her, from which she supplied us very expeditiously. Her boat was rowed by two boys, who delivered to us the articles we had purchased, the price of which we were required first to put into their hands.

"When our guard was not composed of Refugees, we were usually permitted to descend to the foot of the Accommodation–ladder, in order to select from the boat such articles as we wished. While standing there it was distressing to see the faces of hundreds of half–famished wretches, looking over the side of the ship into the boat, without the means of purchasing the most trifling article before their sight, not even so much as a morsel of wholesome bread. None of us possessed the means of generosity, nor had any power to afford them relief. Whenever I bought any articles from the boat I never enjoyed them; for it was impossible to do so in the presence of so many needy wretches, eagerly gazing at my purchase, and almost dying for want of it.

"We frequently furnished Dame Grant with a memorandum of such articles as we wished her to procure for us, such as pipes, tobacco, needles, thread, and combs. These she always faithfully procured and brought to us, never omitting the assurance that she afforded them exactly at cost.

"Her arrival was always a subject of interest to us; but at length she did not make her appearance for several days, and her appearance was awaited in extreme anxiety. But, alas! we were no longer to enjoy this little gratification. Her traffic was ended. She had taken the fever from the hulk, and died * * * leaving a void which was never afterwards filled up."

CHAPTER XXXVIII. THE SUPPLIES FOR THE PRISONERS

"After the death of Dame Grant, we were under the necessity of puchasing from the Sutler such small supplies as we needed. This man was one of the Mates of the ship, and occupied one of the apartments under the quarter–deck, through the bulkhead of which an opening had been cut, from which he delivered his goods. He here kept for sale a variety of articles, among which was usually a supply of ardent spirits, which was not allowed to be brought alongside the ship, for sale. It could, therefore, only be procured from the Sutler, whose price was two dollars per gallon. Except in relation to this article, no regular price was fixed for what he sold us. We were first obliged to hand him the money, and he then gave us such a quantity as he pleased of the article which we needed; there was on our part no bargain to be made, but to be supplied even in this manner was, to those of us who had means of payment, a great convenience. * * *

"Our own people afforded us no relief. O my country! Why were we thus neglected in this hour of our misery, why was not a little food and raiment given to the dying martyrs of thy cause?

"Although the supplies which some of us were enabled to procure from the Sutler were highly conducive to our comfort, yet one most necessary article neither himself nor any other person could furnish. This was wood for our daily cooking, to procure a sufficient quantity of which was to us a source of continual trouble and anxiety. The Cooks would indeed steal small quantities, and sell them to us at the hazard of certain punishment if detected; but it was not in their power to embezzle a sufficient quantity to meet our daily necessities. As the disgust at swallowing any food which had been cooked in the Great Copper was universal, each person used every exertion to procure as much wood as possible, for the private cooking of his own mess.

"During my excursion to the shore to assist in the interment of Mr. Carver, it was my good fortune to find a hogshead stave floating in the water. This was truly a prize I conveyed the treasure on board, and in the economical manner in which it was used, it furnished the mess to which I belonged with a supply of fuel for a considerable time.

"I was also truly fortunate on another occasion. I had, one day, commanded the Working–party, which was then employed in taking on board a sloop–load of wood for the sailors' use. This was carefully conveyed below, under a guard, to prevent embezzlement. I nevertheless found means, with the assistance of my associates, to convey a cleft of it into the Gunroom, where it was immediately secreted. Our mess was thereby supplied with a sufficient quantity for a long time, and its members were considered by far the most wealthy persons in all this republic of misery. We had enough for our own use, and were enabled, occasionally, to supply our neighbors with a few splinters.

"Our mode of preparing the wood was to cut it with a jack–knife into pieces about four inches long. This labor occupied much of our time, and was performed by the different members of our mess in rotation, which employment was to us a source of no little pleasure.

"After a sufficient quantity had been thus prepared for the next day's use, it was deposited in the chest. The main stock was guarded by day and night, with the most scrupulous and anxious care. We kept it at night within our enclosure, and by day it was always watched by some one of its proprietors. So highly did we value it that we went into mathematical calculation to ascertain how long it would supply us, if a given quantity was each day consumed."

OUR BY-LAWS

"Soon after the Jersey was first used as a place of confinement a code of by-laws had been established by the prisoners, for their own regulation and government; to which a willing submission was paid, so far as circumstances would permit. I much regret my inability to give these rules verbatim, but I cannot at this distant period of time recollect them with a sufficient degree of distinctness. They were chiefly directed to the preservation of personal cleanliness, and the prevention of immorality. For a refusal to comply with any of them, the refractory person was subjected to a stated punishment. It is an astonishing fact that any rules, thus made, should have so long existed and been enforced among a multitude of men situated as we were, so numerous and composed of that class of human beings who are not easily controlled, and usually not the most ardent supporters of good order. There were many foreigners among our number, over whom we had no control, except so far as they chose, voluntarily, to submit to our regulations, which they cheerfully did, in almost every instance, so far as their condition would allow. Among our rules were the following. That personal cleanliness should be preserved, as far as was practicable; that profane language should be avoided; that drunkenness should not be allowed; that theft should be severely punished, and that no smoking should be permitted between decks, by day or night, on account of the annoyance which it caused the sick.

"A due observance of the Sabbath was also strongly enjoined; and it was recommended to every individual to appear cleanly shaved on Sunday morning, and to refrain from all recreation during the day.

"This rule was particularly recommended to the attention of the officers, and the remainder of the prisoners were desired to follow their example.

"Our By-laws were occasionally read to the assembled prisoners, and always whenever any person was to be punished for their violation. Theft or fraud upon the allowance of a fellow prisoner was always punished, and the infliction was always approved by the whole company. On these occasions the oldest officer among the prisoners presided as Judge. It required much exertion for many of us to comply with the law prohibiting smoking between decks. Being myself much addicted to the habit of smoking, it would have been a great privilege to have enjoyed the liberty of thus indulging it, particularly during the night, while sitting by one of the air-ports; but as this was inadmissible, I of

244

course submitted to the prohibition. * * * We were not allowed means of striking a fire, and were obliged to procure it from the Cook employed for the ship's officers, through a small window in the bulkhead, near the caboose. After one had thus procured fire the rest were also soon supplied, and our pipes were all in full operation in the course of a few minutes. The smoke which rose around us appeared to purify the pestilent air by which we were surrounded; and I attribute the preservation of my health, in a great degree, to the exercise of this habit. Our greatest difficulty was to procure tobacco. This, to some of the prisoners, was impossible, and it must have been an aggravation to their sufferings to see us apparently puffing away our sorrows, while they had no means of procuring the enjoyment of a similar gratification.

"We dared not often apply at this Cook's caboose for fire, and the surly wretch would not willingly repeat the supply. One morning I went to the window of his den, and requested leave to light my pipe, and the miscreant, without making any reply, threw a shovel full of burning cinders in my face. I was almost blinded by the pain; and several days elapsed before I fully regained my sight. My feelings on this occasion may be imagined, but redress was impossible, as we were allowed no means of even seeking it. I mention this occurrence to show to what a wretched condition we were reduced."

THE ORATOR OF THE JERSEY

"During the period of my confinement the Jersey was never visited by any regular clergyman, nor was Divine service ever performed on board, and among the whole multitude of prisoners there was but one individual who ever attempted to deliver a set speech, or to exhort his fellow sufferers. This individual was a young man named Cooper, whose station in life was apparently that of a common sailor. He evidently possessed talents of a very high order. His manners were pleasing, and he had every appearance of having received an excellent education. He was a Virginian; but I never learned the exact place of his nativity. He told us that he had been a very unmanageable youth, and that he had left his family, contrary to their wishes and advice; that he had been often assured by them that the Old Jersey would bring him up at last, and the Waleboght be his place of burial. 'The first of these predictions,' said he, 'has been verified; and I care not how soon the second proves equally true, for I am prepared for the event. Death, for me, has lost its terrors, for with them I have been too long familiar.'

"On several Sunday mornings Cooper harangued the prisoners in a very forcible yet pleasing manner, which, together with his language, made a lasting impression upon my memory. On one of these occasions, having mounted upon a temporary elevation upon the Spar–deck, he, in an audible voice, requested the attention of the prisoners, who having immediately gathered around him in silence, he commenced his discourse.

"He began by saying that he hoped no one would suppose he had taken that station by way of derision or mockery of the holy day, for that such was not his object; on the contrary he was pleased to find that the good regulations established by the former prisoners, obliged us to refrain even from recreation on the Sabbath; that his object, however, was not to preach to us, nor to discourse upon any sacred subject; he wished to read us our By–laws, a copy of which he held in his hand, the framers of which were then, in all probability, sleeping in death, beneath the sand of the shore before our eyes. That these laws had been framed in wisdom, and were well fitted to preserve order and decorum in a community like ours: that his present object was to impress upon our minds the absolute necessity of a strict adherence to those wholesome regulations; that he should briefly comment upon each article, which might be thus considered as the particular text of that part of his discourse.

"He proceeded to point out the extreme necessity of a full observance of these Rules of Conduct, and portrayed the evil consequences which would inevitably result to us if we neglected or suffered them to fall into disuse. He enforced the necessity of our unremitting attention to personal cleanliness, and to the duties of morality; he dwelt upon the degradation and sin of drunkeness; described the meanness and atrocity of theft; and the high degree of caution against temptation necessary for men who were perhaps standing on the very brink of the grave; and added that, in his opinion, even sailors might as well refrain from profane language, while they were actually suffering in Purgatory.

"He said that our present torments, in that abode of misery, were a proper retribution for our former sins and transgressions; that Satan had been permitted to send out his messengers and inferior demons in every direction to collect us together, and that among the most active of these infernal agents was David Sproat, Commissary of Prisoners.

"He then made some just and suitable observations on the fortitude with which we had sustained the weight of our accumulated miseries; of our firmness in refusing to accept the bribes of our invaders, and desert the banners of our country. During this part of his discourse the sentinels on the gangways occasionally stopped and listened attentively. We much feared that by some imprudent remark, he might expose himself to their resentment, and cautioned him not to proceed too far. He replied our keepers could do nothing more, unless they should put him to the torture, and that he should proceed.

"He touched on the fact that no clergyman had ever visited us; that this was probably owing to the fear of contagion; but it was much to be regretted that no one had ever come to afford a ray of hope, or to administer the Word of Life in that terrific abode; that if any Minister of the Gospel desired to do so, there could be no obstacles in the way, for that even David Sproat himself, bad as he was, would not dare to oppose it.

"He closed with a merited tribute to the memory of our fellow–sufferers, who had already passed away. 'The time,' said he, 'will come when their bones will be collected, when their rites of sepulchre will be performed, and a monument erected over the remains of those who have here suffered, the victims of barbarity, and who have died in vindication of the rights of man.'

"The remarks of our Orator were well adapted to our situation, and produced much effect on the prisoners, who at length began to accost him as Elder or Parson Cooper. But this he would not allow; and told us, if we would insist on giving him a title, we might call him Doctor, by which name he was ever afterwards saluted, so long as he remained among us.

"He had been a prisoner for about the period of three months when one day the Commissary of Prisoners came on board, accompanied by a stranger, and inquired for Cooper, who having made his appearance, a letter was put in his hand, which he perused, and immediately after left the ship, without even going below for his clothing. While in the boat he waived his hand, and bade us be of good cheer. We could only return a mute farewell; and in a few minutes the boat had left the ship, and was on its way to New York.

"Thus we lost our Orator, for whom I had a very high regard, at the time, and whose character and manners have, ever since, been to me a subject of pleasing recollection.

"Various were the conjectures which the sudden manner of his departure caused on board. Some asserted that poor Cooper had drawn upon himself the vengeance of old

Sproat, and that he had been carried on shore to be punished. No certain information was ever received respecting him, but I have always thought that he was a member of some highly influential and respectable family, and that his release had been effected through the agency of his friends. This was often done by the influence of the Royalists or Refugees of New York, who were sometimes the connections or personal friends of those who applied for their assistance in procuring the liberation of a son or a brother from captivity. Such kind offices were thus frequently rendered to those who had chosen opposite sides in the great revolutionary contest, and to whom, though directly opposed to themselves in political proceedings, they were willing to render every personal service in their power."

CHAPTER XXXIX. FOURTH OF JULY ON THE JERSEY

A few days before the fourth of July we had made such preparations as our circumstances would admit for an observance of the anniversary of American Independence. We had procured some supplies with which to make ourselves merry on the occasion, and intended to spend the day in such innocent pastimes as our situation would afford, not dreaming that our proceeding would give umbrage to our keepers, as it was far from our intention to trouble or insult them. We thought that, though prisoners, we had a right, on that day at least, to sing and be merry. As soon as we were permitted to go on deck in the morning thirteen little national flags were displayed in a row on the boom. We were soon ordered by the guards to take them away; and as we neglected to obey the command, they triumphantly demolished, and trampled them under foot. Unfortunately for us our guards at that time were Scotch, who, next to the Refugees, were the objects of our greatest hatred; but their destruction of our flags was merely viewed in silence, with the contempt which it merited.

"During the time we remained on deck several patriotic songs were sung, and choruses repeated; but not a word was intentionally spoken to give offence to our guards. They were, nevertheless, evidently dissatisfied with our proceedings, as will soon appear. Their moroseness was a prelude to what was to follow. We were, in a short time, forbidden to pass along the common gangway, and every attempt to do so was repelled by the bayonet. Although thus incommoded our mirth still continued. Songs were still sung, accompanied by occasional cheers. Things thus proceeded until about four o'clock; when the guards were ordered out, and we received orders to descend between decks, where we were immediately driven, at the point of the bayonet.

"After being thus sent below in the greatest confusion, at that early and unusual hour, and having heard the gratings closed and fastened above us, we supposed that the barbarous resentment of our guards was fully satisfied; but we were mistaken, for they had further vengeance in store, and merely waited for an opportunity to make us feel its weight.

"The prisoners continued their singing between decks, and were, of course, more noisy than usual, but forbore even under their existing temptations, to utter any insulting or aggravating expressions. At least, I heard nothing of the kind, unless our patriotic songs could be thus constructed. In the course of the evening we were ordered to desist from making any further noise. This order not being fully complied with, at about nine o'clock the gratings were removed, and the guards descended among us, with lanterns and drawn cutlasses in their hands. The poor, helpless prisoners retreated from the hatchways, as far as their crowded situation would permit, while their cowardly assailants followed as far as they dared, cutting and wounding every one within reach, and then ascended to the upper deck, exulting in the gratification of their revenge.

"Many of the prisoners were wounded, but from the total darkness, neither their number, nor their situation could be ascertained; and, if this had been possible, it was not in the power of their compatriots to afford them the least relief. During the whole of that tragic night, their groans and lamentations were dreadful in the extreme. Being in the Gun–room I was at some distance from the immediate scene of this bloody outrage, but the distance was by no means far enough to prevent my hearing their continual cries from the extremity of pain, their appeals for assistance, and their curses upon the heads of their brutal assailants.

"It had been the usual custom for each person to carry below, when he descended at sunset, a pint of water, to quench his thirst during the night. But, on this occasion, we had thus been driven to our dungeon three hours before the setting of the sun, and without our usual supply of water.

"Of this night I cannot describe the horror. The day had been sultry, and the heat was extreme throughout the ship. The unusual number of hours during which we had been crowded together between decks; the foul atmosphere and sickening heat; the additional excitement and restlessness caused by the unwonted wanton attack which had been made;

above all, the want of water, not a drop of which could be obtained during the whole night, to cool our parched lips; the imprecations of those who were half distracted with their burning thirst; the shrieks and wails of the wounded; the struggles and groans of the dying; together formed a combination of horrors which no pen can describe.

"In the agonies of their sufferings the prisoners invited, and even challenged their inhuman guards to descend once more among them, but this they were prudent enough not to attempt.

"Their cries and supplications for water were terrible, and were of themselves sufficient to render sleep impossible. Oppressed with the heat, I found my way to the grating of the main hatchway, where on former nights I had frequently passed some time, for the benefit of the little current of air which circulated through the bars. I obtained a place on the larboard side of the hatchway, where I stood facing the East, and endeavored, as much as possible, to withdraw my attention from the terrible sounds below me, by watching, through the grating, the progress of the stars. I there spent hour after hour, in following with my eyes the motion of a particular star, as it rose and ascended until it passed over beyond my sight.

"How I longed for the day to dawn! At length the morning light began to appear, but still our torments were increasing every moment. As the usual hour for us to ascend to the upper deck approached, the Working–party were mustered near the hatchway, and we were all anxiously waiting for the opportunity to cool our weary frames, to breathe for awhile the pure air, and, above all, to procure water to quench our intolerable thirst. The time arrived, but still the gratings were not removed. Hour after hour passed on, and still we were not released. Our minds were at length seized with horror, suspicious that our tyrants had determined to make a finishing stroke of their cruelty, and rid themselves of us altogether.

"It was not until ten o'clock in the forenoon that the gratings were at last removed. We hurried on deck and thronged to the water cask, which was completely exhausted before our thirst was allayed. So great was the struggle around the cask that the guards were again turned out to disperse the crowd.

"In a few hours, however, we received a new supply of water, but it seemed impossible to allay our thirst, and the applications at the cask were incessant until sunset. Our rations were delivered to us, but of course long after the usual hour. During the whole day, however, no fire was kindled for cooking in the galley. All the food which we consumed that day we were obliged to swallow raw. Everything, indeed, had been entirely deranged by the events of the past night, and several days elapsed before order was restored. This was at last obtained by a change of the guard, who, to our great joy, were relieved by a party of Hessians. The average number who died during a period of 24 hours on board the Jersey was about six, [Footnote: This was in 1782. The mortality had been much greater in former years.] but on the morning of the fifth of July eight or ten corpses were found below. Many had been badly wounded, to whom, in the total darkness of the night, it was impossible for their companions to render any assistance; and even during the next day they received no attention, except that which was afforded by their fellow prisoners, who had nothing to administer to their companions, not even bandages for their wounds. I was not personally acquainted with any of those who died or were wounded on that night. No equal number had ever died in the same period of time since my confinement. This unusual mortality was of course caused by the increased sufferings of the night. Since that time I have often, while standing on the deck of a good ship under my command, and viewing the rising stars, thought upon the horrors of that night, when I stood watching their progress through the gratings of the Old Jersey, and when I now contrast my former wretchedness with my present situation, in the full enjoyment of liberty, health, and every earthly comfort, I cannot but muse upon the contrast, and bless the good and great Being from whom my comforts have been derived. I do not now regret my capture nor my sufferings, for the recollection of them has ever taught me how to enjoy my after life with a greater degree of contentment than I should, perhaps, have otherwise ever experienced."

CHAPTER XL. AN ATTEMPT TO ESCAPE

It had been for some time in contemplation among a few inmates of the Gun-room to make a desperate attempt to escape, by cutting a hole through the stern or counter of the ship. In order that their operations might proceed with even the least probability of success, it was absolutely necessary that but few of the prisoners should be admitted to the secret. At the same time it was impossible for them to make any progress in their labor unless they first confided their plan to all the other occupants of the Gun-room, which was accordingly done. In this part of the ship each mess was on terms of more or less intimacy with those whose little sleeping enclosures were immediately adjacent to their own, and the members of each mess frequently interchanged good offices with those in their vicinity, and borrowed or lent such little articles as they possessed, like the good housewives of a sociable neighborhood. I never knew any contention in this apartment, during the whole period of my confinement. Each individual in the Gun–room therefore was willing to assist his comrades, as far as he had the power to do so. When the proposed plan for escape was laid before us, although it met the disapprobation of by far the greater number, still we were all perfectly ready to assist those who thought it practicable. We, however, described to them the difficulties and dangers which must unavoidably attend their undertaking; the prospect of detection while making the aperture in the immediate vicinity of such a multitude of idle men, crowded together, a large proportion of whom were always kept awake by their restlessness and sufferings during the night; the little probability that they would be able to travel, undiscovered, on Long Island, even should they succeed in reaching the shore in safety; and above all, the almost absolute impossibility of obtaining food for their subsistence, as an application for that to our keepers would certainly lead to detection. But, notwithstanding all our arguments, a few of them remained determined to make the attempt. Their only reply to our reasoning was, that they must die if they remained, and that nothing worse could befall them if they failed in their undertaking.

"One of the most sanguine among the adventurers was a young man named Lawrence, the mate of a ship from Philadelphia. He was a member of the mess next to my own, and I had formed with him a very intimate acquaintance. He frequently explained his plans to me; and dwelt much on his hopes. But ardently as I desired to obtain my liberty, and great as were the exertions I could have made, had I seen any probability of gaining it, yet it was not my intention to join in this attempt. I nevertheless agreed to assist in the labor of cutting through the planks, and heartily wished, although I had no hope, that the enterprise might prove successful.

"The work was accordingly commenced, and the laborers concealed, by placing a blanket between them and the prisoners without. The counter of the ship was covered with hard oak plank, four inches thick; and through this we undertook to cut an opening sufficiently large for a man to descend; and to do this with no other tools than our jack knives and a single gimlet. All the occupants of the Gun–room assisted in this labor in rotation; some in confidence that the plan was practicable, and the rest for amusement, or for the sake of being employed. Some one of our number was constantly at work, and we thus continued, wearing a hole through the hard planks, from seam to seam, until at length the solid oak was worn away piecemeal, and nothing remained but a thin sheathing on the outside which could be cut away at any time in a few minutes, whenever a suitable opportunity should occur for making the bold attempt to leave the ship.

"It had been previously agreed that those who should descend through the aperture should drop into the water, and there remain until all those among the inmates of the Gun–room who chose to make the attempt could join them; and that the whole band of adventurers should then swim together to the shore, which was about a quarter of a mile from the ship.

"A proper time at length arrived. On a very dark and rainy night, the exterior sheathing was cut away; and at midnight four of our number having disencumbered themselves of their clothes and tied them across their shoulders, were assisted through the opening, and dropped one after another into the water.

"Ill–fated men! Our guards had long been acquainted with the enterprise. But instead of taking any measures to prevent it, they had permitted us to go on with our labor, keeping a vigilant watch for the moment of our projected escape, in order to gratify their bloodthirsty wishes. No other motive than this could have prompted them to the course which they pursued. A boat was in waiting under the ship's quarter, manned with rowers and a party of the guards. They maintained a profound silence after hearing the prisoners drop from the opening, until having ascertained that no more would probably descend, they pursued the swimmers, whose course they could easily follow by the sparkling of the water,—an effect always produced by the agitation of the waves in a stormy night.

"We were all profoundly silent in the Gun–room, after the departure of our companions, and in anxious suspense as to the issue of the adventure. In a few minutes we were startled by the report of a gun, which was instantly succeeded by a quick and scattering fire of musketry. In the darkness of the night, we could not see the unfortunate victims, but could distinctly hear their shrieks and cries for mercy.

"The noise of the firing had alarmed the prisoners generally, and the report of the attempted escape and its defeat ran like wildfire through the gloomy and crowded dungeons of the hulk, and produced much commotion among the whole body of prisoners. In a few moments, the gratings were raised, and the guards descended, bearing a naked and bleeding man, whom they placed in one of the bunks, and having left a piece of burning candle by his side, they again ascended to the deck, and secured the gratings.

"Information of this circumstance soon reached the Gun–room; and myself, with several others of our number, succeeded in making our way through the crowd to the bunks. The wounded man was my friend, Lawrence. He was severely injured in many places, and one of his arms had been nearly severed from his body by the stroke of a cutlass. This, he said, was done in wanton barbarity, while he was crying for mercy, with his hand on the gunwale of the boat. He was too much exhausted to answer any of our questions; and uttered nothing further, except a single inquiry respecting the fate of Nelson, one of his fellow adventurers. This we could not answer. Indeed, what became of the rest we never knew. They were probably all murdered in the water. This was the first time that I had ever seen a light between decks. The piece of candle had been left by the side of the bunk, in order to produce an additional effect upon the prisoners. Many had been suddenly awakened from their slumbers, and had crowded round the bunk where the sufferer lay. The effect of the partial light upon his bleeding and naked limbs, and upon the pale and haggard countenances, and tattered garments of the wild and crowded groups by whom he was surrounded, was horrid beyond description. We could render the sufferer but little assistance, being only able to furnish him with a few articles of apparel, and to bind a handkerchief around his head. His body was completely covered, and his hair filled with clotted blood; we had not the means of washing the gore from his wounds during the night. We had seen many die, but to view this wretched man expire in that situation, where he had been placed beyond the reach of surgical aid, merely to strike us with terror, was dreadful.

"The gratings were not removed at the usual hour in the morning, but we were all kept below until ten o'clock. This mode of punishment had now become habitual with our keepers, and we were all frequently detained between decks until a late hour in the day, in revenge for the most trifling occasion. This cruelty never failed to produce the torments arising from heat and thirst, with all their attendant miseries.

"The immediate purpose of our tyrants having been answered by leaving Mr. Lawrence below in that situation they promised in the morning that he should have the assistance of a surgeon, but that promise was not fulfilled. The prisoners rendered him every attention in their power, but in vain. Mortification soon commenced; he became delirious and died.

"No inquiry was made by our keepers respecting his situation. They evidently left him thus to suffer, in order that the sight of his agonies might deter the rest of the prisoners from following his example.

"We received not the least reprimand for this transaction. The aperture was again filled up with plank and made perfectly secure, and no similar attempt to escape was made,—at least so long as I remained on board.

"It was always in our power to knock down the guards and throw them overboard, but this would have been of no avail. If we had done so, and had effected our escape to Long Island, it would have been next to impossible for us to have proceeded any further among the number of troops there quartered. Of these there were several regiments, and among them the regiment of Refugees before mentioned, who were vigilant in the highest degree, and would have been delighted at the opportunity of apprehending and returning us to our dungeons.

"There were, however, several instances of individuals making their escape. One in particular, I well recollect,—James Pitcher, one of the crew of the Chance, was placed on the sick list and conveyed to Blackwell's Island. He effected his escape from thence to Long Island; from whence, after having used the greatest precaution, he contrived to cross the Sound, and arrived safe at home. He is now one of the three survivors of the crew of the Chance."

CHAPTER XLI. THE MEMORIAL TO GENERAL WASHINGTON

"The body maddened by the spirit's pain;
The wild, wild working of the breast and brain;
The haggard eye, that, horror widened, sees
Death take the start of hunger and disease.
Here, such were seen and heard;—so close at hand,
A cable's length had reached them from the land;
Yet farther off than ocean ever bore;—
Eternity between them and the shore!"
—W. Read.

"Notwithstanding the destroying pestilence which was now raging to a degree hitherto unknown on board, new companies of victims were continually arriving; so that, although the mortality was very great, our numbers were increasing daily. Thus situated, and seeing no prospect of our liberty by exchange, we began to despair, and to believe that our certain fate was rapidly approaching.

"One expedient was at length proposed among us and adopted. We petitioned General Clinton, who was then in command of the British forces at New York, for leave to transmit a Memorial to General Washington, describing our deplorable situation, and requesting his interference in our behalf. We further desired that our Memorial might be examined by the British General, and, if approved by him, that it might be carried by one of our own number to General Washington. Our petition was laid before the British commander and was granted by the Commissary of Prisoners. We received permission to choose three from our number, to whom was promised a pass–port, with leave to proceed immediately on their embassy.

"Our choice was accordingly made, and I had the satisfaction to find that two of those elected were from among the former officers of the Chance, Captain Aborn and our Surgeon, Mr. Joseph Bowen.

"The Memorial was soon completed and signed in the name of all the prisoners, by a Committee appointed for that purpose. It contained an account of the extreme wretchedness of our condition, and stated that although we were sensible that the subject was one over which General Washington had no direct control, as it was not usual for soldiers to be exchanged for seamen, and his authority not extending to the Marine Department of the American service; yet still, although it might not be in his power to effect an exchange, we hoped he would be able to devise some means to lighten or relieve our sufferings.

"Our messengers were further charged with a verbal commission to General Washington, which, for obvious reasons, was not included in the written Memorial. They were directed to state, in a manner more circumstantial than we had dared to write, the peculiar horrors of our situation; to discover the miserable food and putrid water on which we were doomed to subsist; and finally to assure the General that in case he could effect our release, we would agree to enter the American service as soldiers, and remain during the war. Thus instructed our messengers departed.

256

"We waited in alternate hope and fear, the event of their mission. Most of our number, who were natives of the Eastern States, were strongly impressed with the idea that some means would be devised for our relief, after such a representation of our condition should be made. This class of the prisoners, indeed, felt most interested in the success of the application; for many of the sufferers appeared to give themselves but little trouble respecting it, and some among the foreigners did not commonly know that such an appeal had been made, or that it had even been in contemplation. The long endurance of their privations had rendered them almost indifferent to their fate, and they appeared to look forward to death as the only probable termination of their captivity.

"In a few days our messengers returned to New York, with a letter from General Washington, addressed to the Committee of Prisoners who had signed the Memorial. The prisoners were all summoned to the Spar–deck where this letter was read. Its purport was as follows:—That he had perused our communication, and had received, with due consideration, the account which our messengers had laid before him; that he viewed our situation with a high degree of interest, and that although our application, as we had stated, was made in relation to a subject over which he had no direct control, yet that it was his intention to lay our Memorial before Congress; and that, in the mean time, we might be assured that no exertions on his part should be spared which could tend to a mitigation of our sufferings.

"He observed to our messengers, during their interview, that our long detention in confinement was owing to a combination of circumstances, against which it was very difficult, if not impossible, to provide. That, in the first place, but little exertion was made on the part of our countrymen to secure and detain their British prisoners for the sake of exchange, many of the British seamen being captured by privateers, on board which, he understood, it was a common practice for them to enter as seamen; and that when this was not the case, they were usually set at liberty as soon as the privateers arrived in port; as neither the owners, nor the town or State where they were landed, would be at the expense of their confinement and maintenance; and that the officers of the General Government only took charge of those seamen who were captured by the vessels in public service. All which circumstances combined to render the number of prisoners, at all times, by far too small for a regular and equal exchange.

"General Washington also transmitted to our Committee copies of letters which he had sent to General Clinton and to the Commissary of Prisoners, which were also read to us.

He therein expressed an ardent desire that a general exchange of prisoners might be effected; and if this could not be accomplished, he wished that something might be done to lessen the weight of our sufferings, that, if it was absolutely necessary that we should be confined on the water, he desired that we might at least be removed to clean ships. He added if the Americans should be driven to the necessity of placing the British prisoners in situations similar to our own, similar effects must be the inevitable results; and that he therefore hoped they would afford us better treatment from motives of humanity. He concluded by saying, that as a correspondence on the subject had thus begun between them, he ardently wished it might eventually result in the liberation of the unfortunate men whose situation had called for its commencement.

"Our three messengers did not return on board as prisoners, but were all to remain on parole at Flatbush, on Long Island.

"We soon found an improvement in our fare. The bread which we received was of a better quality, and we were furnished with butter, instead of rancid oil. An awning was provided, and a wind−sail furnished to conduct fresh air between the decks during the day. But of this we were always deprived at night, when we most needed it, as the gratings must always be fastened over the hatchway and I presume that our keepers were fearful if it was allowed to run, we might use it as a means of escape.

"We were, however, obliged to submit to all our privations, consoling ourselves only with the faint hope that the favorable change in our situation, which we had observed for the last few days, might lead to something still more beneficial, although we saw little prospect of escape from the raging pestilence, except through the immediate interposition of divine Providence, or by a removal from the scene of contagion."

Note. From the *New Jersey Gazette*, July 24th, 1782. "New London. July 21st. We are informed that Sir Guy Carleton has visited all the prison ships at New York, minutely examined into the situation of the prisoners, and expressed his intention of having them better provided for. That they were to be landed on Blackwell's Island, in New York harbour, in the daytime, during the hot season."

CHAPTER XLII. THE EXCHANGE

"Soon after Captain Aborn had been permitted to go to Long Island on his parole, he sent a message on board the Jersey, informing us that his parole had been extended so far as to allow him to return home, but that he should visit us previous to his departure. He requested our First Lieutenant, Mr. John Tillinghast, to provide a list of the names of those captured in the Chance who had died, and also a list of the survivors, noting where each survivor was then confined, whether on board the Jersey, or one of the Hospital ships.

"He also requested that those of our number who wished to write to their friends at home, would have their letters ready for delivery to him, whenever he should come on board. The occupants of the Gun–room, and such of the other prisoners as could procure the necessary materials were, therefore, soon busily engaged in writing as particular descriptions of our situation as they thought it prudent to do, without the risk of the destruction of the letters; as we were always obliged to submit our writing for inspection previous to its being allowed to pass from the ship. We, however, afterwards regretted that on this occasion our descriptions were not more minute, as these letters were not examined.

"The next day Captain Aborn came on board, accompanied by several other persons, who had also been liberated on parole; but they came no nearer to the prisoners than the head of the gangway–ladder, and passed through the door of the barricade to the Quarter–deck. This was perhaps a necessary precaution against the contagion, as they were more liable to be affected by it than if they had always remained on board; but we were much disappointed at not having an opportunity to speak to them. Our letters were delivered to Captain Aborn by our Lieutenant, through whom he sent us assurances of his determination to do everything in his power for our relief, and that if a sufficient number of British prisoners could be procured, every survivor of his vessel's crew should be exchanged; and if this could not be effected we might depend upon receiving clothing and such other necessary articles as could be sent for our use.

"About this time some of the sick were sent on shore on Blackwell's Island. This was considered a great indulgence. I endeavored to obtain leave to join them by feigning sickness, but did not succeed.

American Prisoners of the Revolution

"The removal of the sick was a great relief to us, as the air was less foul between decks, and we had more room for motion. Some of the bunks were removed, and the sick were carried on shore as soon as their condition was known. Still, however, the pestilence did not abate on board, as the weather was extremely warm. In the daytime the heat was excessive, but at night it was intolerable.

"But we lived on hope, knowing that, in all probability, our friends at home had ere then been apprised of our condition, and that some relief might perhaps be soon afforded us.

"Such was our situation when, one day, a short time before sunset, we described a sloop approaching us, with a white flag at her mast–head, and knew, by that signal, that she was a Cartel, and from the direction in which she came supposed her to be from some of the Eastern States. She did not approach near enough to satisfy our curiosity, until we were ordered below for the night.

"Long were the hours of the night to the survivors of our crew. Slight as was the foundation on which our hopes had been raised, we had clung to them as our last resource. No sooner were the gratings removed in the morning than we were all upon deck, gazing at the Cartel. Her deck was crowded with men, whom we supposed to be British prisoners. In a few moments they began to enter the Commissary's boats, and proceeded to New York.

"In the afternoon a boat from the Cartel came alongside the hulk, having on board the Commissary of Prisoners, and by his side sat our townsman, Captain William Corey, who came on board with the joyful information that the sloop was from Providence with English prisoners to be exchanged for the crew of the Chance. The number which she had brought was forty, being more than sufficient to redeem every survivor of our crew then on board the Jersey.

"I immediately began to prepare for my departure. Having placed the few articles of clothing which I possessed in a bag (for, by one of our By–laws, no prisoner, when liberated, could remove his chest) I proceeded to dispose of my other property on board, and after having made sundry small donations of less value, I concluded by giving my tin kettle to one of my friends, and to another the remnant of my cleft of firewood.

"I then hurried to the upper deck, in order to be ready to answer to my name, well knowing that I should hear no second call, and that no delay would be allowed.

"The Commissary and Captain Corey were standing together on the Quarter–deck; and as the list of names was read, our Lieutenant, Mr. Tillinghast, was directed to say whether the person called was one of the crew of the Chance. As soon as this assurance was given, the individual was ordered to pass down the Accommodation ladder into the boat. Cheerfully was the word 'Here!' responded by each survivor as his name was called. My own turn at length came, and the Commissary pointed to the boat. I never moved with a lighter step, for that moment was the happiest of my life. In the excess and overflowing of my joy, I even forgot, for awhile, the detestable character of the Commissary himself, and even, Heaven forgive me! bestowed a bow upon him as I passed.

"We took our stations in the boat in silence. No congratulations were heard among us. Our feelings were too deep for utterance. For my own part, I could not refrain from bursting into tears of joy.

"Still there were moments when it seemed impossible that we were in reality without the limits of the Old Jersey. We dreaded the idea that some unforeseen event might still detain us; and shuddered with the apprehension that we might yet be returned to our dungeons.

"When the Cartel arrived the surviving number of our crew on board the Old Jersey was but thirty–five. This fact being well known to Mr. Tillinghast, and finding that the Cartel had brought forty prisoners, he allowed five of our comrades in the Gun–room to answer to the names of the same number of our crew who had died; and having disguised them in the garb of common seamen, they passed unsuspected.

"It was nearly sunset when we had all arrived on board the Cartel. No sooner had the exchange been completed than the Commissary left us, with our prayers that we might never behold him more. I then cast my eyes towards the hulk, as the horizontal rays of the sunset glanced on her polluted sides, where, from the bend upwards, filth of every description had been permitted to accumulate for years; and the feeling of disgust which the sight occasioned was indescribable. The multitude on her Spar–deck and Fore–castle were in motion, and in the act of descending for the night; presenting the same appearance that met my sight when, nearly five months before, I had, at the same hour, approached her as a prisoner."

It appears that many other seamen on board the Jersey and the Hospital ships were exchanged as a good result of the Memorial addressed to General Washington. An issue of the *Royal Gazette* of New York, published on the 17th of July, 1782, contains the following statement:

"The following is a Statement of the Navy Prisoners who have, within the last few days, been exchanged and brought to this city, viz:

"From Boston, 102 British Seamen. "From Rhode Island, 40 British Seamen. "From New London, Conn., 84 British Seamen. "From Baltimore, Md, 23 British Seamen. "Total 249.

"The exertions of those American Captains who published to the world in this *Gazette*, dated July 3rd, the real state and condition of their countrymen, prisoners here, and the true cause of their durance and sufferings, we are informed was greatly conducive to the bringing this exchange into a happy effect. We have only to lament that the endeavors of those who went, for the same laudable purpose, to Philadelphia, have not hitherto been so fortunate."

This was published before the release of Captain Dring and the crew of the Chance, and shows that they were not the only prisoners who were so happy as to be exchanged that summer. It is possible that the crew of the Chance is referred to in this extract from the *Pennsylvania Packet*, Philadelphia, Thursday, August 15th, 1782: "Providence, July 27th. Sunday last a flag of truce returned here from New York, and brought 39 prisoners."

CHAPTER XLIII. THE CARTEL—CAPTAIN DRING'S NARRATIVE (CONTINUED)

"On his arrival in Providence Captain Aborn had lost no time in making the details of our sufferings publicly known; and a feeling of deep commiseration was excited among our fellow citizens. Messrs. Clarke and Nightingale, the former owners of the Chance, in conjunction with other gentlemen, expressed their determination to spare no exertion or expense necessary to procure our liberty. It was found that forty British prisoners were at that time in Boston. These were immediately procured, and marched to Providence, where a sloop owned and commanded by a Captain Gladding of Bristol was chartered, to proceed with the prisoners forthwith to New York, that they might be exchanged for an equal number of our crew. Captain Corey was appointed as an Agent to effect the exchange, and to receive us from the Jersey; and having taken on board a supply of good provisions and water, he hastened to our relief. He received much assistance in effecting his object from our townsman, Mr. John Creed, at that time Deputy Commissary of Prisoners. I do not recollect the exact day of our deliverance, but think it was early in the month of October * * * We were obliged to pass near the shore of Blackwell's Island, where were several of our crew, who had been sent on shore among the sick. They had learned that the Cartel had arrived from Providence for the purpose of redeeming the crew of the Chance, and expected to be taken on board. Seeing us approaching they had, in order to cause no delay, prepared for their departure, and stood together on the shore, with their bundles in their hands; but, to their unutterable disappointment and dismay, they saw us pass by. We knew them and bitterly did we lament the necessity of leaving them behind. We could only wave our hands as we passed; but they could not return the salutation, and stood as if petrified with horror, like statues fixed immovably to the earth, until we had vanished from their sight.

"I have since seen and conversed with one of these unfortunate men, who afterwards made his escape. He informed me that their removal from the Jersey to the Island was productive of the most beneficial effects upon their health, and that they had been exulting at the improvement of their condition; but their terrible disappointment overwhelmed them with despair. They then considered their fate inevitable, believing that in a few days they must again be conveyed on board the hulk; there to undergo all the agonies of a second death. * * * Several of our crew were sick when we entered the Cartel, and the sudden change of air and diet caused some new cases of fever. One of our number, thus seized by the fever, was a young man named Bicknell of Barrington, R. I. He was unwell when we left the Jersey, and his symptoms indicated the approaching fever; and when we entered Narragansett Bay, he was apparently dying. Being informed that we were in the Bay he begged to be taken on deck, or at least to the hatchway, that he might look once more upon his native land. He said that he was sensible of his condition; that the hand of death was upon him; but that he was consoled by the thought that he should be decently interred, and be suffered to rest among his friends and kindred. I was astonished at the degree of resignation and composure with which he spoke. He pointed to his father's house, as we approached it, and said it contained all that was dear to him upon earth. He requested to be put on shore.

"Our Captain was intimately acquainted with the family of the sufferer; and as the wind was light we dropped our anchor, and complied with his request. He was placed in the boat, where I took a seat by his side; in order to support him; and, with two boys at the oars, we left the sloop. In a few minutes his strength began rapidly to fail. He laid his fainting head upon my shoulder, and said he was going to the shore to be buried with his ancestors; that this had long been his ardent desire, and that God had heard his prayers. No sooner had we touched the shore than one of the boys was sent to inform his family of the event. They hastened to the boat to receive their long lost son and brother, but we could only give them his yet warm and lifeless corpse."

OUR ARRIVAL HOME

"After remaining a few moments with the friends of our deceased comrade we returned to the sloop and proceeded up the river. It was about eight o'clock in the evening when we reached Providence. There were no quarantine regulations to detain us; but, as the yellow fever was raging among us, we took the precaution to anchor in the middle of the stream. It was a beautiful moonlit evening, and the intelligence of our arrival having spread through the town, the nearest wharf was in a short time crowded with people drawn together by curiosity, and a desire for information relative to the fate of their friends and connections.

"Continual inquiries were made from the anxious crowd on the land respecting the condition of several different individuals on board. At length the information was given that some of our number were below, sick with the yellow fever. No sooner was this fact announced than the wharf was totally deserted, and in a few moments not a human being remained in sight. The Old Jersey fever as it was called, was well known throughout the whole country. All were acquainted with its terrible effects; and it was shunned as if its presence were certain destruction.

"After the departure of the crowd, the sloop was brought alongside the wharf, and every one who could walk immediately sprang on shore. So great was the dread of the pestilence, and so squalid and emaciated were the figures which we presented, that those among us whose families did not reside in Providence found it almost impossible to gain admittance into any dwelling. There being at that time no hospital in or near the town, and no preparations having been made for the reception of the sick, they were abandoned for that night. They were, however, supplied in a few hours with many small articles necessary for their immediate comfort, by the humane people in the vicinity of the wharf. The friends of the sick who belonged in the vicinity of the town were immediately informed of our arrival, and in the course of the following day these were removed from the vessel. For the remainder of the sufferers ample provision was made through the generous exertions of Messrs. Clarke and Nightingale.

"Solemn indeed are the reflections which crowd upon my mind as I review the events which are here recorded. Forty–two years have passed away since this remnant of our ill–fated crew were thus liberated from their wasting captivity. In that time what changes have taken place! Of their whole number but three are now alive. James Pitcher, Dr. Joseph Bowen, and myself, are the sole survivors. Of the officers I alone remain."

CHAPTER XLIV. CORRESPONDENCE OF WASHINGTON AND OTHERS

General Washington cannot with justice be blamed for any part of the sufferings inflicted upon the naval prisoners on board the prison ships. Although he had nothing whatever to do with the American Navy, or the crews of privateers captured by the British, yet he exerted himself in every way open to him to endeavor to obtain their exchange, or, at least, a mitigation of their sufferings, and this in spite of the immense weight of cares and anxieties that devolved upon him in his conduct of the war. Much of his correspondence on the subject of these unfortunate prisoners has been given to the world. We deem it necessary, in a work of this character, to reproduce some of it here, not only because this correspondence is his most perfect vindication from the charge of neglect that has been brought against him, but also because it has much to do with the proper understanding of this chronicle.

One of the first of the letters from which we shall quote was written by Washington from his headquarters to Admiral Arbuthnot, then stationed at New York, on the 25th of January 1781.

Sir:

American Prisoners of the Revolution

Through a variety of channels, representations of too serious a nature to be disregarded have come to us, that the American naval prisoners in the harbor of New York are suffering all the extremity of distress, from a too crowded and in all respects disagreeable and unwholesome situation, on board the Prison—ships, and from the want of food and other necessaries. The picture given us of their sufferings is truly calamitous and deplorable. If just, it is the obvious interest of both parties, omitting the plea of humanity, that the causes should be without delay inquired into and removed; and if false, it is equally desirable that effectual measures should be taken to obviate misapprehensions. This can only be done by permitting an officer, of confidence on both sides, to visit the prisoners in their respective confinements, and to examine into their true condition. This will either at once satisfy you that by some abuse of trust in the persons immediately charged with the care of the prisoners, their treatment is really such as has been described to us and requires a change; or it will convince us that the clamors are ill—grounded. A disposition to aggravate the miseries of captivity is too illiberal to be imputed to any but those subordinate characters, who, in every service, are too often remiss and unprincipled. This reflection assures me that you will acquiesce in the mode proposed for ascertaining the truth and detecting delinquency on one side, or falsehood on the other. The discussions and asperities which have had too much place on the subject of prisoners are so irksome in themselves, and have had so many ill consequences, that it is infinitely to be wished that there may be no room given for reviving them. The mode I have suggested appears to me calculated to bring the present case to a fair, direct, and satisfactory issue. I am not sensible of any inconvenience it can be attended with, and I therefore hope for your concurrence.

I should be glad, as soon as possible, to hear from you on the subject.

I have the honor to be, etc., George Washington.

To this letter, written in January, Admiral Arbuthnot did not reply until the latter part of April. He then wrote:

Royal Oak Office April 2lst. 1781.

Sir:

American Prisoners of the Revolution

If I had not been very busy when I received your letter dated the 25 of Jan. last, complaining of the treatment of the naval prisoners at this place, I certainly should have answered it before this time; and, notwithstanding that I then thought, as I now do, that my own testimony would have been sufficient to put the truth past a doubt, I ordered the strictest scrutiny to be made into the condition of all parties concerned in the victualling and treatment of those unfortunate people. Their several testimonies you must have seen, and I give you my honor that the transaction was conducted with such strict care and impartiality that you may rely on its validity.

Permit me now, Sir, to request that you will take the proper steps to cause Mr. Bradford, your Commissary, and the Jailor at Philadelphia, to abate the inhumanity which they exercise indiscriminately upon all people who are so unfortunate as to be carried into that place.

I will not trouble you, Sir, with a catalogue of grievances, further than to request that the unfortunate may feel as little of the severities of war as the circumstances of the time will permit, that in future they may not be fed in winter with salted clams, and that they may be afforded a sufficiency of fuel.

I am, Sir, your most obdt and hble srvt M. Arbuthnot.

Probably the American prisoners would have been glad to eat salted clams, rather than diseased pork, and, as has been shown, they were sometimes frozen to death on board the prison ships, where no fire except for cooking purposes seems ever to have been allowed.

In August, 1781, a committee appointed by Congress to examine into the condition of naval prisoners reported among other things as follows: "The Committee consisting of Mr. Boudinot, Mr. Sharpe, Mr. Clymer, appointed to take into consideration the state of the American prisoners in the power of the enemy report:

"That they have collected together and cursorily looked into various evidences of the treatment our unhappy fellow–citizens, prisoners with the enemy, have heretofore and do still meet with, and find the subject of so important and serious a nature as to demand much greater attention, and fuller consideration than the present distant situation of those confined on board the Prison–ships at New York will now admit of, wherefor they beg leave to make a partial representation, and desire leave to sit again. * * *"

PART OF THE REPORT OF THE COMMITTEE

"A very large number of marine prisoners and citizens of these United States taken by the enemy, are now closely confined on board Prison–ships in the harbor of New York.

"That the said Prison–ships are so unequal in size to the number of prisoners, as not to admit of a possibility of preserving life in this warm season of the year, they being crowded together in such a manner as to be in danger of suffocation, as well as exposed to every kind of putrid, pestilential disorder:

"That no circumstances of the enemy's particular situation can justify this outrage on humanity, it being contrary to the usage and customs of civilizations, thus deliberately to murder their captives in cold blood, as the enemy will not assert that Prison–ships, equal to the number of prisoners, cannot be obtained so as to afford room sufficient for the necessary purposes of life:

"That the enemy do daily improve these distresses to enlist and compel many of our citizens to enter on board their ships of war, and thus to fight against their fellow citizens, and dearest connections.

"That the said Marine prisoners, until they can be exchanged should be supplied with such necessaries of clothing and provisions as can be obtained to mitigate their present sufferings.

"That, therefor, the Commander–in–chief be and he is hereby instructed to remonstrate to the proper officer within the enemy's lines, on the said unjustifiable treatment of our Marine prisoners, and demand, in the most express terms, to know the reasons of this unnecessary severity towards them; and that the Commander–in–chief transmit such answer as may be received thereon to Congress, that decided measures for due retaliation may be adopted, if a redress of these evils be not immediately given.

"That the Commander–in–chief be and he is hereby also instructed to direct to supply the said prisoners with such provisions and light clothing for their present more comfortable subsistence as may be in his power to obtain, and in such manner as he may judge most advantageous for the United States."

Accordingly Washington wrote to the officer then commanding at New York, Commodore Affleck, as follows:

Headquarters, August 21 1781

Sir:

The almost daily complaints of the severities exercised towards the American marine prisoners in New York have induced the Hon. the Congress of the United States to direct me to remonstrate to the commanding officer of his British Majesty's ships of war in the harbor upon the subject; and to report to them his answer. The principal complaint now is, the inadequacy of the room in the Prison–ships to the number of prisoners, confined on board of them, which causes the death of many, and is the occasion of most intolerable inconvenience and distresses to those who survive. This line of conduct is the more aggravating, as the want of a greater number of Prison–ships, or of sufficient room on shore, can hardly be pleaded in excuse.

As a bare denial of what has been asserted by so many individuals who have unfortunately experienced the miseries I have mentioned, will not be satisfactory, I have to propose that our Commissary–general of prisoners, or any other officer, who shall be agreed upon, shall have liberty to visit the ships, inspect the situation of the prisoners, and make a report, from an exact survey of the situation in which they may be found, whether, in his opinion, there has been any just cause of complaint.

I shall be glad to be favored with an answer as soon as convenient.

I have the honor to be yr most obdt srvt George Washington

AFFLECK'S REPLY

New York 30 August 1781

Sir:

I intend not either to deny or to assert, for it will neither facilitate business, nor alleviate distress. The subject of your letter seems to turn on two points, namely the inconvenience and distresses which the American prisoners suffer from the inadequacy of room in the Prison–ships, which occasions the death of many of them, as you are told; and that a Commissary–general of prisoners from you should have liberty to visit the ships, inspect the situation of the prisoners, and make a report from an actual survey. I take leave to assure you that I feel for the distresses of mankind as much as any man; and since my commission to the naval command of the department, one of my principal endeavors has been to regulate the Prison and hospital ships.

The Government having made no other provision for naval prisoners than shipping, it is impossible that the greater inconvenience which people confined on board ships experience beyond those confined on shore can be avoided, and a sudden accumulation of people often aggravates the evil.

But I assure you that every attention is shown that is possible, and that the Prison–ships are under the very same Regulations here that have been constantly observed towards the prisoners of all nations in Europe. Tables of diet are publicly affixed; officers visit every week, redress and report grievances, and the numbers are thinned as they can provide shipping, and no attention has been wanting.

The latter point cannot be admitted to its full extent; but if you think fit to send an officer of character to the lines for that purpose, he will be conducted to me, and he shall be accompanied by an officer, and become a witness to the manner in which we treat the prisoners, and I shall expect to have my officer visit the prisoners detained in your jails and dungeons in like manner, as well as in the mines, where I am informed many an unhappy victim languishes out his days. I must remark, had Congress ever been inclined, they might have contributed to relieve the distress of those whom we are under the necessity of holding as prisoners, by sending in all in their possession towards the payment of the large debt they owe us on that head, which might have been an inducement towards liberating many now in captivity. I have the honor to be, Sir, with due respect, etc,

Edmund Affleck

Much correspondence passed between the English and American Commissaries of Prisoners, as well as between Washington and the commanding officer at New York on the subject of the naval prisoners, but little good seems to have been effected thereby until late in the war, when negotiations for peace had almost progressed to a finish. We have seen that, in the summer of 1782, the hard conditions on board the prison ships were in some measure mitigated, and that the sick were sent to Blackwell's Island, where they had a chance for life. We might go on presenting much more of the correspondence on both sides, and detail all the squabbles about the number of prisoners exchanged; their treatment while in prison; and other subjects of dispute, but the conclusion of the whole matter was eloquently written in the sands of the Wallabout, where the corpses of thousands of victims to British cruelty lay for so many years. We will therefore give only a few further extracts from the correspondence and reports on the subject, as so much of it was tedious and barren of any good result.

In December of the year 1781 Washington, on whom the duty devolved of writing so many of the letters, and receiving so many insulting replies, wrote to the President of Congress as follows:

"I have taken the liberty of enclosing the copies of two letters from the Commissary–general of Prisoners setting forth the debt which is due from us on account of naval prisoners; the number remaining in captivity, their miserable situation, and the little probability there is of procuring their release for the want of proper subjects in our hands.

"Before we proceed into an inquiry into the measures that ought to be adopted to enable us to pay our debt, and to affect the exchange of those who still remain in captivity, a matter which it may take some time to determine, humanity and policy point out the necessity of administering to the pressing wants of a number of the most valuable subjects of the republic.

"Had they been taken in the Continental service, I should have thought myself authorized in conjunction with the Minister of War to apply a remedy, but as the greater part of them were not thus taken, as appears by Mr. Skinner's representation, I must await the decision of Congress upon the subject.

"Had a system, some time ago planned by Congress and recommended to the several States, been adopted and carried fully into execution, I mean that of obliging all Captains of private vessels to deliver over their prisoners to the Continental Commissioners upon certain conditions, I am persuaded that the numbers taken and brought into the many ports of the United States would have amounted to a sufficiency to have exchanged those taken from us; but instead of that, it is to be feared, that few in proportion were secured, and that the few who are sent in, are so partially applied, that it creates great disgust in those remaining. The consequence of which is, that conceiving themselves neglected, and seeing no prospect of relief, many of them entered into the enemy's service, to the very great loss of our trading interest. Congress will, therefore, I hope, see the necessity of renewing their former, or making some similar recommendation to the States.

"In addition to the motives above mentioned, for wishing that the whole business of prisoners of war might be brought under one general regulation, there is another of no small consideration, which is, that it would probably put a stop to those mutual complaints of ill treatment which are frequently urged on each part. For it is a fact that, for above two years, we have had no occasion to complain of the treatment of the Continental land prisoners in New York, neither have we been charged with any improper conduct towards those in our hands. I consider the sufferings of the seamen, for some time past, as arising in great measure from the want of that general regulation which has been spoken of, and without which there will constantly be a great number remaining in the hands of the enemy. * * *"

Again in February of the year 1782 Washington wrote to Congress from Philadelphia as follows:

Feb. 18, 1782.

* * * "Mr. Sproat's proposition of the exchange of British soldiers for American seamen, if acceded to, will immediately give the enemy a very considerable re–enforcement, and will be a constant draft hereafter upon the prisoners of war in our hands. It ought also to be considered that few or none of the Continental naval prisoners in New York or elsewhere belong to the Continental service. I, however, feel for the situation of these unfortunate people, and wish to see them relieved by any mode, which will not materially affect the public good. In some former letters upon this subject I have mentioned a plan, by which I am certain they might be liberated nearly as fast as they are captured. It is by obliging the Captains of all armed vessels, both public and private, to throw their prisoners into common stock, under the direction of the Commissary–general of prisoners. By this means they would be taken care of, and regularly applied to the exchange of those in the hands of the enemy. Now the greater part are dissipated, and the

few that remain are applied partially. * * *"

James Rivington edited a paper in New York during the Revolution, and, in 1782, the American prisoners on board the Jersey addressed a letter to him for publication, which is given below.

"On Board the Prison–ship Jersey, June 11, 1782.

"Sir:

Enclosed are five letters, which if you will give a place in your newspaper will greatly oblige a number of poor prisoners who seem to be deserted by our own countrymen, who has it in their power, and will not exchange us. In behalf of the whole we beg leave to subscribe ourselves, Sir, yr much obliged srvts,

"John Cooper "John Sheffield "William Chad "Richard Eccleston "John Baas"

ENCLOSURES OF THE FOREGOING LETTER

David Sproat, Commissary of Prisoners, to the prisoners on board the Jersey, New York.

"June 11 1782

"This will be handed you by Captain Daniel Aborn, and Dr, Joseph Bowen, who, agreeable to your petition to his Excellency, Rear–Admiral Digby, have been permitted to go out, and are now returned from General Washington's Head–quarters, where they delivered your petition to him, representing your disagreeable situation at this extreme hot season of the year, and in your names solicited his Excellency to grant your speedy relief, by exchanging you for a part of the British *soldiers* in his hands, the only possible means in his power to effect it. Mr. Aborn and the Doctor waits on you with his answer, which I am sorry to say is a flat denial.

"Enclosed I send you copies of three letters which have passed between Mr. Skinner and me, on the occasion, which will convince you that everything has been done on the part of Admiral Digby, to bring about a fair and general exchange of prisoners on both sides. I am "your most hble Srvt, "David Sproat "Comm. Gen. for Naval Prisoners."

ENCLOSURES SENT BY D. SPROAT

David Sproat to Abraham Skinner, American Commissary of Prisoners.

New York lst June 1782

"Sir:

"When I last saw you at Elizabeth Town I mentioned the bad consequences which, in all probability, would take place in the hot weather if an exchange of prisoners was not agreed to by the commissioners on the part of General Washington. His Excellency Rear–Admiral Digby has ordered me to inform you, that the very great increase of prisoners and heat of the weather now baffles all our care and attention to keep them healthy. Five ships have been taken up for their reception, to prevent being crowded, and a great number permitted to go on parole.

"In Winter, and during the cold weather, they lived comfortably, being fully supplied with warm cloathing, blankets, etc, purchased with the money which I collected from the charitable people of this city; but now the weather requires a fresh supply—something light and suitable for the season—for which you will be pleased to make the necessary provision, as it is impossible for them to be healthy in the rags they now wear, without a single shift of cloathing to keep themselves clean. Humanity, sympathy, my duty and orders obliges me to trouble you again on this disagreeable subject, to request you will lose no time in laying their situation before his Excellency General Washington, who, I hope, will listen to the cries of a distressed people, and grant them, (as well as the British prisoners in his hands) relief, by consenting to a general and immediate exchange.

"I am, sir, etc, "David Sproat."

It is scarcely necessary to point out to the intelligent reader the inconsistencies in this letter. The comfortable prisoners, abundantly supplied with blankets and clothing in the winter by the charity of the citizens of New York, were so inconsiderate as to go on starving and freezing to death throughout that season. Not only so, but their abundant supply of clothing was reduced to tattered rags in a surprisingly short time, and they were unable to be healthy, "without a single shift of clothing to keep themselves clean."

We have already seen to what straits they were in reality reduced, in spite of the private charity of the citizens of New York. We do not doubt that the few blankets and other new clothing, if any such were ever sent on board the Jersey, were the gifts of private charity, and not the donation of the British Government.

No one, we believe, can blame General Washington for his unwillingness to add to the British forces arrayed against his country by exchanging the captured troops in the hands of the Americans for the crews of American privateers, who were not in the Continental service. As we have already seen, the blame does not rest with that great commander, whose compassion never blinded his judgment, but with the captains and owners of American privateers themselves, and often with the towns of New England, who were unwilling to burden themselves with prisoners taken on the ocean.

The next letter we will quote is the answer of Commissary Skinner to David Sproat:

"New York June 9th. 1782

"Sir:

From the present situation of the American naval prisoners on board your prison—ships, I am induced to propose to you the exchange of as many as I can give you British naval prisoners for, leaving the balance already due you to be paid when in our power. I could wish this to be represented to his Excellency, Rear Admiral Digby, and that the proposal could be acceded to, as it would relieve many of these distrest men and be consistent with the humane purposes of our office.

"I will admit that we are unable at present to give you seaman for seaman, and thereby relieve the prison—ships of their dreadful burthen, but it ought to be remembered there is a large balance of British soldiers due to the United States, since February last, and that as we have it in our power we may be disposed to place the British soldiers who are now in our possession in as disagreeable a situation as those men are on board the prison ships.

"I am yr obdt hble srvt "Abraham Skinner"

COMMISSARY SPROAT'S REPLY

"New York June 9th 1782

"Sir:

"I have received your letter of this date and laid it before his Excellency Rear Admiral Digby, Commander in charge, etc, who has directed me to give for answer that the balance of prisoners, owing to the British having proceeded, from lenity and humanity, on the part of himself and those who commanded before his arrival, is surprized you have not been induced to offer to exchange them first; and until this is done can't consent to your proposal of a partial exchange, leaving the remainder as well as the British prisoners in your hands, to linger in confinement. Conscious of the American prisoners under my direction, being in every respect taken as good care of as their situation and ours will admit. You must not believe that Admiral Digby will depart from the justice of this measure because you have it in your power to make the British prisoners with you more miserable than there is any necessity for. I am, Sir,

"yr hble servt "David Sproat."

The prisoners on board the Jersey published in the *Royal Gazette* the following

ADDRESS TO THEIR COUNTRYMEN

"Prison Ship Jersey, June 11th 1782

"Friends and Fellow Citizens of America:

"You may bid a final adieu to all your friends and relatives who are now on board the Jersey prison ships at New York, unless you rouse the government to comply with the just and honorable proposals, which has already been done on the part of Britons, but alas! it is with pain we inform you, that our petition to his Excellency General Washington, offering our services to the country during the present campaign, if he would send soldiers in exchange for us, is frankly denied.

"What is to be done? Are we to lie here and share the fate of our unhappy brothers who are dying daily? No, unless you relieve us immediately, we shall be under the necessity of leaving our country, in preservation of our lives.

"Signed in behalf of prisoners

"John Cooper "John Sheffield "William Chad "Richard Eccleston "George Wanton "John Baas.

"To Mr James Rivington, Printer N. Y."

This address was reproduced in Hugh Gaines's *New York Gazette*, June 17, 1782.

Whether the John Cooper who signed his name to this address is the Mr. Cooper mentioned by Dring as the orator of the Jersey we do not know, but it is not improbable. Nine Coopers are included in the list, given in the appendix to this volume, of prisoners on the Jersey, but no John Cooper is among them. The list is exceedingly imperfect. Of the other signers of the address only two, George Wanton and John Sheffield, can be found within its pages. It is very certain that it is incomplete, and it probably does not contain more than half the names of the prisoners who suffered on board that dreadful place. David Sproat won the hatred and contempt of all the American prisoners who had anything to do with him. One of his most dastardly acts was the paper which he drew up in June, 1782, and submitted to a number of American sea captains for their signature, which he obtained from them by threats of taking away their parole in case of their refusal, and sending them back to a captivity worse than death. This paper, *which they signed without reading* was to the following effect:

LETTER PURPORTING TO BE FROM A COMMITTEE OF CAPTAINS, NAVAL PRISONERS OF WAR TO J. RIVINGTON, WITH A REPRESENTATION OF A COMMITTEE ON THE CONDITION OF THE PRISONERS ON BOARD THE JERSEY

New York, June 22, 1782.

Sir:

We beg you will be pleased to give the inclosed Report and Resolve of a number of Masters of American Vessels, a place in your next Newspaper, for the information of the public. In order to undeceive numbers of our countrymen without the British lines, who have not had an opportunity of seeing the state and situation of the prisoners of New York as we have done. We are, Sir,

yr most obdt, hble srvts,

Robert Harris, Captain of the sloop Industry John Chace Charles Collins, Captain of the Sword–fish Philemon Haskell Jonathan Carnes

REPORT

We whose names are hereunto subscribed, late Masters of American vessels, which have been captured by the British cruisers and brought into this port, having obtained the enlargement of our paroles from Admiral Digby, to return to our respective homes, being anxious before our departure to know the true state and situation of the prisoners confined on board the prison ships and hospital ships for that purpose, have requested and appointed six of our number, viz, R. Harris, J. Chace, Ch. Collins, P. Haskell, J. Carnes and Christopher Smith, to go on board the said prison ships for that purpose and the said six officers aforesaid having gone on board five of the vessels, attended by Mr. D. Sproat, Com. Gen. for Naval Prisoners, and Mr. George Rutherford, Surgeon to the hospital ships, do report to us that they have found them in as comfortable a situation as it is possible for prisoners to be on board of ships at this season of the year, and much more so than they had any idea of, and that anything said to the contrary is false and without foundation. That they inspected their beef, pork, flour, bread, oatmeal, pease, butter, liquors, and indeed every species of provisions which is issued on board his British Majesty's ships of war, and found them all good of their kind, which survey being made before the prisoners, they acknowledged the same and declared they had no complaint to make but the want of cloaths and a speedy exchange. We therefore from this report and what we have all seen and known, *Do Declare* that great commendation is due to his Excellency Rear Admiral Digby, for his humane disposition and indulgence to his prisoners, and also to those he entrusts the care of them to; viz: To the Captain and officers of his Majesty's prison–ship Jersey, for their attention in preserving good order, having the ship kept clean and awnings spread over *the whole* of her, fore and aft: To Dr Rutherford, and the Gentlemen acting under him * * *, for their constant care and attendance on the sick, whom we found in wholesome, clean sheets, also covered with awnings, fore and aft, every man furnished with a cradle, bed, and sheets, made of good Russia linen, to lay in; the best of fresh provisions, vegetables, wine, rice, barley, etc, which was served out to them. And we further do declare in justice to Mr. Sproat, and the gentlemen acting under him in his department, that they conscientiously do their duty with great humanity and indulgence to the prisoners, and reputation to themselves; And we unanimously do agree that nothing is wanting to preserve the lives and health of those unfortunate prisoners but clean cloaths and a speedy exchange, which testimony we freely give without restriction and covenant each with the other to endeavor to effect their exchange as soon as possible:

For the remembrance of this our engagement we have furnished ourselves with copies of this instrument of writing. Given under our hands in New York the 22 of June, 1782.

Signed:

Robert Harris John Chace Charles Collins Philemon Haskell]. Carnes Christopher Smith James Gaston John Tanner Daniel Aborn Richard Mumford Robert Clifton John McKeever Dr. J. Bowen.

The publication of this infamously false circular roused much indignation among patriotic Americans, and no one believed it a trustworthy statement. The *Independent Chronicle*, in its issue for August, 1782, had the following refutation: [Footnote: This letter is said to have been written by Captain Manly, *five times* a prisoner during the Revolution.]

"Mr Printer:

"Happening to be at Mr. Bracket's tavern last Saturday, and hearing two gentlemen conversing on the surprising alteration in regard to the treatment our prisoners met with in New York, and as I have had the misfortune to be more than once a prisoner in England, and in different prison–ships in New York, and having suffered everything but death, I cannot help giving all attention to anything I hear or read relative to the treatment our brave countrymen met with on board the prison–ships of New York. One of the gentlemen observed that the treatment of our prisoners must certainly be much better, as so many of our commanders had signed a paper that was wrote by Mr. David Sproat, the commissary of naval prisoners in New York. The other gentleman answered and told him he could satisfy him in regard to the matter, having seen and conversed with several of the Captains that signed Mr. Sproat's paper, who told him that, although they had put their names to the paper that Mr. Sproat sent them on Long Island, where they were upon parole, yet it was upon these conditions they did it: in order to have leave to go home to their wives and families, and not be sent on board the prison–ships, as Mr. Sproat had threatened to do if they refused to sign the paper that he sent them. These captains further said, that they did not read the paper nor hear it read. The gentleman then asked them how they could sign their names to a paper they did not read; they said it was because they might go home upon parole. He asked one of them why he did not contradict it since it had appeared in the public papers, and was false: he said he dare not at present, for fear of being recalled and sent on board the prison–ship, and there end his days: but as soon as he was exchanged he would do it. If this gentleman, through fear, dare not contradict such a piece of falsehood, I dare, and if I was again confined on board the prison–ship in New York, dare again take the boat and make my escape, although at the risk of my life.

"Some of the captains went on board the prison–ship with Mr. Sproat, a few moments, but did not go off the deck.

"In justice to myself and country I am obliged to publish the above.

"Captain Rover."

Besides this refutation of Sproat's shameful trick there were many others. The *Pennsylvania Packet* of Tuesday, Sept. 10, 1782, published an affidavit of John Kitts, a former prisoner on board the Jersey.

"The voluntary affidavit of John Kitts, of the city of Phila., late mate of the sloop Industry, commanded by Robert Harris, taken before the subscriber, chief justice of the commonwealth of Pa., the 16th day of July, 1782.—This deponent saith, that in the month of November last he was walking in Front St. with the said Harris and saw in his hand a paper, which he told the deponent that he had received from a certain Captain Kuhn, who had been lately from New York, where he had been a prisoner, and that this deponent understood and believed it was a permission or pass to go to New York with any vessel, as it was blank and subscribed by Admiral Arbuthnot: that he does not know that the said Robert Harris ever made any improper use of said paper."

AFFIDAVIT OF JOHN COCHRAN, DENYING THE TRUTH OF THE STATEMENTS CONTAINED IN THE REPORT OF THE COMMITTEE OF CAPTAINS

From the *Pennsylvania Packet*, Phila., Tuesday, Sept. 10, 1782.

"The voluntary Affidavit of John Cochran, of the city of Phila., late mate of the ship, Admiral Youtman, of Phila., taken before the subscriber, the 16 day of July, 1782.

"The said deponent saith, that he was taken prisoner on board the aforesaid ship on the 12 of March last by the ship Garland, belonging to the king of Great Britain, and carried into the city of New York, on the 15 of the same month, when he was immediately put on board the prison–ship Jersey, with the whole crew of the Admiral Youtman, and was close confined there until the first day of this month, when he made his escape; that the people on board the said prison–ship were very sickly insomuch that he is firmly persuaded, out of near 1000 persons, perfectly healthy when put on board the same ship, during the time of his confinement on board, there are not more than but three or four hundred now alive; that when he made his escape there were not three hundred men well on board, but upward of 140 very sick, as he understood and was informed by the physicians: that there were five or six men buried daily under a bank on the shore, without coffins; that all the larboard side of the said ship was made use of as a hospital for the sick, and was so offensive that he was obliged constantly to hold his nose as he passed from the gun–room up the hatchway; that he seen maggots creeping out of a wound of one Sullivan's shoulder, who was the mate of a vessel out of Virginia; and that his wound remained undressed for several days together; that every man was put into the hold a little after sundown every night, and the hatches put over him; and that the tubs which were kept for the use of the sick * * * were placed under the ladder from the hatchway to the hold, and so offensive day and night, that they were almost intolerable, and increased the number of the sick daily. The deponent further saith, that the bilge water was very injurious in the hold, was muddy and dirty, and never was changed or sweetened during the whole time he was there, nor, as he was informed and believes to be true, for many years before; for fear, as it was reported, the provisions might be injured thereby; that the sick in the hospital part of the said ship Jersey, had no sheets of Russia, or any other linen, nor beds nor bedding furnished them; and those who had no beds of their own, of whom there were great numbers, were not even allowed a hammock, but were obliged to lie on the planks; that he was on board the said prison ship when Captain

Robert Harris and others, with David Sproat, the commissary of prisoners, came on board her, and that none of them went or attempted to go below decks, in said ship, to see the situation of the prisoners, nor did they ask a single question respecting the matter, to this deponent's knowledge or belief; for that he was present the whole time they were on board, and further the deponent saith not.

"John Cochran"

"Theodore McKean C. J.

It seems singular that Sproat should have resorted to such a contemptible trick, which deceived few if any persons, for the reputation of the Jersey was too notorious for such a refutation to carry weight on either side.

In the meantime the mortality on board continued, and, by a moderate computation, two–thirds of her wretched occupants died and were buried on the shore, their places being taken by fresh victims, from the many privateers that were captured by the British almost daily.

CHAPTER XLV. GENERAL WASHINGTON AND REAR ADMIRAL DIGBY—COMMISSARIES SPROAT AND SKINNER

Washington's best vindication against the charge of undue neglect of American prisoners is found in the correspondence on the subject. We will therefore give his letter to Rear Admiral Digby, after his interview with the committee of three sent from the Jersey to complain of their treatment by the British, and to endeavor to negotiate an exchange.

GENERAL WASHINGTON TO REAR ADMIRAL DIGBY

Head–Quarters, June 5 1782

Sir:

By a parole, granted to two gentlemen, Messrs. Aborn and Bowen, I perceive that your Excellency granted them permission to come to me with a representation of the sufferings of the American prisoners at New York. As I have no agency on Naval matters, this application to me is made on mistaken grounds. But curiosity leading me to enquire into the nature and cause of their sufferings, I am informed that the prime complaint is that of their being crowded, especially at this season, in great numbers on board of foul and infected prison ships, where disease and death are almost inevitable. This circumstance I am persuaded needs only to be mentioned to your Excellency to obtain that redress which is in your power *only* to afford, and which humanity so strongly prompts.

If the fortune of war, Sir, has thrown a number of these miserable people into your hands, I am certain your Excellency's feelings for fellowmen must induce you to proportion the ships (if they *must* be confined on board ships), to their accommodation and comfort, and not, by crowding them together in a few, bring on disorders which consign them, by half a dozen a day, to the grave.

The soldiers of his British Majesty, prisoners with us, were they (which might be the case), to be equally crowded together in close and confined prisons, at this season, would be exposed to equal loss and misery. I have the honor to be, Sir

Yr Excellency's most obt Hble srvt George Washington

REAR–ADMIRAL DIGBY'S ANSWER

N. Y. June 8 1782

Sir:

My feelings prompted me to grant Messrs. Aborn and Bowen permission to wait on your Excellency to represent their miserable situation, and if your Excellency's feelings on this occasion are like mine, you will not hesitate one moment in relieving both the British and Americans suffering under confinement.

I have the Honor to be your Excellency's Very obdt Srvt

R. Digby

FROM COMMISSARY SKINNER TO COMMISSARY SPROAT

Camp Highlands, June 24th 1782

Sir:

As I perceive by a New York paper of the 12 inst, the last letters which passed between us on the subject of naval prisoners have been committed to print, I must request the same to be done with this which is intended to contain some animadversions on those publications.

The principles and policy which appear to actuate your superiors in their conduct towards the American seamen who unfortunately fall into their power, are too apparent to admit of a doubt or misapprehension. I am sorry to observe, Sir, that notwithstanding the affectation of candour and fairness on your part, from the universal tenor of behaviour on your side of the lines, it is obvious that the designs of the British is, by misrepresenting the state of facts with regard to exchanges, to excite jealousy in the minds of our unfortunate seamen, that they are neglected by their countrymen, and by attempting to make them believe that all the miseries they are now suffering in consequence of a pestilential sickness arise from want of inclination in General Washington to exchange them when he has it in his power to do it; in hopes of being able by this insinuation and by the unrelenting severity you make use of in confining them in the contaminated holds of prison–ships, to compel them, in order to avoid the dreadful alternative of almost inevitable death, to enter the service of the King of Great Britain.

To show that these observations are just and well grounded, I think it necessary to inform you of some facts which have happened within my immediate notice, and to put you in mind of others which you cannot deny. I was myself present at the time when Captain Aborn and Dr. Bowen * * * waited on his Excellency General Washington, and know perfectly well the answer his Excellency gave to that application: he informed them in the first place that he was not directly or indirectly invested with any power of inference respecting the exchange of naval prisoners; that this business was formerly under the direction of the Board of Admiralty, that upon the annihilation of that Board Congress had committed it to the Financier (who has in charge all our naval prisoners) and he to the Secretary at war. That (the General) was notwithstanding disposed to do everything in his power for their assistance and relief: that as exchanging seamen for soldiers was contrary to the original agreement for the exchange of prisoners,—which specified that officers should be exchanged for officers, soldiers for soldiers, citizens for citizens, and seamen for seamen; as it was contrary to the custom and practice of other nations, and as it would be, in his opinion, contrary to the soundest policy, by giving the enemy a great and permanent strength for which we could receive no compensation, or at best but a partial and temporary one, he did not think it would be admissible: but as it appeared to him, from a variety of well authenticated information, the present misery and mortality which prevailed among the naval prisoners were almost entirely, if not altogether produced by the *mode of their confinement*, being closely crowded together in infected prison–ships, where the very air is pregnant with disease, and the ships themselves (never having been cleaned in the course of many years), a mere mass of putrefaction, he would therefor, from motives of humanity, write to Rear–Admiral Digby, in whose power it was to remedy this great evil, by confining them on shore, or having a sufficient number of prison–ships provided for that purpose, for, he observed, it was as preposterously cruel to confine 800 men, at this sultry season, on board the Jersey prison–ship, as it would be to shut up the whole army of Lord Cornwallis to perish in the New Goal of Philadelphia, but if more commodious and healthy accommodations were not afforded we had the means of retaliation in our hands, which he should not hesitate, in that case, to make use of, by confining the land prisoners with as much severity as our seamen were held.—The Gentlemen of the Committee appeared to be sensible of the force of these reasons, however repugnant they might be to the feelings and wishes of the men who had destruction and death staring them in the face.

His Excellency was further pleased to suffer me to go to New York to examine into the grounds of the suffering of the prisoners, and to devise, if possible, some way or another, for their liberation or relief. With this permission I went into your lines: and in consequence of the authority I had been previously invested with, from the Secretary at War, I made the proposition contained in my letter of the ninth instant. Although I could not claim this as a matter of right I flattered myself it would have been granted from the principles of humanity, as well as other motives. There had been a balance of 495 land prisoners due to us ever since the month of February last, when a settlement was made; besides which, to the best of my belief, 400 have been sent in, (this is the true state of the fact, though it differs widely from the account of 250 men, which is falsely stated in the note annexed to my letter in the New York paper:) notwithstanding this balance, I was then about sending into your lines a number of land prisoners, as an equivalent for ours, who were then confined in the Sugar House, without which (though the debt was acknowledged, I could not make interest to have them liberated), this business has since been actually negotiated, and we glory in having our conduct, such as will bear the strictest scrutiny, and be found consonant to the dictates of reason, liberality, and justice. But, Sir, since you would not agree to the proposals I made, since I was refused being permitted to visit the prison–ships: (for which I conclude no other reason can be produced than your being ashamed or afraid of having those graves of our seamen seen by one who dared to represent the horrors of them to his countrymen,) Since the commissioners from your side, at their late meeting, would not enter into an adjustment of the accounts for supplying your naval and land prisoners, on which there are large sums due us; and since your superiors will neither make provision for the support of your prisoners in our hands, nor accommodation for the mere existence of ours, who are now languishing in your prison–ships, it becomes my duty, Sir, to state these pointed facts to you, that the imputations may recoil where they are deserved, and to report to those, under whose authority I have the honor to act, that such measures as they deem proper may be adopted.

And now, Sir, I will conclude this long letter with observing that not having a sufficient number of British seamen in our possession we are not able to release urs by exchange:—this is our misfortune, but it is not a crime, and ought not to operate as a mortal punishment against the unfortunate—we ask no favour, we claim nothing but common justice and humanity, while we assert to the whole world, as a notorious fact, that the unprecedented inhumanity in the *mode* of confining our naval prisoners, to the amount of 800 in one old hulk, which has been made use of as a prison–ship for more than three years, without ever having been once purified, has been the real and sole cause of the deaths of hundreds of brave Americans, who would not have perished in that untimely and barbarous manner, had they, (when prisoners,) been suffered to breathe a purer air, and to enjoy more liberal and convenient accommodations agreeably to the practice of civilized nations when at war, (and) the example which has always been set you by the Americans. You may say, and I shall admit, that if they were placed on islands, and more liberty given them, that some might desert; but is not this the case with your prisoners in our hands? And could we not avoid this also, if we were to adopt the same rigid and inhuman mode of confinement you do?

I beg, Sir, you will be pleased to consider this as addressed to you officially, as the principal executive officer in the department of naval prisoners, and not personally, and that you will attribute any uncommon warmth of style that I may have been led into to my feeling and animation on a subject with which I find myself so much interested, both from the principles of humanity and the duties of office. I am, Sir,

yr most obdt Srvt Abraham Skinner

Letters full of recriminations continued to pass between the commissaries on both sides. In Sproat's reply to the letter we have just quoted, he enclosed a copy of the paper which he had induced the thirteen sea captains and other officers to sign, obtained as we have seen, in such a dastardly manner.

In the meantime the naval prisoners continued to die in great numbers on board the prison and hospital–ships. We have already described the cleansing of the Jersey, on which occasion the prisoners were sent on board of other vessels and exposed to cold and damp in addition to their other sufferings. And while negotiations for peace were pending some relaxation in severity appears to have taken place.

CHAPTER XLVI. SOME OF THE PRISONERS ON BOARD THE JERSEY

We have seen that the crew of the Chance was exchanged in the fall of 1782. A few of the men who composed this crew were ill at the time that the exchange was affected, and had been sent to Blackwell's Island. Among these unfortunate sufferers was the sailing–master of the Chance, whose name was Sylvester Rhodes.

This gentleman was born at Warwick, R. I., November 21, 1745. He married Mary Aborn, youngest sister of Captain Daniel Aborn, and entered the service of his country, in the early part of the war, sometimes on land, and sometimes as a seaman. He was with Commodore Whipple on his first cruise, and as prize–master carried into Boston the first prize captured by that officer. He also served in a Rhode Island regiment.

When the crew of the Jersey was exchanged and he was not among the number, his brother–in–law, Captain Aborn, endeavored to obtain his release, but, as he had been an officer in the army as well as on the privateer, the British refused to release him as a seaman. His father, however, through the influence of some prominent Tories with whom he was connected, finally secured his parole, and Captain Aborn went to New York to bring him home. But it was too late. He had become greatly enfeebled by disease, and died on board the cartel, while on her passage through the Sound, on the 3rd of November, 1782, leaving a widow and five children. Mary Aborn Rhodes lived to be 98, dying in 1852, one of the last survivors of the stirring times of the Revolution.

WILLIAM DROWNE

One of the most adventurous of American seamen was William Drowne, who was taken prisoner more than once. He was born in Providence, R. I., in April 1755. After many adventures he sailed on the 18th of May, 1780, in the General Washington, owned by Mr. John Brown of Providence. In a Journal kept by Mr. Drowne on board of this ship, he writes:

"The cruise is for two months and a half, though should New York fetch us up again, the time may be protracted, but it is not in the bargain to pay that potent city a visit *this bout*. It may easily be imagined what a *sensible mortification* it must be to dispense with the delicious sweets of a Prison–ship. But though the Washington is deemed a prime sailor, and is well armed, I will not be too sanguine in the prospect of escape, as 'the race is not always to the swift, nor the battle to the strong.' But, as I said before, it is not in the articles to go there this time, especially as it is said the prisoners are very much crowded there already, and it would be a piece of unfeeling inhumanity to be adding to their unavoidable inconvenience by our presence. Nor could we, in such a case, by any means expect that Madam Fortune would deign to smile so propitiously as she did before, in the promotion of an exchange so much sooner than our most sanguine expectations flattered us with, as 'tis said to be with no small difficulty that a parole can be obtained, much more an exchange."

This cruise resulted in the capture by the Washington of several vessels, among them the Robust, Lord Sandwich, Barrington, and the Spitfire, a British privateer.

In May, 1781, Mr. Drowne sailed on board the Belisarius, commanded by Captain James Munro, which vessel was captured on the 26th of July and brought into the port of New York. Browne and the other officers were sent to the Jersey, where close confinement and all the horrors of the place soon impaired his vigorous constitution. Although he was, through the influence of his friends, allowed to visit Newport on parole in November, 1781, he was returned to the prison ship, and was not released until some time in 1783.

His brother, who was a physician, nursed him faithfully, but he died on the 9th of August, 1786. Letters written on board the Jersey have a melancholy interest to the student of history, and this one, written by William Drowne to a Mrs. Johnston, of New York, is taken from the appendix to the "Recollections of Captain Dring."

Jersey Prison Ship Sep. 25 1781

Madam:

Your letter to Captain Joshua Sawyer of the 23d Inst, came on board this moment, which I being requested to answer, take the freedom to do, and with sensible regret, as it announces the dissolution of the good man. It was an event very unexpected. Tis true he had been for some days very ill, but a turn in his favor cancel'd all further apprehension of his being dangerous, and but yesterday he was able without assistance to go upon deck; said he felt much better, and without any further Complaints, at the usual time turned into his Hammock, and as was supposed went to sleep. Judge of our Surprise and Astonishment this morning at being informed of his being found a lifeless Corpse.

Could anything nourishing or comfortable have been procured for him during his illness, 'tis possible He might now have been a well man. But Heaven thought proper to take him to itself, and we must not repine.

A Coffin would have been procured in case it could be done seasonably, but his situation render'd a speedy Interment unavoidable. Agreeably to which 10 or 12 Gentlemen of his acquaintance presented a petition to the Commanding Officer on board, requesting the favor that they might be permitted, under the Inspection of a file of Soldiers, to pay the last sad duties to a Gentleman of merit; which he humanely granted, and in the Afternoon his remains were taken on shore, and committed to their native dust in as decent a manner as our situation would admit. Myself, in room of a better, officiated in the sacred office of a Chaplain and read prayers over the Corpse previous to its final close in its gloomy mansion. I have given you these particulars, Madam, as I was sensible it must give you great satisfaction to hear he had some friends on board. Your benevolent and good intentions to him shall, (if Heaven permits my return) be safely delivered to his afflicted wife, to give her the sensible Consolation that her late much esteemed and affectionate Husband was not destitute of a Friend, who had wish'd to do him all the good offices in his power, had not the hand of fate prevented.

If you wish to know anything relative to myself—if you will give Yourself the trouble to call on Mrs. James Selhrig, she will inform You, or Jos. Aplin, Esqre.

You will please to excuse the Liberty I have taken being an entire stranger. I have no Views in it but those of giving, as I said before, satisfaction to one who took a friendly part towards a Gentleman decease'd, whom I very much esteemed. Your goodness will not look with a critical eye over the numerous Imperfections of this Epistle.

I am, Madam, with every sentiment of respect

yr most Obdt Servt

Wm. Drowne

The next letter we will give was written by Dr. Solomon Drowne to his sister Sally. This gentleman was making every effort to obtain his brother's release from captivity.

Providence, Oct. 17 1781

Dear Sally:

We have not forgot you;—but if we think strongly on other objects the memory of you returns, more grateful than the airs which fan the Summer, or all the golden products of ye Autumn. The Cartel is still detained, for what reason is not fully known. Perhaps they meditate an attack upon some unguarded, unsuspecting quarter, and already in idea glut their eyes, with the smoke of burning Towns and Villages, and are soothed by the sounds of deep distress. Forbid it Guardian of America!—and rather let the reason be their fear that we should know the state of their shattered Navy and declining affairs—However, Bill is yet a Prisoner, and still must feel, if not for himself, yet what a mind like his will ever feel for others. In a letter I received from him about three weeks since he mentioned that having a letter to Mr. George Deblois, he sent it, accompanied with one he wrote requesting his influence towards effecting his return the next Flag,—that Mr. Deblois being indisposed, his cousin Captain William Deblois, taken by Monro last year, came on board to see him, with a present from Mr. Deblois of some Tea, Sugar, Wine, Rum, etc, and the offer of any other Civilities that lay in the power of either:—This was beneficence and true Urbanity,—that he was not destitute of Cash, that best friend in

Adversity, except some other best friends,—that as long as he had health, he should, he had like to have said, be happy. In a word he bears up with his wonted fortitude and good spirits, as we say, nor discovers the least repining at his fate. But you and I who sleep on beds of down and inhale the untainted, cherishing air, surrounded by most endeared connexions, know that his cannot be the most delectable of situations: therefor with impatience we look for his happy return to the Circle of his Friends.

Yr aff Bro.

Solomon Drowne

DR. S. DROWNE TO MRS. MARCY DROWNE

Newport Nov. 14 1781

Respected Mother,

I found Billy much better than I expected, the account we received of his situation having been considerably exaggerated: However we ought to be thankful we were not deceived by a too favorable account, and so left him to the care of strangers, when he might most need the soothing aid of close relatives. He is very weak yet, and as a second relapse might endanger his reduced, tottering system, think it advisable not to set off for home with him till the wind is favorable. He is impatient, for the moment of its shifting, as he is anxious to see you all.

The boat is just going, Adieu, yr aff son

Solomon Drowne

We have already quoted from the Recollections of Jeremiah Johnson who lived on the banks of Wallabout Bay during the Revolution. He further says: "The prisoners confined in the Jersey had secretly obtained a crow–bar which was kept concealed in the berth of some confidential officer among the prisoners. The bar was used to break off the *port* gratings. This was done, in windy nights, when good swimmers were ready to leave the ship for the land. In this way a number escaped.

"Captain Doughty, a friend of the writer, had charge of the bar when he was a prisoner on board of the Jersey, and effected his escape by its means. When he left the ship he gave the bar to a confidant to be used for the relief of others. Very few who left the ship were retaken. They knew where to find friends to conceal them, and to help them beyond pursuit.

"A singularly daring and successful escape was effected from the Jersey about 4 o'clock one afternoon in the beginning of Dec. 1780. The best boat of the ship had returned from New York between 3 &4 o'clock, and was left fast at the gangway, with the oars on board. The afternoon was stormy, the wind blew from the north-east, and the tide ran flood. A watchword was given, and a number of prisoners placed themselves carelessly between the ship's waist and the sentinel. At this juncture four Eastern Captains got on board the boat, which was cast off by their friends. The boat passed close under the bows of the ship, and was a considerable distance from her before the sentinel in the fo'castle gave the alarm, and fired at her. The second boat was manned for a chase; she pursued in vain; one man from her bow fired several shots at the boat, and a few guns were fired at her from the Bushwick shore; but all to no effect,—and the boat passed Hell-gate in the evening, and arrived safe in Connecticut next morning.

"A spring of the writer was a favorite watering-place for the British shipping. The water-boat of the Jersey watered from this spring daily when it could be done; four prisoners were generally brought on shore to fill the casks, attended by a guard. The prisoners were frequently permitted to come to the (Johnstons') house to get milk and food; and often brought letters privately from the prisoners. From these the sufferings on board were revealed.

"Supplies of vegetables were frequently collected by Mr. Remsen (the benevolent owner of the mill,) for the prisoners; and small sums of money were sent on board by the writer's father to his friends by means of these watering parties."

AN ESCAPE FROM THE JERSEY

"I was one of 850 souls confined in the Jersey in the summer of 1781, and witnessed several daring attempts to escape. They generally ended tragically. They were always undertaken in the night, after wrenching or filing the bar off the port-holes. Having been on board several weeks, and goaded to death in various ways, four of us concluded to run the hazard. We set to work and got the bars off, and waited impatiently for a dark night. We lay in front of Mr. Remsen's door, inside of the pier head and not more that 20 yards distant. There were several guard sloops, one on our bow, and the other off our quarter a short distance from us. The dark night came, the first two were lowered quietly into the water; and the third made some rumbling. I was the fourth that descended, but had not struck off from the vessel before the guards were alarmed, and fired upon us. The alarm became general, and I was immediately hauled on board (by the other prisoners).

"They manned their boats, and with their lights and implements of death were quick in pursuit of the unfortunates, cursing and swearing, and bellowing and firing. It was awful to witness this deed of blood. It lasted about an hour,—all on board trembling for our shipmates. These desperadoes returned to their different vessels rejoicing that they had killed three damned rebels.

"About three years after this I saw a gentleman in John St., near Nassau, who accosted me thus: 'Manley, how do you do?' I could not recollect him. 'Is it possible you don't know me? Recollect the Old Jersey?' And he opened his vest and bared his breast. I immediately said to him—'You are James McClain.' 'I am,' said he. We both stepped into Mariner's public house, at the corner, and he related his marvellous escape to me.

"They pursued me:—I frequently dived to avoid them, and when I came up they fired on me. I caught my breath, and immediately dived again, and held my breath till I crawled along the mud. They no doubt thought they killed me. I however, with much exertion, though weak and wounded, made out to reach the shore, and got into a barn, not far from the ship, a little north of Mr. Remsen's house. The farmer, the next morning, came into his barn,—saw me lying on the floor, and ran out in a fright. I begged him to come to me, and he did, I gave an account of myself, where I was from, how I was pursued, with several others. He saw my wounds, took pity on me; sent for his wife, and bound up my wounds, and kept me in the barn until night–fall,—took me into his house, nursed me secretly, and then furnished me with clothing, etc., and when I was restored, he took me with him, into his market–boat to this city, and went with me to the west part of the city, provided me with a passage over to Bergen, and I landed somewhere in Communipaw. Some friends helped me across Newark Bay, and then I worked my way, until I reached Baltimore, to the great joy of all my friends." [Footnote: "Recollections of Captain Manley".]

Just what proportion of captives died on board of the Jersey it is now impossible to determine. No doubt there were many escapes of which it is impossible to obtain the particulars. The winter of 1779–80 was excessively cold, and the Wallabout Bay was frozen over. One night a number of prisoners took advantage of this to make their escape by lowering themselves from a port hole on to the ice. It is recorded that the cold was so excessive that one man was frozen to death, that the British pursued the party and brought a few of them back, but that a number succeeded in making their escape to New Jersey. Who these men were we have been unable to discover. Tradition also states that while Wallabout Bay was thus frozen over the Long Island market women skated across it, with supplies of vegetables in large hampers attached to their backs, and that some of them came near enough to throw some of their supplies to the half–famished prisoners on board the Jersey.

It would appear that these poor sufferers had warm friends in the farmers who lived on the shores of the Wallabout. Of these Mr. A. Remsen, who owned a mill at the mouth of a creek which empties into the Bay, was one of the most benevolent, and it was his daughter who is said to have kept a list of the number of bodies that were interred in the sand in the neighborhood of the mill and house. In 1780 Mr Remsen hid an escaped prisoner, Major H. Wyckoff, for several days in one of his upper rooms, while at the same time the young lieutenant of the guard of the Jersey was quartered in the house. Remsen also lent Captain Wyckoff as much money as he needed, and finally, one dark night, safely conveyed him in a sleigh to Cow Neck. From thence he crossed to Poughkeepsie.

Although little mention is made by those prisoners who have left accounts of their experiences while on board the Jersey, of any aid received by them from the American government the following passage from a Connecticut paper would seem to indicate that such aid was tendered them at least for a time. It is possible that Congress sent some provisions to the prison–ships for her imprisoned soldiers, or marines, but made no provision for the crews of privateers.

"New London. September 1st. 1779. D. Stanton testifies that he was taken June 5th, and put in the Jersey prison ship. An allowance from Congress was sent on board. About three or four weeks past we were removed on board the Good Hope, where we found many sick. There is now a hospital ship provided, to which they are removed and good attention paid."

The next extract that we will quote probably refers to the escape of prisoners on the ice referred to above.

"New London. Conn. Feb. 16th. 1780. Fifteen prisoners arrived here who three weeks ago escaped from the prison–ship in the East River. A number of others escaped about the same time from the same ship, some of whom being frost–bitten and unable to endure the cold, were taken up and carried back, one frozen to death before he reached the shore."

"*Rivington's Gazette*, Dec. 19th 1780. George Batterman, who had been a prisoner on board the prison ship at New York, deposes that he had had eight ounces of condemned bread per day; and eight ounces of meat. He was afterwards put on board the Jersey, where were, as was supposed, 1,100 prisoners; recruiting officers came on board and finding that the American officers persuaded the men not to enlist, removed them, as he was told, to the Provost. The prisoners were tempted to enlist to free themselves from confinement, hopeless of exchange. * * * The prisoners had a pint of water per day:—the sick were not sent to the hospitals until they were so weak and ill that they often expired before they got out of the Jersey. The commanding officer said his orders were that if the ship took fire we should all be turned below, and left to perish in the flames. By accident the ship took fire in the steward's room, when the Hessian guards were ordered to drive the prisoners below, and fire among them if they resisted or got in the water."

Talbot in his Memoirs stated that: "When the weather became cool and dry in the fall and the nights frosty the number of deaths on board the Jersey was *reduced* to an average of ten per day! which was *small* compared with the mortality for three months before. The human bones and skulls yet bleaching on the shore of Long Island, and exposed by the falling down of the high bank, on which the prisoners were buried, is a shocking sight." (Talbot, page 106.)

In May, 1808, one William Burke of New York testified that "He was a prisoner in the Jersey 14 months, has known many American prisoners put to death by the bayonet. It was the custom for but one prisoner at a time to go on deck. One night while many prisoners were assembled at the grate, at the hatchway to obtain fresh air, and waiting their turn to go on deck, a sentinel thrust his bayonet down among them, and 25 next morning were found to be dead. This was the case several mornings, when sometimes six, and sometimes eight or ten were found dead by wounds thus received."

A Connecticut paper, some time in May, 1781, stated that. "Eleven hundred French and American prisoners died in New York last winter."

A paper published in Philadelphia, on the 20th of February, 1782, says: "Many of our unfortunate prisoners on board the prison ships in the East River have perished during the late extreme weather, for want of fuel and other necessaries."

"New London. May 3rd. 1782. One thousand of our seamen remain in prison ships in New York, a great part in close confinement for six months past, and in a most deplorable condition. Five hundred have died during the past five or six months, three hundred are sick; many seeing no prospect of release are entering the British service to elude the contagion with which the prison ships are fraught."

Joel Barlow in his Columbiad says that Mr. Elias Boudinot told him that in the Jersey 1,100 prisoners died in eighteen months, almost the whole of them from the barbarous treatment of being stifled in a crowded hold with infected air; and poisoned with unwholesome food, and Mr Barlow adds that the cruelties exercised by the British armies on American prisoners during the first years of the war were unexampled among civilized nations.

CONCLUSION

Such of the prisoners as escaped after months of suffering with health sufficient for future usefulness in the field often re–enlisted, burning for revenge.

Mr. Scharf, in his "History of Western Maryland," speaks of Colonel William Kunkel, who had served in Prussia, and emigrated to America about the year 1732. He first settled in Lancaster, Pa., but afterwards moved to Western Maryland. He had six sons in the Revolution. One of these sons entered the American army at the age of eighteen. Taken prisoner he was sent on board the Jersey, where his sufferings were terrible. On his return home after his exchange he vowed to his father that he would return to the army and fight until the last redcoat was driven out of the country. He did return, and from that time, says Mr Scharf, his family never heard from him again.

Mr. Crimmins in his "Irish–American Historical Miscellany," says: "An especially affecting incident is told regarding one prisoner who died on the Jersey. Two young men, brothers, belonging to a rifle corps were made prisoners, and sent on board the ship. The elder took the fever, and in a few days became delirious. One night as his end was fast approaching, he became calm and sensible, and lamenting his hard fate, and the absence of his mother, begged for a little water. His brother with tears, entreated the guard to give him some, but in vain. The sick youth was soon in his last struggles, when his brother offered the guard a guinea for an inch of candle, only that he might see him die. Even this was denied."

The young rifleman died in the dark.

"Now," said his brother, drying his tears, "if it please God that I ever regain my liberty, I'll be a most bitter enemy!"

He was exchanged, rejoined the army, and when the war ended he is said to have had eight large and one hundred and twenty–seven small notches on his rifle stock. The inference is that he made a notch every time he killed or wounded a British soldier, a large notch for an officer, and a small one for a private.

Mr. Lecky, the English historian, thus speaks of American prisoners: "The American prisoners who had been confined in New York after the battle of Long Island were so emaciated and broken down by scandalous neglect or ill usage that Washington refused to receive them in exchange for an equal number of healthy British and Hessian troops. * * * It is but justice to the Americans to add that their conduct during the war appears to have been almost uniformly humane. No charges of neglect of prisoners, like those which were brought, apparently with too good reason, against the English, were substantiated against them. The conduct of Washington was marked by a careful and steady humanity, and Franklin, also, appears to have done much to mitigate the war."

Our task is now concluded. We have concerned ourselves with the prisoners themselves, not much with the history of the negotiations carried on to effect exchange, but have left this part of the subject to some abler hand. Only a very small part of the story has been told in this volume, and there is much room for future investigations. It is highly probable that if a systematic search is made many unpublished accounts may be discovered, and a great deal of light shed upon the horrors of the British prisons. If we have awakened interest in the sad fate of so many of our brave countrymen, and aroused some readers to a feeling of compassion for their misfortunes, and admiration for their heroism, our task has not been in vain.

APPENDIX A. LIST OF 8000 MEN WHO WERE PRISONERS ON BOARD THE OLD JERSEY

PRINTED BY PERMISSION OF THE SOCIETY OF OLD BROOKLYNITES

This list of names was copied from the papers of the British War Department. There is nothing to indicate what became of any of these prisoners, whether they died, escaped, or were exchanged. The list seems to have been carelessly kept, and is full of obvious mistakes in spelling the names. Yet it shall be given just as it is, except that the names are arranged differently, for easier reference. This list of prisoners is the only one that could be found in the British War Department. What became of the lists of prisoners on the many other prison ships, and prisons, used by the English in America, we do not know.

A

Garret Aarons
John Aarons (2)
Alexander Abbett
John Abbett
James Abben
John Abbott
Daniel Abbott
Abel Abel
George Abel
Jacob Aberry
Jabez Abett
Philip Abing
Thomas Abington

Christopher Abois
William Aboms
Daniel Abrams
Don Meegl (Miguel) Abusure
Gansio Acito
Abel Adams
Amos Adams
Benjamin Adams
David Adams
Isaac Adams
John Adams (4)
Lawrence Adams
Moses Adams
Nathaniel Adams
Pisco Adams
Richard Adams
Stephen Adams
Thomas Adams
Warren Adams
Amos Addams
Thomas Addett
Benjamin Addison
David Addon
John Adlott
Robert Admistad
Noah Administer
Wm Adamson (2)
John Adobon
James Adovie
Sebastian de Aedora
Jean Aenbie
Michael Aessinis
Frances Affille
Joseph Antonio Aguirra
Thomas Aguynoble
John Aires

Robert Aitken
Thomas Aiz
Manuel Ajote
Jacob Akins
Joseph Aker (2)
Richard Akerson
Charles Albert
Piere Albert
Robert Albion
Joachin Alconan
Joseph de Alcorta
Juan Ignacid Alcorta
Pedro Aldaronda
Humphrey Alden
Fred Aldkin
George Aldridge
Jacob Alehipike
Jean Aleslure
Archibald Alexander
John Alexander (2)
Lehle Alexander
William Alexander
Thomas Alger
Christopher Aliet
Joseph Aliev
George Alignott
Joseph Allah
Gideon Allan
Hugh Allan
Francis Allegree
Baeknel Allen
Bancke Allen
Benjamin Allen
Bucknell Allen
Ebeneser Allen
George Allen

Gideon Allen
Isaac Allen
John Allen (5)
Josiah Allen
Murgo Allen
Richard Allen (2)
Samuel Allen (7)
Squire Allen
Thomas Allen (3)
William Allen (4)
Jean Allin
Caleb Allis
Bradby Allison
Bradey Allison
James Allison
Frances Alment
Arrohan Almon
Aceth Almond
William Alpin
Jacob Alsfrugh
Jacob Alsough
Jacob Alstright
Jacob Alsworth
Thomas Alvarey
Miguel Alveras
Don Ambrose Alverd
Joseph Alvey
James Alwhite
George Alwood
James Alwood
Charles Amey
Anthony Amingo
Manuel Amizarma
Nathaniel Anabel
Austin Anaga
Jean Ancette

Charles Anderson
Joseph Anderson
Robert Anderson
William Anderson (3)
George Andre
Benjamin Andrews
Charles Andrews
Dollar Andrews
Ebeneser Andrews
Francis Andrews
Frederick Andrews
Jerediah Andrews
John Andrews (4)
Jonathan Andrews
Pascal Andrews
Philany Andrews
Thomas Andrews
William Andrews
Guillion Andrie
Pashal Andrie
Dominique Angola
Andre D. C. Annapolen
Joseph Anrandes
John Anson
William Anster
David Anthony
Davis Anthony
Samuel Anthony
Pierre Antien
Jacques Antiqua
Jean Anton
Francis Antonf
John Antonio
Daniel Appell
Daniel Apple
Thomas Appleby

Samuel Appleton
Joseph Aquirse
——Arbay
Abraham Archer
James Archer
John Archer
Stephen Archer
Thomas Arcos
Richard Ariel
Asencid Arismane
Ezekiel Arme
Jean Armised
James Armitage
Elijah Armsby
Christian Armstrong
William Armstrong
Samuel Arnibald
Amos Arnold
Ash Arnold
Samuel Arnold
Charles Arnolds
Samuel Arnolds
Thomas Arnold
Andres Arral
Manuel de Artol
Don Pedro Asevasuo
Hosea Asevalado
James Ash
Henry Ash
John Ashbey
John Ashburn
Peter Ashburn
John Ashby
Warren Ashby
John Ashley
Andrew Askill

Francis Aspuro
John Athan
George Atkins
John Atkins
Silas Atkins
John Atkinson
Robert Atkinson
William Atkinson
James Atlin
Duke Attera
Jean Pierre Atton
John Atwood
Henry Auchinlaup
Joseph Audit
Anthony Aiguillia
Igarz Baboo Augusion
Peter Augusta
Thomas Augustine
Laurie Aujit
George Austin
Job Avery
Benjamin Avmey
Francis Ayres
Don Pedro Azoala

B

Franklin Babcock
William Babcock
James Babel
Jeremiah Babell
Jean Babier
Abel Baboard
Vascilla Babtreause

Francis Bachelier
Jonathan Bachelor
Antonio Backalong
Francis Backay
Benjamin Bacon
Esau Bacon
Judah Bacon
Stephen Badante
Laurence Badeno
William Badick
Jonathan Baddock
John Baggar
Barnett Bagges
Adam Bagley
Joseph Bahamony
John Bailey (2)
William Bailey
Moses Baird
Joseph Baisolus
William Baison
William Batho
Christopher Baker
Ebenezer Baker
John Baker (2)
Joseph Baker
Judah Baker
Lemuel Baker
Nathaniel Baker
Pamberton Baker
Pemberton Baker
Pembleton Baker
Thomas Baker (3)
David Baldwin
James Baldwin
John Baldwin
Nathaniel Baldwin

Ralph Baldwin
Thomas Ball
Benjamin Ballard
John Ballast
Joseph Balumatigua
Ralf Bamford
Jacob Bamper
Peter Banaby
James Bandel
Augustine Bandine
Pierre Bandine
John Banister (2)
Matthew Bank
James Banker
John Banks
Matthew Banks
Jean Rio Bapbsta
Jean Baptista
Gale Baptist
Jean Baptist
John Barber
Gilbert Barber
John Barden
William Barenoft
Walter Bargeman
Joseph Bargeron
Charles Bargo
Mabas Bark
Benjamin Barker
Edward Barker
Jacom Barker
John Barker
Peter Barker
Thomas Barker
Benjamin Barkly
Joseph Barkump

John Barley
James Barman
Ethiem Barnell
Charles Barnes
Henry Barnes
Wooding Barnes
John Barnett
Henry Barney
Mons Barney
Samuel Barney
William Barnhouse
James Barracks
Pierre Barratt
Abner Barre
Dennis Barrett
Enoch Barrett
Francis Barrett
Samuel Barrett
William Barrett
Robert Barrol
Bernard Barron
Enoch Barrott
Francis Barsidge
William Bartlet
Joseph Bartley
Charles Barthalemerd
Charles Bartholemew
Joseph Bartholomew
——Bartholomew
Benjamin Bartholoyd
Petrus Bartlemie
Michael Bartol
Thomas Barton
John Basker
William Bason
Donnor Bass

Juvery Bastin
Michael Bastin
Louis Baston
Asa Batcheler
Benjamin Bate
Benjamin Bates
Henry Bates
James Bates
William Batt
John Battersley
John Battesker
Adah Batterman
Adam Batterman
George Batterman (2)
Joseph Batterman
——Baumos
Thomas Bausto
Benjamin Bavedon
George Baxter
Malachi Baxter
Richard Bayan
Joseph Bayde
Thomas Bayess
John Bayley
Joseph Baynes
Jean Baxula
John Bazee
Daniel Beal
Samuel Beal
Joseph Beane
James Beankey
James Bearbank
Jesse Bearbank
Morgan Beard
Moses Beard
Daniel Beatty

Benjamin Beasel
Joseph Beaufort
Perri Beaumont
Andrew Beck
Thomas Beck
William Beckett
Jonathan Beckwith
Francis Bedell
Frederick Bedford
Joseph Bedford
Thomas Bedford
Benjamin Beebe
Elias Beebe
Joshua Beebe
Benjamin Beeford
James Beekman
Walter Beekwith
Lewis Begand
Joseph Begley
Joseph Belcher
John Belding
Pierre Belgard
Aaron Bell
Charles Bell
Robert Bell
Uriah Bell
Alexander Bellard
Joseph Belter
Julian Belugh
Jean Bengier
Joseph Benloyde
John Benn
George Bennett
John Bennett
Joseph Bennett
Peter Bennett

Pierre Bennett
Anthony Benson
Stizer Benson
David Benton
John Benton
Peter Bentler
Nathaniel Bentley (2)
Peter Bentley
William Bentley
Joshua M Berason
Joseoh Berean
Julian Berger
Lewis Bernall
Francis Bernardus
Francis Bercoute
Jean Juquacid Berra
Abner Berry
Alexander Berry
Benjamin Berry
Daniel Berry
Dennis Berry
Edward Berry
John Berry
Peter Berry (2)
Philip Berry
Simon Berry
William Berry (3)
Philip Berrycruise
William Berryman
Jean Bertine
Martin Bertrand
John Bertram
Andrew Besin
Jean Beshire
John Beszick
James Bett

American Prisoners of the Revolution

Samuel Bevan
Jean Bevin
Benjamin Beverley
Robert Bibbistone
John Bice
Andrew Bick
John Bickety
Charles Bierd
David Bierd
Joshua Bievey
Benjamin Bigelow
Oliver Bigelow
Thomas Biggs
Jean Bilarie
Charles Bill (2)
Garden Bill
John Bill (2)
Pierre Bill
John Billard
James Biller
Samuel Billing
Benjamin Billings
Bradford Billings
Ezekiel Billings
Robert Billings
David Billows
Frarey Binnen
Cirretto Biola
Pierre Biran
Alexander Birch
Nathaniel Birch
Joseph Bird
Weldon Bird
Thomas Birket
Samuel Birmingham
Ezekiel Bishop

Israel Bishop
John Bishop (2)
John Bissell
Jack Bissick
Osee Bissole
Pierre Bitgayse
Peter Bitton
Daniel Black
James Black (3)
John Black
Joseph Black
Robert N Black
Samuel Black (2)
Timothy Black
William Black
John Blackburn
Alexander Blackhunt
William Blackpond
V C Blaine
John Blair
Charles Blake
Increase Blake
James Blake
Samuel Blake
Valentine Blake
David Blanch
Robert Blanch
Joseph Blancher
William Blanchet
John Blanney
Gideon Blambo
Jesse Blacque
Joseph Blateley
Lubal Blaynald
Asa Blayner
Edward Blevin

Benjamin Blimbey
William Blimbey
Joseph Blinde
William Bliss
Samuel Blissread
Juan Blodgett
Seth Blodgett
John Blond
Lewis Blone
Louis Blong
Peter Bloome (2)
Samuel Bloomfield
Jomes Blossom
James Blowen
John Bloxand
William Bluard
George Blumbarg
George Blunt (4)
William Blythe
Matthew Boar
John Bobier
John Bobgier
Joseph Bobham
Jonathan Bocross
Lewis Bodin
Peter Bodwayne
John Boelourne
Christopher Boen
Purdon Boen
Roper Bogat
James Boggart
Ralph Bogle
Nicholas Boiad
Pierre Boilon
William Boine
Jacques Bollier

William Bolt
William Bolts
Bartholomew Bonavist
Henry Bone
Anthony Bonea
Jeremiah Boneafoy
James Boney
Thomas Bong
Barnabus Bonus
James Bools
William Books
John Booth
Joseph Borda
Charles Borden
John Borman
James Borrall
Joseph Bortushes
Daniel Borus (2)
Joseph Bosey
Pierre Bosiere
Jacques Bosse
Ebenezer Boswell
Gustavus Boswell
Lewis Bothal
Charles Bottis
James Bottom
Walter Bottom
Augustin Boudery
Augustus Boudery
Anthony Bouea
Theophilus Boulding
Pierre Bounet
Lewis Bourge
John Boursbo
Lawrence Bourshe
Jean Boutilla

Lewis Bouton
Edward Boven
Elijah Bowden
Arden Bowen
Elijah Bowen
Ezekiel Bowen
Paldon Bowen
Thomas Bowen (3)
William Bowen
Willis Bowen
James Bowers
Thomas Bowers
Fulbur Bowes
James Bowles
Daniel Bowman
Benjamin Bowman
Elijah Bowman (2)
John Bowman
Michael Bowner
John Bowrie
P I Bowree
Jean Bowseas
John Boyau
Thomas Boyd
John Boyde
David Boyeau
Francis Boyer
Joseph Boyne
Thomas Bradbridge
Samuel Bradbury
William Braden
James Brader
Samuel Bradfield
William Bradford
Abijah Bradley
Alijah Bradley

Daniel Bradley
James Bradley
Abraham Bradley
John Brady
James Bradyon
Ebenezer Bragg (2)
William Bragley
Nathaniel Braily
Zacheus Brainard
Joseph Bramer
Zachary Bramer
William Bramber
James Branart
Aholibah Branch
William Brand
Ralf Brandford
Charles Branel
William Bransdale
David Branson
Peter Braswan
Peter Brays (2)
Burden Brayton
Peter Brayton
John Bredford
James Brehard
Elijah Bremward
Pierre Brene
George Brent
Pierre Bretton
John Brewer
Samuel Brewer
Joseph Brewett
James Brewster (2)
Seabury Brewster
John Brice
Thomas Bridges

Glond Briges
Cabot Briggs
Alexander Bright
Henry Brim
Peter Brinkley
Ephraim Brion
Louis Brire
Thomas Brisk
Simon Bristo
Jalaher C Briton
Peter Britton
Thomas Britton
Ephraim Broad (3)
Ossia Broadley
Joseph Broaker
Joshua Brocton
Philip Broderick
William Broderick (2)
Joseph Broge
William Brooker
Charles Brooks (2)
Henry Brooks
Paul Brooks
Samuel Brooks (2)
Thomas Brooks
Benjamin Brown
Christopher Brown
David Brown (2)
Francis Brown
Gustavus Brown (3)
Hugh Brown (2)
Jacob Brown
James Brown (3)
Jonathan Brown
John Brown (12)
Joseph Brown (3)

Michael Brown
Nathaniel Brown
Patrick Brown
Peter Brown
Samuel Brown (3)
William Brown (5)
W. Brown
William Boogs Brown
Willis Brown
Essick Brownhill
Wanton Brownhill
Charles Brownwell
Gardner Brownwell
Pierre Brows
James Bruding
Lewis Brun
Daniel Bruton
Edward Bryan
John Bryan
Matthew Bryan
Nathaniel Bryan
William Bryan
Benjamin Bryand
Ephraim Bryand
James Bryant
William Bryant
Nicholas Bryard
Francis Bryean
Richard Bryen
Berr Bryon
Thomas Bryon
Simon Buas
Thomas Buchan
Francis Buchanan
Elias Buck
Elisha Buck

John Buck
Joseph Bucklein
Philip Buckler
Cornelius Buckley
Daniel Buckley (2)
Francis Buckley
Jacob Buckley
John Buckley (3)
Daniel Bucklin (2)
Samuel Buckwith
David Buckworth
Benjamin Bud
Nicholas Budd
Jonathan Buddington
Oliver Buddington
Waller Buddington
William Budgid
John Budica
Joshua Buffins
Lawrence Buffoot
John Bugger
Silas Bugg
John Buldings
Jonathan Bulgedo
Benjamin Bullock
Thomas Bullock
Benjamin Bumbley
Lewis Bunce
Norman Bunce
Thomas Bunch
Antonio Bund
Obadiah Bunke
Jonathan Bunker
Timothy Bunker
William Bunker
Richard Bunson (2)

Murdock Buntine
Frederick Bunwell
Thomas Burch
Michael Burd
Jeremiah Burden
Joseph Burden
William Burden
Jason Burdis
Daniel Burdit
Bleck Burdock
Robert Burdock
Vincent Burdock
Henry Burgess
Theophilus Burgess
Barnard Burgh
Prosper Burgo
Jean Burham
James Burke
Thomas Burke
William Burke
Michael Burkman
William Burn
Frederick Burnett
James Burney
James Burnham
Daniel Burnhill
Archibald Burns
Edward Burns (2)
Henry Burns
John Burns
Thomas Burns
Stephen Burr
Pierre Burra
Francis Burrage
John Burrell
Lewis Burrell

Isaac Burrester
Jonathan Burries
Nathaniel Burris
John Burroughs
Edward Burrow
James Burton
John Burton
Jessee Byanslow
Bartholomew Byi
John Bylight

C

Abel Cable
Louis Cadat
Louis Pierre Cadate
Michael Cadate
John Caddington
Nathan Caddock
Jean Cado
John Cahoon
Jonathan Cahoone
Thomas Caile
David Cain (2)
Thomas Cain
Samuel Caird
Joseph Caivins
Pierre Cajole
Thomas Calbourne
James Calder
Caplin Calfiere
Nathaniel Calhoun
Charles Call
Barnaby Callagham

Daniel Callaghan
William Callehan
James Callingham
Andrew Caiman
Francis Calon
Parpi Calve
Nicholas Calwell
Joseph Cambridge
Edward Cameron
Simon Came
Oseas Camp
Alexander Campbell
Frederick Campbell
James Campbell
Jesse Campbell
John Campbell (2)
Joseph Campbell
Philip Campbell (2)
Robert Campbell
Thomas Campbell (2)
James Canady
Joseph Canana
Satarus Candie
Jacob Canes
Richard Caney
Jacob Canmer
William Cannady
William Canner
Charles Cannon
Francis Cannon
John Cannon
Joseph Cannon
Samuel Cannon
Jean Canute
Francis Cape
Timothy Cape

Daniel Capnell
William Caransame
Robert Carbury
Juan Fernin Cardends
Joseph Carea
Isaac Carelton
Joseph Carender
Ezekiel Carew
Daniel Carey
John Carey (4)
Joshua Carey
Richard Carey
William Cargall
Joseph Cariviot
Edward Garland
Antonio Carles
William Carles
Jean Carlton
Thomas Carlton
John Carlisle
Justan Carlsrun
Benjamin Carman
Benjamin Carmell
William Carmenell
Edward Carmody
Anthony Carney
Hugh Carney
David Carns
Jean Carolin
Pierre Carowan
John Carpenter
Miles Carpenter
Richards Carpenter
Edward Carr
Isaac Carr
John Carr (2)

Philip Carr
William Carr
Robert Carrall
——Carret
Thomas Carrington
Jean Carrllo
James Carroll
John Carroll
Michael Carroll
Perance Carroll
William Carrollton
John Carrow
Peter Carroway
Avil Carson
Batterson Carson
Israel Carson
James Carson
Robert Carson (2)
Samuel Carson
William Carson
Levi Carter
Thomas Carter
William Carter (2)
John Carvell
Joseph Casan
Joseph Casanova
John Case
Thomas Case
Thomas Casewell
Edward Casey
John Casey
William Casey
Stephen Cash
Jacob Cashier
Jean Cashwell
Gosper Cassian

Samuel Casson
John Casp
Anthony Casper
Michael Cassey
John Castel
Joseph Castile
Thomas Castle (2)
John Caswell (3)
Baptist Cavalier
Francis Cavalier
George Cavalier
James Cavalier
Thomas Cavalier
Joseph Augustus Cavell
Gasnito Cavensa
Thomas Caveral
Pierre Cawan
John Cawrier
John Cawrse
Edward Cayman
Anthony Cayner
Oliver Cayaran
John Cerbantin
——Chabbott
Perrie Chalier
Samuel Chalkeley
Hurbin Challigne
John Challoner
William Challoner
Pierre Chalore
Benjamin Chamberlain
Bird Chamberlain
Charles Chamberland
Nancy Chambers
Dore Champion
Lines Champion

Thomas Champion
Clerk Champlin
Isaac Champlin
James Chapin
Joseph Chapley
Joseph Chaplin
Josiah Chaplin
Lodowick Chaplin
Daniel Chapman
James Chapman
Jeremiah Chapman
John Chapman (2)
Lion Chapman
Samuel Chapman
Charles Chappel
Frederick Chappell
John Chappell
John Charbein
Ichabod Chard
William Charfill
James Charles
John Charles
Jean Charoner
Aaron Chase
Augustus Chase (2)
Earl Chase (2)
George Chase (2)
Lonie Chase
Samuel Chase
Jean Chatfield
Jovis Chaurine
John Cheavelin
Christopher Chenaur
Louis Chenet
Andrew Cheesebrook
David Cheesebrook

James Cheesebrook
Pierre Cheesebrook
Samuel Cheesebrook
Britton Cheeseman
James Cheevers
Christopher Chenaur
Benjamin Chencey
Louis Chenet
John Cherry
William Cherry
John Chese
Hiram Chester
Benjamin Chevalier
John Chevalier
Jean Gea Chevalier
Julian Chevalier
Edward Cheveland
Lasar Chien
Silas Childs
Cadet Chiller
Thomas Chilling
Abel Chimney
David Chinks
Leshers Chipley
William Christan
Henry Christian
John Christian (2)
James Christie
Benjamin Chittington
Bartholomew Chivers
Benjamin Chopman
Matthew Chubb
David Chueehook
Benjamin Church (2)
Israel Church
Thomas Church

John Churchill
Pierre Clabe
Edward Clamron
Benjamin Clannan
Edward Clanwell
Supply Clap (2)
Supply Twing Clap
Edward Claring
Charles Clark
Church Clark
James Clark (2)
John Clark
Jubal Clark
William Clark (2)
Emanuel Clarke
Daniel Clarke
Jacob Clarke
James Clarke
Joshua Clarke
Lewis Clarke
Nicholas Clarke
Noel Clarke
Stephen Clarke
Theodore Clarke
Timothy Clarke
William Clarke (2)
Samuel Clarkson
Samuel Claypole
Edward Clayton
William Clayton
David Cleaveland
Michel Clemence
Clement Clements
Alexander Clerk
Gambaton Clerk
Isaac Clerk

Jacob Clerk
Jonathan Clerk
John Clerk (3)
Lardner Clerk
Nathaniel Clerk
Peleg Clerk
Thomas Clerk (3)
Tully Clerk
William Clerk
Thomas Clever
Jean Clineseau
David Clinton
Philip Clire
John Cloud
John Coarsin
Christian Cobb
Christopher Cobb
Francis Cobb
John Cobb
Jonathan Cobb
Nathaniel Cobb
Richard Cobb
Thomas Cobb
Christopher Cobbs
Raymond Cobbs
Timothy Cobley
Moses Cobnan
Eliphas Coburn
James Cochran
John Cochran (2)
Richard Cochran
John Cocker
John Cocklin
Equatius Code
Lewis Codean
Christopher Codman

James Codner
Abel Coffin
Edward Coffin
Elias Coffin
Elisha Coffin (2)
Obadiah Coffin (2)
Richard Coffin
Simon Coffin (2)
Zechariah Coffin
William Cogeshall
John Coggeshall
Robert Coghill
John Cohlen
David Coisten
Guilliam Cokill
James Colbert
Abial Cole
Benjamin Cole (2)
John Cole (2)
Joshua Cole
Rilhard Cole
Thomas Cole (2)
Waller Cole
David Coleman
James Coleman
Nicholas Coleman
Stephen Coleman
James Colford
Miles Colhoon
Lewis Colinett
Alexander Colley
Basquito Colley
Septor en Collie
Candal Collier
John Collings
Joseph Collingwood

Doan Collins
James Collins (2)
John Collins (3)
Joseph Collins
Powell Collins
William Collins
Daniel Collohan
Thomas Collough
Joseph Colloy
Elisha Colman
John Colney
Frederick Colson
James Colting
Julian Columb
Julian Colver
David Colvich
Nathaniel Colwell
Nathaniel Combick
Joseph Combs
Matthew Combs
Joseph Comby
Gilbert Comick
Patrick Condon
Stafford Condon
Philip Cong
Strantly Congdon
Muller Congle
John Connell
John Connelly
George Conner
James Conner
John Conner (2)
Robert Conner
Patrick Connelly
Samuel Connelly
John Connor

William Connor
George Conrad
Frederick Contaney
William Convass
John Conway
Thomas Conway
Robert Conwell
Amos Cook
Anthony Cook
Benjamin Cook
Eashak Cook
Esbric Cook
Ezekiel Cook (2)
Frederick Cook
George Cook
James Cook (3)
John Cook (4)
Joseph Cook
Richard Cook
Samuel Cooke
Stephen Cooke
Abraham Cooper
Ezekiel Cooper
Matthew Cooper (2)
Mot Cooper
Nathaniel Cooper (3)
Richard Cooper
Warren Cooper
William Cooper
Aaron Cooping
Joseph Copeland
Andrew Cord
Joseph Cornean
Peter Cornelius
John Cornell
Matthew Cornell

James Corner
Benjamin Corning
Robert Cornwell
William Cornwell
Bernard Corrigan
John Corrigan
John Corroll
Battson Corson
Pomeus Corson
Lewis Cortland
Robert Corwell
Joseph de Costa
Antonio Costo
Noel Cotis
Anghel Cotter
David Cotteral
David Cottrill
James Couch
John Couch
Thomas Coudon
John Coughin
Pierre Coulanson
Nathaniel Connan
Francis Connie
Perrie Coupra
Jean de Course
Leonard Courtney
Louis Couset
Joseph Cousins
Frances Cousnant
Jean Couster
John Coutt
Vizenteausean Covazensa
John Coventry
John Coverley
Peter Covet

Zechariah Coward
James Cowbran
James Cowen
John Cowins
Edward Cownovan
Enoch Cox
Jacob Cox
John Cox
Joseph Cox (2)
Portsmouth Cox
William Cox
Thurmal Coxen
Asesen Craft
Joseph Craft
Matthias Craft (2)
James Craig
Thomas Craig
Henry Crandall
Oliver Crane
Philip Crane
Samuel Crane
William Cranston
Abel Crape (2)
Thomas Craton (2)
Joshua Cratterbrook
Alias Crawford
Benjamin Crawford
John Crawford (4)
Richard Crawford
Samuel Crawford
William Crawford
Basil Crawley
Cornelius Crawley
Isaac Crayton (2)
James Crayton
Amos Creasey

Richard Creech
Thomas Creepman
William Cresean
William Cresley
Henry Cressouson
Michael Crider
John Crim
Others Cringea
William Crispin (2)
George Cristin
Benjamin Crocker
James Crocker
John Crocker
Joshua Crocker (2)
John Croix
Oliver Cromell
Oliver Cromwell (4)
Richmond Cromwell
Robert Cromwell
Hugh Crookt
John Croppen
Bunsby Crorker
Peter Crosbury
Daniel Crosby (3)
William Crosley
Joseph Cross
Thomas Crough
Christian Crowdy
Matthew Crow
Bissell Crowell
Seth Crowell
William Crowell
George Crown
Michael Crowyar
William Crozier
Janeise Cubalod

Benjamin Cuffey
Philip Cuish
Thomas Culbarth
Daniel Culbert
William Cullen (2)
David Cullett
Willis Culpper
Levi Culver
Samuel Culvin
Josea Comnano
Cornelius Cumstock
Isaac Cuningham
James Cunican
Barnabas Cunningham
Cornelius Cunningham
John Cunningham
Jacob Currel
Anthony Curry
Augustine Curry
Robert Curry
Daniel Curtis
Frederick Curtis
Joseph Curtis
Henry Curtis
Joseph Cushing
Robert Cushing
Eimnan Cushing

D

Guilliam Dabuican
Jean Dabuican
John Daccarmell
Isaac Dade (2)

Jean Dadica
Silas Daggott
John Dagure
Benjamin Dail
James Daily (2)
Patrick Daily
Robert Daily
Samuel Daily (2)
William Daily
James Dalcahide
Jeremiah Dalley
Reuben Damon
Thomas Danby
Christopher Daniel
John Daniel (3)
Samuel Daniss
Benjamin Dannison
William Dannison
William Dannivan
Benjamin Darby
William Darby
W Darcey
Thomas Darley
Henry Darling (2)
Richard Darling
William Darling
Charles Darrough
Robert Dart
Samuel Daun
Basteen Davan
James Daveick
Lot Davenport
Christopher Davids
John Davidson
Samuel Davidson
Pierre Davie

Benjamin Davies (2)
Christopher Davies
Edward Davies
Eliga Davies
Elijah Davies
Felton Davies
John Davies (9)
Henry Davies
Lewis Davies
Richard Davies (2)
Samuel Davies (3)
Thomas Davies (3)
William Davies (3)
Benjamin Davies (2)
Charles Davis
Christopher Davis
Curtis Davis
Henry Davis
Isaac Davis
James Davis
John Davis (2)
Lewis Davis
Samuel Davis
Thomas Davis
William Davis
Thomas Dawn
Henry Dawne
Samuel Dawson
John Day
Joseph Day
Michael Day
Thomas Day (2)
William Day
Joseph Days
William Dayton
Demond Deaboney

Jonathan Deakons
Isaac Deal
John Deal
Elias Deale (2)
Daniel Dealing
Benjamin Deamond
Benjamin Dean
Levi Dean
Lewis Dean
Orlando Dean
Philip Dean
Archibald Deane
George Deane
Joseph Deane
Thomas Deane
Michael Debong
James Debland
Peter Deboy
Benorey Deck
Joseph de Costa
Jean de Course
Francis Dedd
——Defourgue
Jean Degle
Pierre Degoniere
Pierre Guiseppe Degue
William Degue
Louis Degune
Pratus Dehango
Jacob Dehart
Jasper Deinay
Domingo Delace
Zabulon Delano
Gare Delare
Gaspin Delary
Anthony Delas

Amos Delavan
Pierre Delavas
Joseph Delcosta
Francis Delgada
Henry Delone
Anthony Delore
James Demay
David Demeny
Israel Deming
Josiah Demmay
Element Demen
Jean Demolot
Richard Dempsey
Avery Denauf
Daniel Denica
Beebe Denison
Deverick Dennis
James Dennis
John Dennis (3)
Jonas Dennis
Joseph Dennis (2)
Moses Dennis
Paine Dennis
Lemuel Dennison
John Denoc
David Denroron
John Denronons
Lewis Depue
Manuel Deralia
John Derboise
Daniel Deroro
Daniel Derry
William Derry
Louis Deshea
John Desiter
Jacob Dessino

Jeane Devaratte
Isaac Devay
Gabriel Devay
James Devereux
Robert Devereux
James Deverick
John Devericks
Honor Devey
Joseph Deville
Frances Devise
Daniel Devoe
Thomas Devoy
Aaron Dexter
Benjamin Dexter
Simon Dexter
Elerouant Diabery
Jonah Diah
David Diber
Archibald Dick
Benjamin Dickenson
Benjamin Dickinson
Edward Dickinson
Ichabod Dickinson
John Dickinson
Edward Dickerson
Joseph Diers
Thomas Diggenson
Rone Digon
Joseph Dillons
John Dillow
Benjamin Dimon
Charles Dimon
James Dimon
Robert Dingee
Elisha Dingo
John Dingo

Pierre Disaablan
Mitchael Dissell
John Diver
Victoire Divie
Christian Dixon
Christopher Dixon
Daniel Dixon
James Dixon (2)
John Dixon
Nicholas Dixon
Robert Dixon (2)
William Dixon
Etamin Dluice
John Doan
Joseph Dobbs
John Dobiee
Henry Docherty
Hugh Docherty
William Dodd (2)
James Dodge
George Doget
Matthew Doggett
Samuel Doggett (2)
Timothy Doggle
John Doherty (2)
Thomas Doherty
Josiah Dohn
Samuel Dohn
Robert Doin
Frances Doisu
John Dolbear
Elisha Dolbuy
John Dole
Elisha Doleby
Nathaniel Dolloway
Pierre Dominica

Jean Domrean
Barton Donald
Anthony Donalds
Daniel Donaldson
Mc Donalm
Solomon Donan
John Dongan
Peter C Dongue
Anthony Dongues
Benjamin Donham
Devereux Donies
George Donkin
Francis Dora
John McDora Dora
Nathaniel Dorcey
Patrick Dorgan (3)
Timothy Dorgan
Joseph Dority
Paul Paulding Dorson
Joseph Doscemer
Jay Doudney
Francis Douglas
Robert Douglass
William Douglass
Iseno Douting
Thomas Douval
James Dowdey
William Dowden
Hezekiah Dowen (2)
John Dower
Henry Dowling
Francis Downenroux
Henry Dowling
John Downey
John Downing
Peter Downing

John Dowray
James Doxbury
Peter Doyle
Murray Drabb
Thomas Drake
Jean Draullard
James Drawberry
Samuel Drawere
James Drayton
William Dredge
Abadiah Drew
John Drew (2)
Thomas Drewry
John Driver
Simeon Drown
William Drown
Jean Dubison
Tames Dublands
Thomas Dubois
Henry Dubtoe
Michael Duchaee
Archibald Ducker
Jean Duckie
Martin Ducloy
Abner Dudley
Doulram Duffey
Ezekiel Duffey
Thomas Duffield
Michael Duffin
Thomas Duffy
Jacques Duforte
Franes Dugree
Chemuel Duke
John Duke
William Duke
Isaac Dukerson

Michael Duless
Terrence Dumraven
James Dunbar
George Duncan
John Duncan
James Duncan
William Duncan
Thomas Dung
John Dunhire
John Dunison
James Dunkin
Pierre Dunkwater
Thomas Dunlope
John Dunlope
Thomas Dunlope
Archibald Dunlopp
Allan Dunlot
John Dunmerhay
Arthur Dunn
Joseph Dunn
Peter Dunn
Sylvester Dunnam
John Dunning
Peter Dunning
Thomas Dunnon
Edene Dunreas
Allen Dunslope
William Dunton
Stephen Dunwell
Ehenne Dupee
Thomas Duphane
Francis Duplessis
France Dupue
Charles Duran
Henry Duran
Lewis Duran

Glase Durand
Jacques Durant
Sylvester Durham
Israel Durphey
Jonathan J Durvana
Robert Duscasson
Anthony Duskin
Andrew Duss
William Dussell
Raoul Dutchell
James Duverick
Timothy Dwier
William Dwine
John Dwyer
Timothy Dwyer (2)
William Dwyman
Alexander Dyer
Fitch Dyer
Hat Dyer
Hubert Dyer
Jonathan Dyer
Nathan Dyer
Patrick Dyer
Robert Dyer
Roger Dyer
Samuel Dyer

E

David Each
Simon Eachforsh
David Eadoe
Benjamin Earle
Isaac Earle

Lewis Earle
Pardon Earle (2)
Michael Eason
Amos Easterbrook
Charles Easterbrook
John Eaves
Joseph Ebben
John Ebbinstone
Avico Ecbeveste
Joseph Echangueid
Francis Echauegud
Amorois Echave
Lorendo Echerauid
Francis Echesevria
Ignatius Echesevria
Manuel de Echeverale
Fermin Echeuarria
Joseph Nicola Echoa
Thoman Ecley —Edbron
Thomas Eddison
William Ede
Butler Edelin
Jessie Edgar
John Edgar
Thomas Edgar
William Edgar (2)
James Edgarton
Philip Edgarton
Doum Edmondo
Henry Edmund
John Edmund
Alexander Edwards
Charles Edwards
Daniel Edwards
Edward Edwards
Henry Edwards

James Edwards
John Edwards
Michael Edwards
Rollo Edwards
Thomas Edwards
William Edwards (2)
James Eggleston
Samuel Eggleston
James Egrant
James Ekkleston
Jonathan Elbridge
Nathan Elder
Luther Elderkin
Daniel Elderton
Aldub Eldred
Daniel Eldridge (2)
Ezra Eldridge
James Eldridge
Thomas Eldridge
William Eldridge
William Eleves
Richard Elgin
John Eli
Benjamin Elias
Benjamin Elith
James Elkins
Nicholas Ellery
Cornelius Elliott
Daniel Elliott
John Elliott
Joseph Elliott
Nathaniel Elliott
Jonathan Ellis
John Ellison (2)
Theodore Ellsworth
Stephen Elns

Nathaniel Elridge
Isaac Elwell
John Elwell
Samuel Elwell (3)
James Emanuel (2)
George Emery
Jean Emilgon
John Engrum
John Eoon
Samuel Epworth
John Erexson
Ignaus Ergua
Martin Eronte
James Esk
Walford Eskridge
Antony Esward
Anthony Eticore
Joseph Eton
Francis Eugalind
Joseph Eugalind
Nicholas Euston
Alias Evans
Pierre Evans
Francis Eveane
Lewis Eveane
Lewis Even
Peni Evena
Pierre Evena
Even Evens
William Evens
Jeremiah Everett
Ebenezer Everall
Robert Everley
George Everson
John Everson
Benjamin Eves

David Evins
John Evins
Peter Ewen
Thomas Ewell
William Ewell
Peter Ewen
Thomas Ewen
James Ewing
Thomas Ewing
Juan Vicente Expassa
Christian Eyes

F

Jean Paul Fabalue
John Faber
Ashan Fairfield
Benjamin Fairfield
John Fairfield (2)
William Faithful
Henry Falam
Ephraim Falkender
George Falker
Robert Fall
Thomas Fallen
Henry Falls
Francis Fanch
Jean Fanum
John Farland
William Farmer
John Faroe
Michael Farrean
William Farrow
Thomas Fary

American Prisoners of the Revolution

Henry Fatem
Jacob Faulke
Robert Fauntroy
Joseph Feebe
Martin Feller
James Fellows
Nathaniel Fellows
John Felpig
Peter Felpig
Benjamin Felt
David Felter
Thomas Fennall
Cable Fennell
John Fenton
Cable Fenwell
Joseph Ferarld
Domigo Ferbon
David Fere
Matthew Fergoe
Pierre Fermang
Noah Fernal
Francis Fernanda
Thomas Fernandis
Matthew Fernay
Ephraim Fernon
Fountain Fernray
Ehemre Ferote
Joseph Ferre
Lewis Ferret
Toseph Ferria
Kennedy Ferril
Conway Ferris
Paul Ferris
William Fester
Elisha Fettian
Manuel Fevmandez

Frederick Fiarde
John Ficket
Charles Field
John Fielding
W Fielding
William Fielding
John Fife
Edwin Fifer
Nathaniel Figg
Benjamin Files
Jean Francis Fillear
Patrick Filler
Ward Filton
John Fimsey
Bartholomew Finagan
David Finch
John Fincher
George Finer
Dennis Finesy
Francis Finley
James Finley
Dennis Finn
John Finn
Jeremiah Finner
Jonathan Finney (3)
Seth Finney
Thomas Finney
Robert Firmie
Joseph Firth
Asel Fish
Daniel Fish
Ezekiel Fish
John Fish
Nathaniel Fish (2)
John Fisham
Abraham Fisher

Archibald Fisher
Isaac Fisher
Jonathan Fisher
Nathan Fisher
Robert Fisher (3)
Simon Fisher
William Fisher (2)
William Fisk
John Fist
Solomon Fist
Ebenezer Fitch
Jedeiah Fitch
Josiah Fitch
Peter Fitch
Theopilus Fitch
Timothy Fitch
Henry Fitchett
William Fithin
Cristopher Fitts
Patrick Faroh Fitz
Edward Fitzgerald
Patrick Fitzgerald
Thomas Fleet
John Fletcher
John Fling
William Fling
John Flinn
Berry Floyd
Michael Fluort
Thomas Fogg
Francis Follard
Jonathan Follett
Stephen Follows
John Folsom
John Folston
Joseph Fomster

Louis Fongue
Daniel Foot
Samuel Foot
Zakiel Foot
John Footman
Peter Forbes
Bartholomew Ford (3)
Daniel Ford
George Ford (2)
John Ford
Philip Ford
William Ford
Benjamin Fordham
Daniel Fore
Hugh Foresyth
Vancom Forque
Matthew Forgough
George Forket
Samuel Forquer
Nathaniel Forrest
Francis Forster
Timothy Forsythe
John Fort
Anthony Fortash
Emanuel Fortaud
Tohn Fortune
Thomas Fosdick
Andrew Foster
Asa Foster
Boston Foster
Conrad Foster
Edward Foster
Ephraim Poster
Henry Foster (2)
George Foster
Jacob Foster

Jebediah Foster
Josiah Foster (2)
John Foster (6)
Nathaniel Foster
Nicholas Foster
William Foster
Ephraim Fostman
John Fouber
Francis Foubert
William Foulyer
Edward Fousler
Pruden Fouvnary
Gideon Fowler
James Fowler (2)
John Fowler (2)
Joseph Fowler
Michael Fowler
John Butler Foy
William Foy
Jared Foyer
Ebenezer Fox
William Fox (3)
Jacob Frailey (2)
Fortain Frances
John Frances
Joseph Frances
Scobud Frances
John Francis
Thomas Francis (2)
William Francis
Manuel Francisco
Jean Franco
Jean Francois
Anthony Frankie
Pernell Franklin
Christopher Franks

Michael Franks
John Frasier
Thomas Frasier
Nathaniel Frask
John F Fravers
John Fravi
William Frey
Andrew Frazer
Thomas Frazier
Pierre Freasi
Iman Frebel
William Freebal
Charles Freeman
David Freeman
Henry Freeman
Humphrey Freeman
John Freeman
Thomas Freeman (2)
Zebediah Freeman
James French
Jonathan French
Michael French
Josias Frett
John Fretto
Juban Freway
Anthony Frick
Post Friend
Shadrach Friend
James Frieris
Ebenezer Frisby
Isaac Frisby
Josiah Frith
John Frost
Joseph Frost (2)
Peter Frume
James Fry (2)

Robert Fry
Abijah Fryske
Joseph Fubre
Joseph Fuganey
Joshua Fulger
Reuben Fulger
Stephen Fulger
Benjamin Fuller
James Fuller
Joseph Fuller
Thaddeus Fuller
Thomas Fuller (2)
George Fullum
James Fulton
Thomas Fulton
Abner Furguson
Samuel Furguson
John Furse
John Fury
Iman Futter

G

Eudrid Gabria
Francis Gabriel
Franes Gabriel
Hernan Gage
Isaac Gage
Matthew Gage
Stephen Gage
Jonas Gale
Joseph Galina
Andrew Gallager
John Gallard

John Gallaspie
Richard Galley
William Gallway
Anthony Gallys
James Gamband
James Gamble
Joseph Gamble
Peter Gambo
Pierre Ganart
William Gandee
William Gandel
Francis Gandway
John Gandy
Hosea Garards
Antony Gardil
Silas Gardiner
William Gardiner
Alexander Gardner (3)
Dominic Gardner
James Gardner (3)
Joseph Gardner (5)
Larry Gardner
Robert Gardner
Samuel Gardner
Silas Gardner
Thomas Gardner
Uriah Gardner
William Gardner
Dominico Gardon
John Garey
Manolet Garico
James Garish
Paul Garish
John Garland (2)
Barney Garlena
Joseph Garley

——Garner
Silas Garner
John Garnet
Sylvester Garnett
Isaac Garret
Michael Garret
John Garretson
Antonio Garrett
Jacques Garrett
Richard Garrett
William Garrett
Louis C. Garrier
Jacob Garrison (2)
Joseph Garrison (3)
Joseph Garrit
Thomas Garriway
Jean Garrow
Roman Garsea
William Garty
Job Gascin
Daniel Gasett
Jacob Gasker
Simon Gason (2)
Manot Gasse
John Gassers
Francis Gater
Charles Gates
Peter Gaypey
John Gault
Paul Gaur
Thomas Gaurmon
Thomas Gawner
Solomon Gay
William Gay
Charles Gayford
John Gaylor

Robert Geddes
George George (2)
George Georgean
Hooper Gerard
Riviere de Ggoslin
George Gill
John Gibbens
Edward Gibbertson
John Gibbons
Charles Gibbs (3)
John Gibbs (2)
Andrew Gibson
Benjamin Gibson
George Gibson
James Gibson
William Gibson
Stephen Giddron
Archibald Gifford
George Gilbert
Timothy Gilbert
George Gilchrist
Robert Gilchrist
John Giles
Samuel Giles (2)
Thomas Giles
William Giles
John Gill
Philip Gill
William Gill
John Gilladen
Jean B. Gillen
Richard Gilleny
William Gillespie
John Gillis
John Gillison
David Gillispie

David Gillot
Toby Gilmay
John Gilmont
Nathaniel Gilson
Thomas Gimray
Peter Ginnis
Jean Ginnow
Baptist Giraud
Joseph Girca
William Gisburn
Francis Gissia
Jean Glaied
Charles Glates
Jean Glease
Jean Gleasie
Gabriel Glenn
Thomas Glerner
William Glesson
James Gloacque
William Glorman
Edward Gloss
Michael Glosses
Daniel Gloud
Jonathan Glover
William Glover
Thomas Goat
Ebenezer Goddard
Nicholas Goddard
Thomas Goddard
Joseph Godfrey
Nathaniel Godfrey
Samuel Godfrey
Simon Godfrey
Thomas Godfrey
William Godfrey (4)
Francis Godfry

Pierre Godt
Vincent Goertin
Patrick Goff
John Going
Ebenezer Gold
John Golston
William Golston
Robert Gomer
Pierre Goodall
George Goodby
Simon Goodfrey
Eli Goodfry
Lemuel Gooding
George Goodley
Francis Goodman
Eli Goodnow
Elizer Goodrich
Jesse Goodrich
Solomon Goodrich
James Goodwick
Charles Goodwin
Daniel Goodwin
George Goodwin
Gideon Goodwin
Ozeas Goodwin
Abel Goose
James Gootman
Abel Goove
——Goquie
Jonathan Goram (2)
John Gord
Andrew Gordan
Andrew Gordon
James Gordon (2)
Peter Gordon
Stephen Gordon

Jesse Gore
Jonathan Goreham
James Gorham
Jonathan Gorham
Shubert Gorham
Joseph Gormia
Christian Goson
William Goss
Jean Gotea
George Gothe
Charles Gotson
Francis Goudin
Lewis Gouire
Augustus Goute
Francis Goutiere
Joseph Goveir
Sylverter Govell
George Gowell (2)
Henry Gowyall
Jean Goyear
Matthew Grace
William Grafton
Alexander Graham
Robert Graham
Samuel Graham
David Graines
Robert Grame
L. A. Granada
William Granby
Adam Grandell
Alexander Grant
Thomas Grant
William Grant
Thomas Grassing
William Gratton
Ebenezer Graub

Dingley Gray
Franes Gray
Joseph Gray (2)
James Gray
Samuel Gray
Simeon Gray
Simon Gray
William Gray
Isaac Greeman
Allen Green
Elijah Green (2)
Elisha Green
Henry Green
John Green (9)
Joseph Green (2)
Robert Green
Rufus Green
William Green (3)
Green Greenbury
Enoch Greencafe
James Greene (3)
John Greene (4)
Samuel Greene
John Greenes
Richard Greenfield
Abner Greenleaf
John Greenoth
William Greenville
Barton Greenville
Malum Greenwell
Robert Greenwold
Jacob Greenwood
David Gregory
Stephen Gregory (2)
Ebenezer Grenach
William Grennis

Ebenezer Grenyard
Samuel Grey
Charles Grier
Isaac Grier
Mather Grier
William Grierson
Moses Griffen
Alexander Griffin
Daniel Griffin
Elias Griffin
James Griffin (2)
Jasper Griffin
Joseph Griffin
Moses Griffin (2)
Peter Griffin
Rosetta Griffin
James Griffith
William Griffith
James Grig
John Griggs
Thomas Grilley
Peter Grinn
Philip Griskin
Edward Grissell
Elijah Griswold
Jotun Griswold
John Grogan
Joseph Grogan
Josiah Grose
Peter Grosper
Benjamin Gross
Michael Gross
Simon P. Gross
Tonos Gross
Peleg Grotfield
John Grothon

Andrew Grottis
Joseph Grouan
Michael Grout
Stephen Grove
Thomas Grover (2)
John Gruba
Samuel Grudge
Peter Gruin
George Grymes
John Guae
Cyrus Guan
Elisha Guarde
John Guason
John Guay
Bense Guenar
Nathaniel Gugg
Pierre Guilber
John Guilley
Peter Guin
William Guinep
Joseph Guiness
Joseph Guinet
William Gulirant
Joseph Gullion
Souran Gult
Jean Gumeuse
Antonio Gundas
Julian Gunder
William Gunnup
Jean Gunteer
Pierre Gurad
Anthony Gurdell
Franes Gusboro
George Guster
Jean Joseph Guthand
Francis Guvare

William Gwinnup

H

Samuel Hacker
John Hackett
Benjamin Haddock
Caraway Hagan
Anthony de la Hage
James Haggarty
John Haglus
Ebenezer Hail
David Halbort
William Haldron
Matthew Hales
Aaron Hall
Ebenezer Hall
Isaac Hall
James Hall
John Hall (3)
Joseph Hall
London Hall
Lyman Hall
Millen Hall
Moses Hall
Nathan Hall
Samuel Hall
Spence Hall
Thomas Hall (3)
William Hall
Willis Hall
Thomas Hallahan
James Hallaughan
Benjamin Hallett (2)

James Hallett (2)
Ephraim Halley
John Halley
Joseph Halley (2)
Samuel Halley
Richard Halley
Charles Hallwell
Henry Halman
William Halsey
Moses Halton
Jesse Halts
Byron Halway
Benjamin Halwell
James Ham
Levi Ham
Reuben Hambell
William Hamber
Empsen Hamilton
Henry Hamilton (2)
John Hamilton (2)
William Hamilton (2)
Flint Hammer
Charles Hammond
Elijah Hammond
Homer Hammond
James Hammond
Joseph Hammond
Thomas Hamsby
James Hanagan
Stephen Hanagan
Henry Hance
Abraham Hancock
Samuel Hancock
Elias Hand
Elijah Hand
Gideon Hand

Joseph Hand (2)
Thomas Hand
William Hand
Levi Handy
Thomas Handy (3)
John Hanegan
Josiah Hanes
Patrick Hanes
Samuel Hanes
John Haney
Gideon Hanfield
Peter Hankley
Every Hanks
John Hannings
Hugh Hanson
James Hanwagon
Jonathan Hanwood
John Hanwright
Neil Harbert
John Harbine
Daniel Harbley
Augustus Harborough
Peter Harcourt
Jean Hard
Lewis Harden
Richard Harden
William Harden
Turner Hardin
Frances Harding
Nathaniel Harding (2)
George Hardy
James Hardy
Joseph Hardy (2)
Thomas Harens
John Harfun
Joel Hargeshonor

Jacob Hargous
Abraham Hargus
Thomas Harkasy
John Harket
Solomon Harkey
Thomas Harkins
Charles Harlin
Selden Harley
Solomon Harley
Byron Harlow
John Harman
Richard Harman
John Harmon
Joseph Harner
William Harragall
John Harragall
Lewis Harrett
Bartholomew Harrington
Daniel Harrington
Charles Harris
Edward Harris
Francis Harris
George Harris
Hugh Harris
James Harris (2)
John Harris (2)
Joseph Harris
Nathaniel Harris (2)
Robert Harris
William Harris
Charles Harrison
Elijah Harrison
Gilbert Harrison
John Harrison
William Harron
Charles Harroon

Cornelius Hart
Jacob de Hart
John Hart
Samuel Hartley
Jacob Hartman
James Hartshorne
Thomas Hartus
John Harwood
John Harvey
Peter Haselton
Michael Hashley
Philip Hashton
John Hasker
Jacob Hassa
John Hassett
John Hassey
Benjamin Hatam
Charles Hatbor
Edward Hatch
Jason Hatch
Nailor Hatch
Prince Hatch
Reuben Hatch
William Hatch
Edward Hatchway
Burton Hathaway
Jacob Hathaway
Russell Hathaway
Woolsey Hathaway
Andrew Hatt
Shadrach Hatway
Michael Haupe
Jacob Hauser
William Hawke
Jacob Hawker
John Hawker

John Hawkin
Christopher Hawkins
Jabez Hawkins
John Hawkins (2)
Thomas Hawkins
Jacob Hawstick
John Hawston
George Haybud
Benjamin Hayden
Nicholas Hayman
David Hayne
Joseph Haynes
Peter Haynes (2)
Thomas Haynes
William Haynes
David Hays
Patrick Hays
Thomas Hays
William Hays
William Haysford
Benjamin Hazard
John Hazard
Samuel Heageork
Gilbert Heart
Samuel Heart
Joseph Hearth
Charles Heath
Joseph Heath
Seren Heath
Seson Heath
Jack Hebell
Heraclus Hedges
George Heft
Edmund Helbow
Matthias Hellman
Lacy Helman

Thomas Helman
Odera Hemana
Daniel Hemdy
Jared Hemingway
Alexander Henderson
Ephraim Henderson
Joseph Henderson
Michael Henderson
Robert Henderson
William Henderson
Archibald Hendray
Robert Hengry
Leeman Henley
Butler Henry
James Henry
John Henry (3)
Joseph Henry
Michael Henry (2)
William Henry (2)
John Hensby
Patrick Hensey (2)
Enos Henumway
Dennis Henyard
Samson Herart
Thomas Herbert
Philip Herewux
Ephraim Herrick
John Herrick (2)
William Herrick
Michael Herring
William Herring
Robert Herrow
Robert Herson
Robert Hertson
Augustin Hertros
Stephen Heskils

John Hetherington
John Hewengs
Lewis Hewit
William Heysham
Diah Hibbett
John Hibell
Michael Hick
Daniel Hickey
Baptist Hicks
Benjamin Hicks
John Hicks
Isaac Higgano
George Higgins
Ichabod Higgins
Samuel Higgins
Stoutly Higgins
William Higgins (3)
Henry Highlander
John Highlenede
John Hill (2)
James Hill
Joshua Hill (2)
Thomas Hill (2)
Edward Hilley
James Hilliard
Joseph Hilliard
Nicholas Hillory
Hale Hilton
Nathaniel Hilton
Benjamin Himsley
Peter Hinch
James Hines
William Hinley
Aaron Hinman
William Hinman
Nathaniel Hinnran

Jonathan Hint
John Hirich
Christian Hiris
Samuel Hiron
John Hisburn
Nathaniel Hise
Samuel Hiskman
John Hislop
Philip Hiss
Loren Hitch
Robert Hitch
Joseph Hitchband
Edward Hitchcock
Robert Hitcher
John Hitching
Arthur Hives
Willis Hoag
Edwin Hoane
Henry Hobbs
William Hobbs
Jacob Hobby
Nathaniel Hobby
Joseph Hockless
Hugh Hodge
Hercules Hodges (2)
Benjamin Hodgkinson
Samuel Hodgson
Conrad Hoffman
Cornelius Hoffman
Roger Hogan
Stephen Hogan
Stephen Hoggan
Alexander Hogsart
Jacob Hogworthy
Ephraim Hoist
Humphrey Hoites

Lemuel Hokey
William Hold
William Holden
Thomas Holdridge
John Holland
Michael Holland
William Holland (2)
Nicholas Hollen
William Holliday
Michael Holloway
Myburn Holloway
Grandless Holly
Henry Holman
Isaac Holmes
James Holmes
Joseph Holmes
Nathaniel Holmes
Thomas Holmes (3)
George Holmstead
Charles Hole
Samuel Holt
James Home
Jacob Homer
William Homer
William Honeyman
Simon Hong
Warren Honlap
Daniel Hood (2)
Nicholas Hoogland (2)
George Hook
John Hook (2)
George Hooker
Ezekiel Hooper
John Hooper (3)
Michael Hooper (3)
Sweet Hooper

Caleb Hopkins
Christopher Hopkins
John Hopkins
Michael Hopkins
Stephen Hopkins
William Hopkins
Edward Hopper
John Hopper
Richard Hopping
Levi Hoppins
Joseph Horn (2)
Jacob Horne
John Horne
Ralph Horne
Samuel Horne
Augusta Horns
Michael Horoe
Charles Horsine
Ephraim Hort
Jean Hosea
John Hosey
Jean Hoskins
James Hottahon
Ebenezer Hough
Enos House
Seren House
Noah Hovard
Joseph Hovey
John Howe
Absalom Howard
Ebenezer Howard
John Howard
Richard Howard
Thomas Howard
William Howard (3)
James Howburn

Edward Howe
John Howe
Thomas Howe
Ebenezer Howell
Jesse Howell
Jonathan Howell
John Howell
Luke Howell
Michael Howell
Thomas Howell
Waller Howell
William Howell
Daniel Howland
Joseph Howman
Benjamin Hoyde
Dolphin Hubbard
Jacob Hubbard
James Hubbard
Joel Hubbard
Moses Hubbard
William Hubbard
Abel Hubbell
William Huddle
John Hudman
Fawrons Hudson
John Hudson
Phineas Hudson
John Huet
Conrad Huffman
Stephen Huggand
John Huggins
Abraham Hughes
Felix Hughes
Greenberry Hughes
Greenord Hughes
Jesse Hughes

John Hughes
Peter Hughes
Thomas Hughes
Pierre Hujuon
Richard Humphrey
Clement Humphries
W W Humphries
Ephraim Hunn
Cephas Hunt
John Hunt (2)
Robert Hunt
Alexander Hunter
Ezekiel Hunter
George Hunter
Robert Hunter
Turtle Hunter
Rechariah Hunter
Elisha Huntington
Joseph Harand
Benjamin Hurd
Joseph Hurd
Simon Hurd
Asa Hurlbut
George Husband
John Husband
Negro Huson
Charles Huss
Isaac Huss
Jesse Hussey
James Huston
Zechariah Hutchins
Esau Hutchinson
John Hutchison
Abraham Smith Hyde
Vincent Hyer

I

Joseph Ignacis
Ivede Sousis Illiumbe
Benjamin Indecot
Isaac Indegon
John Ingersall
Henry Ingersoll (2)
John Ingraham
Joseph Ingraham
Joshua Ingraham
Philip Ignissita
Joseph Irasetto
David Ireland
James Ireland
Joseph Ireland
Michael Irvin
George Irwin
Michael Irwin
Isaac Isaacs
George Ismay
Gospar Israel
James Ivans
John Ivington
Francis D Izoguirre

J

Michael Jacen
Black Jack
John Jack (2)
John Jacks (2)
Frederick Jacks (2)

George Jacks (2)
Henry Jacks
John Jacks
John Jackson
James Jackson
Josiah Jackson
Nathaniel Jackson
Peter Jackson
Robert Jackson
Jean Jacobs
Bella Jacobs
Joseph Jacobs
Wilson Jacobs
Andrew Jacobus
Guitman Jacques
Guitner Jacques
Lewis Jacques
Peter Jadan
John Jaikes
Benjamin James
John James (2)
Ryan James
William James
Daniel Jamison
Josiah Janes
Jean Jardin
Francis Jarnan
Edward Jarvis
Petuna Jarvis
Negro Jask
John Jassey
Francis Jatiel
Clement Jean
Joseph Jean
William Jean
Benjamin Jeanesary

Roswell Jeffers
Samuel Jeffers
James Jeffrey
John Jeffries
Joseph Jeffries
Philip Jeffries
George Jemrey
Pierre Jengoux
David Jenkin
Enoch Jenkins
George Jenkins
Solomon Jenkins
George Jenney
John Jenney
Langdon Jenney
Langhorn Jenney
Nathaniel Jennings
Thomas Jennings
William Jennings
John Jenny
Langhorn Jenny
Frances Jerun
Abel Jesbank
Oliver Jethsam
Germain Jeune
Silas Jiles
Nathan Jinks
Moses Jinney
Verd Joamra
Manuel Joaquire
Robert Job
——Joe
Thomas Joel
Elias Johnson (2)
Francis Johnson
George Johnson

James Johnson (3)
John Johnson (3)
Joseph Johnson
Major Johnson
Samuel Johnson
Stephen Johnson
William Johnson (8)
Ebenezer Johnston
Edward Johnston
George Johnston
John Johnston (2)
Joseph Johnston
Major Johnston
Michael Johnston
Miller Johnston
Paul Johnston
Peter Johnston
Robert Johnston (3)
Samuel Johnston
Simon Johnston
Stephen Johnston
William Johnston (8)
William B. Johnston
James Johnstone
John Joie
Thomas Joil
Adam Jolt
———Joan
Benjamin Jonas
Abraham Jones
Alexander Jones
Benjamin Jones (3)
Beal Jones
Clayton Jones
Darl Jones
Edward Jones (2)

James Jones
Jib Jones
John Jones (7)
Thomas Jones (2)
Richard Jones (2)
Samuel Jones (3)
William Jones (10)
Jean Jordan
John Jordan
Philip Jordan
Nicholas Jordon (2)
Anthony Joseph
Antonio Joseph
Emanuel Joseph
Thomas Joseph
William Joslitt
Antonio Jouest
Thomas Joulet
Jean Jourdana
Mousa Jousegh
Jean Jowe
Thomas Jowe
Curtis Joy
Josiah Joy
Peter Joy (2)
Samuel Joy
Samuel Joyce
Conrad Joycelin
Randon Jucba
Manuel Joseph Jucerria
Peter Julian
Henry Junas
Henry Junus (2)
Jacques Jurdant
George Juster
Samuel Justice

Simeon Justive
George Justus
Philip Justus

K

Mark Kadoody
Jonn Kam
Lewis Kale
Barney Kane
Edward Kane
John Kane
Patrick Kane
Thomas Kane
Sprague Kean
Thomas Kean
Nathaniel Keard
William Keary
Tuson Keath
Daniel Keaton
Samuel Kelbey
Samuel Kelby
John Keller
Abner Kelley
John Kelley (5)
Michael Kelley (2)
Oliver Kelley
Patrick Kelley
Samuel Kelley
William Kelley
Roy Kellrey
Abner Kelly (2)
Hugh Kelly
James Kelly

John Kelly
Roger Kelly
Seth Kelly
Timothy Kelly
Nehemiah Kelivan
Olgas Kilter
William Kemplin
Simon Kenim
Charles Kenneday
James Kenneday
Jonathan Kenneday
Nathaniel Kenneday
Robert Kenneday (2)
Thomas Kenneday
William Kenneday (2)
David Kennedy
James Kennedy
John Kenney (2)
William Kensey
Elisha Kenyon
Joson Ker
John Kerril
William Kersey (2)
Edward Ketcham
Samuel Ketcham
William Keyborn
Anthony Keys
John Keys
Michael Keys
Jean Kiblano
James Kickson
George Kidd
John Kidd
James Kidney
Manuel Kidtona
Thomas Kilbourne

John Kilby
Lewis Kildare
John Kilfundy
Samuel Killen
William Killenhouse
Samuel Killer
Charles Killis
Gustavus Killman
Daniel Kilray
John Kilts
Nathaniel Kimberell
Charles King
Gilbert King
Jonathan King
John King (4)
Joseph King (4)
Michael King
Richard King
William King
Nathaniel Kingsbury
William Kingsley
Samuel Kinney
Josiah Kinsland
Benjamin Kinsman
Charles Kirby
John Kirk
William Kirk
Jacob Kisler
Edward Kitchen
John Kitler
Ebenezer Knapp
James Knapp
Benjamin Knight (2)
Job Knight
Reuben Knight
Thomas Knight (2)

James Knowles (2)
Nathaniel Knowles
James Knowls
Edward Knowlton
William Knowlton
Jeremiah Knox (2)
John Knox
Ezekiel Kuthoopen
Louis Kyer

L

Basil Laban
Pierre Labon
Francois Labone
Deman Labordas
Fortne Laborde
Frederick Laborde
Anton Laca
Michael La Casawyne
John Lack
Christopher Lacon
Oliver Lacope
Guilham La Coque
Anthony Lafart
Dennis Lafferty
Pierre La Fille
Anthony Lagarvet
Jeff Laggolf
Samuel Laighton
Thomas Laigue
Peter Lain
Christopher Laird (3)
John Laird (2)

Simon Lake
Thomas Lake
Nathan Lakeman
Thomas Laley
Samson Lalley
John Lalour
David Lamb
William Lamb
Pierre Lambert
Richard Lambert (2)
Cayelland Lambra
Thomas Lambuda
Evena Lame
Thomas Lame
Jean Lameari
Michael Lameova
Alexander Lamere (2)
Roque Lamie
Henry Land
Stephen Landart
George Landon
Peter Landon
William Lane
John Langdon
Jonathan Langer
Darius Langford
William Langford
John Langler
Obadiah Langley
Thomas Langley (2)
James Langlord
Joseph Langola
Andrew Langolle
Thomas Langstaff
Franes Langum
Francois Lan Hubere

Samuel Lanman
Nicholas Lanmand
William Lanvath
David Lapham
Bundirk Laplaine
Joseph La Plan
James Lapthorn
Pierre Laquise
Francis Larada
Matthew La Raison
Charles Larbys
Thomas Larkin
James Larkins
Gillian Laroache
Bundirk Larplairne
Pierre Larquan
Benjamin Larrick
Lewis Larsolan
Guillemot Lascope
Julian Lascope
Joseph Laselieve
John Lasheity
William Lasken
Jachery Lasoca
David Lassan
Michael Lassly
Pierre Lastio
David Latham
Edward Latham
James Latham
Thomas Latham
Elisha Lathrop
John Lathrop
Hezekiah Lathrop
Solomon Lathrop
James Latover

Lorenzo Lattam
Peter Lattimer
Thomas Lattimer
William Lattimer
William Lattimore
Frederick Lasker
William Lathmore
Samuel Laura
John Laureny
Homer Laury
Michael Lased
Daniel Lavet
Pierre Lavigne
Michael Lavona
Ezekiel Law (2)
John Law
Richard Law
Thomas Law
Michael Lawbridge
Thomas Lawrance
Antonio Lawrence
Isaac Lawrence
James Lawrence
John Lawrence (2)
Joseph Lawrence
Michael Lawrence
Robert Lawrence
Samuel Lawrence (3)
Thomas Lawrence
William Lawrence (2)
John Lawrie
Andrew Lawson
Joseph Lawson
Joseph Lawton
Edward Lay
Lenolen Layfield

William Layne
John Layons
Colsie Layton
Jessie Layton
Anthony Layzar
Ezekiel Leach
Thomas Leach (3)
William Leach
William Leachs
John Leafeat
Cornelius Leary
John Leasear
John Leatherby
Louis Leblanc
Philip Le Caq
William Le Cose
Baptist Le Cour
Benjamin Lecraft
Joseph Lecree
Aaron Lee
Adam Lee
David Lee
Henry Lee
James Lee
John Lee
Josiah Lee
Peter Lee
Richard Lee (3)
Stephen Lee
Thomas Lee (3)
James Leech
John Leech (2)
George Leechman
Jack Leeme
Joseph Leera
Jean Lefant

——Le Fargue
Michael Lefen
Samuel Le Fever
Nathaniel Le Fevere
Alexander Le Fongue
Jean Le Ford
Hezekiah Legrange
Thomas Legrange
Joseph Legro
Samuel Legro
George Lehman
Gerge Lehman
George Leish
Jacob Lelande
Jeremiah Leman
John Lemee
Rothe Lemee
Abraham Lemon
Peter Lernonas
Pierre Lemons
John Lemont
Powell Lemosk
John Lemot
James Lenard
Joseph Lenard
John Lenham
Tuft Lenock
Joseph Lenoze
John Leonard
Simon Leonard
Louis Le Pach
Joshua Le Poore
Pierre Le Port
Francis Lepord
Pierre Lepord
Pierre Lerandier

Jean Le Rean
Joseph Peccanti Lescimia
John Lessington
John Lessell
Christian Lester
Henry Lester
Lion Lesteren
Ezekiel Letts (2)
James Leuard
Anthony Levanden
Thomas Leverett
John Leversey
Joseph Levett
Nathaniel Levi
Bineva Levzie
Jean Baptiste Leynac
Nicholas L'Herox
Pierre Liar
John Lidman
George Lichmond
Charles Liekerada
Charles Liekeradan
Louis Light
John Lightwell
Homer Ligond
Joseph Lilihorn
Jonathan Lillabridge
Joseph Lillehorn
Thomas Lilliabridge
Armistead Lillie
John Lilling
John Limberick
Christopher Limbourne (2)
Lewis Lincoln
Samuel Lindsay
James Lindsey

Matthew Lindsley
William Lindsley
Lamb Lines
Charles Linn
Lewis Linot
Richard Linthorn
Nicholas Linva
Samuel Linzey
William Linzey
Jesse Lipp
Henry Lisby
Francis Little
George Little
John Little (3)
Philip Little
Thomas Little
Thomas Littlejohn
William Littleton
Thomas Livet
Licomi Lizarn
James Lloyd
Simon Lloyd
William Lloyd
Lones Lochare
John Logan
Patrick Logard
Eve Logoff
Samuel Lombard
John London
Richard London
Adam Lone
Christian Long
Enoch Long
Jeremiah Long
William Long
Martin Longue

Emanuel Loper
Joseph Lopez
Daniel Loran
John Lorand
Nathaniel Lord
William Loreman
Francis Loring
John Lort
Thomas Lorton
Jean Lossett
William Lott
David Louis
John Love (2)
Stephen Love
Thomas Love
John Loveberry
William Loverin
James Lovett
Thomas Lovett (2)
James Low
William Low
John Lowe
Abner Lowell (2)
Israel Lowell
Jonathan Lowell
John Lowering
Jacob Lowerre
Robert Lowerre (2)
Robert Lowerry
John Lowery
Philip Lowett
John Lowring
Pierre Lozalie
Jacques Lubard
James Lucas
Lucian Lucas

Jean Lucie
William Lucker
William Luckey (2)
W. Ludds
Samuel Luder
David Ludwith
Peter Lumbard
Francois Lumbrick
Joseph Lunt (3)
Skipper Lunt
Philip Lute
Nehemiah Luther
Reuben Luther
Benjamin Luyster
Augustin Luzard
Alexander Lyelar
Charles Lyle
Witsby Linbick
Jean Lynton
Peter Lyon
Samuel Lyon
Archibald Lyons
Daniel Lyons
Ephraim Lyons
Ezekiel Lyons
Jonathan Lyons
Samuel Lyons

M

Jean Franco Mabugera
John Macay
Nicholas McCant
John Mace

Anthony Macguire
Pierre Marker
William Macgneol
Romulus Mackroy
John Madding (2)
Peter Madding
Peter Maggot
John Maginon
Stringe Mahlan
Peter Mahrin
Jean Maikser
William Main
Joseph Mainwright
Simon Majo
Pierre Malaque
John Maleon
Lewis Malcom
Maurice Malcom
John Male
William Malen
Francis Maler
Matthew Malkellan
Enoch Mall
Daniel Malleby
Thomas Malleby
Frederick Malleneux
John Mallet
Daniel Mallory
John Malone
Paul Malory
Thomas Makend
Nathaniel Mamford
——Mamney
Peter Manaford
Josiah Manars
John Manchester

Silas Manchester
Thaddeus Manchester
Edward Mand
Edward Manda
Jonathan Mandevineur
Sylvester Manein
Pierre Maneit
Etien Manett
George Manett
George Mangoose
John Manhee
William Manilla
Anthony Mankan
Jacob Manlore
William Manlove
John Manly
James Mann
John Manor
Isaac Mans
Benjamin Mansfield
Hemas Mansfield
William Mansfield
Joseph Mantsea
Jonathan Maples
Jean Mapson
Auree Marand
——Marbinnea
Mary Marblyn
Etom Marcais
James Marcey
Jean Margabta
Jean Marguie
Timothy Mariarty
John Mariner (2)
Hercules Mariner (2)
Elias Markham

Thomas Marle
James Marley
Jean Marlgan
Francis Marmilla
David Marney
James Marriott
Zachary Marrall
William Marran
James Marriott
Alexander Marse
Jarnes Marsh
Benjamin Marshall
James Marshall
John Marshall
Joseph Marshall
Samuel Marshall
Thomas Marshall
Timothy Marson
Thomas Marston
Adam Martellus
Antonio Marti
Ananias Martin
Damon Martin
Daniel Martin
Daniel F. Martin
Emanuel Martin
Embey Martin
Francis Martin
George Martin
Gilow Martin
Jacob Martin
James Martin
Jesse Martin
John Martin (4)
Joseph Martin (3)
Lewis Martin

Martin Martin
Michael Martin
Peter Martin
Philip Martin
Samuel Martin (2)
Simon Martin
Thomas Martin (2)
William Martin (3)
Jose Martine (2)
Thomas Martine
Pierre Martinett
Philip Marting
Martin Martins
Oliver Marton
John Marton
Baptist Marvellon
Anthony Marwin
Andrew Masar
Thomas Mash
Matthew Maskillon
Thomas Masley
Jean Maso
Augustus Mason
Francis Mason
Gerard B. Mason
Halbert Mason
James Mason
Louis Mason
Charles Massaa
James Massey
James Maston
Pierre Mathamice
James Mathes
Jeffrey Mathews
John Mathews
Joseph Mathews (2)

Josiah Mathews
Richard Mathews (2)
Robert Mathews
Thomas Mathews
William Mathews (2)
Thomas Mathewson
Robert Mathias
Joseph Matre
James Matson
William Matterga
George Matthews
Joseph Matthews
Josiah Matthews
Richard Matthias
Thomas Maun
James Maurice
John Mawdole
Patrick Maxfield
Daniel Maxwell
David Maxwell
George Maxwell
James Maxwell (6)
John Maxwell (3)
William Maxwell (5)
George May
John Maye (3)
John Maygehan
Pierre Maywer (3)
Parick McAllister
Charles McArthur
John McArthur
Peter McCalpan
Nathaniel McCampsey
William McCanery
Edward McCann
Daniel McCape (2)

Andrew McCarty
Cornelius McCarty
William McCarty
John M. McCash
Francis McClain
James McClanagan
Daniel McClary
Henry McCleaf
Patrick McClemens
John McClesh
Patrick McCloskey
Murphy McCloud
Peter McCloud
James McClure
William McClure
Johnston McCollister
James McComb
Paul McCome
James McConnell
Hugh McCormac
James McCormick
William McCowan
Donald McCoy
George McCoy
Peter McCoy
Samuel McCoy
John McCrady
Gilbert McCray
John McCray
Roderick McCrea
Patrick McCuila
Francis McCullam
William McCullock
Daniel McCullough
William McCullough
Patrick McCullum

Caleb McCully
Archibald McCunn
James McDaniel (3)
John McDaniel
John McDavid
William McDermott
Alexander McDonald
Donald McDonald
John McDonald
Petre McDonald
William McDonald (2)
Patrick McDonough (2)
William McDougall
Ebenezer McEntire
John McEvan
John McFaggins
James McFall
Bradford McFarlan
Daniel McFarland
William McFarland (2)
Bradford McFarling
Bushford McFarling
John McFamon
William McGandy
John McGee (2)
Andrew McGelpin (3)
James McGeer
John McGey (3)
Arthur McGill
James McGill
Henry McGinness
James McGinniss
John McGoggin
Robert McGonnegray
James McGowan
John McGoy

Barnaby McHenry
Duncan McIntire
Patrick McKay
Matthew McKellum
Barnaby McKenry
John McKensie
Thomas McKeon
Patrick McKey
James McKinney (2)
John McKinsey
George McKinsle
William McKinsley
Benjamin McLachlan
Edward McLain
Lewis McLain
Philip McLaughlin
Daniel McLayne
James McMichael
Philip McMonough
Francis McName
John McNauch
Archibald McNeal
John McNeal
James McNeil
William McNeil
John McNish
Molcolm McPherman
William McQueen
Charles McQuillian
Samuel McWaters
Samuel Mecury
John Medaff
John Mede
Joshua Medisabel
Joseph Meack
John Meak

Usell Meechen
Abraham Meek
Joseph Meek
Timothy Meek
John Mego
Springale Meins
William Melch
Joseph Mellins
Harvey Mellville
William Melone
Adam Meltward
George Melvin
Lewis Meneal
John Menelick
Jean Baptist Menlich
William Mellwood
John Mercaten
James Mercer
Robert Mercer (2)
Jean Merchant (2)
John Merchant
Peter Merchant
William Merchant
John Merchaud
Sylvester Mercy
Bistin Mereff
Jean Meritwell
Francis Merlin
John Merlin
Augustus Merrick
John Merrick
Joseph Merrick
Samuel Merrick
Nimrod Merrill
John Merritt
John Merry

John Mersean
Clifton Merser
John Mersey
Abner Mersick
William Messdone
Thomas Messell
George Messingburg
George Messmong
Thomas Metsard
Job Meyrick
Roger Mickey
Thomas Migill
James Migley
Jean Milcher
John Miles (2)
Segur Miles
Thomas Miles
Timothy Miles
George Mildred
James Millbown
Robert Millburn
John Millen
Christopher Miller
David Miller
Ebenezer Miller
Elijah Miller (2)
George Miller
Jacob Miller
John Miller (3)
John James Miller
Jonathan Miller
Michael Miller
Peter Miller
Samuel Miller (2)
William Miller (2)
Maurice Millet

Thomas Millet
Francis Mills
John Mills (2)
William Mills
Dirk Miners
John Mink
Renard Mink
Lawrence Minnharm
Arnold Minow
Kiele Mires
Koel Mires
Anthony Mitchell
Benjamin Mitchell
James Mitchell
Jean Mitchell
John Mitchell (2)
Joseph Mitchell
David P. Mite
Elijah Mix
Joseph Mix
Paul Mix
James Moet
William Moffat
David Moffet
Emanuel Moguera
Peter Moizan
Joseph Molisan
Alexander Molla
Mark Mollian
Ethkin Mollinas
Bartholomew Molling
Daniel Mollond
James Molloy
John Molny
Gilman Molose
Enoch Molton

George Molton
Isaac Money
Perry Mongender
William Monrass
James Monro
Abraham Monroe
John Monroe
Thomas Monroe
David Montague
Norman Montague
William Montague
Lewis Montaire
Matthew Morgan
Francis Montesdague
George Montgomery (2)
James Montgomery (3)
John Montgomery (2)
James Moody
Silas Moody
Hugh Mooney
Abraham Moore (2)
Adam Moore
Frederick Moore
Henry Moore
Israel Moore
James Moore
John Moore (2)
Joseph Moore
Nathaniel Moore
Patrick Moore
Ralph Moore
Richard Moore
Samuel Moore
Stephen Moore
Thomas Moore (6)
Wardman Moore

William Moore (6)
Charles Moosey
John Mooton
Acri Morana
John Morant
Adam Morare
John Baptist Moraw
W. Morce
Gilmot Morea
Toby Morean
Joseph Morehand
Abel Morehouse (2)
Grosseo Moreo
Jonathan Morey
Lewis Morey
Louis Morey
Abel Morgan
Henry Morgan
John Morgan (3)
Joseph Morgan
Matthew Morgan
John Moride
Edward Moritz
William Morein
James Morley
John Morrell
Osborne Morrell
Robert Morrell (3)
Francis Morrice
Andrew Morris (2)
Daniel Morris
David Morris
Easins Morris
Edward Morris
Foster Morris
Gouverneur Morris

John Morris (3)
Matthew Morris
Philip Morris
Robert Morris
W Morris
William Morris
Hugh Morrisin
James Morrison
Murdock Morrison
Norman Morrison
Samuel Morrison
Richard Morse
Sheren Morselander
William Morselander
Benjamin Mortimer
Robert Mortimer (2)
Abner Morton (2)
George Morton
James Morton
Philip Morton (2)
Robert Morton
Samuel Morton
Philip Mortong
Simon Morzin
Negro Moses
Daniel Mosiah
Sharon Moslander
William Moslander
John Moss (2)
Alexander Motley
William Motley
Elkinar Mothe
Enoch Motion
Benjamin Motte
Francis Moucan
Jean Moucan

George Moulton
John Moulton
Richard Mount
John Muanbet
Hezekiah Muck
Jacob Muckleroy
Philip Muckleroy (2)
Jacob Mullen
Eleme Mullent
Jean Muller
Leonard Muller
Robert Muller
Abraham Mullet
Jonathan Mullin
Leonard Mullin
Jonathan Mullin
Robert Mullin
William Mullin
Edward Mulloy (2)
Francis Mulloy
Richard Mumford
Timothy Mumford
Michael Mungen
John Mungon
John Munro
Henry Munrow
Royal Munrow
Thomas Munthbowk
Hosea Munul
James Murdock (2)
John Murdock
Peter Murlow
Daniel Murphy (2)
John Murphy
Nicholas Murphy
Patrick Murphy

Thomas Murphy (2)
Bryan Murray
Charles Murray
Daniel Murray (2)
John Murray (4)
Silas Murray
Thomas Murray
William Murray
Antonio Murria (2)
David Murrow
John Murrow
Samuel Murrow
Adam Murtilus
Richard Murus
Antonio Musqui
Ebenezer Mutter
Jean Myatt
Adam Myers (2)
George Myles
Henry Myres

N

Ebenezer Nabb
Dippen Nack
Archibald Nailer
Thomas Nandiva
Hosea Nandus
Richard Nash
Jean Natalt
Benjamin Nathan
Joseph Nathan
John Nathey (2)
Nathaniel Naval

Simon Navane
Francis Navas
Pierre Navey
David Neal (2)
George Neal
William Nealson
Ebenezer Neating
Gideon Necar
Joseph Negbel
Michael Negg
John Negis
James Neglee
Frank Negroe
James Negroe
James Negus
Thomas Negus
Abraham Neilson
Alexander Neilson
James Neilson
Joseph Neilson
Alexander Nelson
Andrew Nelson
John Nelson (2)
Joseph Nelson
Thomas Nelson (2)
William Nelson
Thomas Nesbitt
Bartholomew Nestora
Francis Neville
Jean Neville
Michael Neville
Ebenezer Newall
Sucreason Newall
William Neward
Elisha Newbury
Andrew Newcomb

John Newcomb
Andrew Newell
Amos Newell
Joseph Newell
Nathaniel Newell
Robert Newell
Nicholas Newgal
Joseph Newhall
Joseph Newille
Francis Newman
Moses Newman
Nathaniel Newman
Samuel Newman
Thomas Newman (4)
Adam Newton (2)
John Newton
William Newton
Adam Newtown
William Newtown
John Niester
James Nigley
Richard Nich
Thomas Nicher
Martin Nichets
Richard Nicholas
Allen Nichols
George Nichols
James Nichols
John Nichols
Richard Nichols
Alexander Nicholson
George Nicholson
Samuel Nicholson
Thomas Nicholson
George Nicks
Gideon Nigh

William Nightingale
James Nigley
Frank Niles
Robert Nixon
Jean Noblat
Arnox Noble
James Noble
John Mary Noblet
John Nocker
William Noel
William Nore
John Norfleet
Proper Norgand
John Norie
James Norman
John Norman
Joseph Norman
Peter Norman
Joseph Normay
Henry Norris
Anfield North
Daniel Northron
Harris Northrup
William Northrup
Elijah Norton
Jacob Norton
John Norton (3)
Nicholas Norton
Peter Norton
William Norton
Jacques Norva (2)
William Nourse
Nathaniel Nowell
Joseph Noyes
William Nurse
Pierre Nutern

David Nutter (2)
Joseph Nutter
John Nuttin (2)
Ebenezer Nutting
Robert Nyles

O

Charles Oakford
Solomon Oakley
John Oakman
Israel Oat
Joseph Oates
John Obey (2)
Cornelius O'Brien
Edward O'Brien
John O'Brien
William O'Bryan
Daniel Obourne
Samuel Oderon
Samuel Odiron
Pierre Ogee
John Ogillon
Richard Ogner
Patrick O'Hara
Robert O'Hara
Patrick O'Harra
Daniel Olbro
George Oldham
John Oldsmith
Raymond O'Larra
Devoe Olaya
Zebulon Olaya
Don R. Antonio Olive

Anthony Oliver
James Oliver (5)
Zebulon Oliver
Ebenezer Onsware
Allan Ord
John Ord
John Orgall
Sebastian Orman
Edward Ormunde
William Orr
John Orrock
Emanuel Orseat
Patrick Orsley
John Osborn
Joseph Osbourne
John Oseglass
Stephen Osena
John Osgood
Gabriel Oshire
Jean Oshire
Louis Oshire
John Osman
Henry Oswald
Gregorian Othes
Andre Otine (2)
Samuel Otis
Benjamin Otter
John Oubler
Charles Ousanon
Samuel Ousey
William Ousey
Jay Outon
John Outton
Jonathan Ovans
Samuel Ovell
Vincent Overatt

Samuel Overgorm
Lewis Owal
John Owen
Anthony Owens
Archibald Owens
Barnick Owens
James Owens
John Owens
Samuel Owens

P

Jean Packet
Abel Paddock
Joseph Paddock
Silas Paddock
Daniel Paddock
Journey Padouan
B. Pain
Jacob Painter
Henry Painter
John Palicut
Daniel Palmer
Elisha Palmer
Gay Palmer
George Palmer
James Palmer
John Palmer
Jonas Palmer
Joshua Palmer
Lemuel Palmer
Matthew Palmer
Moses Palmer
Philip Palmer

William Palmer (4)
Peter Palot
Moses Palot
Nicholas Pamphillion
Emea Panier
Anthony Panks
Joseph Parde
Christopher Pardindes
Jacob Pardley
John Parish
George Park
John Parkard
Thomas Parkard
George L. Parke
Joseph Parkens
Amos Parker
Ebenezer Parker
Edward Parker
George Parker (2)
John Parker (4)
Luther Parker (2)
Peter Parker
Samuel Parker (2)
Thaddeus Parker
Timothy Parker
George Parks
Richard Parks
Thomas Parkson
Joseph Parlot
Thomas Parnell
Jean Parol
Sebastian Parong
Dominick Parpot
Gabriel Parrie
Francis Parshall
James Parsons (3)

Jeremiah Parsons
John Parsons
Joseph Parsons
Samuel Parsons
Stephen Parsons
William Parsons (2)
James Partridge
Roman Pascan
Edmund Paschal
Leroy Pasehall
Richard Pass
William Pass
Israel Patch
Joseph Patrick
David Patridge
Edward Patterson
Hance Patterson
John Patterson (2)
Peter Patterson
W. Patterson
William Patterson
William Paul
Pierre Payatt
James Payne
Josiah Payne
Oliver Payne
Thomas Payne (3)
William Payne (2)
William Payton
John Peacock
Benjamin Peade
Benjamin Peal
Samuel Pealer
William Peals
John Pear
Amos Pearce

Benjamin Pearce
John Pearce
Jonathan Pearce
Edward Pearsol
John Pearson
George Peasood
Elisha Pease
Estrant Pease
Guliel Pechin
Andrew Peck (2)
Benjamin Peck
James Peck
Joseph Peck (2)
Simon Peck
William Peck
Benjamin Pecke
Gardner Peckham
John Peckworth
Zachary Peddlefoot
Solomon Pedgore
Edward Pedlock
Alexander Pees
John Pees
Silas Pegget
Jean Pegit
John Pelit
Pierre Pelit
Samuel Pell
Sebastian Pelle
Jacques Peloneuse
——Pelrice
Gothard Pelrice
John Pelvert
Amos Pemberton (2)
Thomas Pemberton
William Pemberton

John Pendleton
Sylvester Pendleton (2)
——Penfield
Peter Penoy
James Penwell
John Baptist Peomond
Alfred Peose
Michael Pepper
Thomas Perall
James Peril
Charles Perinell
Peter Perieu
Charles Perkinell
Charles Perkmell
Jabez Perkins
Jonathan Perkins
Joseph Perkins
William Perkins
Antonio Permanouf
Peter Perons
Peter Perora
Pierre Perout
John Perry
Joseph Perry
Raymond Perry
Richard Perry
William Perry (7)
Manuel Person
Jabez Pervis
Jean Peshire
John Peterkin (2)
Francis Peters
John Peters (2)
Aaron Peterson
Hance Peterson
Joseph Peterson (2)

James Petre
William Pett
Daniel Pettis
Ephraim Pettis
Nathan Pettis
Isaac Pettit
Joseph Antonio Pezes
Thomas Philbrook
John Philip (2)
Joseph Philip
Lewis Philip
Pierre Philip
John Philips
Lewin Philips
Nathan Philips
Thomas Philips
Edward Phillips
John Phillips (2)
Samuel Phillips
James Phimmer
Joseph Phipise
Nathaniel Phippin
Thomas Phippin
Jean Picher
Juan Picko
Pierre Pickolet
Richard Pierce (2)
Stephen Pierce
Jeremiah Pierel
Jean Pierre
Jesse Pierre
Jucah Pierre
Joseph Pierson
Amos Pike
John Pike
George Pill

Joseph Pillion
Truston Pilsbury
John Pimelton
Simeon Pimelton
James Pine (2)
Charles Pinkel
Jonathan Pinkman
Robert Pinkman
Augustus Pion
Henry Pipon
Jean Pisung
Elias Pitchcock
Sele Pitkins
John Pitman
Jonathan Pitman (2)
Thomas Pitt
John Pittman
W. Pitts
Nathaniel Plachores
Elton Planet
Etena Planett
John Platte
William Plemate
Francis Plenty
John Ploughman
Thomas Plunkett
James Plumer
John Plumstead
Thomas Plunkett
Motthew Poble
Henry Pogan
Daniel Poges
Salvador Pogsin
Michael Poinchet
Gilman Poirant
William Poke

John Poland
John Pollard
Peter Pollard
Jonathas Pollin
Elham Poloski
Samuel Polse
William Polse
Charles Pond
Pennell Pond
Peter Pond
Culman Poni
Fancis Ponsard
Hosea Pontar
Joseph Pontesty
Robert Pool
David Poole
Hosea Poole
John Poole
Richard Poole
Robert Poole
Morris Poor
Thomas Poor
Henry Poore
Morris Poore
William Poore
Alexander Pope
John Pope
Etienne Porlacu
Nathaniel Porson
Anthony Port
Charles Porter (3)
David Porter (3)
Edward Porter
Frederick Porter
Howard Porter
John Porter (2)

Thomas Porter
William Porter
Frank Portois
Seren Poseter
Jeremiah Post
Jean Postian
Edward Posture
Thomas Posture
Thomas Poteer
Abijah Potter
Charles Potter
Ephraim Potter
Rufus Potter
Mark Pouchett
Jean Poullain
Mark B Poullam
William Powder
John Powell
Thomas Powell
William Powder
Patrick Power
Richard Powers
Stephen Powers
Nicholas Prande (2)
Benjamin Prate
James Prate
Ebenezer Pratt
Ezra Pratt (2)
Andre Preno
Nathaniel Prentiss
Robert Prentiss
Stanton Prentiss
Andrew Presson
Isaac Presson
Benjamin Prettyman
John Pribble (2)

Edward Price (2)
Joseph Price
Nathaniel Price
Reason Price (2)
Richard Price
Samuel Price
William Price
John Prichard
Jonathan Pride
William Priel
Henry Primm
Edward Primus
Charles Prince
Negro Prince
Nicholas Priston
James Proby
James Proctor
Joseph Proctor
Samuel Proctor
Claud Provost
Paul Provost
John Proud (2)
Joseph Proud
Joseph Prought
Lewis de Pue
James Pullet
Pierre Punce
Peter Purlett
William Purnell
Edward Pursell
Abraham Putnam
Creece Putnam

Q

James Quality (3)
Joseph Quality
Josiah Quality
Samuel Quamer
Thomas Quand
Louis Quelgrise
Duncan Quigg (2)
James Quinch
Samuel Quinn
Charles Quiot
Samuel Quomer

R

Thomas Race
Antonio Rackalong
Patrick Rafferty
Daniel Raiden
Michael Raingul
Richard Rainham
Thomas Rainiot
George Rambert
Peter Ramlies
Joseph Ramsdale
Abner Ramsden
Jean C. Ran
Benjamin Randall
Charles Randall
Edward Randall
Jesse Randall
Joseph Randall

Nathaniel Randall (2)
Thomas Randall
William Randall (2)
Dolly Randel
Paul Randell
Joseph Randell (2)
Joses Randell
George Randell
Paul Randell
George Randels
Nathaniel Randol
Jean Baptiste Rano
Benjamin Ranshaw
James Rant
Norman Rathbun
Roger Rathbun
Peter Rathburn
Samuel Rathburn
Rogers Rathburne
Peter Rattan
Arthur Rawson
Francis Rawson
James Rawson
Alexander Ray
John Ray
Nathaniel Ray
Nathaniel Raye
George Raymond
James Raymond
William Raymond
William Raymons
Jean Raynor
Benjamin Read
Oliver Reade
Jeremiah Reardon
Lewis Recour

John Red
James Redfield
Edward Redick
Benjamin Redman
Andre Read
Barnard Reed
Christian Reed
Curtis Reed
Eliphaz Reed
George Reed
Jeremiah Reed
Job Reed
John Reed (2)
Jonathan Reed
Joseph Reed
Levi Reed
Thomas Reed (2)
William Reed (2)
John Reef
Nicholas Reen
Thomas Reeves
Jacques Refitter
Julian Regan
Hugh Reid
Jacob Reiton
Jean Remong
Jean Nosta Renan
Louis Renand
John Renean
Pierre Renear
Thomas Renee
Thomas Rennick
Frederick Reno
Jean Renovil
Michael Renow
Jean Reo

Barton Repent
Jean Requal
Jesse Rester
Louis Rewof
Thomas Reynelds
Elisha Reynolds
Nathaniel Reynolds
Richard Reynolds (2)
Thomas Reynolds
Thomas Reyzick
Sylvester Rhodes
Thomas de Ribas
George Ribble
Benjamin Rice
Edward Rice
James Rice
John Rice (2)
Nathaniel Rice
Noah Rice
William Rice
Elisha Rich
Freeman Rich
John Rich
Matthew Rich
Nathan Rich
Benjamin Richard
Diah Richards
Gilbert Richards
James Richards
John Richards
Oliver Richards
Pierre Richards
William Richards
David Richardson
John Richardson
Pierre Richardson

William Richardson
Cussing Richman
Ebenezer Richman
Benjamin Richmond
Seth Richmond
Clement Ricker
John Rickett
Nathaniel Rickman
Lewis Ridden
Isaac Riddler
Lewis Rider
John Riders
John Ridge
John Ridgway
Isaac Ridler
Amos Ridley
Thomas Ridley
David Rieve
Israel Rieves
Jacob Right
James Rigmorse
Joseph Rigo
Henry Riker
R. Riker
James Riley
Philip Riley
Philip Rilly
Pierre Ringurd
John Rion
Daniel Riordan
Paul Ripley
Ramble Ripley
Thomas Ripley
Ebenezer Ritch
John River
Joseph River

Paul Rivers
Thomas Rivers
John Rivington
Joseph Roach
Lawrence Roach
William Roas
Thomas Robb
James Robehaird
Arthur Robert
John Robert
Julian Robert
Aaron Roberts (2)
Edward Roberts
Epaphras Roberts
James Roberts (2)
Joseph Roberts
Moses Roberts (2)
William Roberts (4)
Charles Robertson (2)
Elisha Robertson
Esau Robertson
George Robertson
James Robertson (3)
Jeremiah Robertson
John Robertson (6)
Joseph Robertson
Samuel Robertson
Thomas Robertson
Daniel Robins
Enoch Robins
James Robins
William Robins
Anthony Robinson
Ebenezer Robinson
Enoch Robinson
James Robinson (2)

Jehu Robinson
John Robinson (3)
Joseph Robinson
Mark Robinson
Nathaniel Robinson
Thomas Robinson
William Robinson
John Rockway
Daniel Rockwell
Jabez Rockwell
Elisha Rockwood
Anthony Roderick
Jean Raptist Rodent
James Rodgers
Michael Rodieu
Francis Rodrigo
Franco Rogeas
Robert Roger
Dudson Rogers
Ebenezer Rogers
Emanuel Rogers
George Rogers (3)
John Rogers (5)
Nicholas Rogers
Paul Rogers
Thomas Rogers
William Rogers
John Rogert
Joseph Roget
Jean Rogue
John Francis Rogue
John Roke
John Rollin
Paul Rollins
Toby Rollins
Francis Roman

Petre Romary
Diego Romeria
Benjamin Romulus
Lewis Ronder
Jack Rone
Paul Ropeley
Bartram Ropper
Gideon Rose (2)
John Rose (2)
Philip Rose
Prosper Rose
Jean Rosea
Augustus Roseau
Guilliam Roseau
Jean Baptist Rosua
William Rose
Andrew Ross
Archibald Ross
Daniel Ross (3)
David Ross
James Ross
Malone Ross
Thomas Ross
William Ross (3)
Bostion Roteslar
John Roth
Samuel Rothburn
Benjamin Rothers
Jean Baptist Rouge
Jean James Rouge
Charles Roulong
Hampton Round
John Round
Nathan Round
Samuel Round
Andrew Rouse

Claud Rouse
Daniel Roush
Hampton Rowe
John Rowe
William Rowe
George Rowen
George Rowing
Patrick Rowland
John Rowley
Shter Rowley
John Frederick Rowlin
William Rowsery
James Rowson
Augustus Royen
John Royster
Richard Royster
Blost Rozea
Lawrence Rozis
Peter Ruban
Ebenezer Rube
Thomas Rubin
Eden Ruddock
Ezekiel Rude
John Ruffeway
Lewis Ruffie
Henry Rumsower
Joseph Runyan
Nathaniel Ruper
John Rupper
Daniel Ruse
Daniel Rush
Edward Russell
Jacob Russell
Pierre Russell
Samuel Russell
Valentine Russell

William Russell
John Rust
William Rust (2)
John Ruth (2)
Pompey Rutley
Pierre Ryer
Jacob Ryan
Frank Ryan
Michael Ryan
Peter Ryan
Thomas Ryan
Renee Ryon

S

Francisco Sablong
John Sachel
Jonathan Sachell
George Sadden
George Saddler
John Sadens
Abraham Sage
Edward Sailly
John Saint
Elena Saldat
Gilbert Salinstall
Luther Salisbury
Michael Sallibie
John Salmon
John Salter
Thomas Salter
Edward Same
Pierre Samleigh
Jacob Sammian

Stephen Sampson (2)
Charles Sand
Henry Sanders
Manuel Sandovah
Ewing Sands
Stephen Sands
Daniel Sanford
Anthony Santis
Thomas Sarbett
Louis Sarde
Peter Sarfe
Juan Sassett
David Sasson
Jonathan Satchell
William Saterly
Johns Sathele
Joseph Satton
Edward Sauce
Augustus Saunders
Daniel Saunders
John Saunders
Allen Savage
Belias Savage
Nathaniel Savage(2)
Joseph Savot
Benjamin Sawyer
Daniel Sawyer
Ephraim Sawyer(3)
James Sawyer
Jeremiah Sawyer
John Sawyer
Peter Sawyer
Thomas Sawyer
William Sawyer
Cuffy Savers
Joseph Sayers

Henry Scees
Peter Schafer
Melchior Scheldorope
Peter Schwoob
Julian Scope
Christopher Scott
George Scott
James Scott
John Scott (4)
Robert Scott
Thomas Scott
William Scott
Daniel Scovell
David Scudder
Nutchell Scull
Lamb Seabury
Samuel Seabury
Adam Seager
George Seager
Thomas Sealey (2)
Robert Seares
George Seaton
Antonio Sebasta
Benjamin Secraft
Thomas Seeley
Jean Baptist Sego
Elias Seldon
Edward Sellers
Anthony Selwind
William Semell
John Senior
Adam Sentelume
Abraham Sentilier
Leonard Sepolo
Emanuel Seerus
Anthony Serals

James Seramo
John Serant
Francis Seratte
Francis Sergeant
Thomas Sergeant
Joel Serles
Sebastian Serrea
William Service
Jonathan Setchell
Otis Sevethith
Francis Seyeant
Solomon Shad
Matthew Shappo
Elisha Share
John Sharke
Philip Sharp
Peter Sharpe
Philip Sharper
John Sharpley
Joseph Sharpley
Joseph Shatille
Joseph Shatillier
Archibald Shaver
Jacob Shaver
Abner Shaw
Daniel Shaw
James Shaw
Jeremiah Shaw
Joseph Shaw
Samuel Shaw
Thomas Shaw (3)
William Shaw
Patrick Shea
Jean Shean
Brittle Sheans
Gideon Shearman

Henry Shearman
Stephen Shearman
Philip Shebzain
John Sheffield
William Sheilds
Nicholas Sheilow
Jeremiah Shell
Benjamin Shelton
James Shepherd
John Shepherd (4)
Robert Shepherd (3)
Thomas Sherburn
William Sherburne
Gilbert Sherer
James Sheridan
John Sheridan
John Sherman
Samuel Sherman (3)
Andrew Sherns
Andrew Sherre
George Shetline
John Shewin
Jacob Shibley
George Shiffen
Louis de Shille
Jack Shilling
Jacob Shindle
Frederick Shiner (2)
John Shirkley
Joseph Shoakley (2)
Edward Shoemaker
James Shoemaker
Samuel Shokley
John Short (2)
Joseph Short
Thomas Short

Enoch Shout
Christopher Shoving
Jacob Shroak
James Shuckley
Thomas Shuman
Francis Shun
Enoch Shulte
John Shute
Richard Sickes
Francis Silver
James Simes
Chapman Simmons
David Simmons
Hilldoves Simmons
John Simmons
Joshua Simms
James Simon
William Simon
Francis Simonds
Boswell Simons
Champion Simons
Elijah Simons
Francis Simons
Joseph Simons
Nathaniel Simons
Nero Simons
Samuel Simons
William Simpkins
Benjamin Simpson
Charles Simpson
Thomas Simpson
John Sindee
John Singer
John Sitchell
John Skay
John Skelton

Samuel Skinner (2)
Richard Skinner
Peter Skull (2)
David Slac
Benjamin Slade
Thomas Slager
John Slane
Jean Louis Slarick
Measer Slater
Matthew Slaughter
John Slee
Thomas Slewman
Samuel Slide
Joseph Slight
Josiah Slikes
Christopher Sloakum
Edward Sloan
Timothy Sloan
Andrew Sloeman
Thomas Slough
Ebenezer Slow
Isaac Slowell
William Slown
Henry Sluddard
Samuel Slyde
Richard Slykes
William Smack
Joseph Small
Robert Smallpiece
John Smallwood (2)
Peter Smart
John Smight
William Smiley
Abraham Smith
Alexander Smith
Allan Smith

Andrew Smith (2)
Anthony Smith
Archibald Smith
Basil Smith
Benjamin Smith (2)
Burrell Smith
Buskin Smith
Charles Smith
Clement Smith
Clemont Smith
Daniel Smith (3)
David Smith
Easoph Smith
Edward Smith
Eleazar Smith
Enoch Smith
Epaphras Smith
Ezekiel Smith
George Smith
Gideon Smith
Haymond Smith
Henry Smith
Hugh Smith
Jack Smith
James Smith (7)
Jasper Smith
John Smith (12)
Jonathan Smith (5}
Joshua Smith
Joseph Smith (3)
Laban Smith
Martin Smith
Richard Smith (3)
Rockwell Smith
Roger Smith (2)
Samuel Smith (6)

Stephen Smith
Sullivan Smith
Thomas Smith (8)
Walter Smith
William Smith (4)
Zebediah Smith
Thomas Smithson
Peter Smothers
Samuel Snare
John Snellin
John Sneyders
Peter Snider
William Snider
Ebenezer Snow
Seth Snow
Sylvanus Snow
Abraham Soft
Raymond Sogue
Assia Sole
Nathan Solley
Ebenezer Solomon
Thomas Solomon
James Sooper
Christian Soudower
Moses Soul
Nathaniel Southam
William Southard
Henry Space
Enoch Spalding
Joshua Spaner
Charles Sparefoot
James Sparrows
John Speake
Martin Speakl
James Spear
Eliphaz Speck

Elchie Spellman
William Spellman
James Spencer
Joseph Spencer
Nicholas Spencer
Thomas Spencer
Solomon Spenser
Henry Spice
John Spicer (2)
Lancaster Spicewood
John Spier (2)
Richard Spigeman
John Spinks
Caleb Spooner
David Spooner
Shubab Spooner
William Spooner
Jonathan Sprague
Simon Sprague
Philip Spratt
Charles Spring
Richard Springer
John Spriggs
Joshua Spriggs
Thomas Spriggs
William Springer
Alexander Sproat
Thomas Sproat
Gideon Spry
Long Sprywood
Nathaniel Spur
Joshua Squibb
David Squire
John St. Clair
Francisco St. Domingo
John St. Thomas

John Staagers
Thomas Stacy
Thomas Stacey
Christian Stafford
Conrad Stagger
Edward Stagger
Samuel Stalkweather
John Standard
Lemuel Standard
Butler Stanford
Richard Stanford
Robert Stanford
John Stanhope
William Stannard
Daniel Stanton
Nathaniel Stanton (2)
William Stanton
Joseph Stanley
Peter Stanley
Starkweather Stanley
W Stanley
William Stanley
Abijah Stapler
Timothy Star
Samuel Starke
Benjamin Starks
Woodbury Starkweather
John Stearns
William Stearny
Daniel Stedham
Thomas Steele
James Steelman
John Steer
Stephen Sleevman
John Stephen
Benjamin Stephens

John Stephens (2)
Henry Stephens
William Stephens (3)
David Stephenson
John Stephenson
John Sterns
William Sterry
David Stevens
James Stevens
Joseph Stevens
Levert Stevens
William Stevens
Robert Stevenson
Charles Steward
Joseph Steward
Lewis Steward
Samuel Steward
Daniel Stewart
Edward Stewart (2)
Elijah Stewart
Hugh Stewart
Jabez Stewart (2)
John Stewart
Samuel Stewart
Stephen Stewart
Thomas Stewart
William Stewart
John Stiger
John Stikes
Daniel Stiles
Israel Stiles
John Stiles
Joshua Stiles
Josiah Stiles
Ashley Stillman
Theodore Stillman

Enoch Stillwell
John Stillwell
Jacob Stober
Hugh Stocker
William Stocker
Simeon Stockwell
Israel Stoddard
Noah Stoddard
Thomas Stoddard
Edward Stoddart
Israel Stoddart
Nathaniel Stoey
Abney Stone
Amos Stone
Donald Stone
Elijah Stone
Richard Stone
Thomas Stone (5)
William Stone
Boston Stoneford
Job Stones
John Stones
Matthew Stoney
Jonathan Stott
Seren Stott
John Stoughton
Daniel Stout
George Stout
William Stout
Andrew Stowers
Blair Stove
Joseph Strand
James Strange
Joshua Bla Stratia
James Stridges
John Stringe

John Stringer
Joseph Stroad
Samuel Stroller
Joseph Stroud
Benjamin Stubbe
John Sturtivant
Smith Stutson
James Suabilty
Benjamin Subbs
Jacquer Suffaraire
Manuel Sugasta
Miles Suldan
Parks Sullevan
Dennis Sullivan
Patrick Sullivan
Thomas Sullivan
George Summers
Rufus Sumner
Amos Sunderland
Edward Sunderland (3)
Francis Suneneau
John Suneneaux
Andre Surado
Godfrey Suret
Jack C. Surf
Francis Surronto
Hugh Surtes
John Surtevant
John Sussett
Franco Deo Suttegraz
Louis John Sutterwis
George Sutton
John Sutton
Thomas Sutton
Jacob Snyder
Roman Suyker

Simon Swaine
Zacharias Swaine
Thomas Swapple
Absolom Swate
James Swayne
Isaac Swean
Peter Swean (2)
Enoch Sweat
John Sweeney (2)
Benjamin Sweet
Godfrey Sweet (2)
Nathaniel Sweeting
Joshua Swellings
Daniel Swery
Martin Swift
William Swire

T

Anthony Tabee
John Taber (2)
Thomas Taber
Samuel Table
John Tabor
Pelack Tabor
Ebenezer Tabowl
Ebenezer Talbot
Silas Talbott
Ebenezer Talbott
Wilham Talbut
James Talketon
Archibald Talley
John Tankason
Caspar Tanner

John Tanner
William Tant
Thomas Tantis
Samuel Tapley
Isaac Tappin
Antonio Tarbour
Townsend Tarena
Edward Target
John Tarrant
Lewis Tarret
Domingo Taugin
Edward Tayender
Samuel Taybor
Alexander Taylor
Andrew Taylor (2)
Gabriel Taylor
Hezekiah Taylor
Isaac Taylor
Jacob Taylor (3)
John Taylor (8)
Captain John Taylor
Joseph Taylor (3)
Major Taylor
Noadiah Taylor
Peter Taylor
Robert Taylor (3)
Tobias Taylor
William Taylor (3)
George Teather
Thomas Tebard
John Teller
Jean Temare
John Templing
Philip Temver
Gilbert Tennant
Thomas Tenny

Henry Teppett
Governe Terrene
Joshua Ternewe
Thomas Terrett
William Terrett
John Terry
Samuel Terry
William Terry
Joshua Teruewe
Zerlan Tesbard
Jean Tessier
Freeborn Thandick
Lewis Thaxter
Seren Thaxter
John Thelston
Robert Therey
Simon Thimagun
Thurdick Thintle
——Thomas
Abner Thomas
Andrew Thomas
Cornelius Thomas
Ebenezer Thomas (2)
Edward Thomas
Green Thomas
Herod Thomas
Jacques Thomas (2)
James Thomas (2)
Jean Supli Thomas
Jesse Thomas (2)
John Thomas (8)
Joseph Thomas
Thomas Thomas
Urias Thomas
William Thomas
Abraham Thompson

Andrew Thompson (3)
Bartholomew Thompson
Benjamin Thompson (2)
Charles Thompson
Eli Thompson
George Thompson
Harvey Thompson
Isaac Thompson
Israel Thompson
John Thompson (8)
Joseph Thompson (2)
Lawrence Thompson
Patrick Thompson
Robert Thompson (3)
Seth Thompson (2)
William Thompson (6)
John Thorian
William Thorner
James Thornhill
Christian Thornton
Christopher Thornton
Jesse Thornton
Samuel Thornton
Thomas Thornton
William Thorpe
Gideon Threwit
Sedon Thurley
Benjamin Thurston
Samuel Thurston
Samuel Tibbards
Richard Tibbet
George Tibbs
Henry Ticket
Harvey Tiffman
Andrew Tillen
Jacob Tillen

Peter Tillender
Thomas Tillinghast
David Tilmouse
John Tilson
Nicholas Tilson
Grale Timcent
George Timford
Jeremiah Timrer
Alexander Tindell
James Tinker
William Tinley
Joseph Tinleys
Anthony Tioffe
Samuel Tippen
Jean Tirve
Stephen Tissina
Michael Titcomb
Moses Titcomb
James Tobin
Thomas Tobin (2)
John Todd
William Todd
Thomas Tolley
Francis Tollings
Henry Tollmot
Thomas Tomay
James Tomkins
Charles Tomped
Benjamin Tompkins
William Tompkins
Thomas Thompson
Henry Too
Andrew Toombs
Rufus Toppin
Christopher Torpin
Francis Torrent

Michael Tosa
Daniel Totton
Pierre Touleau
Robert Toulger
Sylvanus Toulger
Dominic Tour
Jean Tournie
Francis Tovell
Joseph Towbridge
John Towin
Samuel Townhend
James Townley
Samuel Towns
Elwell Townsend
Jacob Townsend
Jeremiah Townsend
William Townsend
Jille Towrand
James Towser
Thomas Toy
Benjamin Tracy
Jesse Tracy
Nathaniel Tracy
Jacob Trailey
William Traine
Thomas Trampe
Nathaniel Trask (2)
Richard Traveno
Christopher Traverse
Solomon Treat
James Treby
James Tredwell
William Treen
Andrew Trefair
Thomas Trenchard
William Trendley

Thomas W Trescott
Andre Treasemas
Edward Trevett
Job Trevo
John Trevor
Thomas Trip
Richard Tripp
Thomas Tripp
Jacob Tripps
John Tritton
Ebenezer Trivet
Jabez Trop
John Trot
John Troth
William Trout
John Trow
Benjamin Trowbridge
David Trowbridge
Stephen Trowbridge
Thomas Trowbridge
Joseph Truck
Peter Truck
William Trunks
Joseph Trust
Robert Trustin
George Trusty
Edward Tryan
Moses Tryon
Saphn Tubbs
Thomas Tubby
John Tucke
Francis Tucker
John Tucker (4)
Joseph Tucker (2)
Nathan Tucker
Nathaniel Tucker

Paul Tucker
Robert Tucker (2)
Seth Tucker
Solomon Tucker
George Tuden
Charles Tully
Casper Tumner
Charles Tunkard
Charles Turad
Elias Turk
Joseph Turk
Caleb Turner
Caspar Turner
Francis Turner
George Turner
James Turner
John Turner (3)
Philip Turner
Thomas Turner (4)
William Turner (2)
Lisby Turpin (2)
Peter Turrine
John Tutten
Daniel Twigg
Charles Twine
Joseph Twogood
Daily Twoomey
Thomas Tyerill
Jean Tyrant
John Tyse

U

Urson Ullaby

Thomas Umthank
Benjamin Uncers
Joseph Union
Obadiah Upton
John Usher
Andre Utinett
Abirnelech Uuncer

V

Peter Vaidel
Pierre Valem
Joseph Valentine
George Vallance
David Vallet
John Valpen
Nathan Vamp
William Vance
Thomas Vandegrist
Francis Vandegrist
Patrick Vandon
John Vandross
Eleazar Van Dyke
John Van Dyke
Nathaniel Van Horn
William Van Horn
Christain Vann
Jean Van Orse
James Vanoster
Barnabus Varley
Patrick Vasse
Richard Vaugh
Aaron Vaughan
Andrew Vaughan

Christian Vaughan
David Veale
Elisha Veale
Toser Vegier
Bruno Velis
David Velow
William Venable
Moses Ventis
Samuel Ventis
Joseph Verdela
Julian Verna
Peter Vesseco
Justin Vestine
Pierre Vettelet
John Vial
Jean Viauf
William Vibert
Anare Vic
John Vickery
Roger Victory
David Viegra
Daniel Viero
William Vierse
Jean Vigo
John Vilvee
Lange Vin
Peter Vinane
Francis Vincent
William Vinnal
Robert Virnon
Jean Vissenbouf
Andrew Vitena
Joseph Vitewell
Juan Albert Vixeaire
John Voe
John Vonkett

William Von Won
Nicholas Vookly
John Vorus
Henry Voss
George Vossery

W

Christian Wadde
Benjamin Wade
Thomas Wade (2)
Christopher Wadler
Richard Wagstaff
Joseph Wainwright
Jacob Wainscott
Matthew Wainscott
Charles Waistcoott
Ezekiel Waistcoat
Jabez Waistcoat
Jacob Waistcoat
John Waistcoat
Joseph Waiterly
Joseph Wakefield
Joseph Walcot
Asa Walden
George Walding
John Waldrick
Ephraim Wales
Samuel Wales
Baldwin Walker
Daniel Walker
Ezekiel Walker
George Walker
Hezekiah Walker

John Walker
Joseph Walker
Michael Walker (4)
Nathaniel Walker (4)
Richard Walker
Samuel Walker (2)
Thomas Walker (2)
William Walker (3)
James Wall
Bartholomew Wallace
John Wallace
Joseph Wallace
Thomas Wallace (2)
Ebenezer Wallar
Joseph Wallen
Caleb Waller
George Wallesly
Anthony Wallis
Benjamin Wallis
Ezekiel Wallis
George Wallis
Hugh Wallis
James Wallis
John Wallis
Jonathan Wallis
John Wallore
Edward Walls
William Wallsey
William Walmer
Robert Walpole
John Walsey
Patrick Walsh
George Walter
John Walter
Joseph Walter
Jonathan Walters

Roger Walters
Henry Walton
John Walton
Jonathan Walton
John Wandall
Ezekiel Wannell
Powers Wansley
Michael Wanstead
George Wanton
Benjamin Ward
Charles Ward
Christenton Ward
David Ward
Joseph Ward
Simon Ward
Thomas Ward
William Ward
John Warde
Benjamin Wardell
John Wardell
James Wardling
Elijah Wareman
William Warf
Unit Warky
Joseph Warley
Joseph Warmesley
William Taylor Warn
Christopher Warne
Andrew Warner
Amos Warner
Berry Warner
John Warner
Obadiah Warner
Samuel Warner (2)
Thomas Warner
Robert Warnock

Christopher Warrell
Benjamin Warren
Jonathan Warren
Obadiah Warren
Richard Warringham
William Warrington
Thomas Warsell
Lloyd Warton
Joseph Wartridge
Townsend Washington
Asher Waterman (2)
Azariah Waterman
Calvin Waterman
John Waterman
Samuel Waterman
Thomas Waterman
William Waterman (3)
Henry Waters
John Waters
Thomas Waters
John Watkins
Thomas Watkins (4)
Edward Watson
Joseph Watson
Henry Watson (2)
John Watson (5)
Nathaniel Watson
Robert Watson
Thomas Watson (5)
William Watson
John Watt
William Wattle
Henry Wattles
Joseph Watts
Samuel Watts
Thomas Watts

Andrew Waymore
James Wear
Jacob Weatherall
Joseph Weatherox
Thomas Weaver
Jacob Webb
James Webb
John Webb (3)
Jonathan Webb
Michael Webb
Nathaniel Webb
Oliver Webb
Thomas Webb (2)
William Webb (2)
Joseph Webber
William Webber (2)
George Webby
Francis Webster
William Wedden
John Wedger
David Wedon
William Weekman
Francis Weeks (2)
James Weeks
Seth Weeks
Thomas Weeks
John Welanck
Ezekiel Welch
George Welch
Isaac Welch
James Welch (5)
Matthew Welch
Moses Welch
Philip Welch
Joseph Wenthoff
Nellum Welk

John Wellis
John Wellman
Matthew Wellman
Timothy Wellman
Cornelius Wells
Ezra Wells
Gideon Wells
Joseph Wells
Peter Wells
Richard Wells
William Wells
Joseph Welpley
David Welsh
John Welsh
Patrick Wen
Isaac Wendell
Robert Wentworth
Joseph Wessel
William Wessel
John Wessells
Benjamin West
Edward West
Jabez West (3)
Richard West (2)
Samuel Wester
Henry Weston
Simon Weston
William Weston
Philip Westward
Jesse Wetherby
Thomas Whade
John Wharfe
Lloyd Wharton
Michael Whater
Jesse Wheaton
Joseph Wheaton

Henry Wheeler
Michael Wheeler
Morrison Wheeler
William Wheeler (2)
Michael Whelan
Michael Whellan
James Whellan
Jesse Whelton
John Whelton
Horatio Whethase
John Whila
Benjamin Whipple (2)
Samuel Whipple
Stephen Whipple
Christopher Whippley
Benjamin White (2)
Ephraim White
Ichabod White
James White
John White (7)
Lemuel White
Joseph White
Lemuel White
Richard White
Robert White
Sampson White (2)
Samuel White (2)
Thomas White (2)
Timothy White
Watson White
William White (3)
Jacob Whitehead
Enoch Whitehouse
Harmon Whiteman
Luther Whitemore
William Whitepair

Card Way Whithousen
George Whiting (2)
James Whiting
William Whiting
John Whitlock
Joseph Whitlock
William Whitlock
Samuel Whitmolk
George Whitney
Isaac Whitney
James Whitney
John Whitney
Peter Whitney
Joseph Whittaker
Jacob Whittemore
Felix Wibert
Conrad Wickery
Joseph Wickman
Samuel Wickward
Leron Widgon
John Wier (2)
John Wigglesworth
Irwin Wigley
Michael Wiglott
Stephen Wigman
John Wigmore
Edward Wilcox (2)
Isaac Wilcox
Obadiah Wilcox
Pardon Wilcox
Robert Wilderidger
Charles Wilkins
Amos Wilkinson
William Wilkinson
George Willard
John Willard

Julian Willard
John Willeman
Benjamin Willeroon
James Willet
Conway Willhouse
Amos Williams
Barley Williams
Benjamin Williams
Cato Williams
Charles Williams
Dodd Williams
Edward Williams
Ephraim Williams
Ethkin Williams
George Williams (3)
Henry Williams (2)
Isaac Williams (2)
James Williams (4)
Jeffrey Williams
John Williams (9)
Jonathan Williams (2)
Moses Williams
Nathaniel Williams
Nicholas Williams
Peter Williams
Richard Williams
Samuel Williams (2)
William Williams (2)
William Williamson
John Foster Willian
John Williman
Day Willin
Abel Willis
Frederick Willis
John Willis (2)
Jesse Willis

Abraham Williston
Joseph Willman
Abraham Willor
Guy Willoson
Benjamin Willshe
Benjamin Willson
Francis Willson
James Willson (2)
John Willson
Martin Willson
Thomas Willson
Timothy Willson
W. Willson
William Willson
Samuel Wilmarth
Luke Wilmot
Benjamin Wilson (2)
Edward Wilson
George Wilson
John Wilson
Lawrence Wilson
Nathaniel Wilson
Patrick Wilson
William Wilson
George Wiltis
Vinrest Wimondesola
Guilliam Wind
Edward Windgate
Joseph Windsor
Stephen Wing
Jacob Wingman
Samuel Winn
Jacob Winnemore
Seth Winslow
Charles Winter
George Winter

Joseph Winters
David Wire
John Wise
Thomas Witham
John Witherley
Solomon Witherton
William Withpane
William Witless
Robert Wittington
W. Wittle
John Woesin
Henry Woist
Henry Wolf
John Wolf
Simon de Wolf
Stephen de Wolf
Champion Wood
Charles Wood (3)
Daniel Wood (4)
Edward Wood (2)
George Wood
Jabez Wood
John Wood
Jonathan Wood
Joseph Wood (2)
Justus Wood
Matthew Wood
Samuel Wood (2)
William Wood
Herbert Woodbury (3)
Jacob Woodbury
Luke Woodbury
Nathaniel Woodbury
Robert Woodbury
William Woodbury
Thomas Woodfall

David Woodhull
Henry Woodly
Nathaniel Woodman
James Woodson
Joseph Woodward
Gideon Woodwell
Abel Woodworth
Edward Woody
John Woody
Michael Woolock
Michael Woomstead
James Woop
William Wooten
James Worthy
John Wright
Robert Wright
Benjamin Wyatt
John Wyatt (2)
Gordon Wyax
Reuben Wyckoff
William Wyer
Henry Wylie

X

John Xmens

Y

Joseph Yalkington
Joseph Yanger
Joseph Yard
Thomas Yates

Francis Yduchare
Adam Yeager
Jacob Yeason
Jacob Yeaston
Pender Yedrab
George Yoannet
Edward Yorke
Peter Yose
Alexander Young
Archibald Young
Charles Young
George Young
Ichabod Young
Jacob Young
John Young (2)
Marquis Young (2)
Seth Young
William Young
Charles Youngans
Louis Younger

Z

Jean Peter Zamiel
Pierre Zuran

APPENDIX B

THE PRISON SHIP MARTYRS OF THE REVOLUTION, AND AN UNPUBLISHED DIARY OF ONE OF THEM, WILLIAM SLADE, NEW CANAAN, CONN., LATER OF CORNWALL, VT.

The following extremely interesting article on the prisoners and prison ships of the Revolution was written by Dr. Longworthy of the United States Department of agriculture for a patriotic society. Through his courtesy I am allowed to publish it here. I am sorry I did not receive it in time to embody it in the first part of this book.

D D

Doubtless all of us are more or less familiar with the prison ship chapter of Revolutionary history, as this is one of the greatest, if not the greatest, tragedies of the struggle for independence. At the beginning of the hostilities the British had in New York Harbor a number of transports on which cattle and stores had been brought over in 1776. These vessels lay in Gravesend Bay and later were taken up the East River and anchored in Wallabout Bay, and to their number were added from time to time vessels in such condition that they were of no use except as prisons for American troops The names of many of these infamous ships have been preserved, the Whitby, the Good Hope, the Hunter, Prince of Wales, and others, and worst of all, the Jersey.

It was proposed to confine captured American seamen in these ships, but they also served as prisons for thousands of patriot soldiers taken in the land engagements in and about New York. The men were crowded in these small vessels under conditions which pass belief. They suffered untold misery and died by hundreds from lack of food, from exposure, smallpox and other dreadful diseases, and from the cruelty of their captors. The average death rate on the Jersey alone was ten per night. A conservative estimate places the total number of victims at 11,500. The dead were carried ashore and thrown into shallow graves or trenches of sand and these conditions of horror continued from the beginning of the war until after peace was declared. Few prisoners escaped and not many were exchanged, for their conditions were such that commanding officers hesitated to exchange healthy British prisoners in fine condition for the wasted, worn–out, human wrecks from the prison ships. A very large proportion of the total number of these prisoners perished. Of the survivors, many never fully recovered from their sufferings.

In 1808, it was said of the prison ship martyrs: "Dreadful, beyond description, was the condition of these unfortunate prisoners of war. Their sufferings and their sorrows were great, and unbounded was their fortitude. Under every privation and every anguish of life, they firmly encountered the terrors of death, rather than desert the cause of their country. * * *

"There was no morsel of wholesome food, nor one drop of pure water. In these black abodes of wretchedness and woe, the grief worn prisoner lay, without a bed to rest his weary limbs, without a pillow to support his aching head—the tattered garment torn from his meager frame, and vermin preying on his flesh—his food was carrion, and his drink foul as the bilge water—there was no balm for his wounds, no cordial to revive his fainting spirits, no friend to comfort his heart, nor the soft hand of affection to close his dying eyes—heaped amongst the dead, while yet the spark of life lingered in his frame, and hurried to the grave before the cold arms of death had embraced him. * * *

"'But,' you will ask, 'was there no relief for these victims of misery?' No—there was no relief—their astonishing sufferings were concealed from the view of the world—and it was only from the few witnesses of the scene who afterwards lived to tell the cruelties they had endured, that our country became acquainted with their deplorable condition. The grim sentinels, faithful to their charge as the fiends of the nether world, barred the doors against the hand of charity, and godlike benevolence never entered there—compassion had fled from these mansions of despair, and pity wept over other woes."

Numerous accounts of survivors of the prison ships have been preserved and some of them have been published. So great was popular sympathy for them that immediately after the close of the Revolutionary War an attempt was made to gather the testimony of the survivors and to provide a fitting memorial for those who had perished. So far as I have been able to learn most of the diaries and journals and other testimony of the prison ship victims relates to the later years of the war and particularly to the Jersey, the largest, most conspicuous, and most horrible of all the prison ships.

I have been so fortunate as to have access to a journal or diary kept by William Slade, of New Canaan, Conn, a young New Englander, who early responded to the call of his country and was captured by the British in 1776, shortly after his enlistment, and confined on one of the prison ships, the Grovner (or Grovesner). From internal evidence it would appear that this was the first or one of the first vessels used for the purpose and that Slade and the other prisoners with him were the first of the American soldiers thus confined. At any rate, throughout his diary he makes no mention of other bands of prisoners in the same condition The few small pages of this little diary, which was always kept in the possession of his family until it was deposited in the Sheldon Museum, of Middlebury, Vt, contain a plain record of every–day life throughout a period of great suffering. They do not discuss questions of State and policy, but they do seem to me to bring clearly before the mind's eye conditions as they existed, and perhaps more clearly than elaborate treatises to give a picture of the sufferings of soldiers and sailors who preferred to endure all privations, hardships, and death itself rather than to renounce their allegiance to their country and enlist under the British flag.

The first entry in the Slade diary was made November 16, 1776, and the last January 28, 1777, so it covers about ten weeks.

The entries were as follows:

Fort Washington the 16th day November A.D. 1776. This day I, William Slade was taken with 2,800 more. We was allowed honours of War. We then marched to Harlem under guard, where we were turned into a barn. We got little rest that night being verry much crowded, as some trouble [illegible]. * * *

Sunday 17th. Such a Sabbath I never saw. We spent it in sorrow and hunger, having no mercy showd.

Munday 18th. We were called out while it was still dark, but was soon marchd to New York, four deep, verry much frownd upon by all we saw. We was called Yankey Rebbels a going to the gallows. We got to York at 9 o'clock, were paraded, counted off and marched to the North Church, where we were confind under guard.

Tuesday 19th. Still confind without provisions till almost night, when we got a little mouldy bisd [biscuit] about four per man. These four days we spent in hunger and sorrow being derided by everry one and calld Rebs.

Wednesday, 20th. We was reinforsd by 300 more. We had 500 before. This causd a continual noise and verry big huddle. Jest at night drawd 6 oz of pork per man. This we eat alone and raw.

Thursday, 21st. We passd the day in sorrow haveing nothing to eat or drink but pump water.

Friday, 22nd. We drawd 3/4 lb of pork, 3/4 lb of bisd, one gil of peas, a little rice and some kittels to cook in. Wet and cold.

Saturday, 23rd. We had camps stews plenty, it being all we had. We had now spent one week under confinement. Sad condition.

Munday, 25th. We drawd 1/2 lb of pork a man, 3/4 of bisd, a little peas and rice, and butter now plenty but not of the right kind.

Tuesday, 26th. We spent in cooking for wood was scarce and the church was verry well broke when done, but verry little to eat.

Wednesday, 27th. Was spent in hunger. We are now dirty as hogs, lying any and every whare. Joys gone, sorrows increase.

Thursday, 28th. Drawd 2 lbs of bread per man, 3/4 lb of pork. A little butter, rice and peas. This we cooked and eat with sorrow and sadness.

Friday, 29th. We bussd [busied] ourselves with trifels haveing but little to do, time spent in vain.

Saturday, 30th. We drawd 1 lb of bread, 1/2 lb of pork, a little butter, rice and peas. This we eat with sorrow, discouragd.

Sunday, 1st of Decembere 1776. About 300 men was took out and carried on board the shipping. Sunday spent in vain.

Munday, 2nd. Early in the morning we was calld out and stood in the cold, about one hour and then marchd to the North River and went on board The Grovnor transport ship. Their was now 500 men on board, this made much confusion. We had to go to bed without supper. This night was verry long, hunger prevaild much. Sorrow more.

Tuesday, 3rd. The whole was made in six men messes. Our mess drawd 4 lb of bisd, 4 oz of butter. Short allow. We now begin to feel like prisoners.

Wednesday, 4th. We drawd 4 lb of bisd. After noon drawd 2 quarts of peas and broth without salt, verry weak.

Thursday, 5th. We drawd 4 lb of bisd at noon, a little meat at night. Some pea broth, about one mouthful per man. We now feel like prisoners.

Friday, 6th. of Decr. 1776. We drawd 1/2 of bisd, 4 oz of butter at noon and 2 quarts of provinder. Called burgo, poor stuff indeed.

Saturday, 7th. We drawd 4 lb of bisd at noon, a piece of meat and rice. This day drawd 2 bisd per man for back allowance (viz) for last Saturday at the church. This day the ships crew weighd anchor and fell down the river below Govnors Island and saild up the East River to Turcle Bay [Turtle Bay is at the foot of 23rd street], and cast anchor for winter months.

Sunday, 8th. This day we were almost discouraged, but considered that would not do. Cast off such thoughts. We drawd our bread and eat with sadness. At noon drawd meat and peas. We spent the day reading and in meditation, hopeing for good news.

Munday, 9th. We drawd bisd and butter at noon, burgo [a kind of porrige] the poorest trade ever man eat. Not so good as provinder or swill.

Tuesday, 10th. We drawd bisd at noon, a little meat and rice. Good news. We hear we are to be exchangd soon. Corpl. Hawl verry bad with small pox.

Wednesday, 11th. We drawd bisd. Last night Corpl Hawl died and this morning is buryd. At noon drawd peas, I mean broth. Still in hopes.

Thursday, 12th. We drawd bisd. This morning is the first time we see snow. At noon drawd a little meat and pea broth. Verry thin. We almost despair of being exchangd.

Friday, 13th of Decr. 1776. We drawd bisd and butter. A little water broth. We now see nothing but the mercy of God to intercede for us. Sorrowful times, all faces look pale, discouraged, discouraged.

Saturday, 14th. We drawd bisd, times look dark. Deaths prevail among us, also hunger and naked. We almost conclude (that we will have) to stay all winter At noon drawd meat and rice. Cold increases. At night suffer with cold and hunger. Nights verry long and tiresome, weakness prevails.

Sunday, 15th. Drawd bisd, paleness attends all faces, the melancholyst day I ever saw. At noon drawd meat and peas. Sunday gone and comfort. As sorrowfull times as I ever saw.

Munday, 16th of Decr. 1776. Drawd bisd and butter at noon. *Burgo poor. Sorrow increases. The tender mercys of men are cruelty.

Tuesday, 17th. Drawd bisd. At noon meat and rice No fire. Suffer with cold and hunger. We are treated worse than cattle and hogs.

Wednesday, 18th. Drawd bisd and butter. At noon peas. I went and got a bole of peas for 4. Cole increases Hunger prevails. Sorrow comes on.

Thursday, 19th., Drawd bisd the ship halld in for winter quarters. At noon drawd meat and peas. People grow sick verry fast. Prisoners verry much frownd upon by all

Friday, 20th. of Decr. 1776. Drawd bisd and butter this morn. Snow and cold. 2 persons dead on deck. Last night verry long and tiresom. At noon drawd burgo Prisoners hang their heads and look pale. No comfort. All sorrow.

Saturday, 31st. Drawd bisd. Last night one of our regt got on shore but got catched. Troubles come on comfort gone. At noon drawd meat and rice. Verry cold Soldiers and sailors verry cross. Such melancholy times I never saw.

Sunday, 22nd. Last night nothing but grones all night of sick and dying. Men amazeing to behold. Such hardness, sickness prevails fast. Deaths multiply. Drawd bisd. At noon meat and peas. Weather cold. Sunday gone and no comfort. Had nothing but sorrow and sadness. All faces sad.

Munday, 23rd. Drawd bisd and butter. This morning Sergt Kieth, Job March and several others broke out with the small pox. About 20 gone from here today that listed in the king's service. Times look verry dark. But we are in hopes of an exchange. One dies

480

almost every day. Cold but pleasant. Burgo for dinner. People gone bad with the pox.

Tuesday, 24th. Last night verry long and tiresom. Bisd. At noon rice and cornmeal. About 30 sick. (They) Were carried to town. Cold but pleasant. No news. All faces gro pale and sad.

Wednesday, 25th. Lastnight was a sorrowful night. Nothing but grones and cries all night. Drawd bisd and butter. At noon peas. Capt Benedict, Leiut Clark and Ensn Smith come on board and brought money for the prisoners. Sad times.

Thursday, 26th. Last night was spent in dying grones and cries. I now gro poorly. Terrible storm as ever I saw. High wind. Drawd bisd. At noon meat and peas. Verry cold and stormey.

Friday, 27th. Three men of our battalion died last night. The most malencholyest night I ever saw. Small pox increases fast. This day I was blooded. Drawd bisd and butter. Stomach all gone. At noon, burgo. Basset is verry sick. Not like to live I think.

Saturday 28th. Drawd bisd. This morning about 10 cl Josiah Basset died. Ensn Smith come here about noon with orders to take me a shore. We got to shore about sunset. I now feel glad. Coffee and bread and cheese.

Sunday, 29th. Cof. and bread and cheese. This day washed my blanket and bkd my cloathes. The small pox now begins to come out.

Munday, 30th. Nothing but bread to eat and coffee to drink. This day got a glass of wine and drinkd. Got some gingerbread and appels to eat.

Tuesday, 31st. Nothing good for breakt. At noon verry good. I grow something poorly all day. No fire and tis cold. Pox comes out verry full for the time. The folks being gone I went into another house and got the man of the same to go and call my brother. When he came he said I wanted looking after. The man concluded to let me stay at his house.

Wednesday 1st of Jany 1777. Pox come out almost full. About this time Job March and Daniel Smith died with the small pox.

Thursday, 2nd. Ensn Smith lookd about and got something to ly on and in. A good deal poorly, but I endeavourd to keep up a good heart, considering that I should have it (the small pox) light for it was verry thin and almost full.

Friday 3d. This morning the pox looks black in my face. This day Robert Arnold and Joshua Hurd died with the small pox. This day Ensn Smith got liberty to go home next morning, but omitted going till Sunday on account of the prisoners going home.

Saturday, 4th. Felt more poor than common. This day the prisoners come on shore so many as was able to travel which was not near all.

Sunday, 5th. This morning Ensn Smith and about 150 prisoners were set out for home. The prisoners lookd verry thin and poor.

Monday 6th. Pox turnd a good deal but I was very poorly, eat but litte. Drink much. Something vapery. Coughd all night.

Tuesday 7th. Nothing reml [remarkable] to write. No stomach to eat at all. Got some bacon.

Wednesday, 8th. Feel better. This day I went out of doors twice. Nothing remarkl to write.

Thursday, 9th. Tryd to git some salts to take but could not. Begin to eat a little better.

Friday, 10th. Took a portion of salts. Eat water porrage. Gain in strength fast.

Saturday, 11th. Walk out. Went and see our Connecticut officers. Travld round. Felt a good deal better.

Sunday, 12th. Went and bought a pint of milk for bread. Verry good dinner. Gain strength fast. Verry fine weather Went and see the small–pox men and Samll.

Munday, 13th. Feel better. Went and see the officer. Talk about going home.

Tuesday, 14th. Went to Fulton market and spent seven coppers for cakes. Eat them up. Washd my blanket.

Wednesday 15. Cleand up all my cloathes. Left Mr. Fenixes and went to the widow Schuylers. Board myself.

Thursday, 16th. Went to Commesary Loring. Have incouragement of going home. Signd the parole.

Friday, 17th. In expectation of going out a Sunday. Verry cold. Buy milk and make milk porrage. Verry good liveing. Had my dinner give.

Saturday, 18t. Verry cold. Went to see Katy and got my dinner. Went to Mr. Loring. Some encouragement of going hom a Munday, to have an answer tomorrow morning. Bought suppawn (some corn?) meal and Yankey.

Sunday, 19th. Went to Mr. Lorings. He sd we should go out in 2 or 3 days. The reason of not going out now is they are a fighting at Kingsbridge. Went to Phenixes and got my dinner. Almost discouraged about going home. To have answer tomorrow.

Munday, 20th. Nothing remarkable. Mr. Loring sd we should have an answer tomorrow. An old story.

Tuesday, 21st. Still follow going to Mr. Lorings. No success. He keeps a saying come tomorrow. Nothing remarkable.

Wednesday, 22. Mr. Loring says we should have a guard tomorrow, but it fell through. The word is we shall go out in 2 or 3 days.

Thursday, 23d. Nothing remarkl. Almost conclude to stay all winter.

Friday, 24th. Encouragement. Mr. Loring say that we shall go tomorrow. We must parade at his quaters tomorrow by 8 oclok.

Saturday, 25th. We paraded at Mr. Lorings by 8 or 9 oclk. Marchd off about 10 oclk. Marchd about 6 miles and the officers got a waggon and 4 or 5 of us rid about 4 miles, then travl'd about 1–1/2, then the offr got a waggon and broght us to the lines. We were blindfolded when we come by Fort Independency. Come about 4/5 of a mile whare we stay all night. Lay on the floor in our cloathes but little rest.

Sunday, 26th. We marchd by sun rise. March but 8 miles whare we got supper and lodging on free cost. This day gave 18 pence for breekft, 19 pence for dinner.

Munday, 27th. Marchd 2 miles. Got breekft cost 19 pence. Travld 2 or 3 miles and a waggon overtook us a going to Stamford. We now got chance to ride. Our dinner cost 11 count lawful. About 3 oclok met with Capt Hinmans company. See Judea folks and heard from home. This day come 13 miles to Horse neck. Supper cost 16. Lodging free.

Tuesday, 28th. Breekft cost 11. Rode to Stamford. Dinner 16. Travld 3 miles, supr and lodg free.

Here the diary ends when Slade was within a few miles of his home at New Canaan, Conn., which he reached next day.

* * * * *

Perhaps a few words of his future life are not without interest. He was one of the early settlers who went from Connecticut to Vermont and made a home in what was then a frontier settlement. He lived and died at Cornwall, Vt., and was successful and respected in the community. From 1801 to 1810 he was sheriff of Addison County. Of his sons, one, William, was especially conspicuous among the men of his generation for his abilities and attainments. After graduation from Middlebury College in 1810, he studied law, was admitted to the bar, and filled many offices in his town and county. After some business reverses he secured a position in the State Department in Washington in 1821. He was on the wrong side politically in General Jackson's campaign for the presidency, being like most Vermonters a supporter of John Quincy Adams. Some time after Jackson's inauguration, Slade was removed from his position in the State Department and this so incensed his friends in Vermont that as soon as a vacancy arose he was elected as Representative to Congress, where he remained from 1831 to 1843. On his return from Washington he was elected Governor of Vermont in 1844, and in his later years was corresponding secretary and general agent of the Board of National and Popular Education, for which he did most valuable work. He was a distinguished speaker and an author of note, his Vermont State Papers being still a standard reference work.

To revert to the prison ship martyrs, their suffering was so great and their bravery so conspicuous that immediately after the War a popular attempt was made in 1792 and 1798 to provide a proper resting place for the bones of the victims, which were scattered in the sands about Wallabout Bay. This effort did not progress very rapidly and it was not until the matter was taken up by the Tammany Society that anything definite was really accomplished. Owing to the efforts of this organization a vault covered by a small building was erected in 1808 and the bones were collected and placed in the vault in thirteen large coffins, one for each of the thirteen colonies, the interment being accompanied by imposing ceremonies. In time the vault was neglected, and it was preserved only by the efforts of a survivor, Benjamin Romaine, who bought the plot of ground on which the monument stood, when it was sold for taxes, and preserved it. He died at an advanced age and was, by his own request, buried in the vault with these Revolutionary heroes.

Early in the last century an attempt was made to interest Congress in a project to erect a suitable monument for the prison ship martyrs but without success. The project has, however, never been abandoned by patriotic and public spirited citizens and the Prison Ship Martyrs' Society of the present time is a lineal descendant in spirit and purpose of the Tammany Club effort, which first honored these Revolutionary heroes. The efforts of the Prison Ship Martyrs' Association have proved successful and a beautiful monument, designed by Stanford White, will soon mark the resting place of these prison ship martyrs.

APPENDIX C. BIBLIOGRAPHY

The writer of this volume has been very much assisted in her task by Mr. Frank Moore's Diary of the Revolution, a collection of extracts from the periodicals of the day. This valuable compilation has saved much time and trouble. Other books that have been useful are the following.

Adventures of Christopher Hawkins.

Adventures of Ebenezer Fox. Published in Boston, by Charles Fox, in 1848.

History of Brooklyn by Stiles.

Bolton's Private Soldier of the Revolution.

Bigelow's Life of B. Franklin, vol II, pages 403 to 411.

Account of Interment of Remains of American Prisoners. Reprint, by Rev. Henry R. Stiles.

Elias Boudinot's Journal and Historical Recollections.

Watson's Annals.

Thomas Dring's Recollections of the Jersey Prison Ship, re-edited by H. B. Dawson, 1865.

Thomas Andros's Old Jersey Captive, Boston, 1833.

Lossing's Field Book of the Revolution.

Memoirs of Ethan Allen, written by himself.

Journal of Dr. Elias Cornelius.

Dunlap's New York.

Narrative of Nathaniel Fanning.

Narrative of Jabez Fitch.

Valentine's Manual of New York.

The Old Martyrs' Prison. A pamphlet.

Jones's New York.

Poems of Philip Freneau.

Prison Ship Martyrs, by Rev. Henry R. Stiles.

A Relic of the Revolution, by Rev. R. Livesey, Published by G. C. Rand, Boston, 1854.

Memoirs of Alexander Graydon.

Memoir of Eli Bickford.

Martyrs of the Revolution, by George Taylor, 1820.

Memoirs of Andrew Sherburne.

Mrs. Ellet's Domestic History of the Revolution, pages 106–116.

Irving's Life of Washington, vol. III, p. 19.

Experiences of Levi Handford. C. I. Bushnell, New York, 1863.

Onderdonk's Suffolk and King's Counties, New York.

Philbrook's Narrative in Rhode Island Historical Society's Proceedings, 1874 and 1875.

Harper's Monthly, vol. XXXVII.

Historical Magazine, vol. VI, p. 147.

Mrs. Lamb's New York.

Jeremiah Johnson's Recollections of Brooklyn and New York.

Life of Silas Talbot, by Tuckerman.

Ramsey's History of the Revolution, vol. II, p. 9.

Narrative of John Blatchford, edited by Charles I, Bushnell, 1865.

Irish–American Hist. Miscellany, published by the author, 1906, by Mr. John D. Crimmins.